DELACORTE WORLD HISTORY

VOLUME II

The Near East:

THE EARLY CIVILIZATIONS

The Near East:
THE EARLY CIVILIZATIONS

EDITORS
Jean Bottéro
Elena Cassin
Jean Vercoutter

CONTRIBUTORS
JEAN BOTTÉRO
DIETZ OTTO EDZARD
ADAM FALKENSTEIN
JEAN VERCOUTTER

TRANSLATED BY
R. F. Tannenbaum

DELACORTE PRESS
NEW YORK

Contents

Illustrations

PORTFOLIO

[between pages 206 and 207]

Maps

Editors' Introduction

There is but one past, yet there are countless histories of it. In presenting still another, the editors offer this explanation to those who may wonder why: There is but one past, but there are countless historians. Which means not only so many eyes professionally turned toward the past, but also so many points of view from which it may be interpreted.

But there is more to it than that, particularly when the object of that examination is ancient history—and no history is more ancient than that with which the following pages are concerned, as history itself was born in the Near East, at the beginning of recorded time. There, the documentary sources are always too sparse, and more and more so the further one goes back in time: They are always difficult to understand, and scholars are constantly reexamining and reinterpreting them in the hope of understanding them better. Research and excavation keep producing new interpretations and new evidence, sometimes giving precious confirmation to opinions already formed, sometimes clarifying them, sometimes overthrowing them entirely and requiring a complete rethinking of everything that had been taken for granted. For an understanding of the history of antiquity, then, it is useful to pause from time to time and survey what is known just at present about a past that reveals more of itself day by day; in fact it is not only useful, it is indispensable.

The reader will therefore find, in the present volume and the two that are to follow it, a synthesis, which we have attempted to make as up-to-date as possible, of what is currently known about the earliest history of the lands where our civilization was born.

There has been no attempt to give this task to a single author: No one man could be expected to master so many difficult and disparate scripts and languages, so many hundreds of thousands of documents of every kind, whose interpretation requires so varied an array of specialized techniques. We have thought it better to assign, to experienced specialists, the territories and periods each knows thoroughly and at first hand. And this we have done.

In preparing the work as a whole, these specialists have worked together, each reading and commenting on the work of his colleagues, but none considering himself obliged to imitate them. Our only common principles have been these: to follow the strict methods that the practice of our profession has always required of us, and to take into account *all* of the important data in each field, including the results of the latest excavations and of the most recent scholarship. And one more: as a general guideline, to attempt to hold, each in our own fashion, the balance between chronological narrative and cultural history, between recording the succession of peoples, rulers, and events and analyzing the civilizations that they produced. We have tried, in both these areas, to include the essential and rigorously to exclude the superfluous, referring the reader with an interest in the original sources or in particular details to a topical bibliography. By so doing we hope that our work will have fulfilled the aim of the series of which it forms a part: to provide, for the ordinary reader, a straightforward, reliable guide through the endless galleries of that enormous museum, history.

JEAN BOTTÉRO
ELENA CASSIN
JEAN VERCOUTTER

DELACORTE WORLD HISTORY

VOLUME II
The Near East:
THE EARLY CIVILIZATIONS

NOTE ON SPELLING

In Sumerian and Semitic words and names, the letter "ḫ", with its underlying sign, indicates a sound for which there is no precise English spelling. It is pronounced like "ch" in German *Bach* or Scottish *loch*. The form "ssh" indicates a double occurrence of the consonant "š" and is pronounced simply "sh." Spellings have otherwise been Anglicized throughout.

1

The Prehistory and Protohistory of Western Asia

The Rediscovery of Ancient Western Asia

Until the end of the eighteenth century A.D., everything men knew about the history of the ancient Near East came either from the Old Testament or from scattered, often fictional traditions preserved in classical authors. In 1802 the decisive step was taken toward reading what the inhabitants of the ancient Near East themselves had to say on the subject. In that year, G. F. Grotefend succeeded in making a partial decipherment of inscriptions in the Old Persian language, written in cuneiform script. These inscriptions, copied in the palace of the Persian kings at Persepolis by C. Niebuhr in 1765, dated back to the reigns of Darius and Xerxes, the unsuccessful invaders of Greece. They had been carved on stone in three scripts and as many languages. Once the Old Persian text was translated, European scholars had the key to the interpretation of the other two in their hands. One was written in Elamite, the language of southwestern Iran, and the other in the language of the Babylonians and Assyrians. This last proved to be an exceptionally complicated system of writing, and it raised exceptional obstacles in the decipherers' path. Not until 1857 were its problems more or less solved. Once done, the decipherment had immense consequences for our understanding of antiquity, for the vast majority of the written tradition of ancient Western

Asia proved to be written in this language. It is a Semitic language, today called Akkadian after the ancient name of its native country.

Attempts to decipher Akkadian cuneiform, even before they achieved success, had aroused an intense interest in the lands where it was written. This led to large-scale excavations by Europeans in the capitals of the New Assyrian empire, whose location was more or less known from Biblical and classical references: Nineveh, near present-day Mosul in Iraq; Khorsabad, the temporary capital of Sargon II (722–705 B.C.); Nimrud, the Biblical Calah (Akk. Kalḫu). In the first half of the nineteenth century, French and English excavators (P. E. Botta, E. Flandin, and A. H. Layard), pioneering the entire art of archaeology, brought back the first reports of magnificent palaces and temples, ornamental reliefs, colossal statues; more, they brought back many of the monuments themselves, to become treasured possessions of the Louvre and the British Museum. A spectacular windfall at Nineveh was the discovery of the state library of the last great Assyrian king, Asshurbanipal (669–627 B.C.), in which the monarch had collected every Babylonian and Assyrian literary and religious work on which his agents could lay their hands, including texts in Sumerian, by then a dead language for nearly 1,500 years.

The ruins of Babylonia—that is, the part of Mesopotamia that lies to the south of Assyria—at first proved less productive. From 1877, however, E. de Sarzec directed excavations at Tello, the ancient Girsu, where the first remains of Sumerian civilization were found. Among them were inscribed statues of the ruler of the city, Gudea (ca. 2143–2124 B.C.), and two inscribed clay cylinders, the oldest extensive literary texts yet found on Babylonian soil. Scholars now had the possibility of retrieving the Sumerian language from documents written when it was a living tongue. American excavators in 1889 discovered what is still the largest find of Sumerian literary texts, unearthed in a private residence of the eighteenth century B.C. at Nippur. German archaeologists have been active in the area since 1899 (R. Koldewey at Babylon) and 1903

(W. Andrae at Assur), their object being to restore to us the remains of the two great Mesopotamian capitals. In 1913, J. Jordan began the excavation of Uruk (the Biblical Erech), the largest archaeological site in southern Babylonia.

Meanwhile, the curiosity of archaeologists had already been drawn to areas outside Mesopotamia. At Susa, J. de Morgan unearthed the civilization of Elam, intimately related to neighboring Babylonia but preserving a character all its own. In 1887, at Amarna in Middle Egypt, there was found the diplomatic correspondence of rulers great and small, from all parts of Western Asia, with the pharaohs Amenhotep III and IV (1400–1344 B.C.), all of it written in cuneiform. H. Winckler in 1907 discovered at Boghazköy in central Anatolia (the ancient Hattusas) a cuneiform archive that made the decipherment of the Hittite language and literature possible. The world's store of cuneiform documents was enriched not only by formal excavations but by illegal private digs, in all parts of the Near East, producing tablets of all ages that made their way, through the hands of dealers, to the great museum collections.

World War I, of course, interrupted archaeology as it did everything else, but soon after, the pace of excavation quickened to the point where we can report only a fraction of the newer finds here. Excavations at Ur under L. Woolley revealed the astonishing royal burials of the Early Dynastic period (ca. 2450 B.C.); at Uruk, continuing excavations first reached the level of the Protoliterate age (ca. 3000–2700 B.C.). American excavations under the direction of H. Frankfort, in the region of the Lower Diyala River, recovered temple sites from every period of the Early Dynastic age. At Nuzi, near modern Kirkuk, a settlement of the fifteenth and fourteenth centuries B.C. was uncovered, with private archives throwing a flood of light on a hitherto dark age. Materials complementing our knowledge of the Early Dynastic period were found at Mari, on the Middle Euphrates, by A. Parrot, as well as a palace of the eighteenth century B.C., whose royal archives for the first time enabled us to see, in concrete and fascinating

3

detail, the age when Hammurabi was building his empire. Earlier, C. F. A. Schaeffer had begun to unearth ancient Ugarit, a Syrian city on the Mediterranean at the modern Ras Shamra, where clay tablets were discovered written in a hitherto unknown alphabetic script. These, on being deciphered, revealed the poetry and mythology of the ancient Canaanite people. Boghazköy was once more investigated under K. Bittel, and the history of the Hittite empire and of ancient Anatolia in general was brought to light. Persepolis, where our story began, was now systematically studied by an American expedition under E. Herzfeld and E. Schmidt, exploring the ruins of the palaces of the Achaemenid kings. And now began the slow and difficult process of investigating, and trying to understand, the earliest stages of human culture, by the excavation of Near Eastern settlements from the Stone Age.

World War II brought another interruption, its aftermath another increase in activity. Many of the major sites previously investigated were worked over again—Boghazköy, Ugarit, Mari, Nimrud, Nippur, Uruk, and Susa—and new excavations were carried out in search of light on prehistoric problems, particularly on the transition to Neolithic society and the origins of agriculture. Now, too, the Near Eastern countries themselves began to participate in the archaeological recovery of their own past, through the staffs of the departments of antiquities in each state.

A lost past, then, has been successfully and extensively brought to light—or so it would seem from the record outlined above. But two things must be borne in mind. First, the influx of new material is incessant and immense, so much so that it is difficult in the extreme for research to keep up with it. Second, in spite of all that has been done, there are still whole areas and whole ages that are blank on our historical charts. Much, then, remains to be done before we can begin to hope that we have succeeded in reconstructing faithfully the history of the ancient Near East.

Ancient Western Asia—Historical Geography

We begin with a difficulty in nomenclature. The terms "Near East" and "Middle East" today cover an area that does not always coincide with what historians mean by "the ancient Near East." First of all, today, "Near East" includes parts of both Asia and Africa; the first five chapters of this book are concerned with Asia alone, and we shall therefore be referring to "ancient Western Asia," i.e. all of the ancient Near East excluding Egypt. Secondly, "ancient Near East" or "Western Asia" mean different things for different periods of historical study, as one area after another enters or drops from our field of vision. At the very beginning, in the stage of early village communities, the focus of interest is limited almost entirely to the "Fertile Crescent," the half-circle of plains and foothills contained by the Zagros mountains to the east of Mesopotamia, and by the ranges of the Taurus, Amanus and Lebanon on the west (see map). Important parts of the Anatolian peninsula border on the Aegean Sea; they generally fall out of our area of interest, to be treated as part of the Aegean, Greek and Balkan cultures. The Black Sea coast of Anatolia was, before the Greek colonization, probably only thinly settled. Northern and southern Arabia have revealed various levels of prehistoric culture up to Neolithic and Chalcolithic times,[1] but do not appear on the historical stage until the period of the New Assyrian Empire, in the first millennium B.C. The eastern borderline of our area fluctuates back and forth into the Iranian highlands, where excavation reveals much for certain periods of time but finds (so far) nothing for others.

The heartland of this oldest East, the region where prehistory first turned into history, is the geologically recent lowland plain between the Tigris and the Euphrates—roughly the area between modern Baghdad and the outlet of the two rivers into the Persian Gulf, the latter probably extending farther inland in antiquity than it does today. This territory we call, geographically, Babylonia. Its climate is lamentable, charac-

5

terized by extremes of heat in the long summer months and rare and irregular rainfall in the late autumn and winter, so that agriculture here was dependent on artificial irrigation from the start. This meant that only a limited area could be utilized for agriculture at all.

To the southeast of this is the modern Khuzistan, the ancient Susiana or Elam, where the climate is very much the same except in places near the hills and mountains, where the chances for a sufficient natural rainfall are improved. On the flanks of the Iranian (Zagros) mountain range, in fact, there are territorial pockets where rain agriculture can succeed. But they are often cut off from each other by the mountains and have very seldom coalesced into major political units. There are a few passes through these mountains to the east and north, facilitating contact between Mesopotamia and the Iranian and Armenian uplands. These routes lead from Susa to Fars, from the region of the Upper Diyala to Hamadan and Kermanshah, from the eastern Assyrian hill country via the Rowanduz Pass to the area around Lake Urmiah. Time and again peoples from Iran have migrated into the Assyrian plains, and onto the Babylonian lowland, through these mountain passses.

Assyria begins, at the south, with the Jebel Hamrin, a range of mountains reaching into the lowland of Iraq, and extends north and east to the Zagros range, a fairly large territory on and east of the Middle Tigris. On the east bank of the Tigris, however, arable land is limited to a narrow strip, broadening near the modern Mosul, with easy access to the hill country nearby.

West and northwest of Babylonia lay the nonarable, semi-desert plain, where only pastoral nomads could live; far into late historical times this was much wider than it is today, for it was only relatively late that the Euphrates shifted its bed toward the west, closer to the edge of the Arabian plateau. Until the camel was domesticated, i.e. up to the end of the second millennium B.C., these nomads could move no more than a few days' journey from the areas of cultivation. Along

6

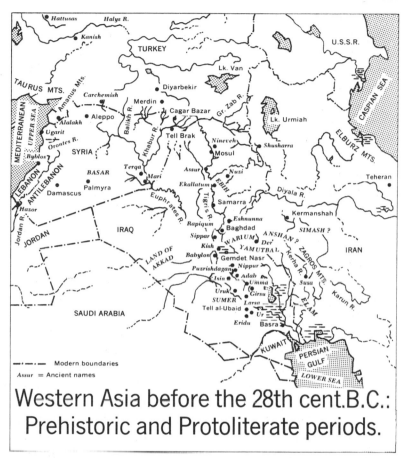

Western Asia before the 28th cent.B.C.: Prehistoric and Protoliterate periods.

the Upper Euphrates these areas are hemmed in on both sides, from the west by the steppelands of the Arabian plateau, from the east by tracts of gypsum-laden desert; the result is a chain of river oases, like the modern Ane, which were all that the upper valley of that river offered for human settlement, until one reached (still going upstream) the region of ancient Mari. There, and along the tributaries Khabur and Balikh, the arable territories grow larger and connect up with the lands around the foothills of the Taurus, where rainfall permits a thickly settled countryside.

South of the Taurus, between the Mediterranean coast and

7

the Upper Euphrates, and farther south into central Syria and Palestine, there are a number of small areas of settlement of varying character. The coastal region is oriented toward the sea; there are many good harbors, especially in what was later to be known as Phoenicia. The Amanus range, the Lebanon and Anti-Lebanon to the south, were in antiquity heavily forested, and provided building timber and aromatic resins to both Egypt and Babylonia, and later to Assyria as well. (A memory of this is preserved in the Gilgamesh cycle, the great epic story of the Sumerians, adopted by Akkadians and Hittites; the heroic King of Uruk goes out to do battle with the monster Ḫuwawa, who is Lord of the Cedar Forest.) The depression between the Lebanon and the Anti-Lebanon ranges, with its southern extension, the Jordan Rift, offered a connective route between north and south much traveled in both directions. Near the eastern slope of the Anti-Lebanon were a few oasis towns, the most important being Damascus, with its fertile surrounding oasis, the modern Ghuta.

Palestine is a geography textbook come to life: There are relatively fertile zones on the western slopes of the Judaean and Galilean hills; there are stretches of desert in the Judaean mountains and in the Negev; in the Rift Valley of the Jordan grow subtropical jungles. The deserts of the Sinai peninsula and the southern Negev isolated the country from Egypt, at least until shortly before 3000 B.C. East of the Jordan are lands which were, in early times as well as under the Roman Empire, more heavily settled than they are today.

The Far West of the ancient Near East was Anatolia's central plateau; good pass routes led there from Upper Mesopotamia and Cilicia. The area in and around the bend of the Halys River (the modern Kizil Irmak) was the main center of settlement. The country around the Upper Sangarius (Sakarya) and the plain of Konya were the only other important ones. At the time of the Hittite Empire the Pontic mountains (i.e. the Black Sea coastal range) were inhabited only by nomadic and seminomadic tribes. Eastern Anatolia was so cut up by mountain ranges that rarely did any major unified state emerge there.

Western Asia, then, is divided into natural regions of, for the most part, quite limited size. The result on the early history of this part of the world is obvious: There were only very limited ethnic and political units in the territories bounded by mountains. Three larger and less obstructed natural regions, however, lend themselves to the formation of great states: Mesopotamia, particularly in Babylonia and Assyria; central Anatolia; and the Iranian plateau. A zone apart is the belt of half-desert steppeland, fitting between the Fertile Crescent and the Arabian plateau; in all periods of which we know, this is the home of Semitic pastoral nomads, constantly on the move. The picture is incomplete unless we recall that, among the nations destined to found great Near Eastern empires, many— the Hittites, the Indo-European Mittanians, the Medes and Persians—came into being as ethnic units, and grew into for- midable populations, in the vast spaces of eastern and south eastern Europe, long before they appeared on the borders of the Near East.

These individual areas, as we have said, are by and large isolated from each other by nature. Counteracting this is the uneven distribution of raw materials essential to settled life. Naturally the demand for these varies in intensity, and the objects sought after are different, in the various stages of the evolution of civilization. Obsidian, flint and bitumen are first sought, then stone for vessels, and metals above all. In the very earliest village settlements, materials have been found that must have been brought from afar. The intensive settlement of Babylonia must have been a tremendous stimulus to trade, for, on the Babylonian plain, there are no good building tim- ber, no proper building stone, no metals whatsoever. By the time Babylonia had a fully developed urban civilization, its commerce extended far beyond the geographical limits of Western Asia: to the shores of the Persian Gulf, to the Indus valley, to Afghanistan (the source of lapis lazuli), to the un- known sources of the tin needed in the making of bronze. Here was no isolated corner, but the commercial center of a whole world.

9

Chronology

It is impossible to give accurate B.C. dates (i.e. "absolute chronology," rendered according to our own system of time-reckoning) for long stretches of the history of ancient Western Asia. The list of Assyrian eponymous officials, after whom successive years were named,[2] does not go back beyond 910 B.C. Assyrian and Babylonian king lists allows us to date events, for Mesopotamia, more or less accurately within a margin of about ten years back to 1450 B.C. For Syria and Asia Minor we have to rely on synchronisms with Babylonia and Assyria, and even more with Egypt, where the chronology of this period is fixed to some degree. We have as a result of such a synchronism one firm point from which we can count forward and backward: the date of the peace treaty between Ramses II and the Hittite king Hattusilis II, 1270 B.C. But the period immediately before 1450 is a kind of chronological dark age extending over all of Western Asia, with a historical tradition so clouded that we cannot tell how many years passed between 1450 and a preceding era, where, for nearly eight centuries, we have a perfectly good idea of what is going on; i.e. we have a well-established "relative chronology" for the era from the Dynasty of Agade to the end of the Dynasty of Hammurabi (First Dynasty of Babylon), which means we know the succession of kings and can add the length of the reigns, but the dark period of unknown length immediately following it leaves a period of more than 700 years floating unanchored in time with respect to our calendar. To solve the problem one would have to have an agreed date for the end of the First Dynasty of Babylon and the beginning of the Kassite domination of Babylonia (i.e. the beginning of the "dark age"), but there is none. Or rather there are several. In this volume we shall follow what is called the "middle chronology" of S. Smith and M. Sidersky, which dates the end of the First Dynasty of Babylon at 1595 B.C. and the reign of Hammurabi at 1792–1750 B.C. The Dynasty of Agade would

CHRONOLOGICAL TABLE I

Prehistory through the Protoliterate Period

Shanidar: Neanderthal man	60,000–40,000
Upper Palaeolithic, Mesolithic and Neolithic	35,000–9000
Origin of animal husbandry and agriculture	ca. 9000–6750
Early Pre-Pottery Jericho	ca. 7000
Earliest settlement at Jarmo	ca. 6750
Beginning of Chalcolithic	ca. 5500
Eridu, Ubaid, Uruk	ca. 5000–3100
Protoliterate Uruk	ca. 3000–2750
"Temple C" in Uruk	2815 ± 85 (?)

then begin at ca. 2340 B.C. An alternative system is offered by the "low chronology" of W. F. Albright and F. Cornelius, with all dates lowered by sixty-four years, i.e. one Venus period, as all these calculations are based on attempts to date certain Babylonian astronomical observations.[3]

Before the Dynasty of Agade we are entirely unable to give anything but approximate dates, and these only for the last phase of the Early Dynastic period; we base these on the succession of rulers of Lagash from Ur-Nanshe to Urukagina, who cover a period of about 120 years. There is a very full *Sumerian King List*, which offers a succession of rulers of Sumer and of Babylonia from the time "when kingship descended from heaven" down to the end of the Dynasty of Isin (1794 B.C.), but it is quite unreliable from the point of view of chronology for anything before the Dynasty of Agade. The names of the rulers are reliably transmitted, to be sure, with only occasional oversights resulting from repeated copying of the text through the centuries. Some of these names from the Early Dynastic period check out perfectly against those given on original documents of the age. That is not the problem. The problem is the attitude of the scribes who drew it up. Their historical information for the early periods is excellent, but the historical assumptions according to which they arranged it are ruinous. They assumed that at any given time only one dynasty could rule in and over all Babylonia. They were also anxious not to omit anything from the store of names handed down to them from what was already, for them, a remote past. The result: Dynasties that ruled simultaneously in different parts of Babylonia were listed by them as ruling successively over the whole. Forty-five rulers are therefore listed from Meshkalamdug of Ur to Lugalzagesi of Uruk, who immediately precedes Sargon, founder of the Dynasty of Agade. In the city-state of Lagash, however, the line of rulers is known to us from contemporary documents without a gap, and there only eight princes reign during the same period, several of whom had reigns lasting no more than a few years. Finally, for all their zeal for completeness, names did drop out of the tradition in the centuries between the Early Dynastic period and the final editing of our text, so that, for example, all the princes of Lagash are missing from the *Sumerian King List*, although several of them at least deserve to be numbered among the masters of Mesopotamia.

Before Ur-Nanshe of Lagash, we are at a loss even for approximate dates; we can but vaguely estimate the length of the various phases of the Early Dynastic period, and of the Protoliterate period that precedes it. Our grounds for these estimates are the thickness of various archaeological levels at early sites and the evolution of the cuneiform script through various early stages. There is a possible synchronism with Egypt at one point: At the very end of the Predynastic period in Egypt (archaeologically, Late Gerzean or "Nagada II"), just before the unification of the Two Lands—in other words at, very roughly, 3000 B.C.—certain works of art appear in the valley of the Nile that are indisputably related to those of Protoliterate Sumer. Further, we have a date for one phase of the Protoliterate period, Uruk level IVa, obtained by the radiocarbon (carbon-14) method:[4] wooden remains from "Temple C" produce a date of 2815 ± 85 years B.C., which is not far from that suggested by the finds in Egypt.

Still further back in time, in the prehistory of Western Asia, a steadily increasing number of carbon-14 dates for settlements in Palestine, Cilicia, Anatolia, Iraq and Iran permit us to set up, in connection with corresponding dates from Egypt and the Balkans, a reasonably reliable chronological scheme for the development of civilization. We can estimate the distance in time between stages of that development and thereby assess its speed. To this study we shall now turn.

Prehistoric Western Asia

For long, there was very little in the way of material evidence for the early existence of man in Western Asia. There still is very little, when compared with the rich yield of European soil. More recently, however, systematic investigation has been applied to the area, and, with the aid of a number of natural sciences, has produced definite results. We now have a fairly clear picture of the stages of human progress in Western Asia during Palaeolithic and Neolithic times. Products of the dexterity of the human hand in the Palaeolithic age have been found in sites all over the region: in the caves of Mount Carmel near Haifa, in the hill country of Judaea, in the coastal areas of Syria and up into southern Turkey, on the western coast of Turkey, in central Anatolia, in Jordan; from the Arabian plateau to the Euphrates valley and western Kurdistan. In Mount Carmel were found skeletons of the type of Neanderthal man, and also at Shanidar in Iraqi Kurdistan, the latter in Mousterian strata said to be 60,000 to 40,000 years old. At Shanidar, the next level up is from the Upper Palaeolithic, an estimated 35,000 years old; a Mesolithic stratum comes next, and another of the pre-pottery Neolithic, at something below 9000 B.C. The Shanidar cave, of course, does not contain every level of this long development, does not record every step: there is a gap after the Mousterian level, corresponding to the period when humans of the Neanderthal type were driven from this area forever, probably by a severe climatic change.[5]

The hunt for the traces of early man in Western Asia has

intensified in the last decade and a half, with spectacular results. We are now in a position to begin to understand one of the most decisive steps taken by the human race, the transition from food collecting to food producing. This transition has been called, and with good reason, the Neolithic Revolution, for it ushered in a stage in man's dominion over nature that was not terminated until less than two centuries ago, by the Industrial Revolution. But "revolution" must not be taken to imply, in the Neolithic Age, a sudden event; rather this was a process extending over several thousand years of prehistory.

Between 9000 and 6750 B.C., climatic conditions in the Near East already approximated those obtaining at present. Man now begins, at least in Western Asia, to domesticate some of the wild animals around him and, a little later, to cultivate selected plants for food. By 6750, sheep, goats, cattle have been tamed and bred to human uses, and emmer wheat, barley and flax have been cross-bred and cultivated for human harvests. The cultivation of grains, when practiced with enough success to make these a staple of the human diet, inevitably led to settled agriculture and the formation of village communities.

Where did this transition begin? Obviously, where animals capable of domestication were to be found, and where the wild grasses that were the ancestors of grain grew in abundance. This describes the mountain valleys and the grass-covered foothill zones of the ranges of Iran, Iraq, Turkey, Syria and Palestine. Here is rain enough for agriculture without irrigation; in the modern Near East, this requires an average annual precipitation of about eight inches.

We are not yet, however, in a position to see the full extent of the changes that the Neolithic Revolution brought about. It is difficult, for instance, to estimate at their true value the consequences of the change to grain production as the principal source of food. There would have been a considerable increase in population with the introduction of a settled life; child mortality would be lower, life expectancy longer, than was the case in former ages. This is brought home to us by one fact: In a few millennia, a span of years which usually produced no noticeable change at all in Palaeolithic times, the original area of settlement on the mountain slopes was extended as far into the plains as the presence of winter rains would allow; a close net of village settlements sprang up there. Also at this time, we may assume, and drawing on the experiences of early settled agriculture, nomadic pastoralism on a small scale began, with its wandering herds of sheep and goats, and men who, living off them, could find a livelihood of sorts even in the high mountains, or on the plains outside the rainfall line—both *terra incognita* to the Neolithic husbandman. These were to be the pioneers of the agricultural revolution, we may imagine, seeking out and opening up new areas of settlement, as their own numbers and the sedentary populations increased.

The earliest villagers, crowded together in unheralded proximity, would have had to hammer out new customs, new legal principles, to allow them to live together amicably in a limited space. Religion, too, would be transformed: Men now had to propitiate the powers that presided over the fertility of their flocks, or released the life-giving rain. The old magical practices that had sufficed for the hunting life were no longer enough; new foods meant new gods, or old gods given new functions.

The transition to agriculture, from 9000 B.C. on, is attested archaeologically in Palestine (the hill slopes facing the Mediterranean as well as drier regions toward the east, e.g. Natufian), in Lebanon and in Syria, in Iraqi and in Iranian Kurdistan. Caves were still used as dwelling places, and, during the warm season, open camps, although some of the latter may have been used the year round. In Palestine (Ain Mallaha), and in Kurdistan (Mlaffaat and Zawi Chemi Shanidar), remains of round huts were found, possibly built in imitation of circular tents used in the open camps. Stone querns for grinding grain indicate cultivation. Goats and sheep were certainly domesticated.

Jarmo, east of Kirkuk in the Kurdish highlands, is a good

example of the early village settlements. There are twelve archaeological levels, but they all display about the same stage of development. There are simple houses, built of packed mud, with foundations of unhewn stones; each has several rectangular rooms. On each level there may have been a total of twenty to twenty-five houses, giving a population estimate for the village of about 150 persons. Crops cultivated include a large-grained barley, developed from the wild *hordeum spontaneum*, and two kinds of emmer wheat. In the later levels, goats, sheep and pigs are the domestic animals—other animal remains do not indicate domestication clearly enough to allow us to decide one way or the other. Most of the stone tools are microliths, and many of these are made of obsidian, volcanic glass that would have had to be imported from a considerable distance, the nearest natural deposit being some 240 miles away. Carefully worked stone vessels are typical of these early villages, and they are found at Jarmo, but there, in the upper third of the archaeological strata, were discovered the first (portable) vessels made of clay. Clay figurines include that of a crouching pregnant woman, reminiscent of a long line of such figures stretching well back into the Old Stone Age, and implying notions of fertility magic. How old was Jarmo, this model Neolithic village? Carbon-14 dates set the beginnings of its earliest level at around 6750 B.C.

At the same period, and even before, the level of development reached by villages like Jarmo was surpassed elsewhere. Jericho, for example, is exceptional—by nature, to begin with, for it is located more than 650 feet below sea level and stands in a well-watered oasis in an otherwise bone-dry territory at the foot of the Judaean hills; by human endeavor, in the second place, for the older Pre-Pottery Neolithic settlement, dated by the carbon-14 method at about 7000 B.C., is surrounded by a wall of undressed stone five feet thick, preserved up to a height of over twelve feet. On one of its inner sides is a solid round tower about twenty-seven feet high, with a staircase cut inside leading to the top.[6] This wall encloses a town of more than eight acres in area. The houses are of mud brick and are round in plan. The dead are buried under the floors, but the heads are removed and the skulls kept separately in the house, a most peculiar custom which is, however, known in other places in the Neolithic Near East. In a later level of the Neolithic walled settlement of Jericho, these skulls are filled and covered with plaster, lifelike features being modeled over the facial bones, and split shells inserted to portray eyes.[7] In this level the houses have large rectangular rooms. There are also, it seems, in various levels, places of worship already to be found.

The Pre-Pottery Neolithic settlement at Ugarit on the Mediterranean was likewise fortified. The wall there is of mud and gravel, with an outside facing of large rocks.[8]

By about 5500 B.C. this culture of villages and towns had developed to the point where it was expanding rapidly into new areas and working out entirely new manufacturing techniques. We have isolated finds of pieces of raw metal, worked by men, from this period, well before what had previously been thought of as the beginning of the Chalcolithic Age. Settlements now appear on the low plains beneath the mountains, probably filling the entire area available to rain agriculture. This is true for every part of Western Asia: There are sites at Catal-hüyük and Hacilar in southwestern Turkey; at Mersin and Tell Judeidah in the Cilician-North Syrian region; at Tell Halaf in central Mesopotamia; at Tell Hassuna near Mosul, Tepe Sialk on the Iranian plateau, and Tell-i-Bakun in south-central Iran (Fars). Amid this general expansion certain local cultural regions are formed; pottery is now made all over the area, and is our best evidence for these local traditions. The vessels are often still quite coarsely made; they are decorated with patterns incised or indented in the surface, with incrustations of white coloring and the beginnings of decorative painting. Houses are still built of compacted clay, but others are now constructed of sun-dried mud brick; both types have rectangular rooms. At Çatal-hüyük, in the plain of Konya, the plastered wall of a building is covered with a large-scale fresco of animals and huntsmen;[9] from the same period in time,

17

probably, but made by men living at a lower cultural level, come striking rock paintings at Kilwa, in Jordan, picturing an ibex hunt. There are a number of female figures in clay from Hacilar, notable for their size (up to nine and a half inches long) and eloquent of both the art and the religion of the early townsmen.

More animals are now domesticated than before; we find goats, sheep, pigs, cattle and dogs, although presumably not all are kept in every area. To grains are now added lentils, peas, vetch, and flax. We do not yet have the evidence that would allow us to decide when grapes, olives and fruits were first grown, but by historical times these are typical of the agriculture of the Fertile Crescent; as all these plants occur there in wild forms, we can assume they were cultivated at an early stage.

At slightly later levels painted pottery is the typical ware, painting having largely replaced the other forms of decoration. The area over which these painted vessels can be found is immense; it includes Anau, in southwestern Turkestan, apparently settled from some Iranian center—the new culture is spreading rapidly and far. In fact, we now get the first settlements outside the zone of rain agriculture, at Baghuz on the Middle Euphrates and at Samarra on the Tigris.

We have spoken of local cultures. For this period they are distinguished according to pottery styles and named after the sites where they were first identified: Tell Halaf near the source of the River Khabur, Samarra on the Tigris, and Tell-i-Bakun in Iran.

The pottery of these cultures is not only technically well made, it is quite literally beautiful. The painted decoration is mostly in the form of geometric patterns, but there are some naturalistic figures, and patterns derived from nature. Tell Halaf ware is the most widespread, reaching from its Mesopotamian center to Syria and Cilicia, to eastern Assyria, and even as far as Armenia. It is painted in polychrome at the peak of its artistic development, the paints producing a glazelike luster when the pottery is fired at great heat. The center of Samarra

18

FIGURE 1. *Pottery of the Tell Halaf culture.*

ware is in the eastern Assyrian region, but it reaches westward beyond the Tigris, with an advanced outpost at Baghuz on the Euphrates: on the whole, a more limited area than that of the Tell Halaf culture. What is the difference between them? All we have are differences in ceramic decoration, in the pat-

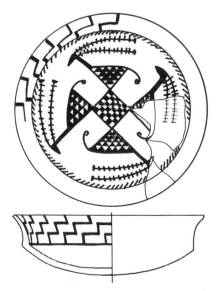

FIGURE 2. *Clay bowl of the Samarra culture.*

terns and figures painted on their pottery. These may signify some ethnic distinction, and some of them certainly signify different religious ideas, namely the apparently symbolic figures that the artists employ: for Tell Halaf, the bull's head ("bucranion") in frontal view, and the Maltese cross; for Samarra, the swastika, either alone or as a compositional motif.

Furthermore, in the Tell Halaf culture, alongside the traditional houses with rectangular rooms, there appear circular buildings, sometimes with a rectangular anteroom added on; traces of such circular houses can be found at Tepe Gawra, at Arpachiyah, at Tell Hassuna near Mosul and at Yunus near Carchemish on the Upper Euphrates;[10] indeed they are of such general occurrence in Mesopotamia at the time that they must be taken as evidence of some importance, particularly in view of the fact that house forms, among any given people, are tradition-bound for extremely long periods of time. There may well be some connection here with the round buildings frequently seen in the Pre-Pottery Neolithic period; in the other direction similar houses are pictured on New Assyrian reliefs, perhaps 5,000 years later on; the "beehive" houses of modern northern Syria complete the tale.

For the religious ideas of the Tell Halaf culture much may be learned, and more imagined, from painted clay female figurines, represented in a crouching position. The arms are joined under the breasts, the latter much emphasized in the modeling; the upper thighs are massive. The head is only barely modeled. There are animal figurines too; terra cottas of cattle are particularly popular, and probably ought to be considered in connection with the "bucranion" sign on the pottery, i.e. as some sort of religious or magical symbol.

What of Babylonia, the alluvial plain of Lower Mesopotamia, the future birthplace of cities, writing, and all the higher arts of civilization? There is nothing here. There is no evidence whatever for human settlement there until the Chalcolithic period, i.e. at the height of the Tell Halaf culture. It is possible, of course, that pastoral nomads may have tented there at an earlier period—this would be a natural prelude to the foundation of settled villages—but there is no evidence of any kind for it. What is certain is that agricultural settlements are late, perhaps as much as 2,000 years after earliest Jericho. There are reasons for this. The climate of the Babylonian lowland is excessively dry, much too dry for rain agriculture. The two great rivers, especially the Tigris, are no advantage in their natural state; quite the reverse; with the spring thaw, melting the snows of the far northern mountains, water streams by the ton into the rivers but does not rush to the sea, as the fall of only 112 feet between the point where it enters the alluvial plain and the point of its discharge into the Persian Gulf, 210 miles away, is insufficient to keep it moving steadily on its course. It therefore tends to wander, and over and over again the rivers changed their beds; it is no accident that the myth of the Flood had its origin in this land. Spreading waters created marshes, in which nothing grew but enormous water reeds, far more extensive than those at the mouth of the rivers today; even in the northern part of the Babylonian plain, the early settlers often had to fill in the land with cut reeds before they could erect their homes, as the Ma'dan Arabs still must do in southern Iraq. But lack of rain is the decisive factor; the area on which eight inches or more of rain falls in a year, the area, that is, in which rain agriculture can be practiced with assurance, has its edge at a line up to 120 miles away from the Babylonian plain—between the two is a belt of land where only migratory herdsmen could live. This means that the first agriculturalists in Babylonia had also to be the first irrigationists; a whole new way of life had to be invented to settle this land. In the beginning, of course, they would set up purely local, limited systems of dikes and canals, but even this would demand a community effort beyond the experience of the villagers of former times. And far more had to be done, centuries of planning and hard labor, to complete, to perfect, and above all to keep in constant repair, an irrigation system that could make of Babylonia the *ager totius orientis fertilissimus*,[11] the most fruitful land of all those in the East.

The work, naturally, that could be put into the creation of an irrigation system depended on the number of the settlers and the degree of their organization. Unfortunately we cannot estimate the density of population in Babylonia at the time. We know that all the regions of Babylonia were soon inhabited. But we cannot learn anything certain about the size of the settlements, nor the thickness of their distribution on the land. This is because many of the sites were continuously inhabited far into historical times, so that the oldest levels of habitation

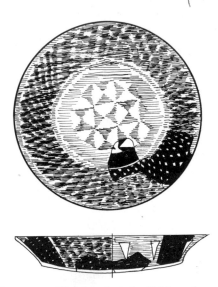

FIGURE 3. *Clay bowl of the Eridu culture.*

lie under layer after layer of later settlement, to be reached only with the greatest difficulty by much too narrow an excavation. Whatever sites may have been abandoned before historical times, all sign of them has long since been buried under alluvial silt, which has raised the level of the plain by about seven feet since the beginning of settlement; we do not know where to look for them.

Fortunately these limitations apply to our knowledge in terms of space, not in terms of time. We are able to follow the development of the earliest settlements in Babylonia through three phases, with pottery, again, providing our most important evidence:

1. The Eridu culture. This is the oldest, as far as we now know, and is documented by a long series of strata at Eridu in the far south of the plain, but is also found, in southern Babylonia, at Ur, at Tell al-Ubaid nearby, and at the Kala[12] of Hajji Muhammad west of Uruk; in central Babylonia, at Nippur and at Ras al-Amiya.[13] The pottery is worked on a slowly turning wheel and is painted, for the most part, in solid colors, occasionally on a white ground, in geometric patterns; the technique is watercolor. Naturalistic figures are rare. The colors differ widely from piece to piece, depending on the firing: dark purple and greenish shades are frequent. The most common form is a large, low bowl heavily painted on the inside (figure 3). Spouts are seldom found, handles never.

2. The Ubaid culture. The remains of this second stage in the development of Babylonia were also found at Eridu, where they coincide with Eridu ware through many levels, as well as at Ur and at Uruk. The Ubaid culture, however, reaches into northern Babylonia as well, where finds have been made in the Diyala region, northeast of Baghdad.[14] Its characteristic pottery is for the most part greenish (a result of its being highly

FIGURE 4. *Pottery of the Ubaid culture.*

23

fired), and painted in black-brown colors. Like Eridu ware, decoration is largely geometric, with only rare naturalistic themes, the latter most often to be found at Girsu and at the northern Babylonian Tell Ukair. As time goes on the patterns grow more and more restricted in motif, the execution becomes more careless, displaying a real degeneration in the art of painted pottery decoration; there is, on the other hand, a greater variety of pottery shapes than ever before. There are many spouted vessels, although handles are still rare. One can see a transition from Eridu ware to Ubaid ware, but the latter shows an originality of its own, which speaks of the individuality of the culture that produced it; we cannot yet determine where and how that culture began.

3. The Uruk culture. This stage is to be observed chiefly at Uruk, but spreads over all Babylonia, and, indeed, as we shall see, reaches far beyond its boundaries. Painted pottery, so long the signature of the cultures of Mesopotamia, now comes to an end. It is replaced by pottery unpainted or coated in red slip or gray. The gray ware is often decorated with incised patterns, frequently "combs." Vessels with twisted handles are typical, and jugs with bent spouts (figure 5). Already this pottery is shaped on a swiftly turning potter's wheel. This unpainted Uruk ware at first coincides with, then slowly replaces, the painted pottery of Ubaid.

These three stages in the development of the Babylonian settlers represent rather a long period of time. At Uruk, a stratification pit reached only late strata of the Ubaid culture; nevertheless above these are layers totaling 53 feet before one reaches the earliest levels of the protohistorical period. A similar depth has been found at Eridu. But here we must bear in mind that the early settlers deliberately raised the level of their villages as rapidly as possible, to put them out of reach of floods. We do have a carbon-14 date for the lowest level at Uruk: 4115 ± 160 B.C. Comparing this with Tell Halaf dates, we get a period, for these three earliest stages in the human record in Babylonia, of ca. 5000–3100 B.C.

In these 2,000 years men live in village communities on the

24

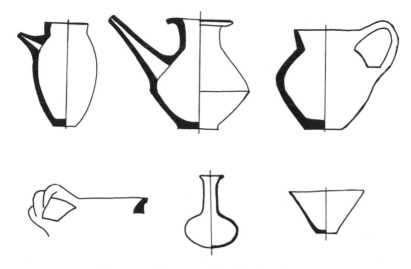

FIGURE 5. *Pottery of the Uruk culture.*

Babylonian plain and practice agriculture, horticulture, stock-raising, fishing and hunting. Cattle, sheep, goats and dogs (and surely also donkeys) are their familiar companions. The crops are the same as those raised in the lands of rain agriculture, except for the olive, for which the climate of the Babylonian plain is too dry. The date palm, however, provided a crop unknown to the north. Its origin? Sumerian tradition names Tilmun as its source, i.e. the island of Bahrain in the Persian Gulf and the Arabian shore nearby; perhaps this preserves a genuine memory. For the Sumerians, astonishingly enough, also remembered that grain first came from the mountains near Babylonia, as we have seen it must have; a Sumerian myth copied in the eighteenth century B.C. reports that An, the sky-god, brought wheat, barley and hemp down from the heavens to the fertile earth. Enlil, the god of royal power, then piled all of it up in the hill country, "barring the mountains as with a door"; then the divinities Ninazu and Ninmada decided to let "Sumer, the land that knows no grain, come to know grain."[15]

This daring experiment, the transplanting of grains native

25

to the mountains and the foothills of the Fertile Crescent onto plains with an entirely different climate, to be grown on artificially irrigated soil, was successful to an amazing degree. Barley had been cultivated in the rain-agriculture zone only in its two-row variety, but mutated under the completely changed conditions of the lowlands into a six-row form that was eventually adopted by the whole of the ancient world. Flax, too, developed considerably larger seeds and therefore produced more linseed oil, probably also more fibers.[16]

Houses, built of compacted clay or mud brick, began as simple huts but by the Ubaid stage were more regular in form. In many places reed huts surrounded by a hurdle serve as dwellings, extraordinarily like those found in the marshes of southern Iraq today. The houses of the gods show greater architectural progress. At Eridu the earliest temples are small,

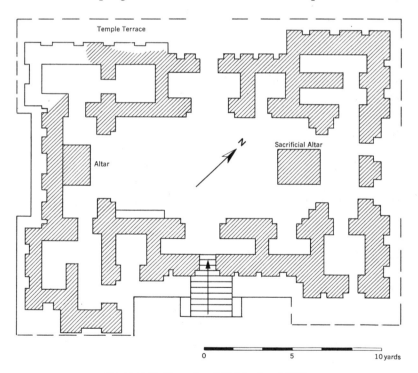

FIGURE 6. *Temple at Eridu, level VII.*

26

one-room buildings; by the time we reach Ubaid levels there is already a type of construction that will be repeated right through the Protoliterate period. On an artificial terrace stands a long rectangular building (80 by 42 feet), in which two side chambers flank a central cella with altar and cult pedestal (figure 6). This may be taken as the first step in the evolution of the ziqqurrat,[16a] the stepped tower that is to be the characteristic sacred building of all the native civilizations of Mesopotamia, down to the great "Tower of Babel" of Nebuchadnezzar at Babylon (605–562 B.C.). This temple stands on a site that was to remain sacred for millennia; under the Third Dynasty of Ur, for example, in about 2050 B.C., there was to be built there, above the ruins of previous shrines, the great ziqqurrat of Enki, Sumerian god of wisdom, showing a continuous tradition of worship on the same spot for more than 2,000 years.

As for the material culture of these villages of the alluvial plain, their implements show the level attained: They have everything required for their particular way of life. Aside from pottery, for which increasing uses are found, they have flint and obsidian knives and saws, sickles of fired clay, and bent clay nails, whose use we find it hard to imagine. Much, of course, in the way of articles made from perishable materials (wood, leather, textile, etc.) has been lost. But we can see, at least, that the inhabitants are not depending on native raw materials alone. Flint came from the Arabian plateau, obsidian from Armenia and Upper Mesopotamia; bitumen, indispensable for the mounting of implements on wooden handles and for calking boats, had to be brought from the Middle Euphrates near Hit,[17] or from the present oil region of Kirkuk and Mosul. There are no signs of metal in the Ubaid stage, but since it was already known in the Tell Halaf culture, to the north, it must certainly have been used from the earliest times in Babylonia too. The clay model of a sailboat found in a tomb toward the end of the Ubaid culture[18] implies that the shores of the Persian Gulf had already been explored. Babylonia, then, had become the center of a considerable trade. What was exported in return for these materials we cannot be sure, but by analogy with historical times we may think of grains, with the new barley no doubt having considerable exchange value, and of dates. Perhaps textiles were already exported then, as they were to be in later ages. For a purely agricultural economy, without industry for export and without foreign trade, can support a steadily growing population only within limits. This is an axiom of economics and would have applied even in these ancient times.

For the religion of early Babylonia we have good evidence in the temples erected in honor of the principal god at Eridu. Sacrifices were mostly of fish, and we have seen that the early temples were located under what historically was the ziqqurrat of the god Enki. Now Enki, in Sumerian art, is typified by streams of water flowing from his shoulders, in which fish are pictured swimming "upstream"; we have here, in other words, further signs of an unbroken tradition going back to prehistoric times.

Terra-cotta figures, too, found in all the settlements of the Ubaid culture, tell us something of religion, though not so clearly. A figure of a woman kneeling in the position of childbirth, found at Uruk, dates back to the Eridu culture there and bears some relationship to the crouching feminine figures of Tell Halaf.[19] The Ubaid figures are usually standing men and women, or at any rate manlike beings of both sexes: The heads are exaggeratedly long and narrow, drawn back to a point, and the eyes are slanted; the whole face is reptilian in expression as a result. The male figures have, for the most part, arms modeled like wings. Animal figures are principally representations of cattle, as was the case in the Tell Halaf culture, but wild animals also occur. Occasionally, these terra cottas are placed in the tombs of the dead.

Burial gifts (where they occur, they are mainly pottery) imply a belief in life after death, without, of course, giving us a hint of the details of that belief. A hunting dog laid across a dead man's chest, or a plate with meat laid next to the dog, are more expressive.[20] We have already spoken of the clay model of a sailing vessel, found in a grave; does this imply that a man might, by magical means, follow his profession in the afterworld? If so, this would tie up with the custom of burying servants along with their master, if the master was one of the leaders of the community; there are a few cases of this known from the Early Dynastic period (see pp. 68 ff.). In the Ubaid era, however, if the dead continue their earthly life elsewhere, they do not do so in the service of a superior.

From the remains of the dead themselves we obtain anthropological data, but very little. Skeletons from a burial ground late in the Ubaid levels at Eridu, where the dead were buried stretched out on their backs in rectangular brick tombs, show a surprisingly large body size, where skeletons from the Early Dynastic period indicate a small-sized population.[21] The Ubaid skeletons, along with the older human remains from Tell Hassuna and Mosul, and those of the oldest Tell Halaf stage from Tepe Gawra, arc ascribed to the Mediterranean racial type;[22] racially, then, we know who the creators of the preliminary stages of civilization in Babylonia were, probably also the creators of village culture as a whole.

But ethnically, we know nothing. All we can do is work backward from the Protoliterate period, when the Sumerians are demonstrably the leading nationality of Babylonia, to arrive at the assumption that they must have entered the country at some earlier date, by the period of the Uruk culture at the latest. The break in pottery traditions, the decay and disappearance of painted pottery, must not, however, be connected with their arrival; this is not ethnical evidence. We also must not exclude the possibility that the Sumerians were there from the beginning, i.e. that they were among the earliest settlers of the land.

If we cannot tell who the earliest settlers were, we have some indication of where they came from. Their material remains show cultural connections with Elam (where finds at Tell Jovi and Jafarabad are identical with Eridu ware) and with the Iranian plateau, especially Fars.[23] On the other hand, there are also clear connections with Tell Halaf levels in Upper Mesopotamia. Consequently one gets the impression that the Babylonian plain was settled by husbandmen from both the east and north, in which case we may further assume that it was the rapid rise in population, in the areas of rain agriculture, that forced these farmers to open up a new frontier.

Note, also, that once the settlement of Babylonia is under way, all through the three early stages we have been studying, changes in the areas to the north and to the northwest coincide curiously with Babylonian developments. After Tell Halaf pottery reaches the peak of its artistic development, there is a distinct degeneration in the painting of these vessels, all over the vast area in which they are to be found; and, all over that area, this is followed by the disappearance of painted pottery altogether and a vogue for unpainted ware like that of Uruk. This coincidence in development is so marked that we can properly speak of Ubaid and Uruk levels far outside Babylonia, even though all the artifacts of culture are not identical over the whole area.[24]

How are we to interpret these broad-scale developments? With the greatest difficulty. All we can say is that in that age close ties connected the individual regions of Western Asia, and that these ties were promoted by reciprocal exchange of goods. But is that enough to explain what we see? Everything we know of the historical ancient Near East, where ethnic groups occupy only limited areas, warns us that we must think in terms of large-scale migrations. But if there were migrations here, on the eve of history, they would not have come from those areas where village culture was as yet unknown; the population density would have been too low, at the level of a hunting and food-gathering existence or of pastoral nomadism. But the original homeland of village culture, the rim of the Fertile Crescent with its fast-rising population, would have been forced to expand. We have seen the example of the settling of Babylonia; in Anatolia and Iran, too, farmers opened up new areas farther and farther away from their starting point. At this time settlements spring up in territories as climatically ill favored as the northern Negev in Palestine. But whether the village cultures of Western Asia participated, decisively, in the development of the Neolithic villages of Europe, or whether these were original creations of the peoples of the Middle and Lower Danube, is undecided. The same is true for the rest of the ancient world.

The Protoliterate Period in Sumer*

And now, something altogether new appears in the world, whose point of departure and motivating force we do not yet understand. We have archaeological evidence, but it does not answer our questions. This is unfortunate, for they concern nothing less than the origins of civilization—the city-civilization of the Sumerians.

The characteristics of this civilization are these: large-scale temple architecture, high achievements in sculpture in the round and in relief, and, finally and decisively, the first writing in the world. But for all this novelty, the new stage grew out of the preceding one, the end of the Uruk culture, without a visible break. The new cities grow on the site of the old village settlements. Their temples follow the ground plan known far back in Ubaid levels. Their pottery, to begin with, is simply a development from Uruk ware.

The earliest stages of the new civilization can best be observed at Uruk. The oldest preserved temple, on the site of the later *Eanna*, the sacred precinct of the city's patron deity Inanna, goddess of love, war and the planet Venus, is to be found at levels V–IVb (the numbering of archaeological strata often begins on the surface; the higher numbers therefore represent chronologically earlier levels, the lower numbers later ones). But already at level VI, beneath this shrine, large stores of clay pegs were found, of the sort later used to fasten wall plaques in important sacred buildings only; and the enclosure wall of the later temple dates back at least to level VI. Cyl-

---

* The author's general term "protohistory" (*Frühgeschichte*) has been translated "Protoliterate period" where the period immediately preceding the historical in Babylonia is concerned, to conform to English scholarly usage. [*Tr.*]

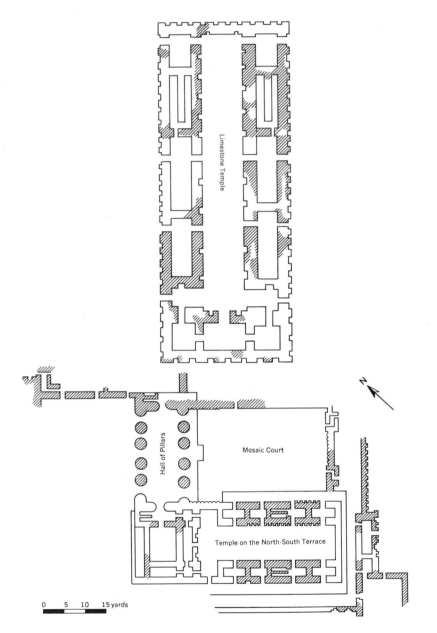

Limestone Temple

Hall of Pillars

Mosaic Court

Temple on the North-South Terrace

0   5   10   15 yards

FIGURE 7. *Temple at Uruk, levels V–IVb.*

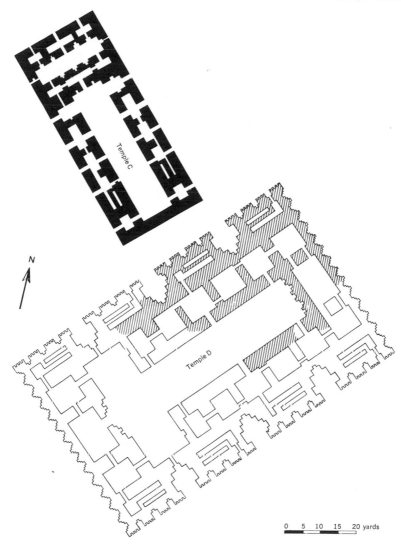

FIGURE 8. *Temple at Uruk, level IVa.*

inder-seal impressions are also found there, of a type much more common in level IVb. In other words, although we do not have its architectural remains, there is a temple typical of Sumerian civilization already in existence.

33

The temple of levels V–IVb is an impressive monument. Erected on a limestone base, to protect it from rain and moisture, it measures 248 by 96 feet—in other words, seven times the area of the last temple of the Ubaid phase at Eridu. The building stone had to be brought from the escarpment of the Arabian plateau, about thirty-six miles away. The temple follows in general the ground plan of the shrine at Eridu, with its central hall and two side chambers. New features are the T-shaped central hall and the addition of an extension with three rooms at the head of the T, the central room probably serving as the Holy of Holies for the goddess and her daily cult. The precisely planned and precisely executed symmetry of this "Limestone Temple" witnesses to a high degree of architectural ability. On a low terrace nearby is a smaller shrine at right angles to the Limestone Temple. Between the two is a court, whose walls are decorated in part with a three-colored mosaic of baked clay cones. This court gave access to a pillared hall and to a terrace. The next level up, IVa, again has two temples linked together, the one (much restored) measuring 275 by 176 feet, the other 182 by 73 feet. With an entrance building, they form a complex laid out on a generous scale. Another temple of level IV was found about a thousand feet northwest of the Limestone Temple. Again set on a limestone platform, its walls are made of plaster alone, poured in place, a building technique highly unusual for Mesopotamia. The outer walls, the central hall and the enclosure wall around the court are all decorated with mosaics of stones and clay cones. The amount of work that must have been required to erect and decorate it is staggering to contemplate.

In the area of the temple of levels V–IV, but higher up at level III, traces of the modest prototype of a ziqqurrat were found (under what was later the center of the Eanna, the ziqqurrat built by Ur-nammu and Shulgi at about 2100 B.C.); but this rapidly developed into a larger construction. At Uruk also, in the area later devoted to the supreme deity of the Sumerian pantheon, the sky-god An, temples have been found that are analogous to the terrace-cum-temple complexes of

Eridu. A precisely similar complex was discovered at Tell Ukair in the north of the Babylonian plain. On its walls, the remains of frescoes show animals, and human figures in a religious procession.[25]

The period that produced these temples has also left us important examples of the art of seal carving. Stamp seals had been used exclusively in the prehistoric periods, in Babylonia and in the neighboring lands, but the cylinder seal (a small tube of stone covered with carved designs, which, when the seal is rolled in wet clay, leave an impression in the form of a long illustrated panel) makes its first appearance no later than level VI at Uruk; it was to remain in use, not only in Babylonia but in nearly all of Western Asia, down to the last stages of the

FIGURE 9. *The Anu ziqqurrat at Uruk (restoration).*

history of the ancient Near East. Compared to the limited format of the stamp seal, the cylinder seal gave the lapidary a much larger surface to work with, providing room for quite extensive and complex scenes. It was used mainly to seal vessels against unauthorized opening; later, it was also used to "sign" inscribed clay tablets.

There are four different classes of cylinder seal in Proto-literate Mesopotamia. We shall go into the differences in content and style and the different areas of distribution in some detail, as useful historical conclusions can be drawn from this. The first class consists mostly of larger seals, on which the lapidary carved extensive naturalistic scenes in intaglio, always aiming at a sculptural effect. Besides scenes of worship before

35

temples and altars and religious processions by boat, there are battle scenes (one involving a chariot) and struggles with or hunting of wild animals for the protection of the herds; also wild animals battling each other, rows of animals, and the "sacred herd" of domestic animals. Scenes from daily life are relatively rare. The most important figure is the ruler, recognizable by his towering size and by his costume and appearance—bearded, his long hair held together by a band, he wears a net kilt that falls from hips to ankles. Seals of this class are in the great majority among those found at Uruk, are rare in northern Babylonia, and are barely present at all in the Diyala region. The second-most-frequent class at Uruk is decorated with "heraldic" compositions, often featuring paired animals facing one another. Snakes or fabulous animals frequently appear, with their long necks intertwined. The third class is widespread in the Diyala region and common in northern Babylonia but appears only in isolated instances at Uruk. These are small, compact seals, carved in materials different from those used for the first class. The patterns picture schematized animals, often dissolved into mere lines: fishes, vessels, pigtailed figures and weird creatures resembling spiders. The execution is crude, roughly drilled without sufficient retouching. There is a fourth class, also common to the Diyala region and northern Babylonia, but distinguishable only toward the end of the Protoliterate period, apparently. Abstract ornaments, deeply incised, characterize these seals: the quatrefoil or the Maltese cross.

On relief sculptures we find themes similar to those of the first class of cylinder seals: the ruler, fighting lions with bow and arrow, or at the head of a procession carrying offerings to a priestess of the goddess Inanna or to the goddess herself. Relief carvings are particularly frequent on stone vessels, on which the artists can give free play to their predilection for working in high relief.[26]

Only a few remains of sculpture in the round have been found so far. The fragment of a statuette seems to have been part of a figure portraying a ruler, of the same type seen on

FIGURE 10. *Protoliterate cylinder-seal impressions.*

seals and reliefs. There is a head of a female figure larger than life size, poorly preserved, unfortunately, for she seems to have been the first example known of the representation of a deity in human form; traces of a cap with a double crown of horns remain, and the horned cap is the normal headgear of the gods in Mesopotamian art.[27] By far the most important work, however, is the head of a woman from Uruk. Even in the damaged condition in which it has come down to us, it lets us sense the capacity for rendering nature that the Protoliterate artists possessed.[28] Small animal sculptures, some of which probably served as amulets, speak of the same degree of talent.[29]

Probably the most significant achievement of the Protoliterate period, the one most pregnant with consequences for the future of mankind, was the development of writing. This marks the age off from everything that had gone before and brings it into the penumbra of history. Indeed we now name the period after this accomplishment: "Protoliterate"—having the first letters. When were the first letters written? Evidently the earliest examples that we possess, clay tablets from level IVa at Uruk, actually represent the very earliest stage of writing. Each character is impressed onto the still-wet clay with a fine reed stylus. Some of these signs are clearly pictorial— pictures whose counterparts we can recognize on the reliefs and on seals of the first class mentioned above (and on those of no other class, which is significant). The majority of the signs, however, deliberately abbreviate the outline of what is represented or meant, abbreviations that could not possibly belong to the repertoire of contemporary artists. The feminine pubic triangle, for example, is enough to signify "wife" or "woman." Complicated signs, human figures in different positions, for instance, of which Egyptian hieroglyphics make so much use, are strictly avoided. What the inventors of this script were striving for, and from the very beginning, was a means of communication that could be put to daily use. The script would soon develop, therefore, into a cursive, entirely nonornamental medium in which, shortly after the end of the Protoliterate period, the signs bear hardly a trace of their pictorial origins.

The number of signs was initially quite high; estimates run to 2,000. About two-thirds of these were eliminated by the end of the Early Dynastic age, by which time the script was fully developed; the losses were made good not by new signs but by the exploitation of the inherent possibilities of the script.

Structurally, cuneiform is logographic; it is a "word-script," in which each sign or group of signs corresponds to a single word. A script based on this principle must soon find ways to increase its clarity and its possibilities for expression. It will use word-signs for homophones (words of the same sound but different meaning) and in this way develop symbols for individual sound-syllables. We find an example of this on a tablet from Jamdet Nasr in northern Sumer, corresponding in time with documents from Uruk's level IIIb; it contains the personal name *En-lil-ti*. Later counterparts help us to interpret this as "(May) Enlil [the chief god of Nippur in central Babylonia] (cause) to live." The sign for "to live," "to keep alive," is a drawing of an arrow. Originally this sign designates the Sumerian word *ti*, "arrow," but it had been shifted to the homophonous *ti(l)*, "to live," which is a little too abstract to have its picture drawn. In the same way Egyptian hieroglyphics borrowed the symbol for *ḫpr*, "to become," "to come into being," from the drawing of the dung beetle or scarab *ḫpr* (the Egyptian system is interested only in consonants). Syllabic writing emphasizes the sound connected with a certain sign and makes the sound rather than the picture carry the meaning. But sound-signs do not replace word-signs (syllabograms do not replace logograms) in cuneiform; both are used in combination. This combination was to remain a characteristic of the script long after the language for which it had been invented had died out, when it was being used to write Akkadian, Hurrian, Hittite and so on. The last cuneiform inscription was composed in the first century A.D.; the experiments of the Protoliterate age were approved by 3,000 years of use.

The very first written documents we have are tallies and records from the economic administration of the large temples: so many cows, so much barley, and the like. There are no literary compositions, no historical information, written down until the middle of the Early Dynastic period. On the other hand we do get, at Uruk, evidence of the manner in which writing was taught in schools or temples, in the form of word lists. At Jamdet Nasr in the north we find word lists with identical texts. These word lists were handed down through centuries, into the period of the Dynasty of Agade (from 2340 B.C.). They were thus the textbooks for instruction in all of Sumer, and were to be the same for Akkad, Elam and Assyria.

In what language are these documents written? Which is as much as to say, who invented writing? The earliest signs, as we have said, are largely logograms, word-signs, and therefore only tell us what the meaning of a word is, not its spoken sound. Only where these signs are used for homophonous words do we learn anything about sound, or where they are used as syllabic symbols. Then we can "hear" what we read, and thus identify the spoken language. By this means, the language has been shown to be Sumerian by level IIIb at Uruk. Our evidence is the name we have cited above, *En-lil-ti*, "(may) Enlil (cause) to live," for only in Sumerian is the word "arrow" homophonous with the verb "to live." But for Uruk IVa, where the earliest documents appear, there has been no certain occurrence found either of the use of a word-sign for a homophone or of a syllabic symbol. We therefore have no linguistic evidence at all for the inventors of writing. However, there is not the slightest archaeological indication of a change in population at Uruk between levels IVa and IIIb. It is therefore perfectly reasonable to assume that the earliest documents, too, were written in Sumerian, and that the Sumerians were therefore the inventors of writing, and of the first historical civilization.

Where had they come from? We shall probably never know. As we have seen, they must have been immigrants, like all inhabitants of the Babylonian plain, and they would have entered the land at some time before the Protoliterate period, i.e. in prehistoric times. But we cannot ask a historical question of prehistoric finds and expect a cogent answer. The archaeological evidence is therefore of no help; neither is the linguistic evidence. Sumerian is an agglutinative language, one, that is, in which words do not change their sound or ending for grammatical purposes but add on other, equally fixed words according to fixed laws. Agglutinative languages known in the ancient Near East are Elamite, Proto-Hattic, and Hurrian-Urartian; not one is related to Sumerian. No ties can be found with any of the modern agglutinative languages either—the Finno-Ugric, Turkic, and Mongolian languages, Basque (this, too, has been tried), or various languages of the Caucasus, such as Georgian. Agglutinative languages can, it is true, be classified according to whether they add on grammatical indicators (1) before or (2) after a word or (3) do both; Sumerian is one of those that uses both prepositions and postpositions, but this class includes Georgian and a few related languages at one end of the map and Basque on the other, too wide a gap to give us any indication of a possible geographical origin. Whatever languages may have been related to Sumerian appear to have died out without leaving a trace. Sumerian is, as far as our knowledge goes, unique.

These Sumerians are, in the Protoliterate period, obviously the leaders of the population then dwelling in the Babylonian plain, culturally according to the evidence, and politically according to all probability. This does not mean that they are the whole population. There are definitely Semitic-speaking settlers there, for there are several very old Semitic loan words in Sumerian (see p. 63). It is very difficult to tell, by the same means, who else was living there. There are many place names on the Babylonian plain for which our knowledge of the Sumerian language provides no interpretation, no etymology, and which have an entirely un-Sumerian appearance, but at the present stage of our knowledge, no safe conclusions can be drawn from this (see p. 67).

On the other hand, it is clear that Sumerian did not spread beyond the Babylonian plain. The Sumerian script was not adopted in neighboring Elam. There, toward the end of the

Protoliterate period, knowledge of the Sumerian innovation sparked the invention of a script of their own, the Proto-Elamite script. That there was no writing in Assyria until the Dynasty of Agade (twenty-fourth and twenty-third centuries) proves that this area differed from Sumer in its ethnic and probably also in its political and economic structure. Differences in the decoration and distribution of the different classes of cylinder seal show that, in the Protoliterate period, even the Diyala region, close as it is to Babylonia proper, did not fully share in its civilization. The areas immediately bordering on the Babylonian plain to the north and east were therefore then inhabited by men living in small local units. This was still the case, in part, in historical times; it would also have been true of prehistoric times, although there were then already large-scale regions with a common cultural tradition.

The Sumerians, then, are the dominant nationality in Babylonia in the Protoliterate period, but not elsewhere. Their country is coextensive with the Babylonian plain. We can therefore now call that plain Sumer, until ethnic and political conditions change.

This they were bound to do, in the long run. The national destiny of the Sumerians was determined by the fact that they could not hope to increase their numbers by welcoming immigrants of their own nationality, or from related ethnic groups. The Semitic-speaking peoples in Sumer, and of the western and northwestern steppes, could count on constant reinforcements from outside; they would surely prevail by sheer weight of numbers. The Sumerians as a nation were doomed to being absorbed by Semites, and their language as a spoken medium was doomed to die out. This is precisely what occurred at about 1900 B.C. Against this background the achievements of the Sumerians, numerically weak and nationally ill fated as they were, influencing the civilization of every people in Western Asia down to the last centuries of ancient Near Eastern history, are all the more impressive and deserving of respect.

The Protoliterate period in Sumer was one of great prosperity. Its centers were the cities of the plain, formed in part by the growing together of several village settlements. It is difficult to determine how many of these cities there were at the time. Probably by the Protoliterate period all places of importance in the first half of the third millennium had already grown out of the village state. From south to north, then, these are the cities of Sumer: Eridu, Ur, Uruk, Badtibira, Lagash, Nina, Girsu, Umma, Nippur, and, lying northward on the plain, Kish, Sippar and Akshak. The center of gravity lay toward the south, where Uruk held the position of greatest importance. These cities were unwalled, strangely enough, although we know of walled settlements in Neolithic times. Political conditions must therefore have been relatively stable.

Life in Sumer is based on the cultivation of grain; the latter is based on an irrigation system already fully developed. Cattle and sheep are also important. This situation is depicted on a relief on a cult vase found at Uruk: Grain of several kinds grows over a wavy line representing water, and in the next row above, sheep advance in line.[30] The themes of seals and stone vessels illustrate further the appreciation of agriculture as the center of life. For work in the fields, wagons, sleds and plows are available. The importance and complexity of animal husbandry appears in art and even more in the script, which developed thirty-one characters for various species of small domesticated animal, all based on the sign "sheep." The pig was not yet taboo, as it was in later times.

In the cities, a great many artisans devoted their energies to a variety of manufactures. Evidently the stoneworkers were particularly numerous; they would have had to be, to produce the masonry of the temples, the stone cones for mosaics, and the many stone vessels of Sumer. Handsome metal vessels and striking animal figures testify to the skills of the metalworkers of the land. Many men were employed at brickmaking; bricks and clay cones for mosaics were in constant demand, as the temples needed constant repair. There was an abundance of imported raw materials on hand for those crafts that had need of them, as the works of art in metal and stone show. For these we may ascribe an origin to those places from which they were imported at a later period: gold from Meluḫḫa, the Indus valley; lapis lazuli from Badakhshan in Afghanistan; fine stone for vessels from the Iranian mountains to the east; silver from the "Silver Mountain," probably in the Cilician Taurus; copper from Magan, the coasts of either side of the Arabian Sea; woods from the eastern mountain ranges, not yet as denuded as they were to be in later ages—already, Sumer was tied by strings of trade to most of the then known world. East and southeast were the preferred directions of trade; the long sea voyages would have required a mastery of the art of sailing before the monsoon winds. But there is some interesting evidence from the northwest. Typically Sumerian finds in the midst of non-Sumerian surroundings, at Tell Brak on the Jagjaga, a tributary of the River Khabur, might be interpreted as evidence for an attempt to control the trade routes of Upper Mesopotamia.

The centers of economic life, both agricultural and industrial, were the temples of the cities. Not all temples, to be sure, can have attained the importance of the E-anna at Uruk, whose buildings covered an area of (at a conservative estimate) twenty-two acres. The Sumerian script had sprung, as we have seen, from the needs of the managers of the temples' economic activities, so widespread and so complex that unaided memory could no longer keep track of them. The oldest clay tablets are all, without exception, found in temple precincts; all, without exception, deal with economic transactions. This is how we know the motivation for the invention of writing. For countries and periods with a different economic structure, writing was unnecessary, therefore neither invented nor, where this was possible, adopted from those who possessed it. On seal impressions and reliefs we see, again and again, herds marked as property of the gods (i.e. of the temples) by symbolic signs. In the great complex of the E-anna at Uruk are to be found workshops of potters, stonecutters, metalsmiths. These, along with the volume and quality of the artifacts found, show the high degree of specialization and the advanced division of labor already achieved; it is a mark even of this earliest city-

44

civilization that a considerable part of the population is freed from direct production of their own food to pursue other tasks —the satisfaction of domestic demand for artifacts, and the production of export goods to pay for the flow of imports from abroad.

At the head of the temple economy is the ruler, the "man in the net kilt" from the cylinder seals and reliefs. We are not sure what title he bore at the time. He was probably called *en*, which we usually translate as "lord"—unsatisfactorily, for this does not express the fact that the title also implies the rank of high priest or priestess. Yet it is precisely this union of sacred and profane functions that the pictorial tradition displays in the scenes featuring the "man in the net kilt." (In any case, the distinction between sacred and profane is ours, not necessarily theirs, and need cause no difficulty in studying this ancient material.) We also meet with the word *lugal*, the term usual in later historical and literary texts for "king" (the word means literally "big man" or "great man"); but we meet with it only once, in a document of Uruk IIIb. The "man in the net kilt" appears, on a cylinder seal, as the "good shepherd" (a title frequently borne by later kings); two sheep, longhorned and maned, feed on the leaves of two branches he holds in his hands. The scene has a religious significance, as is shown by the symbols of the goddess Inanna, the "reed-bundles" or "gateposts" as they are variously called, on either side of the symmetrical composition.

The evidence, then, both archaeological and documentary, allows us to trace back to the Protoliterate period an organizational form that we can perceive clearly, through written sources, only toward the end of the Early Dynastic period— the Sumerian "temple-state."[31] In this system, the head of the temple economy is the city-god's vicar on earth. He supervises the construction and repair of the god's house (temple) and the celebration of all the solemnities of his cult. He also supervises the planning and management of the irrigation works, without which the god's (temple's) fields cannot be tilled, and directs the manifold activities of the god's (temple's) servants.

In addition, he must defend the god's property (the temple-state's territory) against attack from outside. All this will be seen in greater detail when we come to deal with the Early Dynastic period (see pp. ooo ff.).

The reticence of the Protoliterate sources prevents us from learning the size of the political units that these temple-states rule. Sumer is, culturally speaking, a closely knit unity: Writing is found at Kish, in the far north of Sumer, at the same time it appears for the first time at Uruk IVb; by level III it is employed all over the country in the service of the temple economies; the word lists from which the script is learned are uniform in every part of Sumer. None of this proves that a single city dominated the whole. Unfortunately the later Sumerians preserve no direct and reliable knowledge of this formative phase of their history. The *Sumerian King List* ascribes five successive dynasties to the period that began "when kingship descended from heaven" and ended with the Flood. Capitals of these dynasties were Eridu, Badtibira, Larak (a city in central Sumer not yet discovered), Sippar in the north and Shuruppak (the modern Fara) in the center. Shuruppak would have to be the last, as its king, Ziusudra, is the Noah of the Sumerian Flood legend. In fact this tradition of the antediluvian age seems to have come into the *King List* mainly from the Flood myth itself, for there the above five cities are given as the main centers of the land when the gods decided to cleanse it of the human race. But excavations at Shuruppak have yielded no signs of a Protoliterate city even remotely comparable to Uruk, while the extensive remains of Badtibira may well cover another important city of this age. Neither Uruk nor Lagash is mentioned in the antediluvian chapter of the *King List*. Uruk in fact appears only as the capital of the second dynasty after the Flood, preceded by a dynasty of Kish (most of whose rulers bear Akkadian names, a sign of the difference between the south and the already strongly Semiticized north). Both of these dynasties, however, ruling simultaneously as has been shown, belong to the Early Dynastic period. The *King List* has therefore nothing to tell us of the political history of the Protoliterate age.

The religious traditions of the Sumerians, on the other hand, may more faithfully reflect their early past. We have already pointed out that at Eridu cult was offered on the same spot from the Ubaid stage well into historical times, and we may assume that the same is true elsewhere. This does not guarantee that the same gods were always worshiped, under the same names. It does not mean that the conception of the gods would not have gone through basic changes in this long course of time. The deities in the Protoliterate period are represented by symbols, in the great majority of cases, in works of plastic art as well as in script. The most frequent symbols we see are polelike objects; the "gateposts" or "reed-bundles" of Inanna of Uruk and the "buckled post" of Nanna the moon-god of Ur are the best-known. Totems? It is possible. But anthropomorphic representations are not unknown, as we have seen from the fragment of a head with a divine horned cap (see p. 38). A document from Uruk IIIb unites in one square the symbols for "festival," "star," "Inanna," "day," and "to set"; the interpretation would be "festival on the day on which the star of Inanna sets" (heliacal setting is no doubt meant). Inanna here would already be what she is in later texts, goddess of the planet Venus—which would mean that the development of the idea of the divine from an earlier, probably totemic, conception to an anthropomorphic one had already taken place. The symbolic signs now refer to gods in man's image.

The later Sumerian tradition knows several deities who are mentioned with the epithet "old": this may preserve some fragments of ancient religion. "Old" occurs with these names: Gatumdu, "the Mother of Lagash"; Nisiba of Eresh; Nunbarsheguni of Nippur; Belili, the sister of Dumuzi; and Bilulu. All are goddesses. The names that have any meaning we can understand are Sumerian: *Nisaba* is a word for grain, *Nunbarshegunu* contains the Sumerian word for a kind of barley (*hordeum rectum nigrum*). Whether these goddesses were worshiped in Protoliterate times is uncertain. It is worth noting, however, that the pantheons of a number of the oldest cities were headed by a goddess. They had consorts, but of clearly lower rank: in Lagash, Gatumdu-Baba with her consort Ningirsu; in Nina, Nanshe with Nindara; in Kesh, Nintu with Shulpa-ea. Inanna and Dumuzi (the Semitic Ishtar and Tammuz) probably also belong in this category, although the goddess' husband in this case was a mortal. The relative position of male and female in these couples does not correspond to the patriarchal family, normal in Sumer from the time when we have any evidence for such things. But that this had not always been normal appears by an inscription of Urukagina, ruler of Lagash (ca. 2350 B.C.), who speaks of a polyandry permitted in earlier times, but rejected in his own (see p. 000). It would be altogether understandable if, when the idea of anthropomorphic deities first developed, a civilization based on agriculture and stock-breeding were first to ascribe divinity to goddesses who, like Nisaba, represented grain, or, like Turdur, the ewe—or who simply were able to guarantee fertility, in the fields, in the herds, in the homes of men.

While Sumer erected cities and developed the arts of civilization, most of her neighbors remained at the level of village culture. Elam is the exception, making some progress by following the Sumerian example. But the consciousness of a cultural lag must have been brought home to the inhabitants of other parts of Western Asia; far-flung Sumerian trade would ensure it. We have distinct traces of the cultural diffusion that resulted from this. There is a close connection between Sumer and the Diyala region, with its center at Eshnunna, the modern Tell Asmar: several types of cylinder seal and other objects are shared by this territory and northern Babylonia, and to a lesser degree with the south. In Susa, the principal site of Elam, Sumerian influence is so apparent that complete subjection to Sumerian rule has been suggested as an explanation. But the invention of an independent script at the time of Uruk III, although stimulated by the Sumerian model, still proves a degree of independence incompatible with foreign rule. At Susa, too, the seal types of Sumer are common—hunting scenes and above all the heraldic seals—and there are also types that seem to stem from the Diyala country; but, at the same time, quite independent types are developed there. Small animal figures of stone also show a close relationship to Sumerian art.

Contacts with the Assyrian area seem looser. A cylinder seal with a religious boat scene, found at Tell Billa, with exact counterparts at Uruk in levels IV and III, is surely an importation.[32] At Tepe Gawra nearby there are, at levels corresponding to Sumer's Protoliterate period, a series of temples erected in the same form over centuries. They may well be related to the temple compounds we first came to know in Ubaid levels on the Babylonian plain, but they show distinct features of their own. Oddly enough the closest parallel is the temple erected by the Kassite King Karaindash at Uruk, some 1,500 years later (ca. 1430 B.C.). In Assyria in the Protoliterate period stamp seals have yet to be replaced by the cylinder seal; the latter does not appear at Tepe Gawra until the Early Dynastic period and the Dynasty of Agade. The main motif on these stamp seals is the ibex; domestic animals are only rarely represented and human figures very seldom. The Sumerian script makes no appearance.[33]

But, even farther from Sumer, at Tell Brak[34] in the Upper Khabur basin, excavation has produced a quantity of finds authentically Sumerian in style. The level corresponds to late Protoliterate in Sumer. There is a clay-cone mosaic on the outer wall of a temple, which shares other characteristic features with the shrines of Uruk. Spectacle-shaped symbols (they occur also in Sumer and in the Diyala region) have here developed into forms whose upper parts have become large eyes. Some of them also bear high caps and attain a certain human appearance, resembling alabaster heads that have been found there; the latter seem, in turn, related to the fragment of a divine head from Uruk.

When we compare Tell Brak to the contemporary levels of, for example, Nineveh or Tepe Gawra, the quantity of finds that point to Sumer is perfectly extraordinary; the latter sites, although closer to the source, have nothing comparable. Tell Brak is an anomaly in the North. We shall therefore have to consider it a Sumerian enclave, which immediately brings to mind the buildings found there over the Protoliterate ruins: a "palace" of Naram-Sin of Agade (2260–2223 B.C.), reconstructed under the Third Dynasty of Ur (ca. 2100). The so-called "palace" is more in the nature of a fortress, built to uphold Agade's imperial rule in the north and to control the trade route; we should hesitate to assign a similar role to the Protoliterate ruins, which must have stood for a considerable length of time. For, if we were to do so, we should have to posit a military-political expansion of the Sumerians over an area so wide, and at a date so early, that caution would prefer to sound retreat. Nevertheless we may keep in mind the scenes, frequent on the Protoliterate cylinder seals, where captives are presented to the "man in the net kilt." We can hardly think they are the spoil of intra-Sumerian wars; it would then be rather difficult to explain why the cities are not walled.

The influence of Sumer is not limited to Mesopotamia; in northern and central Syria, in Palestine and in Anatolia, isolated finds attest to contacts with the civilization of Sumer. Even in Egypt, quite definite borrowings from Protoliterate Sumer have been revealed, for the Gerzean period just before the first dynasties (see p. 256). This, as we have said, is useful chronologically, but must not be misinterpreted historically. Stimuli from the area of Sumerian civilization were not the decisive factor in the development of civilization in Egypt. The theory, advanced from time to time, that the hieroglyphic script owes its origin to the example of Sumerian cuneiform has little to be said for it.

So momentous an achievement is followed, to our surprise, by the swift decline of Sumerian civilization at the end of the Protoliterate period. In the last stages, the artifacts show unmistakable degeneration from former standards, particularly in cylinder seals and in the animal-figurine amulets. There is a carelessness in execution, a falling away from the original aim of creating sculptural figures, by scratching in rough outlines instead; these are so frequent that this cannot be supposed to be the work of a few clumsy artisans. In any case the age that shortly follows, the Early Dynastic period, is too full of novelties to allow us to accept so easy a solution. Something more important than a lapse in dexterity has occurred. We do not know the details of how Sumerian civilization fell. We do know the cause of it: the massive influx of Semitic-speaking peoples from the north and northwest.

Sumer was a land much harried by its rivers, and therefore in the poetic vocabulary of its people, disasters, even migrations, are often depicted by the image of the Flood. The *King List* places the Flood, the world deluge, at the point where, historically, Protoliterate Sumer comes to an end, to be followed by the changed conditions of the Early Dynastic age.[35] By this it means to convey the influx of Akkadian Semites. Although it is difficult to imagine how the knowledge of these remote events reached the compilers of the *King List*, it is natural to suppose that they would interpret it in the light of their own experience of the Canaanite (or Amorite) migrations, at the beginning of the second millennium B.C.—i.e. that their picture of the first wave of Semites borrows its colors from their vision of the second. In any case this picture perfectly portrays the event as it must have struck Sumerians who experienced it: an inundation of their country by outland immigrants.

2

The Early Dynastic Period

By "Early Dynastic" we mean the age from the end of the Protoliterate period to the founding of the Empire of Agade; an age marked by the infiltration of Sumer by that Semitic population which, anticipating the twenty-fourth century, we call Akkadian. With this age we enter historical times; written records begin to speak to us of men and events. Not, however, that the historian can now find all he needs in the inscriptions; he must still depend in part on archaeological sources. He cannot, for example, ignore the drop in artistic standards to be seen in Sumer after the end of Uruk's level III, particularly in the style of cylinder seals. He cannot but be impressed by the rise, in the Early Dynastic period, of the art of Sumer to new heights of achievement, both in form and in technique. He will note that side by side with innovations appears the temple on a terrace, forerunner of the ziqqurrat, a symbol of continuity pointing back to Protoliterate times. The task of the following chapters is to describe this mixture of old and new, the product of the symbiosis of Sumerians and Akkadians, and to assess the contribution of the Akkadian element to the culture, and the history, of Mesopotamia.

Chronology

We divide the Early Dynastic period into three stages, on the basis of archaeological finds; since their first application, to discoveries in the Diyala region, they have proved of practical use.[36] Early Dynastic I extends from the Protoliterate period to the time of the archaic tablets of Ur. Early Dynastic II begins with the appearance of city walls in Sumer. Early Dynastic III has as its starting point the period of the archive of Shuruppak. In other words these divisions have nothing to do with turning points in political history, of which we know little enough in any case.

Along with "Early Dynastic" as a designation for this age, "Pre-Sargonic" is sometimes used. "Early Dynastic" refers to the plethora of dynasties in Sumer, as reflected by the *Sumerian King List*; "Pre-Sargonic" alludes to the role of the founder of the Empire of Agade, Sargon the Great: his seizure of power, ca. 2340, is the first clearly recognizable decisive event in the history of Mesopotamia.

Before that date, in fact, as we have seen in the previous chapter, chronology can be no exact science. If we date the reign of Hammurabi of Babylon at 1792–1750 B.C.,[37] then it follows that: the Third Dynasty of Ur begins at 2111; the Dynasty of Agade begins ca. 2340[38] (the uncertainty arises from the difficulty of unraveling the overlap between the last kings of Agade and the first Gutian rulers); Lugalzagesi of Umma and Uruk ruled ca. 2350; and Ur-Nanshe of Lagash ruled ca. 2520. Dates for anything older than that can only be vague estimates, and are to be thought of as working hypotheses at best. Mesalim of Kish ruled at roughly the beginning of the twenty-sixth century B.C., perhaps two generations before Ur-Nanshe; Mebaragesi of Kish ruled at approximately the end of the twenty-eighth and the beginning of the twenty-seventh centuries.

The great problem is to apply such absolute dates to the archaeological divisions outlined above. Ur-Nanshe is the earliest king whose date we can estimate with confidence; how to relate him to the archives of Shuruppak, our last archaeological dividing line? Ur-Nanshe's inscriptions are written on stone; we know of no clay tablets that can clearly be assigned to his reign. At Shuruppak we have clay tablets and no stone; any

CHRONOLOGICAL TABLE II
The Early Dynastic Period*

	UR	UMMA	LAGASH	URUK	AGADE	KISH	SHURUPPAK	ADAB
2800						Mebaragesi		
75						Aka		
50								
25								
2700				Gilgamesh				
75	Archaic tablets							
50								
25						(Mesalim)		
2600			LAGASH				Archive	
75			Enhengal (Mesalim)					
50								
25								
2500			Ur-Nanshe ca. 2520					
75	Mesanepada	*Ush*	Akurgal ca. 2490					
50	Meskiangnuna	*Enakale*	Eanatum ca. 2470					
25	Balulu	*Urlumma*	Entemena ca. 2430					
2400			Enanatum II ca. 2400					
75			Lugalanda ca. 2370	*Lugalkin-geneshdudu*				
50		*Lugalzagesi*	Urukagina ca. 2355	*Lugalzagesi*	*Lugalzagesi*			*Meskigala*
25					Sargon 2340–2284			

* The position of names given without dates is based on rough estimates; of names in italics, on synchronisms with other rulers.

clue we might hope for from a comparison of the styles of script is therefore vitiated by the differences that come from writing on different materials. In a word, palaeographic evidence is of little help. However, we do know that the Shuruppak archive has to be several generations older than Eanatum of Lagash, a grandson of Ur-Nanshe. By a cautious estimate we might then date the archive at the beginning or middle of the twenty-sixth century, and with it the beginning of Early Dynastic III. (The archaic tablets at Ur (and the beginning of Early Dynastic II) would be one century or at the most one and a half centuries older than those of Shuruppak.) As the Early Dynastic period begins where the Protoliterate ends, our oldest absolute date would be the carbon-14 determination for Temple C of Uruk IV, i.e. 2815 ± 85 B.C.

Continuous and relatively certain chronology, then, fails above Sargon of Agade. Continuous and approximately certain estimates can still be made back to Ur-Nanshe, as from his time down we have an uninterrupted chain of royal inscriptions indicating that "X is the son of Y," and we count generations to arrive at rough dates for each king. Above that point, all is guesswork. We look for help to developmental study of the cuneiform script (form and order of the signs), and this offers vague chronological clues, when we compare older and younger texts. We also seek support from archaeology (measurement of levels of rubble in tells; stylistic changes in cylinder seals), and, if carefully evaluated, this evidence can be of help to us.

The *Sumerian King List*, as pointed out above, is distorted by the fiction that the area of Babylonia, the Diyala region and the Middle Euphrates (Mari), all were subject to but one ruler at a time, at *all* times. It therefore arranges successively "dynasties" that are in many cases known to have ruled simultaneously. The antediluvian rulers and the kings immediately after the Flood (First Dynasty of Kish) are given reigns of fabulous length, a product of the respect in which the Sumerians held the immense age of civilization in their country. Nevertheless, the *King List* is of value to us, and not only as a witness to the historical conceptions of the age in which it

55

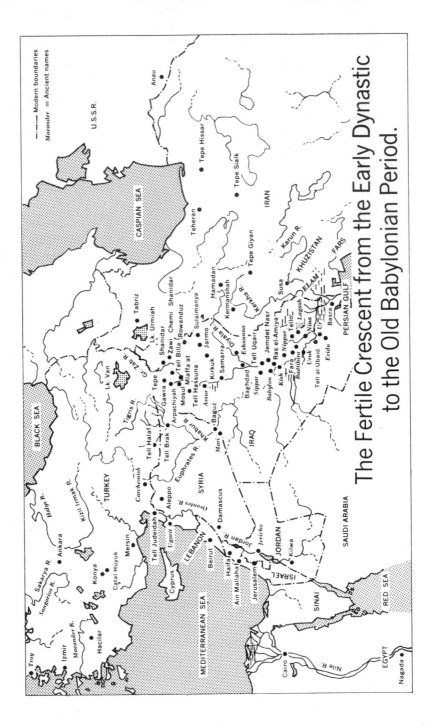

The Fertile Crescent from the Early Dynastic to the Old Babylonian Period.

was composed; its data on the succession of rulers and the length of reigns, wherever it can be checked against other sources, can be an important chronological aid.

What have we, chronologically speaking, for the Early Dynastic period? A reasonably sound structure from the reign of Ur-Nanshe on, i.e. for the major part of Early Dynastic III. As long as we do not attempt to synchronize this with the history of Egypt, we can treat, with some degree of confidence, at least a part of this age as meaningful history, and at last describe the course of events in the order in which they occurred.

Sumerians and Semites in the Early Dynastic Age

Our sources for the beginnings of Early Dynastic history are, as it were, a few stones out of an otherwise vanished mosaic. Written primary sources are royal inscriptions, treaties, administrative documents, and the products of the scribal schools. Written secondary sources are the *Sumerian King List*, the epics of the kings of Uruk, and traditional memories of Early Dynastic rulers preserved in Akkadian omen literature. The reader must take warning that much of what we draw from this is necessarily speculative, and will be so in the following account; let him be warned, also, that new texts may be found at any time, leading to the revision or reversal of opinions held till now. Our knowledge is insufficient and we must be skeptical. But we may not, on that account, be silent; time and again we must try to make sense of what we think we know just now.

The leading role of the Sumerians, among the peoples living on the Babylonian plain, has been discussed in the previous chapter. We need not repeat their extraordinary achievements here. Their invention of writing, however, is crucial to our present theme. For it brought the history of Mesopotamia into our field of vision. It gave us the possibility of a knowledge of personalities and events. An account of the past as political history first becomes possible with royal inscriptions in that

57

script. In this respect the reign of Mebaragesi of Kish (the name is later also written Enmebaragesi), at the end of the twenty-eighth or the beginning of the twenty-seventh century B.C (Early Dynastic II), is the earliest point at which we may begin. The *King List* names him as the twenty-second of the rulers of the "First Dynasty of Kish," which is the first dynasty after the Flood. Most of his predecessors in that dynasty (still according to the *King List*) bear Semitic names. We can hardly hope to prove their historicity; we cannot say that any were authentic rulers of Kish. We may also wonder how reliable the compilers' sources of information can be for so early a period—an age, as we know, when cuneiform was not yet a medium for the expression of complicated facts. Still, we must not underestimate the propensity, and the capacity, of the ancient Semite for the memorization of genealogical lists, and for handing them on orally to his successors, generation after generation. The fact, incidentally, that Mebaragesi himself has a Sumerian name need not speak against his Semitic descent. Sumerian names, like all things Sumerian, must have had high prestige value even outside Sumer itself. In short, we can say little except that Semites appear in the land at the very beginning of the known political history of Sumer. We have already heard (see p. 51) the suspicion voiced that symptoms of decline, at the close of the Protoliterate period, were connected with the flow of Semitic-speaking elements into Sumer. The coexistence of Semites and Sumerians determined Mesopotamian history down to the beginning of the second millennium, when Sumerian as a spoken language quite died out. The results of this contact were effective far beyond that point. Babylonian (and therefore Western Asian) culture was to remain bilingual to the end of its existence.

The influx of Semitic nomads into Iraq continues to this day; it has always been an element of that country's history. With the advantage of hindsight over millennia, we simplify matters by referring to "migratory waves." From time to time these have led to linguistic shifts. In the inscriptions of Assyrian kings of the ninth century B.C. we hear of the Arabs for the first time, as nomadic tribesmen on the move; by the seventh century A.D., they have conquered Mesopotamia, and proceed completely to Arabize the country. From the fourteenth century B.C., we hear of Aramaean nomads intruding; less than 1,000 years later, theirs is the language of the country—Akkadian continued until the time of Christ, but only as a written language. Under the Dynasty of Agade we first hear of the "Martu," as the Sumerians call them, "Amurru" to the Akkadians, and Amorites to us (or Canaanites, in the wider sense of the term, as their language is closely related to Syrian Canaanite).[39] Within a century and a half the Martu are endangering the very existence of the empire of Ur III. By the Old Babylonian period any number of places in Mesopotamia have been seized by Amorite chiefs, who set themselves up as rulers. This, however, did not lead to a shift in language; Akkadian still had such vitality at the time that the Amorites succumbed to its attractions.

What the fate of the Amorites was in the western parts of the Fertile Crescent, to which they also migrated in force at the time, is very difficult to tell, as the sources for the late third and early second millennium in Syria-Palestine are very few indeed.

What about the Akkadians themselves? They call themselves and their language after the capital of the empire founded by Sargon, but were obviously present before he organized his kingdom. They are, in fact, the oldest Semitic people of whom we know in Mesopotamia—which does not necessarily mean that they really were the oldest. They may well have been preceded by Semites sharing in the original settlement of Babylonia, in the fifth millennium B.C. But this we cannot know. Our earliest real evidence for the presence of Akkadians in Sumer is from personal names in the archaic texts of Ur, and from the oldest Semitic loan words in the Sumerian language. By Early Dynastic II we can already assume a heavy Semitic settlement of northern Babylonia and the Diyala region, and the contrast between the Semitic north and the Sumerian south is to be notable from now on.

Where had they come from—the Akkadians, that is, who are the Semites in the north? The question can be answered by comparative means. Considering the course of later Semitic migrations, particularly those of the Amorites, we can assume that the Akkadians moved down from the north, from Syria, the crest of the wave coming to rest in the Diyala region and the northern parts of the Babylonian plain, with Kish as its center. Mari on the Middle Euphrates was also an important center of Akkadian population, in Early Dynastic II, and was to remain a significant one until Hammurabi's time. Inscriptions, personal names, and loan words all give perfectly clear evidence of the ethnical situation; to interpret the archaeological evidence turns out to be more delicate.

Sculpture from the lower basin of the Diyala (Khafaji [=Tutub] Tell Asmar [=Eshnunna], Tell Agrab), discovered in Early Dynastic II levels, makes a strange impression: It is severe and angular and tends toward the abstract. It is therefore not at all like Protoliterate Sumerian work, nor does it resemble that of Sumer in Early Dynastic III, with its rounded, naturalistic forms that may derive from Protoliterate art. This "non-Sumerian" sculpture has, as a particularly frequent type, the votive statuette of a man or woman with hands folded in prayer: the "worshiper." In Early Dynastic II this type also makes its way into the Sumerian south. Such figures are also documented at Mari, at Assur and recently at Tell Khuera, at the headwaters of the Khabur. In other words, there is a connection with Upper Mesopotamia to be observed. Another novelty, again best attested along the Diyala, is the large rectangular votive plaque of stone, in very low relief. The figures represented are in the style of the "worshiper" statuettes. In the same region, at Early Dynastic II levels, appears a temple type imported from the north, technically called the *Herdhaus* temple: The cult pedestal is located at one of the short sides of the temple cella, and the entrance is on the long side and near the opposite end. This does not at all correspond to the symmetrical ground plan of Protoliterate Sumerian shrines. Recently, a *Herdhaus* cella has been found in an Early Dynastic II temple at Nippur. So far this is the only example known in Sumer; but, again, a parallel exists in the north, the archaic Ishtar-temples of Assur.

Ceramics, too, in the Diyala region show an independence of Sumerian influence, in the form of a red-painted pottery, decorated with figures, called "scarlet ware." On the other hand at Khafaji (ancient Tutub) there is a temple showing clear connections with Sumerian architecture: a temple-terrace within a double oval enclosure. Remains of a similar oval precinct wall are preserved at Tell al-Ubaid near Ur, for the Early Dynastic period. The difficulty is that we cannot tell where this type of enclosure originated. We are just as much in the dark concerning the origin of a new type of brick form that is typical for Early Dynastic buildings, common to both the Diyala sites and all of Babylonia, the "plano-convex" brick: It is not the usual rectangular shape, but is flat on one side and cushion-shaped on the other. It was laid on a slant, with the angle of one course opposite to that of the previous one, producing a herringbone pattern in the walls.

All of these innovations point to the arrival of a new population—the Akkadians, certainly; but the question is whether everything new ought to be ascribed to them alone, or whether there is a more complex ethnic background involved. All archaeological indications available so far show a very much greater correspondence between northern Mesopotamian elements and those of the Diyala region than between those of the Diyala region and the south. But caution must be observed: Early Dynastic II is still very ill documented in Sumer, as far as sculpture and temple architecture are concerned. Sumerian art of Early Dynastic III, however, is clearly at opposite poles from the "northern" style of Early Dynastic II, making us think of a reaction against the latter and a renaissance of Protoliterate forms. In this light, a Sumerian hand in the innovations of Early Dynastic II is excluded. There is, however, a definite reassertion of Sumerian influence on the art of the Diyala sites during Early Dynastic III.

As we have seen, these innovations were preceded by a degeneration in forms, chiefly in the art of seal engraving, at the end of the Protoliterate and the beginning of the Early Dynastic period. This is to be attributed, we may assume, to the arrival of the first wave of the Akkadian migration (see p. 51). By the same token ought not the recovery from this fall, with all its new creations, be attributed to the Akkadians as well? If so, there are important consequences for our judgment of the social condition of the Akkadian immigrants by Early Dynastic II. That this population would still be largely nomadic, making the slow transition to settled life in villages or cities only over a stretch of several centuries, as was to be the case with the Amorites and the Armaeans, does not accord with the archaeological evidence. For the Akkadians the process of adaptation to settled life must have been completed as early as Early Dynastic I—which raises questions about the way of life of the Akkadians in their original northern Mesopotamian homes. Only if we assume, for the north, a Semitic population already settled in towns before Early Dynastic II, can we explain the use of Sumerian cuneiform in Mari, at the latter period, for the recording of the Akkadian language. We assume, to go one step further, that the adoption of a settled mode of life by the Akkadians took place in northern Mesopotamia before they settled in the Diyala region and northern Babylonia. If this is true, then we ought, perhaps, to revise our opinions of the examples of Early Dynastic II sculptural style met with in the north, in the figures of the "worshiper": these need not be "offshoots" from the Diyala centers; on the contrary, we may be dealing here with a cultural influence flowing from north to south, with northern Mesopotamia as the point of origin. In all of this, we move through a forest of uncertainties, and two questions must still remain open: Would this northern Mesopotamian art derive from an original Sumerian inspiration? We recall the Sumerian enclave of the Proto-literate period at Tell Brak, at the headwaters of the Khabur. Secondly: Are there still other (non-Semitic) peoples involved in the achievements of this northern Mesopotamian culture? The *Herdhaus* temple of Early Dynastic II in the Diyala region has Assyrian prototypes. Now Assyria in Early Dynastic times was, unlike the Middle Euphrates, settled by Semites either not at all or only sparsely. For there is surely some ethnic reason for the fact that cuneiform was not used there until the age of Agade. In fact we find in Assyria, as late as the twentieth century B.C., traces of an autochthonous, pre-Semitic population.

Let us return, then, to the Babylonian plain, to see what comes of the meeting of Akkadian and Sumerian on the latter's home ground. It led, as such meetings always do, to a mutual borrowing of words. Akkadian, on balance, is the debtor in the exchange; Sumerian loan words from the spheres of cult and technology (Sum. *apin*, "plow," Akk. *epinnum*) appear, and the names of many implements of daily life (Sum. *banshur*, "table," Akk. *passhurum*). There are also many Sumerian loan words to be found among Akkadian names for the professions, and for religious and official functions. An irrigation supervisor in Akkadian is a *kugallum* (Sum. *kungal*), the word for barley is *she'um* (Sum. *she*), the word for emmer wheat is *zizum* (Sum. *ziz*), and the word for farmer is *ikkarum*, which comes from Sumerian *engar*; it is clear that Sumerians led the way in irrigation and agriculture. On the other hand the Sumerian word for garlic bulb, *sum*, is borrowed from the Akkadian *shumum*; Sumerian *sam*, "to buy," is from Akkadian *sha'amum*; a slave, *wardum* in Akkadian, becomes the Sumerian *urd-* or *ird-*. There are, however, cases in which both languages have borrowed words in common from a third, to us unknown, speech. This is the case for copper (Sum. *urudu*, Akk. *weri'um*) and for chair (Sum. *guza*, Akk. *kussi'um*); we know on phonetic grounds that these words are not native to either tongue. For copper, we may think of the name being imported together with the object.

How did these two peoples get on? For this we have completely contradictory hypotheses. They range from a denial of any opposition to an assumption of outright enmity, the latter to be found generally in older histories of the Near East. Between the alternatives of rabid national antagonism and idyllic neighborly relations, it would be foolish to choose, and unwise to seek some fixed median point. Sumerians and Semites represent entirely different traditions, entirely different patterns of culture, as we shall have occasion to see again and again. War, within the confines of the Babylonian plain, will undeniably have occurred between cities of Sumerian and Semitic population. But this is part of a general pattern of rivalry between the cities of the land, which would have led to wars among Sumerians, among Akkadians, and between Akkadians *and* Sumerians, in a manner no different from the other cases. The historical tradition preserved by the *Sumerian King List* knows nothing of a national conflict between the two. At all events the antagonism between nomad and sedentary far overshadowed, at all times, any conscious opposition between Sumerian and Semite. All the settled populations shared the fear of the uncanny, the unstable nomad, and the latter in turn cast hungry eyes on their worldly goods, but never on their way of life. In Sumerian epics and myths we find the term *kur*, meaning both "mountains" and "foreign (or) hostile lands," by which is meant the mountain dwellers of Iran, the nomads of the west and northwest, indeed practically everyone outside Babylonia. The only solution to the conflict between nomad and sedentary (at least the only one satisfactory to the sedentary) was the assimilation of each new threatening tribe to the settled, agricultural mode of life. To repell them, to isolate them, proved only a short-term palliative. Another solution did offer itself, to Sumerians and sedentary Semites alike: to take the tribesmen into the city's service, as mercenary troops.

On the whole, then, this confrontation of two peoples had a salutary effect on both, as is so often the case in history. Akkadian civilization down to its disappearance bears a strong Sumerian stamp; the last, and in many ways the highest, great age of Sumerian civilization, the empire of Ur III, is unimaginable without the legacy of Semitic Agade.

Kish, Uruk and Ur—Political Units

Sumerian epic and hymnal literature retains a tradition of a war fought in this period between Mebaragesi of Kish and his successor Aka on one side, and Gilgamesh of Uruk on the other. (The alternate form of the first name, Enmebaragesi, is a later one, the title *en* having been drawn into the proper name.) The King of Kish, so the story goes, summoned to surrender, besieged Uruk instead. Another version says that Gilgamesh raised the siege by a successful sortie. This, our oldest reference to interstate conflict in Babylonia, has been preserved by posterity's fascination with the heroic figure of Gilgamesh. Gilgamesh is the hero of a cycle of Sumerian epic lays, reworked by the Akkadians into a great epic poem in their own language, after the Old Babylonian period. This Akkadian tradition knows Gilgamesh as the builder of the city wall of Uruk, and as the tyrant who drove his subjects in gangs to labor on it. Excavation has uncovered a wall about five and a half miles long at Uruk. As it is made of plano-convex brick, its construction in the century of Gilgamesh and Mebaragesi is perfectly conceivable. In any case, it is our first evidence of the existence of walled cities in Babylonia.

Gilgamesh is not the only epic hero; in addition to the Sumerian cycle and the Akkadian epic that follow his fortunes, there are Sumerian epic lays that treat of his predecessors on the throne of Uruk, the kings Lugalbanda and Enmerkar. The epic tradition sends its heroes on expeditions to distant lands ("The Cedar Forest," "The Mountain Land of Ḥurrum"); with what care this must be treated, we see from the references to Ḥurrum in the epic story of *Gilgamesh and Ḥuwawa*. Ḥurrum would mean the country of the Ḥurrians, non Semitic invaders of the end of the third millennium. Its presence in the epic is a reflection of the military expeditions mounted in this direction by the rulers of Ur III; it was, in short, injected at a later date. Gilgamesh, according to a Sumerian poem describing the recurring dilapidation and reconstruction of the Tummal, sanctuary of the goddess Ninlil at Nippur, is also supposed to have ruled over that sacred city.

We cannot write a "history" of the city of Uruk in the Early Dynastic age: Mebaragesi is a historically authenticated figure; Gilgamesh, his ancient rival, is not (or at least not yet). The oldest epigraphic occurrence of his name so far known is in a list of gods from Shuruppak (twenty-sixth century), where

Gilgamesh and his father Lugalbanda are named as posthumously deified heroes. The *Sumerian King List* knows the names of the rulers of Uruk only to the fourth generation before Gilgamesh, which thereby falls below the much longer tradition of the rulers of Kish. The First Dynasty of Uruk is placed on the *King List* only after the First Dynasty of Kish, another mark of the precedence, in the eyes of Sumerian tradition, of the ancient city of Kish.

"Low temples" (sanctuaries not erected on a terrace) cease to be built in Sumer after Protoliterate times. This is striking in the light of the usual continuity of sanctuaries. The ziqqurrat, however, continues into the Early Dynastic age. The tradition of the scribal schools also continues unbroken. If nevertheless there is a break in the historical tradition of the Sumerians, obliterating every memory of the great age represented archaeologically by Uruk VI–IV, the cause may perhaps be sought in the effects of the Akkadian migration on Sumer, at the beginning of the Early Dynastic period. Of the historical events accompanying this we know nothing. We may recall, however, that a later Semitic migration, the Amorite invasion, was indirectly responsible for the fall of the Empire of Ur III.

Kish, as we have said, appears to be a Semitic center. We know rather more about it than we do about Uruk, toward the end of Early Dynastic II and in Early Dynastic III. There are two known inscriptions mentioning its king, Mebaragesi. They come from the area east of the Tigris and south of the Diyala. One can be more precisely localized: It was found in the temple oval at Khafaji. The *Sumerian King List*, in a note on "Enmebaragesi," reports a victorious campaign of this king against Elam. This is the oldest indication we have of a conflict between Babylonia and Elam. All of which, to be sure, is very little to work with. But the inscriptions are authentic contemporary documents and permit us to conclude that Kish then ruled a northern Babylonian kingdom, which also included the Diyala area, and which may have gone to war against the Elamite East.

66

The significance of Kish becomes all the more apparent when the custom develops—we can document it from Mesalim[40] on—of rulers, not residing in Kish, nevertheless taking the title of "King of Kish." In addition to Mesalim, Mesanepada of Ur and Eanatum of Lagash are important figures who do the same. The title continued to be used into the Agade period and beyond, but does not occur in Ur III. This is a title of prestige, harking back to a time when Kish held dominion over wide areas of Babylonia, and probably over the Lower Diyala as well. It is not impossible that the power of Mebaragesi himself lies at the basis of this memory of greatness.

Of the Diyala area, and of its significance as a cultural region relatively free of Sumerian influence, we have already spoken at length. It was already urbanized at the beginning of the Early Dynastic age: The temple that in historical times was dedicated to the moon-god Su'en (Sin), located near the temple oval at Khafaji, goes back through level after level to the Jamdet Nasr period, more or less corresponding to Uruk III at the end of the Protoliterate age. A Semitic immigration at the beginning of the Early Dynastic age does not therefore occupy an empty land; there is a non-Semitic element, earlier on the ground, with possible connections with Iran. The oldest place names in the Diyala region are neither Sumerian nor Semitic, e.g. Ishnun and Tutub. The name Ishnun was reinterpreted by folk etymology and transformed into Sumerian Eshnunna, "Prince's Sanctuary," in the Ur III period. In the northern part of Babylonia, too, the toponymy provides place names neither Sumerian nor Semitic: Babilla is one, reinterpreted in Akkadian as Bab-ilim, "Gate of the God"; the Hellenized form is Babylon.

So far we do not know of which city Mesalim was the ruler. He bears the prestige-title of "King of Kish," the first ruler of whom we know to do so. His name is probably Semitic. The *King List* does not include it among the kings of its First Dynasty of Kish. Mesalim's tutelary god was Istaran or Sataran, worshiped at Der on the borders of Iran, near the modern Badrah. We cannot thereby conclude that Mesalim himself came from the Iranian border country. His inscriptions have been found at Adab and Lagash in Sumer. We know that simultaneously local rulers reign in these cities, with the title of *ensi*; we can assume that Mesalim is their overlord. As arbitrator he intervenes in a border dispute between Lagash and Umma, perennial rivals, an event still referred to in the time of Eanatum and Entemena of Lagash.

The rulers of Ur in the far south we meet, for the first time, in the great royal tombs of that city. These tombs are later than the archaic tablets at Ur. (The archaic tablets date from before Mebaragesi, and in terms of the development of cuneiform are halfway between the script of Uruk III–Jamdet Nasr and that of Shuruppak.) Inscriptions on the grave furnishings name the kings Meskalamdug and Akalamdug, and the queen Pu'abi.[41] These royal tombs prove that a ruler, or a member of the ruling house, customarily went to his reward accompanied by a retinue of servitors, buried with him on the occasion. In one of the tomb chambers no less than eighty such servants were found. The only parallel known so far is found at Kish, where the burial of several persons in one tomb points to the same custom. The names of the kings in the tombs of Ur are all in good Sumerian. We should therefore refrain from supposing this a foreign custom imported from abroad, rare though it seems to be in Sumer (it disappeared entirely thereafter). The grave furnishings are of a simply extraordinary splendor—vessels, seals, inlaid furniture, musical instruments, chariots with their teams of donkeys, and so on and on. Gold and silver and lapis lazuli are not spared. These tombs of Ur are therefore one of our most important sources for a knowledge of the art and craftsmanship of Sumer in Early Dynastic III.

The historical tradition of Ur embodied in the *King List* does not reach back as far as the royal tombs; it is in other words rather shorter than that for Kish and Uruk. Mesanepada (ca. 2490 B.C.) leads off the First Dynasty of Ur mentioned by the *King List.* His inscriptions call him "King of Kish," thereby claiming for him the hegemony of Babylonia, perhaps the first time for a king from the south. Ur, by its geographical location, is one of the most important cities in the country. It had, at the time, a harbor on a lagoon joined to the Persian Gulf, and it thus presided over the southern sea trade and all the wealth to be derived from it. Imports reached its quays from Tilmun (Greek Tylos, the modern Bahrain Islands, perhaps also the Arabian coast nearby), a transit harbor of great antiquity, and from Magan and Meluḫḫa (see p. 44). Consequently every major kingdom formed in Babylonia tried to gain possession of Ur. Mesanepada's son is followed by two kings with Akkadian names, Elulu and Balulu. Their reigns coincide, more or less, with the period of Eanatum and Entemena of Lagash.

At present we are able to write the history of a city, and of Babylonia as seen from the point of view of one of its many city-states in Early Dynastic III, only in a single case and only within limits. Lagash is the only place where we have detailed, authentic inscriptions for a relatively long line of rulers, from Ur-Nanshe to Urukagina; Lagash has revealed the only economic archives large enough to give us some insight into the structure of the state. It would therefore be pointless to list here the names of all the other rulers known from the two centuries before Sargon and to stitch together isolated facts known to us more or less by accident. To understand the political situation of the age, or rather of that part of it that is accessible to history, we shall attempt to generalize from the known facts.

Babylonia, as a geographical entity, has no natural center; it therefore had no national capital. Various cities, as we have seen, attempted to take the place of one. We assume an early hegemony of Kish, above all on the basis of the title "King of Kish" as a claim to suzerainty over the whole land. The pre-eminent position of Uruk belongs to an age almost invisible to the historian. It finds expression in the splendid archaeological record of that city in the late Protoliterate period, and in the traditional content of the title *en* (see below). Babylonia did possess a religious center, Nippur, the city of Enlil, the prestige of which was never disputed; but, as the common shrine of all the cities, Nippur was never permitted to develop any political power of its own. Frequently, in fact, it was the bone of contention between rival states.

Geographical conditions in Babylonia invited to particularism. The great cities, sprung from isolated prehistoric settlements, were irrigation oases surrounded by tracts of non-irrigated land; the latter was, potentially, as fertile as any city land, but remained an uninhabited steppe for lack of water. These steppes were the barriers between the city-states. The rivers and the great canals were the links. Main traffic arteries and connecting routes between all the cities, the waterways were bound to counteract the trend to isolation. But they always proved more effective as avenues of trade and, in war, of attack than as means of administrative unification. Thus Babylonia is a congeries of independent little states, whose relationship to each other is one of equality (the "brotherhood" of the treaties of alliance), of suzerainty and vassalage (the overlordship of Mesalim in Adab and Lagash), but never of unity. There are coalitions, but they are always short-term, causing the political situation to change from decade to decade. The same was to be true of the Old Babylonian period, before Hammurabi, to a degree approaching the grotesque. The division of the country in the Early Dynastic period does not, perhaps, reach that point, but it comes uncomfortably near.

We shall return later on to an examination of the history of Lagash, as a model, so to speak, of the political history of Early Dynastic III.

Government and Society in Early Dynastic Sumer

Some conclusions on the internal political structure of these states can be drawn, for the historically knowable periods, from the titles of their rulers. There are three that concern us, all Sumerian: *Lugal*, Sumerian for "big man," to be rendered as "king" according to the evidence of its Akkadian equivalent *sharrum*; *en*, roughly "(priestly) lord"; *ensi*, conventionally translated "city ruler" or "governor" and including in it the title *en* (the exact meaning of the compound is not clear). *Ensi* implied a lower rank than *lugal* or *en*. An independent prince, ruling over a city with its immediate surroundings, would call himself *ensi*; so would the ruler of a city who was vassal to a more powerful monarch. That *ensi* refers to the rule of a limited territory emerges from an inscription of Eanatum of Lagash, who says that he held, "in addition to the *ensi*-ship of Lagash, the kingship of Kish." The rulers of Umma call themselves *lugal* in their own inscriptions, their enemies of Lagash call them *ensi*. *Lugal* is the royal title *par excellence* in the *Sumerian King List*. *Nam-lugal* is "kingship" as a form of government. *Lugal* appears with a ruler's name first at Kish and Ur (Mebaragesi, Meskalamdug); the sign-combination, by itself, is documented as early as the Uruk II–Jamdet Nasr period. *En* as a royal title, unlike *ensi* and *lugal*, is confined to Uruk alone. Enmerkar, Lugalbanda and Gilgamesh are designated as "*en* of Kulaba" (Kulaba is a section of Uruk) in the epic and hymnal literature; Meskianggasher, founder of the First Dynasty of Uruk, is called *en* of Eanna, the temple of Uruk's city deity, by the *Sumerian King List*. King Lugalkingeneshdudu (about the beginning of the twenty-fourth century) says that he exercised *en*-ship (*nam-en*) over Uruk and kingship (*nam-lugal*) over Ur, another indication of the association of the title *en* with the city of Uruk alone. Once only, with Enshakushana of Uruk (about the end of the twenty-fifth century), do we see the style "*en* of Sumer." Epigraphically *en* occurs earlier than *lugal*: The sign is already found on tablets of Uruk IVa, i.e. in the earliest texts of the Protoliterate age. A personal name on an archaic tablet of Ur, translated as "the-*en*-fills-Kulaba," speaks for the prestige that the *en* enjoyed outside of Uruk.

As a priestly and not a royal title, however, *en* appears often at Ur, from the age of Agade onward. Bearer of the title at Ur is the High Priestess of the moon-god Nanna, patron deity of Ur. As the masculine *en* of Uruk ruled a city whose patron deity was a goddess, Inanna, we can conclude that the *en* was of the sex opposite to that of the city's principal divinity.[42] The *en* of Uruk-Kulaba, then, probably had, originally, a religious function more pronounced than that of a *lugal*. The "man in the net kilt" on the cylinder seals of the Uruk IV levels in Sumer should therefore be identified with the *en* (see above, p. 36). But at Uruk, the *en* is not merely a priest, he is also ruler of the city and leader of its troops in war. Precisely this worldly aspect of the office of *en* comes to the fore in the epic accounts of Lugalbanda and Gilgamesh. In cities like Ur and Girsu (royal city of the state of Lagash), *lugal* and *ensi* may not originally have united priestly and worldly functions in their person. Under Entemena we hear of a *sangu*, High Priest of Ningirsu, the city god of Girsu, who stands beside the *ensi*. This is, however, a relatively late document (end of the twenty-fifth century).

The Sumerian names of gods that are formed with *en* (e.g. Enlil, "Lord Wind") are older than those formed with *lugal*, indicating at once the original higher status of an *en* and the greater age of the title of the lords of Uruk. The matter is complicated by the tradition in Sumerian literature (*King List*, epics, hymns) of dignifying rulers like Mebaragesi of Kish by attaching *en* to their names (Enmebaragesi), although, as the patron deity of Kish is a god, Zababa, this would seem to violate the rule of opposite sex. This confuses our efforts to delineate the differences between *en* and *lugal*.

Further, the texts and pictorial documents of the Early Dynastic age assure us that the *lugal* or *ensi* was not exclusively a secular ruler either. A relief plaque of Ur-Nanshe of Lagash (title: *lugal*) shows the king with a carrying basket on his head, a symbol of his prerogative as temple builder. The kings of Ur III deposit statues of themselves bearing baskets as dedication gifts in the temples they have built. According to the hymn of Gudea of Lagash (ca. 2144–2124), written on the occasion of the building of a temple, the *ensi* formed the first brick in the brick mold.

There is, however, no evidence in the Early Dynastic period for the divinization of kings during life, such as we get in the age of Agade. There are cases of posthumous deification (Lugalbanda and Gilgamesh of Uruk), but these are early and are not repeated in Early Dynastic III. But, with Mesalim, and with Eanatum of Lagash, we have the earliest known cases of divine filiation: Mesalim in one inscription calls himself "Beloved Son of Ninḫursanga" (the Sumerian mother-goddess), Eanatum claims to "drink the good milk of Ninḫursanga." None of this means that the ruler regards himself as divine. We also have no clear proof that the Early Dynastic age knew the rite of the sacred marriage (Greek *hieros gamos* is the conventional term used today). The first literary documentation of this is no earlier than the reign of Iddin-Dagan of Isin (1974–1954 B.C.). This rite was celebrated by the ruler and the queen, or the *en*-priestess, magically to promote the fertility of land and herds, a prosperous harvest and a favorable inundation. The literary tradition for Sumerian religion begins, however, quite late (oldest mythological texts from the age of Agade), so that a much older occurrence of this rite is entirely possible.

The complex evidence of royal titles may be summed up as follows: In the beginning, we must assume, different titles are bound to different localities—*en* at Uruk in the Protoliterate period and on into Early Dynastic II, *lugal* or *ensi* in other cities. The religious functions of the *en* extend also to the *lugal* and *ensi*; the *en* of Uruk-Kulaba also has secular duties to attend. During Early Dynastic III even Uruk's ruler takes the title *lugal*, *en* continuing as a priestly title only.

The *lugal* or the *ensi* resides in a palace (Sum. archaic *hai-kal*, later *e-gal*), literally a "big house." Our oldest evidence of this word is from the archaic texts of Ur. Our oldest evidence of the actual existence of royal palaces is from the remains of buildings found in excavations at Eridu (Early Dynastic II/III) and at Kish (Early Dynastic II); these would have to be palaces, as they do not follow the ground plan of temples and are too large for anything else. The *en* at Uruk, however, according to the epic material, lives in a part of the

temple called the *gipar*; this is the name of the temple apart-
ments of *en*-priestesses in other cities. This is consonant with
the religious function of the *en*, but the secular power and
glory of the ruler are also provided for: In the Sumerian lay
of *Enmerkar and the En of Aratta*, the king of Uruk receives
a foreign royal messenger in the courtyard of the temple throne
hall. The Akkadian word for palace, *ekallum*, is a Sumerian
loan word. In the late third and early second millennia this
was adopted by the Semites of Syria. In Ugaritic, Hebrew and
Aramaic, the word means now "palace," now "temple"; however, this is a development extraneous to Mesopotamia, and
offers no evidence for the original meaning of Sumerian
hai-kal.

What do we know of the structure and social conditions of
the Early Dynastic city-state? Only what we can find on the
clay tablets of the age. Tablets, in archives or individually,
have so far been found in the cities of Ur, Shuruppak, Lagash,
Umma, Adab, Nippur and Kish. We are limited not only by
what we can find, but by what we can read. The interpretation
of the script increases in difficulty as we go back in time. The
Lagash archives for the period from Entemena to Urukagina,
and the contemporary tablets from Umma and Adab, are by
and large readable in full; the further removed from these in
time our sources are, the richer are our opportunities for confusion. Many of the signs have yet to yield their meaning.
When we know the meaning of all the signs in a sentence it is
often still extremely difficult to decide what it says, as we have
insufficient clues to its syntax; the earlier texts give us words,
but not their grammatical relationships. For Sumerian cuneiform in its initial stages gives only the stem of a word, and
none of the prefixes and suffixes employed, in an agglutinative
language, to convey such useful information as its person,
number, case, tense, etc. It took several centuries for the script
to develop to the point where the full grammatical context was
available to the reader. As late as the Shuruppak archives
(twenty-sixth century), the sign for a noun may imply any
case. For a reader familiar with the facts recorded, this will
suffice; for us, it represents endless problems of interpretation.

Our oldest class of documents (the oldest we can read well enough to identify), some of which go back to Early Dynastic II, are land-sale contracts. Interestingly enough, these are written not on clay tablets but on stone, for the sake of preservation we may suppose, a sign of the importance attached to the transaction. The very great majority of these come from the area of Akkadian settlement. Akkadian personal names occur often, and we get the first attempts at writing down the Akkadian language. Sales are made, for the most part, not by individuals but by families or clans. These documents on stone are found individually and not in archives, as they are private and not public records.

The earliest archive that we can (with some reservations) interpret is that of Shuruppak, the modern Fara, in the center of the Babylonian plain (beginning of Early Dynastic III). Here we can identify, among other things, lists of persons receiving rations or parcels of land in payment for services to the state. Documents from the sphere of private law include contracts for the purchase of houses and fields, this time on clay. There are administrative documents that make frequent mention of men from other cities, and in which the sign for "battle" frequently occurs. It has therefore been suspected that the archive deals mainly with the military administration of the palace.[43] We also have products of the scribal school at Shuruppak: word lists (a category of texts going back to the levels of Uruk IV), several lists of gods that are enlightening for the history of Sumerian religion, and school exercises in the art of writing that show us, in a sense, the prehistory of Sumerian literature—proverbs, incantations, and isolated phrases from mythology.

For texts, however, that can be made to yield a satisfactory meaning, with the Sumerological knowledge of the present day, we must wait until the archives of Girsu in the city-state of Lagash. From these, far-reaching conclusions have been drawn on the organization of Sumerian cities in general in that and the previous ages. They reveal to us the picture of an extensive, complex, highly organized bureaucratic administration. They deal with temple cult (sacrifices, festivals), management of the temple lands (grain cultivation, vegetable gardening, temple herds, provision of sacrificial animals, sheep shearing), fisheries in fresh water and at sea, crafts and commerce (acquisition of foreign goods by merchants acting for the state), and accounts of wages paid to personnel. The head of the whole machine, often mentioned as receiving revenue, is the *ensi*, or, in the temple of the city goddess, the *ensi*'s wife. No texts so far known give us direct information on the private sphere of the economy. Archives on the management of large estates in private hands do not occur until the Old Babylonian period.

We do, however, have documents for Early Dynastic III from the sphere of private law. We have already mentioned the contracts on stone for the sale of land; contracts on clay record the purchase of houses, slaves, fields; exchanges of real property, the division of inheritance, formal donations, loans and security are attested; we have records of river ordeals (the oldest reference to a judicial ordeal) and of legal proceedings (debt litigation, judicial confirmation of debt). The majority of these private law documents come from the same period as the public archives of Girsu, the last two or three generations before the age of Agade.

In the administrative documents, there is constant reference to the temples: A very large number of persons is mentioned in their service—cult personnel, artisans, laborers, as well as large numbers of men liable for the performance of compulsory public duties. For this reason the social and political system of a Sumerian city such as Lagash has been called the "temple-state."[44] Estimates of the size of the lands held by individual temples vary over a considerable range, as do estimates of the whole territory controlled by a city like Lagash (ca. 1,160 square miles);[45] we cannot yet say what proportion of the state is actually temple-owned land. It is clear, however, that a considerable amount of the arable land in a city is the property of its temples. That very few land-sale contracts have come down to us from the Sumerian south, as opposed to the Semitic north, of Babylonia fits into the picture of a society in which the temples would be the great proprietors of the soil. The few southern examples known are contracts from Girsu, in which rulers or members of the ruling house appear as purchasers. This does not mean that private ownership of land was forbidden; but we must judge the question by the rarity of the transaction and the status, in the available examples, of the purchasers. This is not a matter of one ordinary citizen transferring land to another—at least that much is clear. We are also not dealing with private property in the case of lands issued to individuals in payment of services, the "alimentary fields," for these are inalienable and nonheritable. Not until the time of Lipit-eshtar of Isin (1934–1924 B.C.) do we get land-sale contracts in sizable numbers in southern Babylonia, i.e. in Sumer proper. In view of the number of clay tablets from before the time of Sargon, we should hate to think of these findings as purely accidental. Unless we are quite wrong in this, it would appear that one of the chief differences between Sumerians and Semites, in the Land of the Two Rivers, is in the frequency of private property in land.

In ideal terms, temple land was the property of the god. Secularization, the use of temple lands by the ruler, was prohibited. This we learn from the "reform texts" of Urukagina of Lagash (ca. 2360). The new king there claims to have "re-established Ningirsu, the [legitimate] owner, in the house of the *ensi*, in the field of the *ensi*," and to have done the same for the god's consort, Baba, and their son, Shulshagana. Former rulers had enriched themselves with the gods' property; Urukagina restored it. Unfortunately we know nothing of Urukagina's relation to the dynasty of Ur-Nanshe; it may be that his reforming zeal and his pious restorations are the self-justification of a usurper.

In the Sumerian temple-state, whose citizens are to a large extent in the service of the gods, it is very difficult to say anything meaningful about social stratification. We do the matter less than justice when we speak of "free" and "semi-free," particularly since the latter term makes no appearance in the texts. The Sumerian word we translate as "freedom" (because it renders, in the contracts, the condition of a slave manumitted by his master) is first documented in the reform text of Urukagina: *ama-r-gi*, literally "to return (or allow to return) to one's mother (*ama*)." It may have referred originally to liberation from debt slavery; sale of children by needy parents is not attested until the Agade period. The characteristic quality of freedom, then, would be a life amid one's own family, denied to the slave who worked and lived in a stranger's household. But it is quite another matter to suppose that the authority to requisition men, exercised by the state in the person of the ruler, debased the citizen to an "unfree" status. Modern standards are not to be applied here. A passage in Gudea's hymn describes how the *ensi* mobilized the citizens, "as one man," to work at the rebuilding of Ningirsu's temple. Taken literally, this would mean that the ruler could recruit the entire population (priests and state officials excepted), to labor in the common interest of the city on extensive public works—temples, palaces, fortifications—and on construction and repair of irrigation works. Of a special privileged class, protected by exemptions, the texts have not one word to say.

They do employ technical terms for special groups, but we should not be quick to call these classes: *eren*, *gurush*, and *shub-lugala*. *Eren* is a term applied to those liable for personal service, who can be called up for public works or for war. The corresponding Akkadian word is *sabum*, from the Old Babylonian period, and has the same application. *Gurush* is originally an age designation, meaning an adult, one capable of a man's work. Secondarily, it has the generalized meaning "worker," and in the administrative documents is sometimes interchangeable with *eren*, perhaps as the wider, more comprehensive term. *Shub-lugala* appears in administrative documents and in Urukagina's reform texts; the literal translation would be "subjected to the king," from which, however, we can conclude nothing specific as long as we have no evidence for the details of that condition. To see in this a status of diminished freedom is rash.

From the Girsu archives we learn for the first time of the extent to which the Sumerian city relied on slave labor. The temple of the goddess Baba, according to one tablet, enjoyed the services of 188 female slaves; the temple of Nanshe, of 180. The Sumerian words for "slave" and "female slave," written with the signs for "man + foreign land" or "woman + foreign land," indicate that slaves were originally of foreign origin, kidnapped in raids or taken prisoner in war. But those named in the slave-sale contracts of Early Dynastic III are, as appears by their names, natives of Sumer. The women are set to work at weaving, or at grinding grain. We first hear of female slaves as concubines in the Old Babylonian period. The spoken Sumerian word for slave (masculine) is a loan word from Semitic; that for slave (feminine) is native Sumerian, the cuneiform sign for the latter going back to the texts of Uruk IVa. We can surely assume that there was also a native Sumerian word for "male slave"; why was it replaced by a loan word? Perhaps the Semitic word entered the vocabulary at the beginning of the Early Dynastic age, when the incidents of the Akkadian migration produced a crop of slaves for the Sumerian cities. It is interesting to note that the characterization of the relation of subject to ruler, of worshiper to god, as that of a "slave" seems to stem from Semitic ideas. With regard to slaves, at any rate, we are face to face with a class that really *is* "unfree," in that the Sumerian slave has an owner who can sell him, bequeath him, or simply give him away.

In the past two decades the question has arisen, with regard to the Sumerian city-state of Early Dynastic times, to what degree the people participated in its government. The point of departure for the whole discussion was the occurrence of terms for "assembly" and for "elders," principally in a passage of the Sumerian poem *Gilgamesh and Aka of Kish*. Messengers from the king of Kish appear in Uruk, and Gilgamesh, the *en*, submits the alternatives of war or dishonorable subjection, first to an "assembly of the elders" and second to an "assembly of the young men (*gurush*)." The old urge surrender, the young are eager for the fight. Attempts have been made to see in this a kind of plebiscite.[46] But it is probably a literary convention for displaying the *hubris* of a king.[47] That such assemblies did exist is something that we should not doubt; that they were a prototype of popular democracy, however, is something that we must not imagine. If the gods meet in mythological assembly, this is surely an earthly institution translated, by the religious imagination, to the realm of heaven. But what is the procedure in the assembly of the gods? It is customary, it appears, to acclaim the proposals of the presiding deity (who, of course, will have tried to give expression to the opinion of the majority) with a resounding shout of "So be it!" If this, too, reflects the ways of men, then the Sumerian assembly is a sounding board for public opinion. The purpose of the assembly would have been, above all, to air questions of organization and justice and to receive the directions of the ruler. *Unken* is the Sumerian word for assembly, replaced in the period of Ur III by an Akkadian loan word *puḫrum*, of which the meaning is the same.

Lagash and Umma—Lugalzagesi

By good fortune we have the materials to allow us to reconstruct the political history of a part of Sumer in Early Dynastic III, in relatively close detail. Our documents describe stages in the rivalry of the two city-states of Umma and Lagash, bad neighbors in the south of Babylonia. We owe them to the kings of Lagash. Before Ur-Nanshe, we know of a King Enḥengal from a stone tablet recording land purchases by the ruler. An inscription of Mesalim also mentions an *ensi* of Lagash, who may have reigned a generation or two before Ur-Nanshe. With Ur-Nanshe himself (ca. 2550) begins a hereditary line of six kings, ruling Lagash for nearly two centuries; a seventh, not in the direct line, closes the count. These kings have left us royal inscriptions, sometimes quite detailed, sometimes also affording synchronisms with the kings of Umma. Our story of the conflict between Umma and Lagash will therefore be quite biased—of necessity, for we read of it in Lagash texts. The quarrel of these two states, over the line of their common boundary, over the exploitation of their common watercourse, over the possession of certain steppe and grazing lands (Gu-edena, "the edge of Eden"[48]), goes back before the reign of Mesalim. Mesalim, as overlord of both cities, arbitrated the conflict and fixed the borderline. Nevertheless the dispute raged from generation to generation, often leading to war, never to a settlement. Victory adorned the arms of one side or the other, quite impartially, until, under their King Lugal-zagesi, the troops of Umma sacked the city of Lagash and looted the riches of its temples. Still their rivalry was not extinguished until the Empire of Agade absorbed them both.

Outstanding among the kings of Lagash of the dynasty of Ur-Nanshe was Eanatum (ca. 2460), who took the title of "King of Kish"; in a few inscriptions he styles himself, simply, "*ensi* of Lagash." What we hear of his wars—with Ur, with Uruk, with Kish, with Akshak (northern Babylonia), even with Mari, then engaged in an advance on Babylonia—all of this is but a fraction of the interplay of coalitions and enmities of the states of the Babylonian plain. Nevertheless from his inscriptions emerges the picture of a ruler so far above the average, in power and in achievement, that we understand on what he based his claim as "King of Kish."

"For Ningirsu" (in accordance with the Sumerian idea of the ruler acting on the mandate of the god), Eanatum conquered Elam, the traditional enemy of Sumer, and rewarded himself with the title "He Who Subjects All the [foreign] Lands." The "Vulture Stele" of the Louvre, both sides carved in relief, is a monument to his victories that has come down to us. One side portrays the king, his chariot and his phalanx, the other the god Ningirsu, holding the ruler's enemies in an enormous net in his hand.

The brevity of the tenure of a "King of Kish" is shown by the fact that Eanatum's successors once more held the title of *ensi* alone. But they had not lost all their external power: Inscriptions of Enanatum I have been found at Ur and Uruk; of his successor Entemena at Ur and Badtibira. These cities therefore continued to be subject to Lagash. Otherwise the city's external affairs are dominated by the struggle with Umma. The shifting alliances of the age are illustrated by a building inscription of Entemena, recording that he and the *ensi* Lugalkingeneshdudu of Uruk (whom the *Sumerian King List* names as *lugal*, "king") have pledged mutual "brother-hood."

Urukagina succeeds, by what means we are not sure, the last of the descendants of Ur-Nanshe. His "reform texts" we have already mentioned; they are of the utmost importance for the legal and social history of Sumer. In slightly different versions they appear in various building inscriptions of the king. They contrast old, discarded practices with the new order introduced by Urukagina "at the bidding of Ningirsu." Their main tenor is the abolition of prerogatives assumed by the ruler and his family at the expense of the city god: misappropriation of temple lands for the uses of the palace, misdirection of temple personnel to employments in the palace. Encroachments of officials are also curbed—the fees, for example, for official services, funerals and so on, are reduced and fixed. Exploitation of the weak and lowly by the well-to-do, such as forced sales of house lots or cattle on unfavorable terms, is forbidden. The citizens of Lagash are acquitted of certain debts, their "freedom" is decreed. Reforms in family law are also promulgated: Dyandry, the marriage of one woman to two men, is abolished. Probably this alludes to relics of an original Sumerian polyandry, now grown objectionable to contemporary taste. In this text we meet, for the first time, with a theme that will recur constantly in the legal enactments of subsequent Mesopotamian kings: the ruler as the protector of the widow and the orphan. Urukagina's measures, his grants of tax relief and abolition (if the particular passage is correctly read) of debts, head a long list of royal edicts issued in later ages; these, by permanent or palliative measures of a similar kind, sought to stem the tide of impoverishment and indebtedness that periodically recurred, in times of speculation or economic disturbance. For the particular social and economic circumstances to which Urukagina's texts allude, we have unfortunately no other evidence; we therefore cannot be sure, as we have said above (p. 77), what motivated or necessitated his decrees.

The last great ruler of the Sumerian south, before it was subjected by Sargon of Agade, is Lugalzagesi. From his father's name, Bubu, he would be of Akkadian descent. Bubu had been "ecstatic-priest" (the conventional translation of a Sumerian term) of the goddess Nisaba of Umma; his son also held this office. Lugalzagesi appears to have usurped the throne of Umma—like Urukagina, he has no connection with the previous royal line.

With the sack of the city of Lagash, with the plundering and burning of its temples, Lugalzagesi dealt the enemy state a stunning blow. His adversary Urukagina complains bitterly of this sacrilege. He addresses the city goddess of Umma in these words: "may his goddess Nisaba bear on her neck these crimes committed by Lugalzagesi, the *ensi* of Umma!" By this victory Lugalzagesi freed himself for greater things. He conquered Uruk, where he assumed the title "King of Uruk and King of the Land of Sumer." A new political spirit speaks out from the great royal inscription of Lugalzagesi, our sole source for his extraordinary career; it asserts the conception of a state beyond the city-state in a manner far more distinct than that of his predecessors, whose ideal of suzerainty is expressed only by the title "King of Kish." Lugalzagesi on the other hand relates himself to the city gods of every major state under his control: "Purification-priest of An" (the sky-god of Uruk), "Senior *ensi* of Enlil" (the national god at Nippur), "Grand Vizier of Su'en" (the moon-god of Ur—Su'en is the Akkadian equivalent of Nanna), "Vicar of Utu" (the sun-god of Larsa). Adab and Eridu, too, fall under his dominion. His claims are national; they even seem imperial. "From the Lower Sea [i.e. the Persian Gulf] along the Euphrates and the Tigris to the Upper Sea [the Mediterranean], Enlil made all lands go directly to him." Here expressed in words for the first time is the extent of the Sumerian known world. The kings of Agade ruled this world. But Lugalzagesi's phrase is not to be understood in this sense. He does not claim that his political influence extends to the Mediterranean; the opening of direct trade is what is meant. From an inscription of Meskigala, the *ensi* of Adab and a contemporary of Lugalzagesi, comes our first documentation of the importation of timber from the "Land of the Cedar Mountain," which is the Amanus range on the Mediterranean coast. This is a report of the particulars of what Lugalzagesi simply expresses in generalities. A comparison with similar phrases in the inscriptions of Gudea of Lagash points in the same direction.

In this, the oldest Sumerian royal inscription in fully literary style, Lugalzagesi's titles and phraseology anticipate in many ways the royal inscriptions of the Sargonids. And yet we are in error if we call him a precursor of the Empire of Agade. The unification of the civilized world, as known to the Babylonians, under a single imperial administration was first accomplished by Sargon and his successors. Sargon began by conquering the cities of Sumer. To do so, he had first to destroy, by protracted war, the power of Lugalzagesi.

Babylonia and Her Neighbors

As the previous chapter demonstrated, Sumer's civilizing influence had already reached outside Babylonia in the Proto-literate period. By the beginning of the Early Dynastic age, Elam, a country capable of great originality, at once the enemy and emulator of the cities of the plain, had drawn on Sumerian inspiration to invent a script of its own. Our first report of a clash of arms between Elam and Babylonia comes from a note to the name "Enmebaragesi" in the *Sumerian King List*. Eanatum prides himself, as we have seen, on his conquest of Elam. But the oldest visible trace we have of the supremacy of a Mesopotamian state in Elam comes from the Agade period, when an imperial garrison was stationed at Susa. In the same period cuneiform is adopted for the first time on Iranian soil, displacing entirely the native Proto-Elamite script.

Of decisive influence on the history of the Early Dynastic

age was the region of Syria and northwest Mesopotamia: The Akkadian migration originated there. Sumerian influence had reached and stimulated the area in Protoliterate times, but nevertheless its cultural independence and inventiveness were great. We have outlined above a theory of this independence and its effects that, if correct, accounts for the novel archaeological findings of Early Dynastic II, particularly on the Lower Diyala. These innovations stem from the north. Royal inscriptions of Mari (dating back to the time of Mesalim, about the beginning of the twenty-sixth century, to judge by the form of the signs employed) are already written in the Akkadian language. The linguistic distribution of Akkadian in the Old Babylonian period, if retrojected to Early Dynastic II and III, would show us a strongly homogeneous Semitic population in northern Babylonia, in the Diyala region and on the Middle Euphrates. The *Sumerian King List*, by listing a Dynasty of Mari, informs us indirectly that the area of the Middle Euphrates was closely linked to Babylonia. This connection was promoted by easy access via the great waterway of the Euphrates, and the land route following its course that had no natural obstacles to cross.

For the regions of the Middle Tigris, the later Assyria, the reverse is the case. Connections with Babylonia are blocked, to some degree, by the Jebel Hamrin, an offshoot of the Zagros range, and the desert to the south of it. These natural barriers also affected language. The Assyrian dialect of Akkadian, attested from the beginning of the second millennium, differs considerably from the dialect, which we call Babylonian, common to the Middle Euphrates, the Diyala region and Babylonia itself. The dialect map of modern Iraqi Arabic is divided along precisely the same lines. Because of its isolation Assyria acquired writing very much later than its neighbors; occasional Akkadian texts appear at Assur only in the Agade period. Asia Minor, like Assyria, is outside the Babylonian sphere in the Early Dynastic period. Lugalzagesi and Meskigala of Adab mention the Mediterranean and the Amanus mountains for the first time around the middle of the twenty-fourth century. Of the two countries representing, for later Mesopotamians, the end of the world toward the east, Magan and Meluḫḫa (the coasts of Oman and Makran in the first case, the mouth of the Indus in the second, if the identifications recently backed by sound arguments are correct),[49] only Magan is named, once, by Ur-Nanshe of Lagash, in the Early Dynastic period.

Already in Protoliterate times, however, and increasingly in the Early Dynastic period, trade reached beyond the bounds of the world known to Babylonia. Trade routes to the lands that produced the materials that Babylonia lacked (gold, silver, copper, tin, precious and semiprecious stones) were actively in use as early as the fourth millennium, although the trade probably was not carried on by direct caravans from and to the cities of Babylonia, but by intermediate stages. The funerary deposits of the royal tombs of Ur, the gilded bulls with lapis-lazuli beards, are impressive evidence of the wealth of Sumer in this age, derived from trade with a world beyond its ken.

Conclusion

At the beginning of the Early Dynastic period, Sumerian civilization is in decline; at its end, all of Babylonia, and, indeed, the greater part of the Fertile Crescent, is about to be united in a single empire. The migration of the Akkadians onto Babylonian soil and their rise there to imperial power occupy the entire period. Hand in hand with the creation of the first Semitic states in Babylonia—the kingdoms of Mebaragesi and Mesalim are the first of which we know, but probably not the first to exist—there is an increasing interchange between Sumerians and Semites. Akkadian contributions to the civilization of Babylonia and of the Diyala region were numerous and significant. To the new arrivals we have already attributed the style of sculpture characteristic of Early Dynastic II. A new element in the art of stone engraving, the

86

"figure band," is also an Akkadian creation. It was they who introduced the *Herdhaus* temple into the Diyala region and Babylonia (at Nippur). Akkadian loan words enter the Sumerian language. Theirs is already an outstanding role in Babylonian civilization.

And yet there is no question that, in the interchange between the two peoples, the Sumerians gave far more than they received. The style of the Sumerian sculpture of Early Dynastic III, perhaps deliberately recalling Protoliterate forms, was diffused toward the north and had its influence there. Sumerian loan words in the Akkadian language outnumber by far those that traveled in the other direction. The phonetic system of Akkadian diverges from the Semitic norm for reasons that might best, perhaps, be explained by a Sumerian substrate. Sumerian is the language of the written monuments of the Early Dynastic period. Hesitant attempts to write Akkadian with cuneiform, in contracts and in royal inscriptions, are in no way the equal in quality of Sumerian texts. Not until the time of the Kings of Agade did Akkadian become a written language worthy of the name.

The organization and administration of the state, characteristic of the southern half of Babylonia, is Sumerian—the "temple-state," with its scribal tradition stretching back to Protoliterate times. The later administrative bureaucracy of the Akkadian empires is based upon it. The scribal schools, the education are Sumerian. In religion, Sumer is the donor; the Sumerian pantheon is simply superimposed on the Akkadian, which in any case is quite limited in number. Nippur with its national god, Enlil, becomes the great religious center of the Akkadians too. Long after the Sumerians disappeared, the Akkadians were to remain in their debt.

' The social history of Babylonia is not restricted to these themes of nationality. The institution of the temple, with its immense lands, its crowd of dependents devoted to the service of the deities, could not but lead to social tensions. As Urukagina's reform texts show, secularizing tendencies arose, encroaching on the idea of the theocratic state. The ruler sought to secure a power independent of the temple and its priesthood by acquiring landed wealth in his own right. Officials became autocratic and abused their powers; Urukagina had to put down excessive public fees. To be sure, the texts tell us of the social tensions that must underlie this only by way of implication. Furthermore, with the reform texts we are already in the last or the next-to-last generation of the Early Dynastic period. We can, however, suspect that the arrival of the Akkadians is responsible (although not exclusively) for the rapid decline of the Sumerian temple-state.

There is little that we can learn, from the cuneiform documents, of the spiritual and intellectual life of the Early Dynastic age. The reason for this is that literature, in the strict sense, which ought to be our main source of information, is late in arriving on the Babylonian plain, considering the antiquity of writing there. Isolated quotations of a literary nature appear in the Shuruppak archive; we can barely interpret them. The oldest coherent mythological text in Sumerian does not appear until the twenty-third century. The bulk of Sumerian literary texts date only from the last days of the living language—the time of Gudea, Ur III, and the two and a half centuries that follow. Certainly this does not imply that before this time the Sumerians had no poetry, no tales of gods and heroes, no creativity in words. All it tells us is that they simply did not write them down.[49a]

For this reason, to learn something of Sumerian religion we must turn to other sources: to economic texts recording sacrificial offerings, which tell us something about cult practices; to theophoric personal names that are small sentences about the gods ("The-Sun-God-Decides-the-Right" or "The-King-Does-Not-Act-in-Violence"); to descriptive epithets sometimes applied to the gods in royal inscriptions; or to magical practices, as mentioned on the inscription of the Vulture Stele of Eanatum of Lagash. Pictorial art complements this fragmentary evidence in a manner indispensable to the student. Where the ruler is represented with a carrying basket on his head, his religious responsibility for the building of the temple is expressed. Statuettes of men in the attitude of prayer give us some impression of the usages of cult. Later literary texts help us to interpret symbols: the lion-headed eagle holding two herd animals in his claws is the emblem of Ningirsu, god of Lagash. Many of these illustrative works, however, do not make it clear to us what they illustrate. The heroic figure wrestling with a wild beast or two, a common motif of the cylinder seals, is conventionally identified with Gilgamesh; unfortunately there is no sure literary documentation for this, early or late. That the gods are thought of, and depicted, anthropomorphically is already the case in late Protoliterate times (see p. 38); this holds true for the Early Dynastic period. The occasional representation of a god by a symbol, abstract or animal, does not really detract from this.

There is, by the time of the Shuruppak archive at the latest, a common pantheon for all of Sumer. The great list of gods at Shuruppak has at its head the deities An (sky), Enlil (wind), Inanna (Venus), Enki (sub-soil water), Nanna (moon) and Utu (sun). These, as can be seen, are the great cosmic gods of the Sumerians (the weather-god and the mother-goddess are missing; they appear later on in the list). Old Babylonian lists of gods follow much the same initial order, which speaks for a continuous tradition. This is a national pantheon, superimposed on the groups of gods preferred in each city-state: The universally acknowledged religious primacy of Nippur, and of its city god Enlil, corresponds to this. Enlil took over the position of his father, An, the sky-god and king of the gods (the succession of the younger generation is typical of the mythologies of Mesopotamia); Enlil became the chief executive of the gods, An retired to honored inactivity. We cannot know for certain whether this reflects a political event in the human world. We might, perhaps, recall that the power of Uruk, whose city god was An, was waning during Early Dynastic II.

Intellectual life centered on the school, the "tablet house," where future scribes were introduced to the difficult script, and to all the things that it was used to record. The word lists that originated in Uruk IVa are still present, in much the same form but now often enlarged, in the archives of Jamdet Nasr and Shuruppak. The tradition of the scribal school is tenacious. Indeed it was to be the intellectual tie, effective through time and devastation, lasting into the second and the first millennia, that bound Babylonia to her Sumerian past, and bound Western Asia to Sumero-Akkadian civilization.

3

The First Semitic Empire

About the middle of the twenty-fourth century B.C., the map of the Near East, as the historian sees it, is very different from the Near East that we know today. Only one area at the center can be more or less clearly made out: Lower Mesopotamia. Its immediate neighbors to the southeast (Elam) and to the northwest (the Middle Euphrates area around Mari) can be seen only in a shadowed light. Everywhere else, except for the briefest flashes, there is total darkness. In other words it is Babylonia alone, still the center of an original and highly developed civilization, that makes increasing use of one of the discoveries of half a millennium before, to provide us with the written documents we need for a precise knowledge of the past. In fact, most of what we know about Elam and Mari comes from Babylonian documents, although these areas, having borrowed their script and even their written language from Babylonia, now begin to give us a few texts of their own. But it is entirely from Babylonian documents, and only insofar as they make any mention of them, that we know anything about the other areas on the periphery: from the east coast of Arabia to Iran, from the Zagros mountains to Assyria and Syria. To be sure, for all these countries, and for Babylonia as well, there are the silent witnesses summoned by archaeology. But they are far too few for what we want to ask of them (only a few minor sites have been explored, in the "provincial" areas), and it is difficult to get precise answers from them.

So we are forced to content ourselves, still, for the period considered here, with a "Mesopotamocentric" view of history. And we must constantly bear this in mind as a corrective to our distorted vision. But in itself this optical illusion represents a prime historical fact: the overwhelming, irradiating influence of Babylonia on all its surrounding world—on all of Western Asia.

Mesopotamia

1. Sources

The sources for a reconstruction of the history of these two or three centuries are, basically, whatever we have been able to find in the way of native written records.

The sequence of reigns and dynasties, the general outline for the history of the whole age, is preserved by the *Sumerian King List* (see p. 55)—an incomplete source, to be used with caution, whose basic accuracy is nevertheless both probable for a period so close to the date of its composition and proved by comparison with the facts given by contemporary documents.

The latter help us to fill in many of the gaps in the *King List* and to flesh out the bare outline that it gives us. They are, above all, royal inscriptions—stelae of victories, dedications of votive objects or buildings. The geographical area over which inscriptions signed by a particular ruler can be found tells us something of the extent of his territory. The date formulae by which he dates each document (for lack of any common or continuous system of chronology, each ruler named the years of his reign by some memorable occurrence) tell us something of the events of his time. However, no great number of these documents has been found on the monuments to which they were originally affixed, and many of them have been found, unfortunately, already shattered by time.

Sometimes, however, in the case of the Akkadian kings, the historical curiosity of scribes of a few centuries later has preserved what would otherwise be lost. From the Old Babylonian period onward, possibly for political reasons, a certain number of these royal inscriptions were recopied here and there, generally with care, sometimes arranged in an order that seems to represent the contemporary notion of the sequence of events. (Some of these copies have by chance come down to us, especially at Nippur and at Ur.) They are found side by side with similar but less trustworthy documents, which are more imitations than copies of an original. The true copies, however, fill the place of their lost models. But even with their aid, the chronological outline is far from easy to complete, leaving us as it does with enormous gaps scattered through the record, and with vital questions to which there is no answer.

For this reason the historian has to seek his nourishment elsewhere, in a much richer class of documents—which, unfortunately, has the defect of being later, sometimes much later, in date. This makes them difficult and hazardous to use. We refer, first of all, to works that, at first glance, appear to be genuine historical literature: lists of noteworthy events arranged in chronicles, or arranged, by the authors of books of divination, according to the omens that were supposed to have marked their occurrence. The documentary basis for these lists *might* go back to the events they claim to recall, and therefore one might, after critical examination, be able to draw upon them for a few important facts unattested elsewhere. And then again, one might not, for their literary genre is dedicated to signs and wonders, and they must in the course of time have picked up, by way of enrichment, details that spring from fantasy and a taste for the marvelous.

Rich in details of this kind is another class of literature, obviously imaginative literature in this case, of which we hear from the beginning of the second millennium on. The ancient Mesopotamians seem to have been aware quite early that the era in which their country, for the first time, carried its renown so far afield would forever be one of the high points of their history. This saga and its heroes soon became the subject of a tradition of folklore, then of literature, beginning perhaps

AGADE	GUTIUM	URUK	LAGASH	ELAM
Sargon: 2340–2284				*Luḫḫishan:* ca. 2300
Rimush: 2284–2275			*Ki-KU-id:* ca. 2280	
Manishtushu: 2275–2260			*Engilsa:* ca. 2270	
Naram-Sin: 2260–2223			*Ur-a:* ca. 2250	*Hita:* ca. 2220
Shar-kali-sharri: 2223–2198			*Lugalushumgal:* ca. 2215	*Kutik-Inshushinak:* ca. 2200
	(Erridupizir) (Imta') (Inkishush)	(Urnigin) (Urgigir) (Kudda) (Puzurili)	(Puzur-Mama) (Ur-Utu)	
	Sarlagab: ca. 2210			
	(Shulme')	(Lugalmelam?)	(Ur-Mama)	
Igigi Nanum Imi Elulu } 2198–2195	Elulumesh	(Ur-Utu)	(Lu-Baba) (Lu-Gula)	

Dudu: 2195–2174	(Inimabakesh)	(Kaku)
Shu-DURUL: 2174–2159	(Igeshaush)	*Ur-Baba:* ca. 2164–2144
	(Iarlagab)	
	(Ibate)	
	(Iarlangab)	
	(Kurum)	*Gudea:* ca. 2144–2124
	(Ḫabilkin?)	
	(La'erabum)	*Ur-Ningirsu:* ca. 2124–2119
	(Irarum)	
	(Ibranum)	
		Pirigme: ca. 2119–2117
	(Ḫablum)	*Ur-GAR:* ca. 2117–2113
	(Puzur-Sin)	
	(Iarlaganda)	*Utuḫengal:* 2116–2110
		Nammaḫani: ca. 2113–2109
	(Si'um)	
	Tiriqan: 2116	

* Names in italics are those of rulers known from contemporary inscriptions; names in parentheses, those of rulers who cannot be dated. Names with dates preceded by "ca." are only roughly dated, by synchronism with known rulers or by conjecture.

directly after the fall of Agade. To this tradition we owe the existence of poems, of actual short epics, which often point the moral or theological lesson to be learned from the fates of the exceptional beings they celebrate, Sargon and Naram-Sin especially. Some of these works direct our attention to the glories of the age, others to its catastrophic end, as if the literary tradition had been in doubt (the historian may wonder whether he should not be also) as to the true significance of this ancient adventure. From the beginning, we may be sure, and increasingly as the events receded in time, the fabulous mixed with the factual in this tradition; it is a difficult, sometimes a hopeless task to disentangle them, particularly in the absence of any trustworthy document to aid us. Doubtless only the principal turning points in that drama, stripped bare of (probably imaginary) details, can be given any color of more or less clear descent from the real past. But it is not always easy to isolate, from such a floodtide of legends, even that much. Here a judicious skepticism is probably the soundest attitude the historian can take.

He is on much firmer ground in attempting to reconstruct the social, economic, and intellectual history of the age. For he is able to add, to all of the foregoing, a sizable quantity of documents of every kind, particularly business letters and contracts and legal documentation. Further, there are a few literary and religious texts, still rather rare in this period. Finally, he may have recourse to personal names, which provide not only ethnographic information, but also irreplaceable evidence for the religious psychology and theological conceptions of Mesopotamian man. All of these original documents put together do not come near the amount we should like to have, and the archaeologist's luck has given them to us with a very unequal distribution in time, space and range: One reign or another, one site, one area of daily life is brilliantly lighted, while others are barely or not at all known, despite their importance to our knowledge of the age.

If, then, what we can reconstruct out of these materials does not yet represent genuine history, in the full sense of the word, i.e. a sufficiently clear and uninterrupted series of sufficiently certain events, nevertheless it does give us a much surer and more complete picture than that afforded by the centuries that precede it, of the general trend of development of ancient Western Asia, of the identity and succession of those who presided over it, and of the major events of their reigns.

2. *Chronology*

The chronology of the age, both relative and absolute, we approach by establishing the succession of these reigns. And, since the *King List* must serve as our guiding thread, here is its version of the history of the land after Lugalzagesi:

Uruk having been defeated, kingship passed to Agade.[50] There, Sargon, adopted son of a palm-grower, then cup-bearer to Ur-Zababa, then king of Agade, built the city of Agade and, having become king, reigned fifty-six years. Then Rimush, Sargon's son, reigned nine years. Then Manish-tushu, elder brother of Rimush and Sargon's son, reigned fifteen years. Then Naram-Sin, Manish-tushu's son, reigned thirty-seven years. Then Shar-kali-sharri, Naram-Sin's son, reigned twenty-five years. Then: who was king? Who was not king? Was Igigi king? Was Nanum king? Was Imi king? Was Elulu king? The four of them at once held kingship and reigned three years. Then Dudu reigned twenty-one years. Then shu-DURUL,[51] Dudu's son, reigned fifteen years. All told, eleven kings, who reigned 181 years.

Agade having been defeated, kingship passed to Uruk. At Uruk, Urnigin became king and reigned seven years. Then Urgigir, Urnigin's son, reigned six years. Then Kudda reigned six years. Then Puzur-Ili reigned five years. Then Ur-Utu reigned five years. All told, five kings, who reigned thirty years.

Uruk having been defeated, kingship passed to the hordes of Gutium. Among the hordes of Gutium, there was first a king whose name is not preserved.[52] Then Imta' became king and reigned three years. Then Inkishush reigned six years. Then Sarlagab reigned three years. Then Shulme' reigned six years. Then Elulumesh reigned six years. Then Inimabakesh ruled five years. Then Igeshaush reigned six years. Then Iarlagab reigned fifteen years. Then Ibate reigned three years. Then Iarlangab reigned three years. Then Kurum reigned one year. Then Ḫabil-Kin [?] reigned three years. Then La'erabum reigned two years. Then Irarum reigned two years. Then Ibranum reigned one year. Then Ḫablum reigned two years. Then Puzur-Sin, Ḫablum's son, reigned seven years. Then Iarlaganda [?] reigned seven years. Then Si'um reigned seven years. Then Tiriqan reigned forty days. All told, twenty-one kings, who reigned ninety-one years and forty days.

The hordes of Gutium having been defeated, kingship passed to Uruk. At Uruk, Utuḫengal became king and reigned seven years, six months and fifteen days . . .[53]

It must be noted in passing that another textual tradition, represented by a few tablets, entirely overlooks the paragraph devoted to the Gutians; between the Dynasty of Agade and the Third Dynasty of Ur, a Fourth Dynasty of Uruk is inserted, whose duration is stretched to a hundred years.

In this scheme, for which we have no contemporary confirmation as a whole, but which may well be correct after its own fashion (we shall see what that fashion is), we must distinguish between the following:

(a) *Relative chronology*: the enumeration of the kings and the succession of their reigns. To begin with, the names of the first five kings of Agade are amply attested elsewhere, and if there are some points that might make us doubt the relative position of one or the other (why does Manishtushu *succeed* his *younger* brother Rimush? On the other hand, the thing is not inherently impossible), still the evidence we have conclusively confirms the *King List*'s ordering. The same applies to their successors, although we know only three from contemporary documents. We shall see that, after a period of supremacy under its first five kings, Agade fell onto evil times, opened by a brief moment of anarchy (the rule of the four competitors) and followed by a longer period when an apparent recovery of power did nothing to slow her inevitable decline.

The five kings of Uruk who follow are another story. We know absolutely nothing about them, except for a certain preponderance of their city in "the land" at the time; all of the literary tradition attributes the destruction of Agade to the Gutians, barbarous mountaineers from the Zagros range. Of the Gutian rulers, two at least of the earliest kings named in the *King List* seem to have been contemporaries of the dynasty of Agade: the fourth, Sarlagab, whom Shar-kali-sharri boasts of having beaten (he calls him Sarlag), and the sixth, Elulu-mesh, whom one ought to be justified in recognizing as Elulu, one of the four competitors of the anarchic years, with his name spelled according to the Gutian pronunciation. We can only conclude, then, that the Gutian Dynasty directly replaced the Dynasty of Agade, perhaps after a war or series of wars fought between them. The reason for placing the Dynasty of Uruk first in the *King List* may be a result of the schematic notions that clearly influence its compilers, one of the most obvious of these, to anyone who reads the list straight through, being that of an alternation between south and north in "king-ship over the land"; Agade represents the north, and ought therefore to be followed by Uruk, a city of the south. The authors of the best-represented textual tradition of the *King List* do no ignore the Gutians, but split the Fourth Dynasty of Uruk in two, so to speak, to make room for the northern barbarians, before again turning to the south, where, as every-one knew, Utuḫengal had arisen to expel them forever.

It may be that the choice of Uruk to precede the Gutians was motivated by real events unknown to us; it may be that this city, after or, for all we know, just before the fall of Agade, had succeeded, perhaps by a revolt that she had raised and led herself, in carving out a more or less important position of power. But it is quite improbable that any such power extended over anything but the south of Babylonia: the north at the time lay under the hand of the Gutians; and we know that the *King List* quite often lists contemporary dynasties, ruling in different parts of the country, as if they were consecutive (see p. 55). Finally, the domination of Uruk, if ever there were one, could have lasted only for a time, and certainly a short one: The *King List* gives it only thirty years, as against ninety for the Gutians. The Sumerian cities "liberated" from

Agade, whether or not at first under the rule of Uruk, ended by falling into the power of one of their own number. This city we know, although the *King List* speaks not a word of it, from other sources—it was Lagash.[54]

Between Rimush and Utuhengal we have over fifteen names of *ensi*'s of Lagash, and for some of them we can supply a very full dossier of inscriptions. Nammahani, the last of them, was overcome by Utuhengal's own conqueror, Ur-Nammu, founder of the Third Dynasty of Ur. Before Nammahani, Ur-GAR, preceded by Pirigme, must have reigned rather a short time over an already less powerful Lagash. But Pirigme's father, Ur-Ningirsu, and the latter's father, Gudea, and Gudea's father-in-law Ur-Baba, seem to have founded, and held for nearly half a century, a true hegemony over all Sumer on behalf of Lagash. We cannot accurately put their predecessors into chronological order, nor estimate their political importance, but it is quite clear that it is the Dynasty of Lagash, or at least the succession of *ensi*'s between Ur-Baba and Nammahani, that properly belongs in the place of the *King List*'s Fourth Dynasty of Uruk—and might, indeed, have figured in that place on that list, had not its compilers sworn, as it would appear, never to name the city that the early monarchs of Ur III (for whom the *King List* must have been composed) regarded as their deadly and natural enemy.

Be that as it may, with Utuhengal, at the very end of our period, we are on much firmer ground. Tradition, at least, is unanimous: It was he who wrote *finis* to the domination of the Gutians, and restored Babylonia to native rule.

(b) *Absolute chronology*: To add up the length of the reigns whose succession we have more or less established, and to reduce these figures to dates in our own era of time reckoning, we might, it seems, begin by finding the dates for the kings of Agade on one side and for Utuhengal on the other, setting the *King List*'s figures for the Fourth Dynasty of Uruk and the Gutians aside for the time being.

If, as seems possible, the *King List* was composed no great time after Utuhengal, there is hardly any reason to doubt its exceptionally precise "seven years, six months and fifteen days" assigned to the reign of that monarch. Furthermore it is highly likely that the *List*'s figures for the reigns of the kings of Agade (containing, as they do, no improbabilities in themselves) had as their source, and our guarantee of their reliability, the archives of that very dynasty, whose sizable administration had to keep the list of year names up to date. Admitting, for the sake of caution, a possible slippage of a few years in one direction or another, one can accept the evidence of the *King List* on this point, particularly since here its manuscript tradition does not vary. From the accession of Sargon, then, to the passing of Shu-DURUL, one would be able to reckon about 180 years.

Another matter entirely are the figures for the dynasties of Uruk and Gutium. Quite aside from the figures for individual reigns, curiously low and harping on the number six (base number of the Sumerian sexagesimal system), resembling an artificial series of round numbers and thereby arousing our suspicions, there is the fact that both versions of the *King List* (the one including, the other suppressing the Gutian rulers) offer the same total of around a hundred years for the period after Agade—i.e. that of the rule of the Gutians in the north, and the prominence of the Fourth Dynasty of Uruk and the Second Dynasty of Lagash in the south. There can be no doubt that this was the original figure in the archetype from which our two versions derive, which lends the common total some authenticity (although it relieves none of our doubts as to the individual figures that make it up).

Now we have already noticed the contemporaneity of the first Gutian kings (who in turn are contemporaries of the Fourth Dynasty of Uruk) with Shar-kali-sharri. So, from the total of 180 years for Agade plus a hundred years for the parallel dynasties Gutium-Uruk IV—Lagash II, we must subtract the fifty years, roughly, that lie between Shar-kali-sharri and the last of his successors, Shu-DURUL. This brings the time elapsed between Sargon of Agade and the victory of Utuhengal over the Gutians down to about 230 years. This is of course a round figure, but it ought to be within ten or twenty years of the true one, and, in the present state of our evidence, one would not be able to hope for more.

To turn all this into dates according to our era, we take as a base point the year of the accession to the throne of Ur-Nammu, Utuḥengal's successor, which, according to the system of chronology adopted for the present volume (see p. 10), would be 2110 B.C. From this we may draw up the scheme of absolute chronology given in chronological table III on pp. 94–5.

Dates of this kind, we must repeat, are only probable (and only probable if the system of calculations on which they are based is accepted) and always approximate. In themselves, however, they are of only secondary importance: Primary from the point of view of historical certainty is the internal sequence of the events, which such dates merely set in temporal relation to ourselves. Reduced to essentials, the sequence is a simple one: Of the 230 years or so with which this chapter is concerned, roughly half saw the birth, the growth and the death of the Empire of Agade; the other half saw the independent development of north and south, toward diverging destinies.

3. The Empire of Agade

The Empire of Agade (ca. 2340–2198) was the work of a *dynasty* in the true sense of the word, in that the five kings who built and sustained it succeeded one another in a direct line from fathers to sons for nearly a century and a half; this continuity was both a cause and a sign of the long stability of their state. This, to be sure, does not seem to have been entirely free of difficulty, for the literary tradition refers to the violent deaths of at least Rimush and Manishtushu in palace revolutions; the same is true for Shar-kali-sharri, but then the monarchy never recovered from his fall.

Their names (at least the first is a "throne name," Sargon= Sharru-kin, "True King"; perhaps also Shar-kali-sharri, meaning "King of all Kings") are nearly all that we know for certain as far as the personalities of these monarchs is concerned; except for a few facts about their immediate families and their courts, their original inscriptions have preserved to us not a single "biographical" detail.

Even with Sargon (2340–2284 B.C.), the first and greatest of the line, we know precious little about his origins or the manner in which he reached his throne. By the end of the third millennium men still knew only that he had appeared, as it were, full-grown on the historical scene. Later on, he was given a nomad for a father and a temple votary for a mother, the latter having cast him adrift on the river in a basket of rushes, which bore him to a peasant who adopted him. Here we have a folklore motif known the world over, from Moses to Romulus and Remus, as a means of filling in the obscure origins of great men, sons of their own accomplishments. But it is worth our while to examine the legend more closely, for there appear to be a few valuable facts embedded in it. The city of the birth or bringing-up of the future king is given as Azupiranu, "The City of Saffron" (of which there is not another mention elsewhere), located "on the banks of the Euphrates"; and the territory traveled by his ancestors on the father's side is called "The Mountain." This last may be understood as applying to the fringes of the desert, and "the banks of the Euphrates" is the name of a definite area around the mouth of the River Khabur or Balikh. In this period the area was occupied by Semites, most of them still seminomads leading a pastoral life, who from time to time would leave their semidesert plateaus and their wandering existence, either singly or in groups, to settle among the river towns, particularly among the rich cities of Babylonia. This had been going on since prehistoric times. The northern parts of Babylonia particularly had long been occupied by scattered groups of Semites, in settlements of greater or lesser importance, the principal one apparently being Kish. All had been, up to Sargon's time, in a state of strict dependence, cultural and often political, on their Sumerian neighbors (see pp. 57 ff.).

The legend of Sargon's origins, then, highlights his Semitic

103

background: He was one of that long line of immigrants whose lives had left no mark on history until himself. So much does he represent them all that, after the sensational rise in status that he and his successors brought them, the Babylonian Semites have no other national name than Akkadians, from the name of the capital he founded: Agade. This name, too, in the form of "Akkad," was applied to all the northern part of Lower Mesopotamia, the south alone retaining the name of Sumer. With Sargon, the Semites emerge from the shadows: He and his successors glory in Semitic names; their language, "Akkadian," begins to replace the Sumerian tongue; long-haired, bearded faces replace the generally round, shaven Sumerian heads on the reliefs. In the history of Babylonia, shot through with the coexistence, to a certain extent even the cultural rivalry, of Sumerians and Semites, this is a prime development, whose importance we shall have to weigh later on.

If we follow the same legend, Sargon was born into one of the already settled Semitic groups, although his ancestors would still have been seminomadic at some earlier point in time. He entered political life, we have no idea how, in the great Semitic center of Kish; the *King List* figures him as "cup-bearer" to the second king of the Third Dynasty of Kish, Ur-Zababa. No doubt he later on led a revolt against his sovereign, perhaps on the occasion of the king's defeat in a war that had destroyed the power of Kish. Favored by extraordinary luck (the literary tradition attributes it to a special fondness toward him on the part of the great Semitic goddess Ishtar), Sargon succeeded in carving out a personal domain around the site of Agade, where he either constructed a new or expanded an existing city as his capital—a sin of pride, as men said later on. We do not know the exact location of Agade (its ruins have never been found), but a contemporary document situates it near Kish, and the literary tradition places it not far from Babylon, so we can infer that it must have been somewhere in the territory of the ancient city of Sippar (to give one possibility), and probably on the banks of the Euphrates.

We are deplorably short of details on the great work of

Sargon, namely the creation of an empire ruled from Agade. Or, better put, we do not have the guiding thread that would tie known events together to give us a chronologically ordered picture of the growth of that empire. We can attempt to supply this by following the order in which the scribes of Nippur arranged their copies of his inscriptions, or we might, where this fails us, fall back on "historical logic"—if only history behaved logically.

What we do know is that his empire began with Agade, which remained its center; "King of Agade" was always the first in line of his titles. He adds "King of Kish." The old Semitic capital, that is, even in its fallen state, still had all of its prestige, and the new king's first task was to assure himself of the primacy of all northern Babylonia by conquering it. Perhaps he carried this out under the color of "liberating" it from Uruk, and "restoring" it to its former glory.

Now master of the north and confident of his power, Sargon could hardly have resisted the temptation to strike at the greatest conqueror of the time in his own lands. An attack on Lugalzagesi, with his "fifty governors" to support him, may very well have required more than one campaign; there are allusions in the inscriptions to a threefold invasion and to Sargon's "thirty-four battles"; having finally vanquished the king of Uruk, having cast him down with a stock around his neck before the national sanctuary of Sumer (the Enlil temple at Nippur), Sargon, at the end of these wars, found himself master of Uruk, Ur, Eninmar, Lagash and Umma—in a word of all the Sumerian states "up to the shores of the sea." From now on, the king of Agade and Kish could add, to his titles, "King of the Land."

What had his motive been? The idea of imitating Lugalzagesi, perhaps? Or the need, at first, to respond to threats from the surrounding states, made uneasy by the rise of a new power so near their borders? We simply have no idea. In any case his next steps took him westward, once the land was united under his rule. The chronicles claim to know that his conquest of the northwest, Sargon's most extraordinary exploit, was carried out in two great campaigns: the first in the year one, the second in the year eleven of his reign. Perhaps he restricted himself, in the first, to the conquest of Tuttul (the present-day Hit) on the Euphrates, the gateway to the "Upper Land," and of Mari. By the end of his second campaign, in any case, the king had led his armies as far as northern Syria (Ebla), the shores of the Mediterranean (Iarmuti?), the Lebanon or Amanus mountains ("The Cedar Forest") and the Taurus range, or at least its eastern foothills ("The Silver Mountains"?). Legend early set to work to embroider this great adventure, so that we are now unable to tell where it retains and where it invents historical fact. Not only is Sargon made the conqueror of cities that our inscriptions know nothing about, such as Carchemish, but he is represented as crossing the Mediterranean to conquer the "Land of Tin" (Cyprus, perhaps, or some seaboard country in southern Asia Minor) and to subject the island of Crete; then again, he is shown marching far into Anatolia, to Burushkhanda, to the south of the Great Salt Lake (the modern Tuz Gölu). Without more solid evidence, caution counsels us not to take these stories at face value. Since the story of the Anatolian campaign, for one, turns on the presence of Akkadian merchants in Asia Minor, very like the well-known Assyrian *tamkaru* who appear there some centuries later, we may wonder whether folklore has not transformed the dispatch of simple trading missions into a military conquest. What we can know with assurance, then, is this: Sargon had brought together under his control territories stretching from the "Lower Sea" (the Persian Gulf) to the "Upper Sea" (the Mediterranean), a distance slightly under 900 miles.

Nor was this all: The king may have taken offense at an alliance between his eastern neighbors, Elam and Warahshe, whose object was surely the hope of discouraging the conqueror. In a double inscription (representing a twofold campaign?) Sargon boasts of having defeated the two allies together, proudly listing their kings, governors and great officers of state, and the cities from which he had taken rich booty.

The omen literature contains a reference to Sargon's conquest of the "Land of Subartu," a place we have difficulty locating—perhaps Upper Mesopotamia from the Zagros mountains to the Khabur or the Balikh River, perhaps something farther west. We cannot be entirely sure that this project was ever more than planned by the great Akkadian. Yet one of the date formulae of his reign names a year by a campaign in Simurru, toward the Zagros range; his immediate successors controlled both the region around the modern Kirkuk and Assyria proper; which leads us to think that, in the course of his endless reign, Sargon had himself brought northern Mesopotamia under his rule.

Even if the "fifty-six" years that the *King List* grants him include, which is possible, the early and more insignificant stages of his career—as Ur-Zababa's officer, or as ruler of a pocket principality around Agade—still his time on earth was long enough to allow for countless prodigies of action, of which we would have no trace. He called himself "He Who Keeps Traveling [?] the Four Lands," an Akkadian expression meaning the universe. The imagination of people and poets alike was thunderstruck by the enormity of his accomplishments, by the immensity of his conquest. Surely it was of him that men thought when they came, a little later, to set down the great deeds of Gilgamesh. Someone took the trouble to list the sixty-five countries and great cities of his unbounded empire, the thousand-mile distances that separated its four corners from its center. A mythological map was drawn up, to show the distant and miraculous countries whose soil he alone had trod, save for two others only—both figures of the age of legend.

And yet his long reign must have seen revolts among so many peoples subjected to an alien rule, and defeats, even disasters, which the literary tradition attributes to his immoderacy. And it was not an untroubled legacy he left behind him. Down to the end of the empire he had founded, rebellion never ceased to break out everywhere, putting the extent and cohesion of the state constantly to the test, forcing his succes-

sors constantly to recapitulate, in a sense, the astonishing conquests of Sargon the Great.

Rimush (2284–2275 B.C.), to begin with, immediately on
his accession had to put down a chain reaction of revolts in
the Land of Sumer (Ur, Lagash, Umma, Adab, Uruk and
Kazallu). Then, in the year three of his reign, in a pitiless
war marked by bloodbaths, by cities shorn of their walls or
razed to the ground, he faced his father's old enemies to the
east: Elam and Warahshe had allied again, trying to shake off
the overlordship of Agade. Rimush's presence to the north of
Nineveh is also attested, by his foundation of a city to which
he gave his own name.

Manishtushu (2275–2260 B.C.) had, it seems, other pre-
occupations to start out with, i.e. a revolt by his eastern vassals,
Anshan and Sheriku, in which he had to take "thirty-two cities"
by force to retain his suzerainty over Elam; then, on the western shore of the Persian Gulf, the conquest (reconquest?) of
the quarries of "black stone." An inscription of his found at
Assur, and the memory persisting, half a millennium later,
of his founding of the temple of Ishtar at Nineveh, show him
active in the northern part of his inheritance.

An Akkadian poem of the beginning of the second millennium B.C. lists the Mesopotamian cities in revolt against
Naram-Sin (2260–2223) at the beginning of his reign: Kish,
Kutha, Kazallu, Marad, Umma, Nippur, Uruk, Sippar, to
which it adds the countries of Magan, to the south, of Elam,
Warahshe, Mardaman and Simurru to the east and northeast,
of Mamar and Apishal to the north and Mari to the west. So
many rebellions, breaking out all at once at the very outset of
his reign—the hand of the poet is apparent. But we have not
the least reason to doubt that each of these cities and countries
broke into revolt at *some* time during the thirty-seven-year
reign of Sargon's grandson; his own inscriptions corroborate
it. It is for this reason, we may suppose, that Naram-Sin
had to retrace everywhere his forebear's footsteps—was led,
perhaps, to go beyond them, north, south, east and west, bringing under his scepter "lands that no king before him had ever

conquered," until finally, more than any other of his line, he was compared by later ages to the great Sargon, both for his glory and for the pride that went before so terrible a fall. For, more than Sargon, he felt himself to be the conqueror and master of the universe: He it was who took unto himself a truly "imperial" title, never employed in all the ages before him: "King of the Four Quarters." His royal inscriptions reveal an unbroken succession of victories—royal inscriptions always do. But we must read between the lines, and then we cannot escape the impression, in the midst of all these triumphs, of total disaster to come. Naram-Sin, for instance, concludes a treaty with the King of Elam—meaning he no longer feels himself strong enough to crush him, he has to accommodate him. Naram-Sin, for instance, carries his arms far into the Zagros range, where we may have traces of his passage at Darband-i-Gawr: Why has he gone there? Not for the glory or the profit to be gained by crushing the worthless Lullu who live there, but because these fierce mountaineers, by the boldness and destructiveness of their raids, have begun to represent a real danger to the city dwellers of the plain. Everywhere, appearances of imperial glory: beneath them, so many signs of the way in which the real weaknesses of the Akkadian Empire were growing more pronounced with time, even under the leadership of a sovereign so energetic as Naram-Sin. It may well be that the dismemberment of the empire begins in his reign.

For his son and successor, Shar-kali-sharri (2223–2198 B.C.), no longer bears the title of "King of the Four Quarters." He has returned to the more modest style of "King of Agade," and we must suppose he has good reason for it. Uruk, in his reign, seeks to throw off the rule of Agade, this time perhaps successfully; Elam wins its independence at last; the Amurrum, a western Semitic people, probably still seminomadic, are "defeated at the mountain of Basar" (Jebel Bishri)—probably in the course of a disquieting advance on the northwestern marches of the empire. Finally, and above all, a new threat from the northeast becomes clearly discernible: the Gutians,

to whom coming ages will attribute the final ruin of all that
Sargon had created.

4. State and Civilization in the Age of the Empire

Before we watch its disappearance, let us examine the nature, the *modus operandi*, the originality and the historical
importance of the Empire of Agade.

To begin with, it is clear that the motive for so many wars
and conquests, the real *raison d'être* of the empire created and
maintained by them, was economic in nature. No document
of the age tells us so frankly, but all reveal it. Sargon's ambition for himself and his country was power and glory, to be
sure, but riches before all, for they were the indispensable
foundation for all the rest. They were to be gained—a system
as old as warfare itself—in the form of loot torn from the
hands of defeated enemies, and heavy tribute laid upon their
lands. More certain, more profitable in the long run was the
method he principally employed, that of a monopoly on trade
in the goods most indispensable and most unavailable to the
Babylonians in their own country: wood, stones, and metals
in particular. After listing his conquests on the shores of
the Persian Gulf, he adds, to his victory communiqué: "May
the fleets of Meluḫḫa, of Magan and of Tilmun henceforth
freely sail to the river-port of Agade." Or, to put it in modern
terms, Agade attracts all the sea trade of India and Oman, and
becomes the *entrepôt* for all the metals and stones that are
brought to it from the East. When Sargon wants to give the
limits reached by his expedition to the northwest, he names
"The Cedar Forest" and "The Silver Mountains,"[55] as if to
define his true aim—the wood, the metal, and the stones, with
which these distant regions were so well endowed. We may
guess that the Akkadian kings set certain of their campaigns
on foot for similar reasons, even more narrowly defined. For
instance, it has been noticed that the bronze objects of the time
are made with an alloy containing less tin, and therefore providing less strength, than those of former centuries. It seems
likely, then, that the old sources for this metal either had been

or very nearly were exhausted, so that the Akkadian kings cast about for new ones: this, perhaps, is the reality behind the legend of the "conquest" of the "Land of Tin" (see p. 106).

Under circumstances such as these, it was unnecessary (indeed for geographical reasons it was impractical) to build an empire in the *political* sense of the word, overturning the ethnic, institutional or administrative structure of the conquered nations to annex them to Agade as so many new provinces. It was enough to ensure that the conqueror's presence would be everywhere visible, and everywhere strong enough to prevent the subject peoples from refusing what was required of them: heavy contributions in the native products, and free access by the conqueror's agents to the native natural resources, which must at their direction flow freely toward the capital. It was enough, that is, in an *economic* empire of this kind, to add to the native political and administrative machinery a military occupation force, intended to hold it to obedience. We can, in fact, see quite clearly, in the inscriptions of the kings of Agade, that the conquered cities and countries retained their own native rulers and their high officials (with the exception, obviously, of the more dangerous sovereigns, Lugalzagesi for one, who had to be put out of the way or rendered powerless). Ur, conquered by Sargon, keeps Kaku as her king, for he reappears leading the revolt against Rimush; Waraḫshe makes war on Rimush under Sidgau, who had originally surrendered his state to Sargon.

Sargon himself may be revealing one of the principles of his imperial administration, when he tells us that "from the Lower Sea to the Upper Sea, from now on citizens of Agade held the post of governor [*ensi*]." "Citizens of Agade" may mean not only royal agents, but also members of the royal family: Lipit-ili, a son of Naram-Sin, was named *ensi* of Marad by him. The daughters held religious offices which also carried real political powers, e.g. Enheduanna, whom Sargon, her father, made high priestess of Nanna, the city god of Ur; or her successor in that office, Enmenana, daughter to Naram-Sin.

What the conquerors imposed on all the annexed territories

was not, then, new heads of state, but new officials, set up beside them to represent the king of Agade in matters of local government. It goes without saying that each of these "governors" had to be supported, if the king of Agade's wishes were to be carried out, by armed forces, of varying size but always of Akkadian origin. There is eloquent archaeological testimony to this, found at Tell-Brak, on the Upper Khabur. On this site, which dominated the principal routes of the northwest and allowed its occupants to keep all the "Upper Land" under surveillance, Naram-Sin (perhaps one of his predecessors) had put up a sizable edifice, over two acres in extent; its solid architecture and numerous storerooms speak of a large garrison, among whose tasks the collection and storage of goods to be sent to the capital ranked high.

An administrative system of this kind implies an extreme concentration of power and an extremely high number of officials to exercise it. But in actual fact only the king exercises real power: there is the king, and aside from him nothing but "representatives" (ensi's),[56] who exercise a fragment of his power at his pleasure.

This extraordinary elevation of the position of the monarch, alone responsible from this time forward for all the "Four Quarters" of the universe, was one of the greatest innovations of the Akkadian period. The old Sumerian system of rule by the city and the temple was forever erased: Mesopotamia from now on is ruled by monarchies. More, the personality of the monarch now came to be thought of as a cosmic force, as surrounded by a superhuman aura hitherto reserved to the only beings who, until now, had taken the entire universe as their province—the gods. We are therefore not surprised to find evidence, from the era of Ur III, of a cult offered to Sargon, Rimush, Manishtushu and Naram-Sin; that Naram-Sin, in his inscriptions, calls himself "God of Agade," "Husband of Ishtar Annunit," and precedes his name with the cuneiform sign for "divinity," does not amaze us. Particularly if we take the trouble to understand in just what this "divinization" consists: not a change in the king's nature, but in his function, for he now fulfills for his subjects the same role—creator, organizer, master for good and evil of their destinies—as the gods had fulfilled for mankind. For he too, from now on, has as his subjects all mankind. We see the Akkadian kings exercising this "functional divinity," for example, when they order men to add their royal names to the names of the gods by whom contractual oaths are sworn—as if to affirm that kings now take responsibility for the sanctity of contracts, and thereby for the whole network of obligations by which men live in an ordered society. Law and justice was something the Semites had always considered the province of the gods; henceforth it was to be the care of kings. This had enormous consequences for the legal development of Mesopotamia; the royal "codes" of the future were one outcome of it.

We have spoken above of the great number of officials in the imperial administration. For this we have no direct proofs, but it follows directly from the king's new position. Sargon boasts of feeding "5,400 men at his table" every day, by which we must understand the servants, soldiers and scribes who flooded his palace at Agade. To recall the organization of the empire is to confirm the absolute need of a huge bureaucracy —this would be the only binding link between the king, sole master of all, and all the territories and organizations that awaited and obeyed his orders. Civil and military officials, scribes and overseers, clerks and storekeepers, soldiers and officers, artisans and laborers, in fact a high proportion of the population of the capital, at the very least, would have had to be mobilized in the service of a machine as vast, and as complex, as was the Akkadian state.

They were paid, we may be sure, by the standard Mesopotamian method, i.e. by grants of consumer goods. The king's servants lived at his expense, fed, clothed and laundered by him. To this outpouring of the king's resources add all the other matters for which the king assumed financial responsibility: the founding, reconstruction and maintenance of temples, walls, fortresses, whole cities; the purchase of necessities and luxuries for his court; a tremendous movement of goods, pointing to a vast accumulation of wealth in the king's name. Not the city nor the temple, as in Sumerian times, but the king himself was the greatest capitalist in the land.

His capital consisted not only of movable goods but also of lands. The Akkadian age sees the extension if not the introduction of the system of paying royal servants, not only by feeding them directly, but also by granting them cultivable lands. These the recipients would either farm themselves or sublet to some peasant for a share of the crop. We have an obelisk of Manishtushu that may refer to the practice, a record of a tremendous spate of land transactions by the king: He lists the lands he has acquired for sums adding up to something like 650 pounds of silver; there are about 650-odd acres of arable land in four large lots, each made up of parcels bought from individual proprietors (ninety-eight in all) and handed out again to forty-nine new occupants, all citizens of Agade. The recipients include the king's nephew and the sons of former rulers of conquered Mesopotamian towns; the latter must have been transferred to Agade, either as hostages or as entrants into the king's service. Does the king give away, outright, real estate that has cost him so dear? More likely it is a grant of the use of the land, and the enjoyment of its income, to the king's servants, with the king retaining title to the property. Whatever the case, we have here definite evidence for the existence of private property in land in Agade (an institution that was to spread to all Mesopotamia), and for the preeminence of the king as chief landowner in the country, a final proof of his colossal wealth.

The creation of the Akkadian Empire, then, touched off a vast redistribution of wealth, and it also fostered the spread of a new way of possessing it. Economic individualism would, as it increased, little by little alter the relations between man and man, until, in the end, society would be divided into a system of classes based on property and measured by economic independence.

Such were the innovations that the very structure of the Empire of Agade imposed. Others of no less importance sprang from the Semitic character of its rulers and of the people whom they had raised to the leadership of the world.

Fundamental for the history of the land was the expansion of Akkadian, a Semitic language, at the expense of the Sumerian speech. (The expansion of Babylonian civilization northward to Semitic Assyria is discussed elsewhere—see pp. 129 ff.) From now on, Sumerian is hardly ever seen on official inscriptions, particularly in the north, without an Akkadian translation alongside (when the text is not simply written in Akkadian alone); for nonofficial uses it is entirely restricted to the south of Babylonia. And Akkadian, little by little, becomes the spoken language even there; within a few generations, Sumerian would be reduced to the state of a scholarly and liturgical jargon. Under the kings of Agade a tremendous labor, begun before their time, is carried forward: the adaptation to a Semitic language of the script the Sumerians had invented for their own, entirely different, vocabulary. Here, too, the Akkadians brought the style of writing, the calligraphy of cuneiform, to a point of elegance and perfection never equaled in the three millennia in which the script was employed.

All the subsequent development of Mesopotamian religion is marked by the influence of this age. The most important influence was not the introduction of new Semitic divinities to the old pantheon of the Semites—Aba (written A.MAL), Annunit and Dagan, and, Semitic despite his Sumerian name, Ea. More important by far was the Akkadians' extensive syncretism, by which all of their native divinities were matched and identified with their Sumerian counterparts. The result was that the characters, if not the very lineaments of the gods were, in the long run, greatly altered on both sides. The Sumerian Inanna, for example, the essence of femininity and the goddess of love, had added to this the warlike and almost mannish personality of the Semitic Ishtar. But above all the Semites brought with them a new spirit, slowly filling and changing from within the old Sumerian forms, and new conceptions that would alter the nature of divinity itself. The gods, purely local personifications of the forces of nature as far as the ancient Sumerians were concerned, were to become cosmic powers, charged with maintaining the orderly course not only of nature, but of history; and, at the same time, they were to become moral beings, preoccupied with the social order and with the sanctity of law. Kings of the Universe, in a word. For if the Akkadian monarchs had taken on traits of divinity, they had given the gods royal and imperial traits in return. They conceived gods in their own image, imagined a divine world organized by analogy with the kingdom of men, laying greater and greater stress on ideas of monarchy and hierarchy in the realm of heaven. The very ritual of divine worship was to be altered and enriched, by an assimilation to the forms of court étiquette (or so a fragment of an inscription attributable to Rimush suggests). Profound changes, these, whose effects would not be fully apparent for two or three centuries to come; and yet, for the most part, we can but point to them, we cannot trace them, for lack of sufficient sources of evidence.

The quantity of genuinely religious and literary texts that has been so far found is, to put it simply, pitiful. But the quality of these few forces us to assume, for the century and a half after Sargon, an intense intellectual activity, productive of changes as vital as any we have seen so far. For instance, we possess a hymn of sorts written in Sumerian, found at Nippur and quite probably the oldest Mesopotamian religious text now known. It is full of gaps and it puts up stiff resistance to interpretation, but it demonstrates that mythology, the hoary ancestor of our metaphysics and our theology, was already in flower. We have incantations (a few), in Sumerian and in Akkadian, that show us a less theoretical side of the religious thought of the time. Royal inscriptions are no novelty, but those of Agade are written in a more concise style, composed with greater artistry and lucidity than before, testifying not only to a real command of the language, but to a genuine concern for literary values. How these were fostered we have some idea, from fragments of "dictionaries" for the use of scribes and certain schoolboy exercises. Schools, then, were in full operation. And there was, in the land, around the palace and the temples, a class of men devoted by profession to the arts of reading and writing, and to the cultural life to which these were the key. Who will say that they produced no literary or intellectual results? We cannot imagine, for instance, that so many distant travels on the part of kings and armies did not arouse the geographical curiosity of the learned, nor can we suppose that the unmatched exploits of Sargon and his successors did not stimulate an urge to write them down. To this the requirements of so highly organized an administration would add a concern for chronology:[57] the art of history was being born.

Agade, the city, has yet to be discovered, and in general the small number of excavations of Akkadian sites leaves us very largely in the dark where the age's architecture is concerned. Examples of the stonecarver's art, however, sculptures and above all cylinder seals, we have in quantity, and these allow us to form an opinion of Akkadian art. It is the highest possible. We have here such a regeneration of taste, such an extraordinary mastery of materials, that this must mark the high point in the long history of the arts of Mesopotamia. For Sumerian stiffness and hieratic coldness the Akkadians substituted life and imagination, along with a splendid sense of foreshortening and composition. The power and majesty of the kings of Agade passed, in some sort, into the work of their sculptors in stone and bronze, to produce a truly royal art. This is true even of works in the constricted format of the cylinder seal: The outline and modeling is perfect on the hardest stones; the realism, the power of suggestion of these figures, is as great in its impact as if they were in fact sculptures in the round. And, where men had formerly carved onto their seals mere decorative elements, Akkadian lapidaries began to cover them with mythological scenes—whose composition and variety, by the way, hint at the prolific creation of new mythical material that must then have been going on.

"After the age of Agade, even in the period of Sumerian dominance, there is not a work of art to be found in Mesopotamia that does not bear at least some trace of the great art of the dynasty of Agade . . ."[58] A verdict that would hold true for every other aspect of Akkadian culture. The empire whose foundations were laid by Sargon changed the entire course of development of Mesopotamia, and marked the civilization of that country with an indelible seal.

5. Disruption of the Empire

But, remarkable as this empire was, in its achievements and its influence, a structure so enormous was fragile to the same degree. When and how its disruption occurred, we do not clearly know. Probably by progressive steps. From the end of Naram-Sin's reign onward, possibly as an effect of vast movements of peoples in Hither Asia, various parts of the empire were able to free themselves of the Akkadian yoke. The *King List*, as we have seen, shows Uruk regaining its independence, and taking a good part of Sumer with it. A date formula of Shar-kali-sharri's reign records an expedition of the king "to Uruk and Naksu," perhaps in direct or indirect connection with the same revolt. The first of the Gutian rulers on the *King List*, Erridupizir, set up an inscription in which he hailed himself as "King of the Four Quarters," as if in fact laying claim to the imperial throne, and to the succession to Naram-Sin. The literary tradition, in any case, recalls that Naram-Sin had to fight the Gutians. Their boldness reaped better advantage in Shar-kali-sharri's weaker reign. He, to be sure, records his victory over Sarlag (or Sarlagab), Erridupizir's third successor; but his resistance to the invaders must have monopolized his entire reign. For we have a private letter from his time that represents the Gutians as a permanent danger, seizing the herds and the possessions of the king's subjects, preventing them from cultivating the land. Shar-kali-sharri, "King of All Kings" in name only, constantly pinned down by the pressure of savage raids, can only have ruled a limited or a disintegrating empire, and he must have fought for mere survival.

This was not to be granted to him. His tragic death in

2198 B.C. (in a palace intrigue, the literary tradition tells us) dealt a terrible blow to the monarchy; "for three years" (2198–2195 B.C.) anarchy prevailed, four competitors scrabbling for the throne, and perhaps carving up the national territory among them in the process. That the Gutians had a hand in the matter appears from the name of one of the four rivals, Elul or Elulu, whom the *King List* places, under the (Gutian?) variant of Elulumesh, in its catalogue of Gutian kings. Elul is the only one of the compeitors known to us from a source other than the *King List*, an inscription of his own in which he grants himself the title of "Mighty One, King of Agade."[59] To Dudu (2195–2174 B.C.) is attributed the restoration of order, and perhaps of Agade's independence and power, to some degree; a dedicatory inscription of his found at Nippur and two more at Adab encourage us to think that he had regained control over northern Sumer at the very least. That some sort of stability had been regained is shown by the succession to his throne of a son, Shu-DURUL (2174–2159 B.C.). From the latter we possess certain documents that would indicate suzerainty over Kish and Tutub (modern Khafaji), sixty miles to the north. Would we be right in placing in his reign what the chronicles and the omen texts call the "destruction" (*shaḫluqtum*) of Agade? Not if we take that to mean, as the literary tradition does from the beginning of the second millennium on, the sack of the *city* of Agade, described by a famous poem in Sumerian, *The Curse of Agade*. For this ultimate insult at the invader's hands could have taken place at an earlier date, at any time after the end of the reign of Naram-Sin. But if we take this to mean the destruction of the *Empire* of Agade, its total and final disappearance from the political scene, there is no question that this coincides with the end of the reign of Shu-DURUL (around 2159 B.C.). In either case the tradition is clear on one point: The chief authors of this "destruction" are the Gutians; it is they who rule from now on in the northern half of Babylonia. In memory of a bygone grandeur, men would continue to call it Akkad.

6. The Gutian Occupation

Little is left to us that might help us form an idea of the extent, the duration and the internal history of the Gutian occupation of Akkad and domination of Mesopotamia. The power of the Gutians must have waxed and waned with time. Erridupizir, the first Gutian king, was able to take territory in the south and hold it for a time; he left a long inscription at Nippur, as yet unpublished. The text that celebrates their final expulsion tells us that they posed a real threat to Sumer. But we have good grounds for believing that the north was the only part of the land they occupied permanently, and even that they may have held lightly, with a few troops here and there or garrisons at strategic points. They destroyed much (in the city of Assur, for example) and they built nothing, left nothing of their own behind them, brought nothing new to Mesopotamia. Doubtless they were changed by her instead: in the second half of their stay a number of their kings bore Semitic names (Kurum, Ḥabil-kin, Ibranum, Puzur-Sin, Si'um) or Semitized Gutian names (La'erabum, Irarum). The inscriptions that we have from their monarchs (Erridupizir, Elulu-mesh, La'erabum, Iarlagan, Si'um) are written in cuneiform script and in Akkadian; proving, incidentally, that what civilization they had, they had gotten through Akkad, not directly from Sumer. They may even have adopted some of the Akkadian gods (assimilating them to their own?): La'erabum calls Ishtar and Sin "gods of Gutium." To this, add that La'erabum and, a bit later, Iarlagan and Si'um, call themselves "Mighty One, King of Gutium," and you have everything we now know about the Gutians. We can estimate the duration of their rule, as we have seen, at about a hundred years (2200?–2116 B.C.). The rest is mystery.

7. Sumer in the Gutian Period

In Sumer, for a number of important cities we have nothing, either from the period of Akkadian rule or from its aftermath, but the names of a few "kings" or "governors." At Ur: Ur-Utu (a contemporary of Sargon), Kaku (a contemporary of Rimush), E.LI.LI. (probably under the Gutians). At Adab: Meskigala (a contemporary of Rimush). At Kazallu: Asharid (the same). At Marad: Lipit-Ili, son of Naram-Sin. At Isin, a king whose name is unknown, contemporary with Manish-tushu. At Umma: Mes'e (a contemporary of Sargon), Lu-Damu (under Rimush), Asharid (under Manishtushu), and his son Shurushkin; then, in the Gutian period, Nammaḫani (under Iarlaganda) and Lugalannatum (under Si'um). There are a few other names, which we pass over.

As we already know, this period probably saw a hegemony of Uruk over Sumer for a time, perhaps from the reign of Shar-kali-sharri on; but aside from the five royal names preserved by the *King List* we have no details of it.

The only Sumerian city whose history we are able to reconstruct in some detail, particularly for the Gutian period, is Lagash. And Lagash, in fact, seems to have played a leading role in the land of Sumer at the time.

We know, to begin at the beginning, at least the names of several of the city's *ensi*'s, contemporaries and vassals of the kings of Agade: KI-KU-id, under Rimush; Engilsa under Manishtushu; Ur-a under Naram-Sin; and Lugalushumgal under Naram-Sin and Shar-kali-sharri. After which, we are not sure of the order in which Puzur-Mama, Ur-Utu, Ur-Mama, Lu-Baba, Lu-Gula and Kaku ruled over a city perhaps subordinate to one of her Sumerian neighbors (Uruk?) once Akkadian rule had been shaken off. In any case Lagash played no very important part in Sumerian politics at the time. This state of affairs changes with the last six *ensi*'s: Ur-Baba, Gudea, Ur-Ningirsu, Pirigme, Ur-GAR and Nammaḫani. We can estimate their dates (see Chronological Table III), and we know that son succeeded father (or son-in-law father-in-law) in a true dynasty, which we call the Second Dynasty of Lagash. For they made their city, as the First Dynasty had done (see pp. 80 ff.), the metropolis of Sumer.

Although we continue to speak of "Lagash" for this period, it was not Lagash proper (the modern el-Hiba) that was the capital of this state, but Girsu (the modern Tello). The state comprised a territory, according to a fragmentary but still decipherable document, of 400 acres, in which seventeen "principal towns" and eight "district capitals" were located, to say nothing of villages and hamlets of which we know about forty by their contemporary names. This description gives us a fairly clear idea of what an ancient Sumerian city-state could be, geographically speaking: a veritable tiny kingdom.

From Ur-Baba (ca. 2164–2144 B.C.) on, the rulers of Lagash extended their power over a great part of the Sumerian land. For Ur-Baba could not have set up his daughter, Enanepada, as high priestess of Nanna at Ur, had that city not been his vassal, as it had been Sargon's when he gave his daughter the same post (see p. 111). Eridu, then a dependancy of Ur, must also have had to recognize the suzerainty of Lagash; Gudea (ca. 2144–2124 B.C.) speaks of a processional visit of the city god of Lagash, Ningirsu, to the temples of Eridu as if the god were on his own territory. From Gudea again we have inscriptions that record the erection of temples not only at Ur, but at Nippur, Adab, Uruk, Badtibira. Lagash seems then to have become the ruling power, the mistress of Sumer. We may justly take her princes as the true successors of the kings of Agade—but purely Sumerian successors, both by the extent of their territory and the manner of their rule.

To begin with, Lagash brings a return to the system of city-state rule that was a feature of pre-Akkadian Babylonia, and of Sumer in particular. Their title was the traditional, modest one of *ensi*, although they may have picked up something from Akkadian notions of kingship: Gudea calls himself, once, "God of Lagash." But they were less ambitious, less hot-blooded than their great predecessors, never, for instance, undertaking a war of foreign conquest, or an annexation abroad. Gudea, it is true, reports an expedition against Anshan and Elam, but it must have been a defensive one, for his victory brought no occupation of the enemy's lands.

We have every reason to believe that the *ensi*'s of Lagash aimed at the same goal as Sargon and his successors—the monopoly of trade in certain necessities, and a degree of economic autarky as a result. But they pursued this goal by entirely different means, more traditional in Sumer, and founded more on commercial than on military principles. Gudea's agents appear wherever Sargon's troops had made their way, but as ordinary merchants, with no political intentions. Stone, wood and metals flow to his warehouses: from the south, from Meluḫḫa, from Magan, from Tilmun, from Gubin (which must represent Jebel al-Akhdar on the southern shore of the Gulf of Oman). To the east, he trades, for the same products, with Anshan and Elam, and, farther on, in the mountainous region of the Bakhtiari, with Adamdun and Aratta; to the north with Kimash and Kagalad (north of the Jebel Hamrin), with Magda and Barme, in the area of the modern Kirkuk; to the northwest, with the Middle Euphrates region and even higher up the river toward northern Syria— with Basalla (the Basar of Shar-kali-sharri's inscription), with Tidan (no doubt nearby), with Ursu and Ebla on the Upper Euphrates, and even with the area of the Amanus range. And further still, perhaps: with Menua and Ḫaḫḫum and the mountain Uringeraz, which may have lain on the slopes of the Taurus, or even on the Cappadocian highland in Anatolia. In other words, the map of his commercial network exactly superimposes itself on that of the Akkadian Empire only instead of soldiers, diplomats and traders carried his name abroad. Gudea even appears to have made a treaty guaranteeing free passage for his men through the territory of, of all things, the Gutians.

A smaller quantity of goods, it may be, now came to Lagash than those that had rained on Agade—but they came cheaper. They did not require military expeditions and countless garrisons to collect them, nor an immense administrative machine. The ruler is no longer the unique and formidable being Sargon and his successors were; he is simply the *ensi* of the city, as before. Yet his city is as prosperous as theirs was, and probably much less exposed to danger.

Nothing could better demonstrate this prosperity than the number of public works planned and executed by Ur-Baba

123

and, especially, Gudea. They build in their capital, throughout their state and in many cities subject to their power. Their date formulae name one year after another by the dedication of some new public amenity. There is never a word about war, but we hear of new canals, of irrigation and drainage works (years two and three of Ur-Baba, four of Gudea, three of a ruler with name unknown); of civic improvements and reconstruction (year four of Ur-Baba, three [?] of Gudea); of sanctuaries built in the territory of the city (fifth year of Ur-Baba, second, tenth, fourteenth and fifteenth of Gudea), and also elsewhere (year six of Ur-Baba). Other matters considered worthy of commemoration in year names include the manufacture of cult objects (years five, six, seven [?], nine, eleven and twelve of Gudea), and the nomination of officials and priests (eighth and thirteenth years of Gudea and third, fourth, and fifth of Ur-Ningirsu, second of Pirigme and the second year of an unknown *ensi*). The same peaceful, useful and purposeful occupations are illustrated by the royal inscriptions. Two long poems, written on clay cylinders, were composed by Gudea to celebrate the reconstruction and dedication of the Eninnu, sanctuary of the city god Ningirsu.

That the Second Dynasty of Lagash, particularly under Ur-Baba and Gudea, brought peace and prosperity to its city and to all the land of Sumer, we have just seen: that it also presided over a very great flowering of arts and letters alike, we must now demonstrate. This is easily done, for a great number of texts and monuments testify to it.

The culture of this age is authentically Sumerian. The place names are Sumerian, and the monumental inscriptions are written in Sumerian, as are the tablets that record the transactions of daily life. There are longer compositions, dedications on statues of Gudea and especially his two "cylinders," that are the first texts of respectable length that we have in that language. The language has changed since the time before Sargon, but it is still pure, still "classical." Literature retains the forms originated earlier in Sumer; sculpture retains something of its original hieratic coldness. And yet one can discern

Akkadian influence everywhere. The vocabulary of Sumerian now contains certain new Semitic loan words, written in the Akkadian manner. Certain turns of phrase are clearly adapted from the language of the north. The techniques and aesthetic canons of the sculptors and lapidaries are borrowed from the Akkadian masters. In general, one gets the impression that Sumerian creativity is just beginning to run out, that the artists are imitating more often than they invent.

The same picture is presented by religion: strictly Sumerian forms, under which the legacy of Agade persists and grows. The pantheon is entirely Sumerian, and so are the forms of worship; but religious sentiments and theological thinking on the nature of divine power and the kingly role of the gods seem to be altering under Akkadian influence.

Lagash, therefore, is old Sumer reborn, but reborn with a new heredity in the form of partial, and increasing, Akkadian influence. The empire is gone, but on the cultural level Akkad is in the process of making a more permanent conquest of all Mesopotamia.

After Ur-Ningirsu (ca. 2124–2119 B.C.) and Pirigme (ca. 2119–2117 B.C.), Lagash seems to grow weaker and lose some of its importance, perhaps with a renewal of the power of Uruk. King of that city from 2116 to 2110 is Utuhengal, who restores its supremacy over the south, at least partly at the expense of Lagash. We know, for one thing, that at the beginning of his reign he took the city of Ur, naming one of his generals governor of the place; the general's name was Ur-Nammu, whom time would make a greater king than his master.

8. Expulsion of the Gutians

Utuhengal, however, first had the glory of bringing about the expulsion of the Gutians, by defeating their last king, Tiriqan. Or so an "inscription" of his tells us, actually a literary composition of the beginning of the second millennium. The details of this text make no great sense to us, but it seems, at least, that the decisive conflict took place in the north of Sumer, that is, at the southern limit of Gutian territory as we conceive of its extent at the time. Our text calls the Gutians "mountain dragons" and accuses them of having put the land of Sumer in danger. This last might imply an advance southward by Tiriqan, to seize some of the territories that Lagash was no longer able to protect—it had grown weaker still under Ur-GAR (ca. 2117–2113 B.C.) and Nammaḫani (ca. 2113–2109 B.C.)—and that Uruk was not yet in a position to recover. The only thing of which we can be certain is that the Gutians were thrown back from Sumer once and for all around 2110. But Utuḫengal, liberator of his country, was not himself to retain power for long. Ur-Nammu, his ex-general, soon removed him from the scene. Nammaḫani, last *ensi* of Lagash, was next to fall. A new power was arising, a new era beginning in the history of Mesopotamia.

Western Asia Beyond Babylonia

We have said, at the beginning of this chapter, that our knowledge of the history of this period is almost exclusively "Mesopotamocentric," and our evidence for the surrounding lands exiguous in the extreme. The very few pages devoted to the subject here can do little more than confirm this.

1. The South—The East Coast of Arabia

Of the Meluḫḫa spoken of in Akkadian texts we know little more than the name: It would represent the western shores of India. This leaves Gubin, Magan and Tilmun, also mentioned in the texts, which are probably to be located respectively on the coast of the Gulf of Oman, in Oman itself and in the islands of Bahrain. "Black stone" (basalt?), "precious metal" (gold?) and copper come from these countries, where they are taken out of "holes" (i.e. mines). In Naram-Sin's time, Magan, at least, seems to have been in the power of a single "lord" (*en*), Manium by name.

2. The East—Western Iran (Elam)

We know rather more about this ancient land, at once the traditional enemy and the imitator of Babylonia. There were several divisions; Sheriḫu or Sheriku stretched along the Persian Gulf; farther into the interior lay Anshan; Elam proper directly to the east of Sumer; and, farther north, in the mountains of Luristan, Zaḫara and, notably, Waraḫshe or Baraḫshe (later Marḫashi), which seems to have formed a separate and independent state.

Each of the divisions mentioned contained a certain number of cities, whose rulers called themselves kings or governors; the cities of the whole area seem to have been federated under the leadership of the most powerful among them. In the Akkadian age the leading city was, apparently, Awan (probably the present-day Shushtar). At the beginning of the second millennium the literary tradition knows of a "Dynasty of Awan" with twelve kings, founded by a certain Peli (?). Several of them are mentioned in other sources. The eighth, Luḫḫishan (ca. 2300 B.C.), was a contemporary of Sargon of Agade; Sargon gives his title as "King of Elam" and mentions several of his subordinates, as well as his allies in the land of Waraḫshe (which had its own "king" at its head). Luḫḫishan seems to have been brought to recognize, by force, the suzerainty of Sargon, a condition which lasted in spite of repeated revolts, some of them savagely punished by Akkadian kings, down to the time of Naram-Sin. The latter, perhaps toward the end of his reign, found himself forced to treat with a nation growing continually more powerful and less tractable: From a tablet with twelve columns of Elamite text, we know the treaty he concluded with a King of Awan, perhaps Hita (ca. 2220 B.C.), next-to-the-last of his dynasty. The last king of Awan happens to be the best known to us, largely through his own inscriptions: He is Kutik-Inshushinak,[60] who may have led his country to renewed independence, around 2200, in the reign of Shar-kali-sharri. He was a monarch extremely active in the works of both war and peace, a conqueror, builder and organizer. Can we guess that his power was broken, directly or indirectly, by Gutian attack? The list of kings of Awan ends with him, in any case. There follows a number of kings of Simash (to the north of Susiana, not far from Warahshe), who dominate Elam in the Gutian age. We find brief mention of a campaign in Elam led by Gudea, but otherwise we know nothing more about the history of the country at the time.

The inscriptions we have mentioned and many others, including a good many administrative documents, have been found above all at Susa; they, and a great many archaeological excavations, allow us to form an idea of Elamite civilization. There is much that is original about it. The language, to begin with, resembles no other of which we know, and its grammar and vocabulary are not yet entirely understood. The script, too, is original, at least that first employed in Elam: a pictographic system inspired by, but not directly copied from, that invented by the Sumerians. We are as yet unable to read it. It was abandoned under Akkadian influence, to be replaced by a cuneiform adapted, with some simplifications, to the phonetics of the Elamite tongue. An inscribed fragment found near Bushire is the oldest readable document we have in Elamite; a century before Sargon, it is already written in cuneiform. So is the treaty between Naram-Sin and Hita; Kutik-Inshushinak uses the ancient native script on occasion, perhaps to symbolize the national revival, but he is the last to do so; he himself obviously prefers cuneiform for his inscriptions, and he even uses the Akkadian language. This degree of Akkadian influence can be observed elsewhere: In the peace treaty already mentioned, the Elamite gods are invoked (they are ranged in a pantheon that seems to have a goddess, Pinikir, at its head), but there are several purely Akkadian deities among them; the god of Susa is Inshushinak, a name of Sumerian origin. The religious architecture and ritual of Elam also have features freely borrowed from Mesopotamia. Elam had long lived in clear cultural dependence on its western neighbor, a dependence that grew even greater in the Akkadian age.

3. The Northeast—The Zagros

There are various peoples who haunted these wild peaks; we have outlined above the little that is known about the Gutians. We know even less about their neighbors, perhaps quite near neighbors, the Lullu.[61] They, too, were ruled by "kings." One of them, Anubanini, may be a bit later than the period covered by this chapter, but an inscription left by him shows us that the Lullu, enemies of Agade, conquered by Naram-Sin (according to his famous stele), must have fallen under Akkadian influence too: They have borrowed not only the script and official language of their neighbors, but a good part of their pantheon as well.

4. The North—Assyria

The whole of Upper Mesopotamia, up to the mountains of Kurdistan, had been occupied by the kings of Agade and so thoroughly "Akkadianized" that these territories from now on form part of a single cultural and political world hitherto confined to the south. The area of Mesopotamian civilization, and as a result its vigor and power of expansion, had effectively been doubled by Sargon and his successors. Assur and Nineveh had benefited from the building activities of the Akkadian kings, as we have already seen, and Rimush must have founded, some miles above Nineveh, the city that bore his name. Farther east, in the region of the modern Kirkuk, archives of clay tablets found at Gasur (the later Nuzi) prove that the inhabitants were then (or included) Akkadians. We must probably suppose that, along with these sedentary populations, troops of still seminomadic Semites were to be found in the area. At Assur, in fact, we have found a dagger blade dedicated by a "servant" of Manishtushu who bears the name of Abazu. The same name appears on the Khorsabad list of Assyrian kings, as the thirteenth of those seventeen earliest kings who still "lived under tents." If the two are to be identified (there are those who object to it, perhaps rightly), we should have proof that between the cities of Upper Mesopotamia, inhabited by Sumero-Akkadians, there wandered in nomadic tribes the future conquerors of all the Near East.

5. The Northwest

This is a very large and, from all points of view, complex region. We shall better grasp its complexities by dividing it in two.

(a) *Mari* had stood for a very long time, a major city with a basically Semitic population but under strong Sumerian cultural influence. Akkadian was spoken there, and written in cuneiform. In every area, including art and religion, the city had received and continued to receive its cultural stimuli from Babylonia. The kings of Agade, who understood its strategic and political importance, took care to conquer and to hold it. Its resistance to that conquest by Sargon, and the consequences imposed by the victor, may be attested by the ruin of a part of the city at about this time. The city, once taken, had the usual Akkadian representatives installed in it: Two daughters of Naram-Sin are mentioned there, ME-KIB-BAR and Shumsani, of whom the latter at least had the rank of priestess (probably high priestess) of Shamash. Possibly (as was the case later on) Tuttul, farther south on the Euphrates, was already part of the kingdom of Mari when the latter was taken by Sargon. He speaks of it as an important center of the cult of Dagan, and since it is to Dagan of Tuttul that Sargon says he owes "the gift made to him of all the Upper Land," one may draw the conclusion that the conqueror thought of everything from Tuttul to northern Syria as a single religious, perhaps also ethnic, unit.

(b) *The "Upper Land,"* then, stretched from the upper reaches of the Khabur River to the Mediterranean, and was in fact occupied mainly by Semites, whose country of origin this was. After taking Mari, the kings of Agade conquered all of this territory. We find their traces at Tell-Brak, Chagar-Bazar and, higher still, at Diarbekir. Their inscriptions list the main cities of which they made themselves overlords: Ebla, Arman, and also doubtless Apishal, in the Upper Euphrates region; Iarmuti and Ullis, probably on the Mediterranean; to which one can in all probability add the nearby towns named by Gudea as places good to trade with—Ursu, Menua, Ḥaḫḫum (we have seen that at least the last two may be even farther toward the west—see p. 123). This list of place names, unfortunately, represents the sum of what we know of the history of this part of the world. We can add the name of a "king" of Arman, mentioned by Naram-Sin: Rish-Adad. We can assume that all of these cities were masters of territories, large or small, in their immediate neighborhoods. We can imagine that they warred upon each other and made alliances with each other. But we cannot, at the present point in time, know.

What we can know something about is the ethnography of the region. There were, originally, one or more peoples of unknown provenance in these countries, who have left behind very old place names that fit no language of which we have any record. By our period, however, the population was overwhelmingly and definitely Semitic, and had been for a long time. As we have seen, Sargon's ancestors spring from this area originally—indeed all the Akkadians did before their settlement in Mesopotamia. Another Semite people, more recently arrived on the scene in northern Syria and northwestern Mesopotamia, makes its first appearance in the historical record now. A date formula of Shar-kali-sharri informs us that he had to fight the Amurrum in the area of today's Jebel Bishri; they had probably already posed a threat to Mesopotamia itself. These were probably still wild and seminomadic tribes for the most part, but they were to have a great future—masters of most of the Fertile Crescent, from Jerusalem to Babylon. We refer to them, under the Biblical version of their name, as the Amorites.

Here, too, toward the end of the Akkadian period, we find the first mention of another people, non-Semitic this time also, destined for greatness in the next millennium. The Ḥurrians must have arrived at this time, perhaps from the north or the east, at the northern fringes of the "Upper Land," where they appear to have occupied or founded several towns, in particular Urkish, Nawar and Karḫar (Karkar), in the area of the modern Mardin. We know this from certain inscriptions in which the personal names and even sometimes the language are Ḫurrian. At least once the language, however, is Akkadian, and the script is always cuneiform, a sign of Mesopotamian influence even here, at the edges of the civilized world —an influence certainly imposed by Akkadian conquest.

For here, as everywhere in Western Asia, the Empire of Agade had not only recast Mesopotamian civilization in its own mold, it had made a cultural community of nations out of all the surrounding lands, a community that was to endure and increase for centuries and more to come. Such was the accomplishment, and such the legacy, of Sargon's kingdom of Agade.

4

The Third Dynasty of Ur—
Its Empire and Its Successor States

The Background

The first great empire on Mesopotamian soil, Sargon's Empire of Agade, had faced immense problems with limited resources—small wonder that it did not solve them. The homeland of the Akkadians was small in area; its manpower was not inexhaustible. The task of administering so large an empire was entirely new; there was no backlog of experience to guide its ruling class. The territory that Agade tried to unify had a history of local particularism stretching back to its beginnings; its politics were governed by the ebb and flow of unifying and divisive forces.[62] Its inhabitants were Sumerians and Semites, nomads and city dwellers, with differing traditions and conflicting ways of life. Over a population so far from homogeneous, Agade had to try to impose a single rule. In addition, Sargon and his successors had to guard with Akkadian troops, against enemies from without and within, a territory larger than that of present-day Iraq. The reduction of the rank of *ensi* to that of a local governor, the appontment of "sons of Agade" as *ensi*'s—these were steps consciously taken to attempt to keep the land under control. With what success, we have seen: The weakness of the empire was continually tested, and continualy made evident, by ever recurring revolts. But the idea of Empire had been born. Sumer and the Gutians were its heirs.

Our subject is the Third Dynasty of Ur, so-called according
to the numbering of the *King List*, and the empire it created
in Mesopotamia. The administration of that empire owed much
to the experience of the scribes of the Sumerian "temple-state,"
accumulated in the course of centuries. Agade had had to
apply the arts of administration to a far wider area. Our documentary sources for the age of Agade are still too thin to give
us detailed knowledge of the means they employed. We cannot

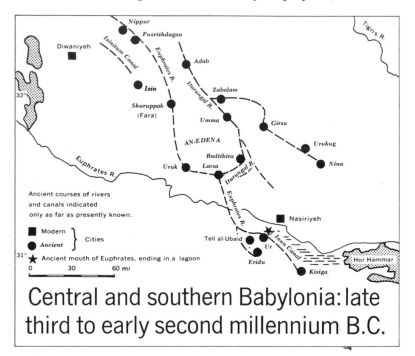

Central and southern Babylonia: late third to early second millennium B.C.

therefore say what the administrative bureaucracy of Ur III
owed to its imperial predecessors—whether the rigid centralization achieved in Ur III had been anticipated, in all its paper-
work perfection, by the servants of the kings of Agade. Insofar
as we can tell, however, the organization of the Sargonids was
very much the looser of the two.

But the elevation of the ruler to "guardian god" of his land
(see pp. 112 ff.) is definitely an innovation of Agade, rein-

stituted under the Third Dynasty of Ur, and leading to an apotheosis of kingship.

Sumer, in part disintegrating into its original component city-states, in part falling under the hegemony of Lagash, had proved able, in one way or another, to reach a *modus vivendi* with the Gutians: Akkad, the north of Babylonia, seems to have fallen to a considerable degree under their rule. A campaign against this foreign domination was led by the Sumerian city of Uruk. Its ruler, Utuḫengal, defeated the Gutian king Tiriqan and his generals Ur-ninazu and Nabi-Enlil. The Gutians ceased to exist as a political factor in Mesopotamian history.

With the power of the invader broken, Utuḫengal looked to a wider sphere. "King of the Four Quarters" is the title he assumed, with its reminiscences of vanished empire (see p. 112). His were, it appears, imperial intentions. But his reign of seven years was to be entirely overshadowed by that of the ruler who replaced him.

Ur-Nammu (2111–2094 B.C.)

Ur, in the period of the Gutian domination, was ruled by *ensi*'s who, from time to time, acknowledged the supremacy of Lagash. Under Utuḫengal, one Ur-Nammu was appointed *shagin* ("military governor" or "governor") of Ur. Ur-Nammu's rise to the throne from a position of military power is a parallel to the later career of Ishbi-Erra of Isin. For the general Ur-Nammu overthrew the king of Uruk. In the *Sumerian King List* the latter city's fall from power is described by the phrase: "Uruk was smitten with weapons, its kingship passed to Ur." But this is the standard formula for a change of dynasty in the *King List*, and tells us nothing.

As king, Ur-Nammu founded a dynasty that, in order to establish its legitimacy, sought to show its relationship to Uruk, with its ancient hero-kings. The kings of Ur call themselves "Son Borne by Ninsun," the divine mother of Gilgamesh, or

"Brother of Gilgamesh." Lugalbanda, Ninsun's human consort who, like his son Gilgamesh, was raised to divine rank after his death, is regarded as the mythical father of the kings of Ur. There is probably more to this than an attempt to capitalize on the historic prestige of Uruk, or to establish a link with Utu-ḫengal's dynasty; it may very well indicate that Ur-Nammu's family came from there. Uruk was at times the residence of the queens of Ur III; administrative texts marked for delivery "to the place of the queen" refer to Uruk. The city of Utu-ḫengal retained a special position in the empire of Ur III.

A recurring theme in Babylonian history is the rise to the throne of a royal official, who shifts the capital to a new city. There is the former cup-bearer of the king of Kish, Sargon of Agade; there is Isḫbi-Erra, rebellious general of Ibbi-Sin of Ur, who transferred his capital to Isin. Ur-Nammu is a third; he made himself independent king of Ur, but he did not immediately oust his former master. There is an overlap between the first years of Ur-Nammu and the last of Utuḫengal: the third year[63] of Ur-Nammu is named: "King Ur-Nammu directed his steps straight from 'below' to 'above' "; this corresponds to Utuḫengal's eighth or ninth year. It also proclaims the new king's intention to extend his power northward from Ur. In the following year the date formula reads: "The son of Ur-Nammu was made en-priest of Inanna at Uruk," by which time Uruk had been absorbed into the new king's dominions. "The return of the ships of Magan and Meluḫḫa into the hands of Nanna" is the name of a year early in Ur-Nammu's reign: this refers to the restoration of Ur's lucrative overseas trade, which had earlier been dominated by Lagash. Perhaps this is the result of a victory by Ur-Nammu over Nammaḫani, the ensi of Lagash, which is mentioned in the prologue to the law code of Ur-Nammu. Ur-Nammu's inscriptions (undated, unfortunately) have been found at Ur, Eridu, Uruk, Lagash, Larsa, Adab and Nippur. But also, as we learn from the boundary text (see p. 138), the districts to the north of Nippur, what had become the land of Akkad, fell under the rule of the lord of Ur. Literary texts report a conquest of the Gutians, which we shall have to regard with a skeptical eye. But there is no question that Ur-Nammu pushed his boundaries beyond the confines of Babylonia: His name is found at Tell-Brak, at the headwaters of the Khabur.

For this new empire, Ur-Nammu invented a new title: "King of Sumer and Akkad" appears now for the first time. This is an express formulation (the first of its kind) of the composite nationality of Babylonia, united under a single state. As a geographical term, "Sumer and Akkad" covers northern and southern Babylonia and the region of the Lower Diyala; as an ethnical term, it reflects the contemporary situation, in which, to be sure, Akkadians have for some time no longer been limited to the north, but in which the majority of the inhabitants of the south are still speakers of the Sumerian language.

Two important documents show us the organizational achievement of Ur-Nammu. We have them in the form of copies made in the Old Babylonian period, but there is no doubt as to their authenticity. The *Code of Ur-Nammu* we possess only in a very fragmentary condition. The major part of the code is, as was to be true of the later royal law codes of Western Asia, a series of conditional sentences on the pattern of: "If a man (does so-and-so), he shall (legally suffer the following penalty, make the following restitution, etc.)." An elaborate prologue precedes this which, among other things, praises the king's concern for the rule of law in his country, but also contains allusions to historical events. The key phrase, ideologically, is "to establish justice in the land," reappearing in the *Code of Lipit-eshtar* of Isin, the *Code of Hammurabi*, and in the date formulae of kings of the Old Babylonian period. We cannot tell whether this phrase, in the time of Ur-Nammu, already refers to an edict of remission of debts, as it quite clearly does in the *Edict of Ammi-Saduqa* of Babylon (1646–1626 B.C.). The few preserved fragments of the law code proper conform closely to the content of the later codes, the rules on river ordeal and on bodily injury, for example. Ur-Nammu's code, then, is either the beginning of a long tradition of legal formulation, or a link in the chain of such a tradition. We are not to think here, however, of legal codification in the modern sense; as we shall see, this is not what an ancient Near Eastern law code represents.

Our second major administrative document from the time of Ur-Nammu is a boundary text, which defines the territories of four districts north of Nippur: SHID-tab,[64] Abiak, Marad, and Akshak (?). (These are probably four different administrative units of the empire.) The section on each district ends with: "Ur-Nammu has confirmed the field of the god X to the god X." In this the king follows the old conception that the god is the real owner of the city's territory. It may be that uncertainties or disputes over the boundaries between these territories arose in the chaos of the Gutian age; this text reports the results of a survey to settle them. And an intensive and exacting survey it was: The borders follow the courses of rivers and canals and trace lines between identifiable points such as fortresses and country shrines, all of which is spelled out in precise detail. Each of the territories so painstakingly defined is, no doubt, the district for which an individual *ensi* bears administrative responsibility. We do not yet know whether similar surveys were made for all the districts in Ur-Nammu's kingdom.

The king's concern for efficient administration is also shown by a burst of activity in the upkeep and extension of the system of canals. These are the arteries that bring life-giving water to the fields, but they are also, along with the rivers, the country's main communication routes. All heavy transportation and military movements are undertaken by boat.

One of the most impressive achievements of Ur-Nammu, particularly impressive to the eye of posterity, is the building program of this monarch. The construction and reconstruction of public edifices fills his reign. Temples and their subordinate outbuildings required constant repair, as, like most Babylonian buildings, they were built of mud brick, which is subject to weathering and wear to a dangerous degree. For buildings as large as those of the temple complexes, this was a major task and an expensive one—only powerful regimes could undertake it. The result seems to have been that, during the period of the Gutian domination,, many temples fell into disrepair. Ur-Nammu set about to remedy this. His efforts, carried forward by his son Shulgi with equal energy, are commemorated in his many building inscriptions. Most of his attention was lavished on his capital, the city of Ur; on Uruk; and on the holy city of Nippur. The ziqqurrat of the moon-god Nanna at Ur was given its final form by Ur-Nammu, as was the ziqqurrat at Uruk. The ziqqurrat, as an architectural form, is a huge square tower rising in receding stages to a broad terrace with a shrine ("high temple") at the top. It originates in the archaic terrace temple; the custom of building new sanctuaries directly over the hallowed ruins of old ones led to higher and higher constructions, as one terrace was laid down above another.[65] But by the period of Ur III at the latest, this accidental growth is taken as the model for monumental towers planned and executed, from the ground up, as a single whole. It may be that this was done as early as the Agade era, but as yet we have no clear archaeological evidence.

An important example of the sculptor's art is the "Ur-Nammu relief" found in the ruins of the Nanna Temple at Ur. On this is figured a motif endlessly repeated on cylinder seals of this and subsequent ages, the "introduction scene." The ruler, in this case, but on the seals a worshiper of any rank, is pictured being introduced to one of the great gods, seated on a throne, by a minor guardian deity who intercedes for him ("personal god"). The art of carving in stone here reaches a new high in technical execution, but lacks, in comparison with the examples of the Agade period, the creative freshness and wider range of motifs of the earlier masters.

Ur-Nammu and his successors were to be favorite subjects of the Sumerian authors. *Ur-Nammu's Journey to the Underworld* describes the deceased ruler's arrival in the "land of no return," where he wins the favor of the deities of the dead, Gilgamesh among them, by lavish gifts. A new literary form, the royal hymn, appears—not a hymn addressed by the king to the gods, but a hymn addressed *to* the king himself: This is quite different from the hymns to the gods we know from the time of Gudea, in which at most a supplication for the reigning king would be inserted. The position of the kings of Ur III was an exalted one, not only in literature but, as we are about to see, in life.

Shulgi and His Successors

1. The Position of the King

Ur III is an absolute monarchy. There are no limitations whatever on the power of the king. This does not mean that the ruler cannot be influenced by his advisers. It means he does not have to be, at any time. The ruler does take consultations before embarking on certain actions, but he consults gods, not men. The selection and appointment of certain high priests is made, as we see by date formulae in Lagash from the Gutian period onward, only after the king has consulted the liver omens. Hepatoscopy, the reading of omens in the markings on the livers of sheep sacrificed to the gods, after the appropriate questions had been asked, was one of the main features of Babylonian religion. Extant omen texts of the Old Babylonian period show that the ruler, and the ordinary man as well, could ask the diviner (a special class of priests was skilled in this pseudoscience and interpreted the markings) for information, confirmation or admonition in almost any situation of public or private life.

The king was supreme judge, head of every branch of administration, and sole arbiter of peace and war. His throne was hereditary: The king of Ur is a dynast. He was absolutely central to the government of the realm, a position illustrated by the strict centralization of the administration of the entire Empire of Ur III. Even though in practice wide authority was delegated to the *ensi*—jurisdiction in the local courts, for example—the *ensi* could take no political action without authority from above. He was a delegate appointed by the king, holding office at the latter's pleasure. Temple building, for example, was a royal prerogative; the *ensi* could construct only shrines dedicated to the cult of the divinized ruler himself.

Divinization of the ruler was the most extreme expression of the exalted position of the king. This practice, first attested under Naram-Sin of Agade (see pp. 112 ff.), reappears once more under Shulgi. On into the age of Hammurabi, there were rulers who had their names written with the divine determinative.[66] Divinization, however, does not in these cases mean that the king is taken as the equal of the divinities of the national pantheon; rather, it is an elevation of the king to the position of a minor guardian deity, here as guardian for the country as a whole. "God," in the singular, in Sumerian, generally refers to the "personal god" of an individual, who has the task of interceding for him with the unapproachable great gods. But even when we define the king's divinity within these limitations, its public lineaments are nonetheless impressive. Shrines for the cult of the king were erected, sacrifices made to him, and local manifestations of the royal god were worshiped, the "Shulgi of Umma" or the "Amar-Su'ena of Kidingira." The king's name becomes part of personal names, as a theophoric element, as it were the name of a cosmic god, e.g. "Shulgi-is-the-Life-of-the-Land-of-Sumer."

There is another factor to the divinization of the king, raising questions we do not yet know how to answer: the identification of the god-king with Dumuzi (Tammuz), the divine lover of Inanna (Ishtar), on the occasion of the rite of the sacred marriage (see p. 73). The first case of which we know is that of Iddin-Dagan of Isin (1974–1954 B.C.). This king, we are told, went as Ama-ushumgal (a name of Dumuzi) to make love to the goddess Inanna. But we do find, in religious texts of the Old Babylonian period, the names of kings of Ur III and Isin added to the names and epithets of Dumuzi; we can therefore conclude that this royal rite was already current in the age of Ur III.[67]

We are not yet fully cognizant of the role played, in the

king's service, by the *sukkal-maḫ*, the "grand vizier." This is the conventional translation; actually *sukkal* originally means "courier" or "messenger." The best-known incumbent of this office is Urdunanna (see pp. 157 ff.), who may, however, be atypical of the *sukkal-maḫ* in that he holds a plurality of offices simultaneously. The *sukkal-maḫ* may intervene in a case under adjudication. In the administration of Ur III he possesses an authority independent of the system of local *ensi*'s and has a rank equal or superior to that of *ensi*. This does not tell us that his office has an influence equal to that of the king, or controls the king's decisions; for an institution of this kind, we have no evidence. From the time of Nammaḫani of Lagash, the last independent *ensi* there, defeated by Ur-Nammu, we know of a *sukkal-maḫ* Ur-abba, who reappears under Ur-Nammu's rule. This, again, does not allow us to say (being an entirely isolated case) that the *sukkal-maḫ* was a Lagashite institution, taken over by the kings of Ur III in their search for means of ruling the empire they were rapidly acquiring.

2. *Military and Foreign Policy*

At first, it seems, the kings of Ur III (in contrast to the kings of Agade) did not have to fight for the retention of the provinces of their empire. The sources available to us show military force applied exclusively to the territories on or beyond its borders; there are no reports of internal unrest before Ibbi-Sin. We cannot be sure, however, that Shulgi, ruler of the empire inherited from his father for forty-eight years (2093–2046 B.C.), held the land peacefully through all that time. Before his twenty-second year on the throne, our textual evidence is extremely slender. Our picture of a golden age of peace and prosperity is based on the abundant sources of the latter half of his reign. The date formula for his twentieth year reads: "The sons of Ur were inducted as bowmen." If the citizens of the capital must be mobilized, there may be unrest within the empire. Still, from the twenty-second year of the reign on, the rich flow of written sources shows us the king firmly in control of his dominions.

Shulgi, in fact, revived the title "King of the Four Quarters," adding it to his father's title of "King of Sumer and Akkad"; he was also divinized in his lifetime. (Ur-Nammu's name, of course, is also written with the determinative sign for a god, in Sumerian literature, but this was a posthumous honor.) Shulgi justified his claim to universal power by military campaigns in the areas bordering Babylonia to the north and northwest: Simurrum, between the river Adhem and the Lower Zab; Karaḥar in the area of modern Kirkuk; the country of the Lullubi around modern Sulaimaniya; Anshan in Iran (to the east of modern Kermanshah and Husainabad); Urbilum or Arbilum, the modern Erbil; Kimash, near Simurrum— these and still other countries and cities are the objects of expeditions, all victorious, of course, for we would not hear of whatever defeats may have taken place. Their purpose was the opening and protection of trade routes, so vital to a country as dependent on the importation of raw materials as Babylonia, but they are also aimed at the prevention of barbarian invasions then beginning to threaten the land. Above all the Hurrians were to be feared, moving inexorably into northern Mesopotamia from the end of the Agade period onward. That they did not penetrate into Babylonia proper, that they did not subject the plain to a new foreign domination, is a measure of the achievement of Shulgi and his successors.

Sumerian literature retains the impress of these wars. One myth gives an account of a campaign of the goddess Inanna in the mountain country of Ebeḥ (i.e. in the Jebel Hamrin). Mention of the "mountain-land of Ḥurrum" in the epic tale of Gilgamesh's journey to the Cedar Mountain to fight the monster Ḥuwawa is probably a reflection of Ur III's struggles with the Hurrians of the north. Our main sources for the wars of Shulgi, however, are date formulae, which only tell us, concisely, "Urbilum destroyed," or the like. Shulgi's second successor, Shu-Sin (2036–2028 B.C.), has left us inscriptions that are more informative. Foreign kings and *ensi*'s (the Sumerian title is here applied to independent rulers) were taken prisoner in his campaigns, and gold was carried by donkey caravan to the shrines of Nippur. The mixed political and economic motive of these campaigns is made apparent. We hear also, for the first time, of what was to be a standard practice of later empires: the transfer of conquered populations. A settlement of such prisoners-of-war sprang up in the vicinity of Nippur; its inhabitants were liable for labor service on public works.

Still we hear of nothing but victories. That setbacks were concealed should not surprise us. So long as they did not take on the dimensions of catastrophe, they were of no interest to the Mesopotamian historical sources. But a threat of just such proportions arises in the reign of Shu-Sin. This king built a wall extending twenty-six "double-hours" march from the Abgal canal in northern Babylonia. Its exact course is uncertain,[68] but its purpose is perfectly obvious. In some texts it is called, simply, the "Martu wall," in others the "Martu Wall that holds off the Tidnum." The Tidnum (also Tidanum) were a specific tribe of the various Semitic nomads who, as a general class, are called "Martu" by the Sumerian texts. Shu-Sin was, by this and other measures, able to hold the Martu temporarily at bay, but in a very short time they were to have a hand in the dissolution of the empire.

Where war was unnecessary or impractical, diplomacy was employed by the kings of Ur III, attempting to bind foreign princes to their cause by royal marriages. A daughter of Shulgi was "raised to the place of Queen of Marhashi" in that king's eighteenth year: Marhashi is the Warahshe of the Agade period, in Iran east of the Diyala and northwest of Elam. The *ensi* of Anshan married another daughter of Shulgi (year thirty-one); the alliance does not appear to have been effective, Shulgi's thirty-fourth year being named after "the destruction of Anshan." Under Ibbi-Sin, an *ensi* of Zabshali married a daughter of the king.

We have no very clear idea of the military organization of Ur III. There appears to have been no great distinction made between the military and the civil services, as military titles sometimes coincide with administrative ones. The Sumerian word *eren* applies to men liable for personal service, members of the free population mobilized for certain tasks—construction and upkeep of dikes and canals, temple building, transportation and military service. They are, to use the term current in France under the Old Regime, *corvéables*. In the Sumerian poem of *Gilgamesh and Ḫuwawa*, the hero, as king of Uruk, calls for fifty men without dependents to accompany him on his expedition to the Land of the Cedar Mountain. The temple-building hymn of Gudea of Lagash, on the other hand, declares that the city labored "as one man" on the *ensi*'s great construction; if exceptions were made, we do not hear of them. In addition to the *eren* we know of the *aga-ush*, a special group (the translation of the term would be something like "gendarme") serving professionally in the armed forces or in the supervision of public construction.

The highest military rank was that of *shagin*. He was responsible for the military security of an administrative district, and had perhaps equal rank with the *ensi*. In a border district like Mari, where so far we have no evidence of an *ensi* in the period of Ur III, the *shagin* is apparently also head of the civil government. That the office was important may be seen by the fact that it is held by heirs to the throne, Shu-Sin, for example, acting as *shagin* at Uruk before his accession.

3. *Extent of the Empire—Main Centers*

To define the boundaries of the Empire of Ur III is no easy task. Obviously the borders will have shifted back and forth in areas of constant warfare like the east and northeast. In the border regions, too, the title *ensi* is ambiguous, since it may mean either an official of the empire or an independent foreign prince. This makes our evidence difficult to interpret. Still, we can take as permanent possessions of Ur III the Babylonian plain, the Diyala region, the Middle Euphrates around Mari, and the Middle Tigris around Assur. At Tell-Brak, in the Upper Khabur basin, over the "palace" of Naram-Sin, were found traces of a compound of the Ur III period probably just as large; the fragment of a tablet containing the name of

Ur-Nammu was discovered there. How much of this territory was inhabited by Semites? Probably pretty much the areas inhabited by Semites in present-day Iraq. The names of persons said to come from what is today Iraqi Kurdistan, the area around Kirkuk, show that this territory was then occupied by a non-Semitic population. An extensive archive of clay tablets at Gasur (the later Nuzi), south of Kirkuk, shows that the city was still, in the age of Agade, Akkadian in population and in language; but the Hurrian migration must have swept over it soon after, for, toward the end of the third or the beginning of the second millennium, the region is lost forever to the Semitic-speaking world. In fact, the Empire of Ur III appears to end at the limits of Semitic speech. The only non-Semitic region permanently under the scepter of the kings of Ur, from Shulgi to the third year of Ibbi-Sin, was Elam with its capital, Susa. Furthermore the external boundaries of the empire do not tell us what the empire ruled: Certain internal areas, regions not accessible by waterways or level land routes, would be unsure—the mountains, the deserts and the steppes. Anything north of Assur and Mari was probably too far removed from the centers of administration to be controlled in any effective way.

Ur, as the royal residence, was the capital of the empire, but there were two subordinate centers, at Uruk and at Nippur. Ibbi-Sin's coronation took place at Ur, Uruk and Nippur, in that order. We have already referred to the importance of Uruk as (perhaps) the place of origin of the dynasty, and as the residence of its queens. Nippur, the sacred city of all Sumerians, was an administrative district governed by an *ensi* in the usual manner, but with marks of special preference, in that it paid no taxes but received deliveries from the *ensi*'s of several other districts in Babylonia instead. The *ensi*'s of Nippur show tendencies toward dynastic succession, which elsewhere the kings of Ur go to any lengths to prevent. The position of Nippur in the country's religion, the pre-eminence of its city-god Enlil, remain untouched: there is no attempt to promote the moon-god of Ur, Nanna, to the chief place in the pantheon. In a Sumerian poem, *The Journey of Nanna to Nippur*, the moon-god travels north from his city by boat, asks for admission to the holy city and is received and entertained by its god. Nanna submits to Enlil requests for blessings on the royal house, and on the fields and herds of the land; the chief executive of the gods graciously grants them. Implicit in this are the ideas that Enlil delegates royal power and that the prosperity of the whole land depends on his favor; the king therefore can successfully rule his country, and secure for it the benefits of nature, only by taking the proper religious steps.

4. *Administration*

The *ensi*, as we have seen, governs an administrative district. He is appointed by the king and must account to him for his actions. His title is all he shares with the rulers of independent states. He is the highest judicial authority for his city; we have record of sentences passed by the *ensi* in his palace. The number of such districts was something over forty, the majority being located in Babylonia proper—in the border regions, as we have said, provinces would drop in and out of the empire according to the variations of military success. In Mari, Uruk, and perhaps also in Der, on the Iranian border, the *shagin* as military governor had civil powers as well. The boundaries of these districts as instituted by Ur-Nammu appear to have held good under his successors—at least we have no sign of internal boundary changes in Babylonia. An *ensi*'s term of office did not coincide with the reign of the ruler who appointed him; a new king would take over the officials of his predecessor, just as in modern monarchies. The term of one Lugalmelam as *ensi* of Nippur did exactly coincide with the nine-year reign of Amar-Su'ena (2045–2037 B.C.), but whether this is the sign of some special position of that city or whether it is simply fortuitous we cannot know. We do know of cases where an *ensi* was transferred once, sometimes twice, from one city to another. This is very likely to be a means of preventing an individual from building up too many connections and too strong a power in one locality, but it may also simply be the transfer of particularly efficient governors to posts where such men were needed, or it may be something else entirely. In several cities we find *ensi*'s whose fathers had also been *ensi*'s, but we have no reason to suppose that this indicates a rule of inheritance of office. Plurality of offices, the entrusting of several districts at once to a single *ensi*, is unknown. The case of Urdunanna in the reign of Shu-Sin is a special one: The impressive string of titles he collected is probably a sign of the slowly weakening authority of the king.

Several *ensi*'s in Babylonia shared in the duty of providing sacrificial animals for the sanctuaries at Nippur, each filling the holy city's needs for a month on a rotating schedule.[69] *Ensi*'s too far from Nippur, the governor of Assur, for example, for whom the delivery of cattle on the hoof was impracticable, were excluded from the roster.

We are much less well informed as to the government of the localities within an *ensi*'s district. In Ur III texts we first meet with the title *rabianum*, "mayor," taken over from the Akkadian. The *rabianum* would perhaps be municipal chief of cities too small to be the residence of an *ensi*. Smaller settlements had a "headman" (*ḫazzanum*, also an Akkadian word).

Administration in general in the Empire of Ur III had two divisions, the palace and the temple. "Palace" does not designate the royal residence alone; it means the residence (of the king, or of an individual *ensi*) plus all of its administrative and economic offices and outbuildings, and therefore includes workshops, storehouses, treasuries, etc.

Our sources for the activities of the palace, in this sense, are immense.[70] And still it is difficult to arrive at a detailed picture of its administration. The reason for this is the unequal distribution of our texts, in terms of subject matter and in terms of geography. Economic texts, for example, are almost totally lacking for northern Babylonia so far. This is regrettable enough in itself; but it also prevents us from discovering whether or not Sumerian is used as the administrative language in all parts of Babylonia. Still, while the number of Akkadian texts so far known is small, it is just large enough to allow us to assume that Akkadian, as the language of administration in the Semitic provinces, had not gone out of use since the Empire of Agade. A number of royal inscriptions in Akkadian by the kings of Ur III point to the same conclusion. The influence of Akkadian on the Sumerian language was, by the way, growing, as can be seen by a number of Semiticisms that appear in Sumerian syntax.

The economic administration of the Empire of Ur III has been the subject of valuable preliminary studies, but a detailed survey of the whole subject has yet to be made. Also still to be done is a study of the great number of technical terms in the documents for crafts and professions, and for official positions. The following rough survey will be limited by these deficiencies.

One of the largest archives of the Ur III period is that of Puzrishdagan, a town established by Shulgi, in his thirty-ninth year, near Nippur. On its outskirts was set up an enormous cattle park, for the receipt of cattle forwarded from Sumer and Akkad to be sacrificed at Nippur. Daily records of arrivals from the provinces and departures for the shrines were kept, with losses through escape or natural death duly reported: Unless the herdsmen could prove their innocence of these losses, they had to provide replacements. Every time cattle arrived, or departed for the shrines, or were received at the shrines, the names of the men involved were meticulously recorded; often the name of the official responsible for the whole process was set down as well. If a dead sheep was delivered as dog food, onto the tablets it went; nothing was too inconsequential to be recorded. And everything was carefully dated, by day, month and year. The scribes of Ur III even invented a daily balance sheet, on which incoming and outgoing deliveries appear together, with the remainder or deficit at the end of the day totted up at the bottom.

Closely joined to the palace or temple herds was a thriving wool and leather industry. Agriculture, too, was subject to the most minute supervision, where palace or temple lands were concerned: amounts of seed grain, size of harvests, crops in storage, supervision of storage, deliveries from granaries— everything was registered, and everything was filed. Deliveries were made to flour mills, cattle fatteners, or persons authorized to receive payments in kind.

Silver was the standard of value (i.e. the value of an object was quoted in terms of standard weights in silver), but in practice payments were frequently made in kind. The grain price that obtained ideally was one *shekel* of silver (a sixtieth of a *mina*, i.e. about nine grams) for one *gur* of barley (about five and a half bushels). The standard of dry measure was the royal *gur* of 300 *sila*, introduced by Shulgi. We can detect no marked fluctuation of prices in the period of Ur III, which is just as we should expect in an internally untroubled age. After the fourth year of Ibbi-Sin, matters change for the worse, as we shall shortly see.

Any metal, in fact, had high value, because of the rarity of metals in Babylonia and the expense of importing them. Metals were sometimes imported as raw ores, but more usually in already refined bars and rings for easier transportation. These would then be manufactured in Babylonia into tools, luxury objects and jewelry. Metal objects for everyday use were of bronze, alloyed in the modern ratio of copper to tin. The copper came from Magan, the tin from the Caucasus or Baluchistan. Our most extensive evidence for metals is from the port city of Ur.

Transportation was highly organized, as was the royal courier system. For shipments by water, the precise number of men towing or poling the vessel is set down on the tablets. Administrative messages went to and from the capital by runner and donkey rider, and we have thousands of little tablets recording their meals, their points of departure and their destinations. The messenger, traveling light, carries no food; his tablet procures his meals along the way. His proper burden is the short administrative directive in letter form, or bulkier reports to the imperial or provincial capital (monthly or annual balance sheets of certain branches of the palace economy, for example). In the bulging files of the administrative centers, the tablets are stored in "tablet baskets," each ticketed with a label showing the category of information it contains and the span of time it covers.

To what degree are the palace and the temple closed economic systems? We do have evidence for the renting of temple lands to members of the ordinary population, i.e. men outside the temple economy.[71] We are not, therefore, dealing with lands granted in lieu of salary to temple personnel, as in the Early Dynastic period. But we are also not dealing with purchase of private property: These are tenures, not sales. As a matter of fact we have no hint, in the documents of Ur III, of the existence of privately owned arable land, except for a few records of donations. We do not, however, have any documentation as yet for northern Babylonia or the Diyala country, where we might expect to find a different situation. Evidence for the granting of temple prebends (incomes from lands set aside for the support of priests) by the *ensi*, very occasionally by the king, indicates only a grant of usufruct for a limited period of time. There is no parallel to what we find in the secularizing movement of Old Babylonian times, an outright sale of the right to dispose of the land at will.

For a knowledge of the law in the Empire of Ur III, we rely more on local court documents than on the fragments of the Code of Ur-Nammu. These are tablets ending with the phrase *di-til-la*, "case closed," and such a tablet is so named by scholarship: *ditilla*. Some are judicial notarizations of marriages, of responsibility for personal support, of sales, donations and the like; some are court reports, a digest of the proceedings and decision in an individual lawsuit. An officer called a *mashkim* held a pretrial investigatory hearing. Sentence was passed by a board of judges, two to seven in number, rarely by a single magistrate. The subject of these suits is family law (action for fulfillment of the terms of a marriage contract, disputed inheritance, divorce and so on), the law of slavery (actions for the restitution of liberty to a native-born slave are remarkably frequent), breach of contract and dis-

CHRONOLOGICAL TABLE IV
Ur III, Isin, Old Babylonian Period

	UR III	ISIN	LARSA	DER	BABYLON	ASSUR	ESHNUNNA	ELAM
2100	Ur-Nammu 2111–2094							
80	Shulgi 2093–2046							
60	Amar-Su'ena 2045–2037							
40	Shu-Sin 2036–2028						Ituriya	
20	Ibbi-Sin 2027–2003	ISIN	Naplanum 2025–2005				Ilshu-iliya	
2000		Ishbi-Erra 2017–1985	Emisum 2004–1977	DER				
80		Shu-ilishu 1984–1975				ASSUR		
60		Iddin-Dagan 1974–1954	Samium 1976–1942	Nidnusha		Puzur-Asshur I		
40		Ishme-Dagan 1953–1935	Zabaya 1941–1933	Anum-muttabbil (20th century)		Shalim-aḫum		
20		Lipit-eshtar 1934–1924	Gungunum 1932–1906			Ilushuma — 15 rulers		
1900	URUK	Ur-Ninurta 1923–1896	Abisare 1905–1895		BABYLON	Erishum I		
80		Bur-Sin 1895–1874	Sumu'el 1894–1866		Sumuabum 1894–1881	Ikunum		ELAM
60	Sin-kashid ca. 1865/60–1833	Lipit-Enlil 1873–1869	Nur-Adad 1865–1850		Sumula'el 1880–1845	Sharrum-ken (=Sargon I)		Eparti ca. 1860

	(Uruk)	(Isin)	(Larsa)	(Babylon)	MARI	(Assyria)	(Eshnunna)	(Elam)
						Ruzur-Asshur II	Ipiq-Adad II	Shilhak ca. 1830
		Enlil-bani 1860–1837	Sin-iddinam 1849–1843	Sabium 1844–1831				
			Sin-eribam, Sin-iqisham 1830–1813	Apil-Sin 1830–1813	Yaggid-Lim ca. 1830	Naram-Sin	Naram-Sin	
			Warad-Sin 1834–1823					
		Zambiya, Iter-pisha, Sin-magir 1827–1817						
	Anam ca. 1821–1817				Yaḫdun-Lim ca. 1825–1810 (Yasmaḫ-Adad)	Erishum II	Dadusha	
	Irdanene ca. 1816–1810		Rim-Sin 1822–1763	Sin-muballit 1812–1793		Shamshi-Adad I 1815–1782		
				Hammurabi 1792–1750	Zimri-Lim 1782–1759	Ishme-Dagan I 1781–1742	Ibal-pi'el II	
			Rim-Sin II SEALAND	Samsu-iluna 1749–1712				Kutir-Naḫ-ḫunte ca. 1730
			Ili-man	Abi-eshuḫ 1711–1684	HANA	Adasi ca. 1700		
				Ammi-ditana 1683–1647	6 kings			
				Ammi-Saduqa 1646–1626				
				Samsu-ditana 1625–1594				
				KASSITES				

40
20
1800
80
60
40
20
1700
80
60
40
20
1600
80
60
40
20

puted property claims. The criminal law is ignorant of the principle of *talion*, the system of "eye for eye, tooth for tooth," and is to remain so down to the *Code of Lipit-eshtar* of Isin (see pp. 168 ff.). From documents dealing with marriage law it is clear that the legal position of the Sumerian woman was by and large equal to that of the men of the land.

The *ditilla*'s provide us either with documentary or with indirect evidence of contracts of sale, donation or debt. Sales are principally of slaves and house property; sales on credit are attested, with the purchase price to be paid after taking possession. There are no contracts for the sale of arable lands, an important piece of negative evidence for our understanding of landholding in the Empire of Ur III.

5. *Social Structure—Sumerians, Akkadians, Amurrum*

In an earlier chapter (pp. 77 ff.), we attempted to draw the outlines of the structure of Sumerian society in the Early Dynastic period. There we encountered the fundamental difficulty of studying the classes of the population, when the sources designate them by names most of which we do not yet know how to define. We also found that terms such as "free" and "semifree" could be applied only in a relative and therefore again necessarily vague sense. For the society of Ur III, some of the same difficulties present themselves: As in pre-Sargonic Lagash, we have massive but one-sided textual evidence, tending to give us the impression of an all-pervading, all-possessing state, in which the role of the individual is modest to the point of self-effacement. Our problem is, can we trust this impression? In other words, can we trust the textual evidence?

Here again the touchstone is the question of the existence of private property in arable land. As we have said, in the Ur III period there are no private contracts of sale for agricultural land, in all the thousands of documents published so far. Does this mean that the greater part of the country, or indeed the entire country, was owned by the state, either through the

154

palace or the temples? For central and southern Babylonia, that is, for Sumer proper, we can be reasonably certain that the answer is yes. As we know, there are, from the Early Dynastic period, what are quite definitely private land-sale contracts in the area of Akkadian settlement. If land was owned, and therefore bought and sold, by individuals in Sumer in the age of Ur III, we should expect to find records of it, for a society with so elaborate a bureaucracy could surely provide the scribes to make them. It would be rather surprising if all scribes were limited to the service of the state. What we have here is an argument from silence; a second argument is more conclusive. The legal documents of Ur III provide us not only with an important insight into the organization and operation of courts of law, they also show us what the objects of litigation were among ordinary men. As we have pointed out, we have no instance of a suit arising from the sale of arable land. We may therefore, perhaps, trust the evidence of the economic texts: There are contracts of lease to private persons, but none of sale, where agricultural land is concerned. After the time of Ur-Ninurta of Isin, private land-sale contracts appear in respectable numbers in the Sumerian south; this can hardly be an accident of archaeology, but points to a change from a previous condition.

A high percentage of the population would therefore be tenants of the state—which tells us nothing of their well-being. We can only guess, where the condition of the ordinary man is concerned, that the economic stability of Ur III—stable grain prices, etc.—produced relatively acceptable conditions of life, if by that we mean the absence of glaring social grievances. As far as we can tell, there is no parallel in Ur III to the typical social plague of the Old Babylonian period, the ever recurring overindebtedness of the lower classes.

There is little to be known about the position of slaves in the Early Dynastic and Agade periods. Ur III provides us with the first adequate documentation. The slave is not free, he is the chattel of another man, but he is a chattel with legal standing and legal rights. He can appear in court as a suitor; he therefore has the right to contest his status and have its legality investigated by the judges. He can testify as a witness, and has legal ownership of personal property. This liberal legal status is not that of all slaves—it applies to natives who have lost their freedom, for the most part through insolvency. Slaves who had entered the country from abroad, as prisoners-of-war or deportees, would have had quite a different position. An inscription of Shu-Sin, as we have pointed out, recorded the establishment of a settlement of deportees near Nippur. Two tablets from Umma, dating from the fifth year of Amar-Su'ena, list rations for foreign women captured in war. There are 150 names on these lists, and it has been suggested that these women are being held in some sort of camp. For the foreign slave, who possessed no legal personality, there was no possibility of suing for his freedom in the courts.

In the Empire of Ur III, there is no question of a difference in social status between Sumerians and Akkadians as such. There is also no question of social separation. How far, indeed, the opposite was true may be seen by the fact that not only queens, but the last two kings of Ur III, Shu-Sin and Ibbi-Sin, bear Akkadian names. The melting-pot had done its work. A high percentage of the royal officials of whom we know from the documents also have Akkadian names. The real contrast in this society is between Sumerians and Akkadians on one side and the nomads called "Martu" (Akk. "Amurrum") on the other. These represent a latent internal danger, and in time they initiated the decline of the Empire of Ur III. But, in the days of that empire's greatness, there was a careful attempt to integrate these newcomers into an ordered society. Martu hold lands in fee from the king and they are not debarred from rising to offices of trust—we know of one Martu who became a royal messenger. Most of our mentions of Martu show them as receiving state rations or as delivering sacrificial offerings. We shall not be wrong in imagining the relation of these nomads to the state as similar to that displayed, for Old Babylonian times, in the archives of Mari, Uruk and the territory around Sippar. The relation takes many forms, but the main thing that we learn from these later texts is that it is perfectly normal for some of these tribesmen to enter the service of the sedentarics—indeed to become assimilated to them to the point where, in Ur III, individual Martu already adopt Sumerian and Akkadian personal names—while, at the same time, the majority of the tribes remain unreconciled to civilization and pose a constant threat to the security of the state.

Decline and Fall of the Empire of Ur III

Under its first four kings—Ur-Nammu, Shulgi, Amar-Su'ena and Shu-Sin—the Empire of Ur III represents a model of continuity, stability and unity unmatched in the early history of Mesopotamia. In contrast to the Empire of Agade, with its pattern of recurring revolts and palace intrigues, this greatest of Sumerian states could offer its subjects the gift of enduring internal peace.

For a time only. What forces brought it to an end? The unquenchable and ever renewed particularism of the Babylonian cities, for one thing, and their unwillingness to acquiesce in the rule of one of their own number for any length of time. Then, too, the increasing influx of Semitic nomads, i.e. the migration of the Amorites. Finally, the always unstable relation between Babylonia and Elam, a country that, for all its willingness to absorb much of Babylonian civilization, refused to be assimilated to it entirely.

Under Shu-Sin, and up to at least the second year of Ibbi-Sin, the security of the eastern flank of Babylonia was entrusted to one man who, considering the number of high offices concentrated in his hands, must have had a personality of unusual power. He is Urdunanna, whose father and grandfather had served Amar-Su'ena and Shulgi as *sukkal-maḫ*, "grand vizier," and who himself held this highest of offices in turn. According to an inscription composed by Urdunanna for his master Shu-Sin on the erection of a temple, this *sukkal-maḫ* was also *ensi* of Lagash, *sangu*-priest of the god Enki of Eridu, *ensi* of

Sabum and of the "Gutian Land," *ensi* of Al-Shusin, Ḥamazi and Karaḥar, as well as military governor of Usargarshana, Bashimi, Dimat-Enlil, Urbilum, Ishar, of the Su-people and of the Land of Kardak. We cannot locate all these places precisely. But the inscription says that Urdunanna's authority extended from Urbilum (the modern Erbil) in the north to the shores of the Persian Gulf. We cannot know whether the extraordinary position Urdunanna enjoyed, in a system that was otherwise devoted to preventing just such a plurality of offices, was the result of his strength of personality or of some other factor; we also cannot know whether he used his powers as a loyal servant of the dynasty or as a potential enemy. His word would certainly carry weight in the politics of the east, but this is no reason to hold him responsible for the revolt of Elam in Ibbi-Sin's fourth year.

We can observe the beginnings of the disintegration of Ur's empire by a simple means: In city after city, administrative documents dated by imperial year formulae cease to present themselves; the *ensi*'s, voluntarily or of necessity, are no longer in communication with the capital. In Eshnunna on the Diyala, this occurs in Ibbi-Sin's third year; in Susa, the year after. As the opening years of the reign still offer an ample supply of documents, their cessation in these cities can have but one explanation: They have left the orbit of the empire. After the fifth and seventh years of Ibbi-Sin the same silence descends on Lagash, Umma and Nippur. A chain reaction seems to be in progress. The historical tradition contained in the Old Babylonian omen texts refers to these events with phrases such as "when the land rose up against Ibbi-Sin." Details are provided by the royal correspondence, letters between the king and his *ensi*'s, which the subsequent generation thought so memorable that they were copied and recopied as *belles-lettres*.

Our best information comes from the correspondence between Ibbi-Sin and Ishbi-Erra, a military commander hailing from Mari on the Middle Euphrates. Ishbi-Erra asks the king to give him the authority he needs to proceed effectively against the Martu, who had broken through the "Martu Wall" and were in the process of conquering one Babylonian citadel after another. An Old Babylonian omen, "He who comes from the steppe will break in and drive out him who sits in the city," gives us a general description of invasion by nomadic tribes, with their sheikhs expelling and replacing the governors in the cities. Ishbi-Erra's request ends in a demand for appointment as commandant of the city of Isin. This is anything but loyal in intention. He blackmails his king into acceding to it; the means that come to his hand are the results of a famine in Sumer, where there has either been a crop failure or a disruption of agricultural work, through fear of the nomads now raiding across the countryside. At Ur, food prices have already skyrocketed: Ishbi-Erra, assigned to procure grain in central Babylonia, has stored 72,000 gur (395,000 bushels) at Isin, and keeps it there under the pretext of preventing the Martu from seizing it. He does nothing on his own about sending it to the capital, but asks for the 600 boats it will take to transport it. The king cannot provide them. The king suggests that Ishbi-Erra ask other *ensi*'s for aid in this matter. Instead, realizing the weakness of the king, Ishbi-Erra seizes his opportunity and sets himself up as independent ruler of Isin. From Ibbi-Sin's tenth or eleventh year, there is an independent Dynasty of Isin, using its own date formulae and rivaling the Empire of Ur to the end of Ibbi-Sin's reign—at which time it attempts to take the place of Ur as ruler of Mesopotamia, a place that disaster had left entirely vacant.

Ishbi-Erra is the classic example, in Mesopotamian history, of a subject betraying his king. But we must remember that our picture of his treasonable career may be greatly oversimplified. We do not know all the details of his quarrel with Ibbi-Sin, which may have lasted many years before it came to a head. And we do not know his motives—there may be more involved than naked ambition. Indeed, we do not really know anything about his personality, or the character of the king he seems so flagrantly to have betrayed.

There were parallels to Ishbi-Erra's rebellion in other cities of the empire. He himself was able gradually to gain control of most of Babylonia, confirming former *ensi*'s of Ibbi-Sin in their offices. But Assur and Susa fell away entirely, to remain free of the Babylonian kingdoms of later times.

When Ishbi-Erra seized Nippur, the Empire of Ur lost its spiritual justification: Ishbi-Erra could now claim, as the proved favorite of the royal god Enlil, the legitimate suzerainty over Sumer and Akkad. Were his victories abetted by collusion with the sheikhs of the Martu? We cannot tell—it may have been a common failing. In a letter to Ishbi-Erra, before the break between them, Ibbi-Sin registers his disapproval of the military governor of the western border fortress of Bad-Igiḥursanga; the latter has been (deliberately?) avoiding battle with the Martu. Other officers, in their correspondence with the king, fill the air with mutual accusations of conspiracy with the enemy, probably to cover their own sins in the same direction.

Ur had now lost control of central and northern Babylonia. But Ibbi-Sin was still able to retain a remnant of his empire, in the vicinity of Ur, for thirteen or fourteen years after the defection of Ishbi-Erra. When the end came, Ishbi-Erra had no hand in it. The death blow fell from the east. Elam unleashed a war of destruction on her former conqueror, enrolling the "Su-people" as auxiliaries. *Su* or *Sua* is a collective term for the peoples of the Zagros north of Elam. The results of this campaign are known to us from the *Lamentation over the Destruction of Ur*, a Sumerian poem in eleven stanzas that still has power to move us after 4,000 years. The wrath of Enlil, its authors report, has conjured up catastrophe for Ur (a note already sounded in the correspondence of Ibbi-Sin); the goddesses hasten to leave their shrines in Sumer. Ningal, the wife of Nanna, has gone to lay a petition before Enlil, pleading for the salvation of her city—unsuccessfully, for once the supreme god has spoken his "So be it!" in the divine assembly, it cannot be recalled. Ur with all its sanctuaries is then utterly destroyed by the Elamites (which archaeology entirely confirms). Ibbi-Sin was led captive to the land of Elam, an event unparalleled in the history of Mesopotamia. What destiny awaited him there, we do not learn. The Elamites left a garrison behind to hold Ur, but it was expelled by Ishbi-

Erra six or seven years later. We cannot tell whether his territory in central Babylonia had also felt the hand of the Elamite; the *Lamentation* mentions cities there as falling prey to the enemy, but our information from Isin implies an uninterrupted development of the new state. The Elamites do not appear to have encroached on the country north of Ur; in extinguishing the remnant of a great empire, they did not build one of their own.

The Successor States

What opinion the usurper Ishbi-Erra (2017–1985 B.C.) had of himself we may read in his titles. A cylinder seal of one of his officials bears the inscription: "Oh Ishbi-Erra, mighty king, King of the Four Quarters: Shu-Erra, 'the military governor [*shagin*], the son of Turam-ili, is your slave." The impression of this seal appears on a tablet dated in the seventh year of Ishbi-Erra, showing that the king of Isin had usurped imperial titles while Ibbi-Sin still ruled in Ur; we also find the name of Ishbi-Erra written with the determinative for a god. On another seal he is called "God of His Land," as the kings of Ur had been; the owner of this seal is one Ishbi-Erra-malik, "Ishbi-Erra is [my] counselor," a name he cannot have borne from birth; his original name has been changed for one that will flatter the king. We meet with many names of the same kind: Ishbi-Erra-bani, ". . . is the Creator," a parallel to such formations as Adad-bani, "[the god] Adad is the Creator"; "Ishbi-Erra is the Life of the Land of Sumer" (cf. "Shulgi is the Life of the Land of Sumer," above); "Praise be to Ishbi-Erra the Strong," and several others in the same vein of adulation.

Ishbi-Erra made the city of Isin, wrested by guile from Ibbi-Sin, the royal residence of his new kingdom; it was to remain the capital to the end of his dynasty. Previously Isin had been a city of very little account, but from Sargon of Agade on we meet with cities of no past prominence that suddenly become, and remain, imperial capitals. Agade itself, from which the "Land of Akkad" and the *Lishanum akkaditum*, the Akkadian language, take their names, had been quite insignificant before Sargon made it his home; the same was true of Babylon (which was to give the whole country its name) until the First Dynasty of Babylon made it a place of conse- -quence. Isin itself has yet to be excavated systematically. The city lies under the Tell Ishan Bahriyat, about eighteen miles south of the ruins of Nippur. We therefore know nothing of the building program of the kings of Isin in their own capital. Isin was the cult center of a goddess Nin-i(n)sina, "The Mis- . tress of I(n)sin," worshipped elsewhere under the name of Gula. She is goddess of healing in the Sumerian pantheon, the "Great Physician of the Land of Sumer." Dagan, too, a god of the Semitic pantheon of Syria, received special devotion from the kings of Isin. The reason for this is Ishbi-Erra's origin at Mari. The cult of Dagan, however, had already taken root in Sumer during the Ur III period—the town of Puzrishdagan near Nippur, for example, founded by King Shulgi of Ur, bears an Akkadian name that signifies: "Under the Protection of Dagan."

How far from Isin the bounds of Ishbi-Erra's influence extended is, unfortunately, nowhere nearly as clear as for the Empire of Ur III. We have, in comparison to the abundance of texts for Ur III, a terribly limited range of cuneiform sources for the Kingdom of Isin. Aside from building inscriptions and votive inscriptions, and a set of year formulae that is not even complete for the dynasty, most of what we know comes from an archive from the city of Isin, covering the reign of Ishbi-Erra and the first years of Shu-ilishu. Its subject is the local leather industry.

As the royal correspondence of Ibbi-Sin shows, when Ishbi-Erra seized the provinces of Babylonia from Ur he also continued in office the *ensi*'s appointed by the empire. He may have begun by making them his allies; he ended by making them his subordinates. Puzur-numushda, the *ensi* of Kazallu, for instance, reports to Ur that Ishbi-Erra has offered him an alliance. In any case Ishbi-Erra was able to take over intact the administrative system elaborated by the kings of Ur, without having to set on foot the sort of radical reorganization required of Ur-Nammu. The administrative texts of Isin follow precisely the forms and formulae of the bureaucrats of Ur III. There are several mentions of messengers from points within and without the kingdom; Ishbi-Erra has taken over the imperial courier system of Ur. The transfer of power, then, from Ur to Isin implies no innovations in the administrative structure. Further, Ishbi-Erra continues the military policy of the later kings of Ur, concentrating on the defense of Babylonia— several of his date formulae commemorate the construction of fortresses. There was reason enough for this; the Amorite nomads continued to press against the northern boundaries, and, as long as Ur was occupied by the Elamites, there was a danger to be warded off in the south as well. In Ishbi-Erra's twenty-second year he expelled the Elamites from the region of Ur, and was henceforth master of central and southern Babylonia.

What role the southern city of Larsa played during the first four reigns of the Dynasty of Isin we are by no means sure. A brief king list from the time of Hammurabi's successor, Samsu-iluna, indicates that a man of Amorite descent, Naplanum (2025–2005 B.C), founded a dynasty at Larsa as early as eight years before Ishbi-Erra's seizure of power. But we have no inscriptions or year dates from Larsa in which its rulers call themselves "kings" before Gungunum (1932–1906 B.C.), a contemporary of Lipit-eshtar and Ur-Ninurta of Isin. It is probably no accident that the long list of date formulae from Larsa, extending down to the end of the reign of Rim-Sin (1763 B.C.), begins only with Gungunum, the fifth "successor" of Naplanum. It is, however, not impossible that Larsa existed as an independent state during the early years of the kingdom of Isin, even though the latter dominated Ur, Eridu and Uruk to the south and west of Larsa itself. Larsa, it is true, was located on the Iturungal Canal where the latter joined the then course of the Euphrates, which put it directly on the river route from Ur to Uruk and Nippur; but a conflict of interest with Isin, which controlled this north-south axis, could be avoided, for as we learn from the sources the expansive energies of Larsa were always directed toward Lagash, that is to say toward the northeast. As for Naplanum, we hear of a man by that name in several administrative documents written toward the end of the Empire of Ur III, in which he is regularly called a "Martu," in other words an Amorite. A *ditilla* of the twentieth century B.C. from Girsu, in the state of Lagash, is confirmed by an oath sworn, by the parties to the lawsuit, by the name of one Samium. The custom is that legally binding oaths are to be sworn by one's city god, one's king or both. Samium must then be a person of political importance, to say the least. If he is taken to be the Samium (1976–1942 B.C.) who is listed as the third "successor" of Naplanum, and the father of Gungunum, this would mean that Larsa was an independent state ruled by her own kings in the mid-twentieth century B.C.

The region of the Diyala was outside the boundaries of the kingdom controlled by Isin. As we have seen, by Ibbi-Sin's third year Eshnunna was no longer in administrative contact with Ur. The secession from the empire probably took place under the leadership of Ituriya, Ibbi-Sin's *ensi* in Eshnunna. Ituriya's son Ilshu-iliya began as a scribe in the service of Ibbi-Sin; later on, an inscription calls him "Mighty King, King of the Land of Warium," Warium being the native name of the district of which Eshnunna was the capital. Ilshu-iliya's successors, however, were content to revert to the title of *ensi*; only Ipiq-Adad II (ca. 1840 B.C.) took up the royal title once more. Further, a few cylinder seals of Ilshu-iliya's time from Eshnunna transfer the royal epithets, as given above, to the city's god Tishpak: one of these seals adds the imperial title "King of the Four Quarters." Eshnunna, then, through its city god, claims universal dominion. Politically, of course, this was patent nonsense, but it is a symptom of the aspirations to independence and expansion that inflamed so many parts of the empire at once, when the imminent collapse of the Dynasty of Ur became apparent. But, under the successors of Ilshu-iliya, it became clear that Eshnunna was not to succeed to the power of that empire, and that it could not hope to be the peer of Isin.

Der, near the modern Badrah, also seized its independence when the weakness of Ibbi-Sin became plain for all to see. Its city god was Sataran, whom we have already met as the god of Mesalim of Kish (see p. 67). Strategically and commercially, Der occupied a position of the first importance on the borderline between Elam and the Babylonian plain. Under the Empire of Ur III it was one of the border districts ruled by a *shagin* or military governor. The independent rulers of Der retained this title in its Akkadian form, *shakkanakkum*. One of them, Nidnusha, had his name written with a divine determinative. Der, like Isin and Eshnunna, is trying to catch a reflection of the fading glory of empire. Another of these kings of Der, Anum-muttabbil, boasts of victory over Elam, Anshan, Simash and Barahshi, Iranian regions near the Mesopotamian borders. Der is another site that has yet to be excavated in a systematic manner. We therefore lack details on the history of this strategic city. We do know, however, that Der fell to the kingdom of Isin under the latter's king Iddin-Dagan (1974-1954 B.C.) at the latest. For Ishme-Dagan was *Shakkanakkum* of Der for his father Iddin-Dagan, before succeeding in turn to the throne of Isin.

The area of Assyria, with its capital, Assur, was now permanently detached from Babylonian rule. The rulers of Assur, on throwing off the domination of Ur, called themselves *isshiakkum*, an Akkadianized equivalent of *ensi*; as at Eshnunna, this title of "governor" now comes to mean an independent prince. Of the history of Assyria in the twentieth century B.C. we know practically nothing. Not until we come to Ilushuma's account of an expedition into Babylonia can we confirm that here too, on the Middle Tigris, is a state that hopes to enter on the inheritance of Ur.

To return to Isin, it appears that, under its first three kings, this state was able to go about its business without serious trouble from outside, despite the number and avidity of its rivals in Mesopotamia. The royal building program proceeded without difficulty and seems to have concentrated on the restoration of the monuments of Ur, destroyed by the Elamites. Ishbi-Erra's successor, Shu-ilishu, succeeded in retrieving the cult statue of Ur's god Nanna from the Elamites, who had carried it off. Whether he accomplished this by diplomacy or by war, we do not know. Further evidence for the relative stability of Sumer at the time is the state of Sumerian literature, whose first flowering had occurred under the Third Dynasty of Ur, but which continued on a high level under the Dynasty of Isin. New hymns to the gods and to the kings were composed, and previous compositions were recopied in the scribal schools; the *Lamentation over the Destruction of Ur* dates from this period. This, and the *Lamentation for Ibbi-Sin*, both works from the same cycle, became the model for a whole class of literature in later times. Under Lipit-eshtar the second great law code of which we know in Mesopotamia was compiled. The royal hymns make frequent reference to the peace and order then reigning in the land. Much of this may be literary cliché—the motif of the reign of peace is already found in a royal hymn devoted to Shulgi of Ur—but there is one passage of a hymn to Iddin-Dagan that deserves our notice. Read in conjunction with the descriptions we have in the historical sources, particularly in Old Babylonian omen texts, of the extreme political turmoil of the succeeding age, it is instructive by contrast. Iddin-Dagan is addressed in the following terms: "You have made safe the ways and paths, caused the land to prosper, set righteousness in all men's mouths. . . . You have raised up terraces and established boundaries . . . oh Iddin-Dagan, your father Shu-ilishu, king of the land of Sumer, laid firm the foundations of Sumer and Akkad for you. At the bidding of An and Enlil you have surpassed even him, you have gathered in all enemies."

The first symptoms of Isin's decline from greatness, the first signs of the coming fragmentation of Babylonia into countless warring states, become visible under Ishme-Dagan, fourth king of the Dynasty of Isin. An Old Babylonian liver omen from Mari preserves the memory of a defeat suffered by Ishme-Dagan before the gates of Kish. This is our first evidence (although not historically authenticated by any means) of warfare between Isin and the north of Babylonia, where, it seems, Kish is once more a leader of the Land of Akkad. A lamentation composed under Ishme-Dagan speaks of unrest raised by Amurrum nomads—the Amorites are again raiding into the settled lands. This poem describes the devastation wrought by the barbarians, particularly in the holy city of Nippur; clearly it is dependent on the *Lamentation for Ur* for its literary form, but we need not doubt that it reflects a historical event.

The Assyrian *isshiakkum* Ilushuma reports an expedition to Babylonia, an account not free of problems of interpretation. Ilushuma was the grandson of Puzur-Ashur, who had founded a dynasty at Assur (see below, pp. 194 ff.). Chronologically, this indicates that Ilushuma was more or less contemporary with Ishme-Dagan, but we cannot supply a firm synchronism. At the end of a building inscription, he states: "From the marshlands [?],[72] from Ur and Nippur, from Awal, Kismar and Der, the city of Sataran, to 'the city' [=Assur], I have decreed freedom from tribute for the Akkadians and their children." Nowhere, however, in the Babylonian sources can we find reference to a ruler of Assur interfering in Babylonian affairs at the time. Other than Ur and Nippur, the cities named by Ilushuma are all located east of the Tigris. This may mean that Ilushuma's primary aim was to bring the trade routes east of that river within his sphere of influence. We have already drawn attention to the key position of the city of Der. It is not impossible that Ilushuma also penetrated into Babylonia proper, but that he was able to decree freedom from tribute in an "empire" stretching from Ur to Assur hardly agrees with the known historical facts.

In one respect, however, Ilushuma's account fits our picture of the age of Ishme-Dagan and his successors. For now, for the first time since Urukagina of Lagash, rulers once more publicly take pride, on their inscriptions, in their endeavors to abolish social grievances. Under the imperial rule of Ur there were hardly grounds for this, for a stable national economy ensured, at least for the greater part of the population, a stable livelihood. Ishme-Dagan "abolished the tribute of the city of

Nippur, and exempted those liable for services from military duty"; formulated in more general terms elsewhere, he "absolved Sumer and Akkad of the tithe." One hymn to Ishme-Dagan informs us that the king, who had freed the *corvéables* (*eren*) of Nippur from military service, set them to work on the temple domains of their city's gods. But our sources are much too thin to give us precise knowledge of these measures. Our understanding of Isin's system of taxation, above all, is still far from satisfactory.

Lipit-eshtar (1934–1924 B.C.) was the last king of the house of Ishbi-Erra. His successor, Ur-Ninurta, was an interloper. Lipit-eshtar is outstanding for his legal enactments, of the kind foreshadowed by Ishme-Dagan. The *Code of Lipit-eshtar* was copied and recopied in the schools, becoming part of Sumerian *belles-lettres*. One of our copies of this code comes from Kish, in northern Babylonian. When we think of the many parallels between the *Code of Lipit-eshtar* and the *Code of Hammurabi*, it is perhaps enlightening to remember just how close Hammurabi's Babylon was to the city of Kish. Like the *Code of Ur-Nammu*, the *Code of Lipit-eshtar* is made up of a collection of legal rules preceded by a prologue and followed by an epilogue. The same structure is to be retained by the *Code of Hammurabi*. The building inscriptions of Lipit-eshtar refer again and again to the king's activities as a guardian of the law, with the phrase "when he had established justice in Sumer and Akkad." We cannot tell whether he means by this primarily an "edict" of debt annulment embodied in his code, as was to be the case with later kings. Lipit-eshtar's code has reached us incomplete, but in a far better state of preservation than that of Ur-Nammu. It is therefore our most valuable source for a knowledge of Sumerian law in its last stages. Was this the first such "codification" made by the kings of Isin? We cannot know. If not, its forerunners were at least not found worthy of transmission by the scribes of later generations. The prologue to the *Code* notes that the king "freed the sons and daughters" of Nippur, Ur, Isin, and of Sumer and Akkad in general. Possibly the king here refers to a remission of debts, decreed to set a limit to social injustice and to a too great accumulation of private capital. The prologue also mentions a reorganization of compulsory personal service by the king. Family status (father of a family, member of a common household of brothers, or bachelor) was to be the deciding factor in assigning either six or ten days' service each month. This was probably a reduction from previous requirements, although the prologue does not expressly say so. The formulation of these measures in the prologue is too vague to allow us to know exactly what was going on. If we ask who exactly was liable for compulsory service (holders of royal land-grants? everyone except priests and officials? everyone excluding some otherwise privileged class?), we must go outside the code entirely for information that might lead to an answer. There is a copy, from Nippur, of another royal edict that states: "I caused the *mashka'en* to serve four days a month." Even this is no great help, as we do not know just which classes of the population were covered by the term *mashka'en* (=Akk. *mushkenum*), and the name of the ruler who issued this edict is fragmented on our copy. Possibly he was one of Lipit-eshtar's successors.

One thing, however, emerges with some clarity from our reading of these edicts, which become more frequent from the time of Ishme-Dagan on: It is no longer considered a matter of course for the ruler to dispose of large parts of the population at will; what was accepted under the Sumerian "temple-state" is now called into question.

But it is also clear that the *Code of Lipit-eshtar* is an outgrowth of the Sumerian past. (To compare it with the *Code of Hammurabi*, and with the court documents of Ur III, is to see this at once.) Consider, for example, once again, the question of landownership. The section of the code dealing with real property does not mention agricultural land. Private ownership of such land was probably still regarded as a deviation from the norm, the norm being the temple and the palace as the principal proprietors of the fields. Or consider the criminal punishments meted out by the code. In contrast to the *Code*

169

of Hammurabi's principle of limb for limb, the last Sumerian code requires, of perpetrators of damages or injuries, reparation in the form of monetary fines. Talion, as we have seen, was also unknown to the courts of law of Ur III, being conspicuous by its absence from the court documents. In Lipit-eshtar's code, in the section on family law, we meet with the term *ni-mi-usa*; the court documents and the Sumerian literary texts tell us what this means: the expenses of the wedding feast, which the bridegroom or his father must defray. In Sumerian law the *ni-mi-usa* is an integral part of a legally contracted marriage. With the Akkadians, the corresponding institution is quite different in intention, the *terḫatum*, which represents an outright price paid by the bridegroom for the bride. The *terḫatum*, for which we have documentation going back to the Agade period, makes the Akkadian marriage a marriage by purchase in the strictest sense. This is a striking difference in the traditions by which Sumerians and Akkadians governed their lives.

Toward the end of Lipit-eshtar's reign, Gungunum of Larsa seized the city of Ur. The south was thereby permanently lost to Isin. This ends the period in which Isin's kingdom can be considered as at least partially the successor of the Empire of Ur. From this point on, Babylonia falls into a congeries of competing city-states. The political structure of the country, from Ur-Ninurta of Isin (1923–1896 B.C.) to Hammurabi of Babylon, is highly reminiscent of that of Early Dynastic Sumer, but its history is to unfold against an utterly different ethnic background. The history of the Sumerians draws inexorably to a close; the history of the Akkadians will be resumed in the next chapter.

The Lands Beyond Babylonia in the Twentieth Century B.C.

The century following the fall of Ur III is once more dark to our inquiries, as far as the history of the rest of Western Asia is concerned. We can dispose of only very limited sources.

We have already mentioned the growing importance of Assyria, but to write a continuous history of this country, called Subur or Subir by the Sumerians, and Subartu by the Akkadians,[73] is beyond our present powers. We are equally ill informed as to the history of Syria and the region of the Middle Euphrates. Ishbi-Erra came from Mari, true, but we do not know whether or for how long this city belonged to the kings of Isin. There are a number of short administrative texts from Mari, and some clay models of sheep livers, inscribed with explanations of the omens that they illustrate, which probably ought to be dated to the end of the twentieth century B.C. They are written in Old Akkadian. These texts give us no information on the political situation of the city in which they were found. The extraordinary archive of letters of Hammurabi's time, found in Mari, throws a flood of light on the complex ethnic and political conditions of Syria, but, until then, purest invisibility reigns. Asia Minor, too, is still beyond the area illuminated by cuneiform sources, as it was in the period of Ur III. We know that, by the beginning of the second millennium B.C., the migration of the Indo-European Hittites into Anatolia had begun. But textual evidence is not available until the following century, where we shall encounter it in the next chapter.

We are somewhat better off for sources on Elam and the neighboring lands. Elam, as we have seen, corresponds geographically to the Susiana of our classical atlases, more or less. North of Elam lay the mountainous country of Anshan, which, unlike Elam, had remained independent of the Empire of Ur. According to a king list found at Susa, a Dynasty of Simash (possibly the area of the modern Khurramabad) lasted from the time, roughly, of Shu-Sin of Ur (2036–2028 B.C.) to about the middle of the nineteenth century B.C. At this point a new dynasty is founded by one Eparti, lasting down to the end of the sixteenth century B.C. Simash was in confederation with Elam; its king may have been leader of this union. The Sumerian sources unite under the name of Su or Sua a number of regions in the northern Zagros, east of Assyria; they, too, had

close connections with Elam, joining with her in the destruction of Ur as we have seen. So far we cannot tell which ruler
of Simash and Elam led the campaign to crush Ur. It may have
been Hutran-tempt of the Dynasty of Simash. At least this
monarch made so strong an impression on the memory of his
people that Shilḫak-Inshushinak of Susa (twelfth century B.C.)
still records him as his ancestor. For the nineteenth and eighteenth centuries we have sources that explain the structure of
the confederation Elam-Anshan-Simash (see pp. 210 ff.); for
the political situation in the twenty-first and twentieth centuries, we have hardly any certainty at all.

Elam's triumph over Ibbi-Sin, the deportation of Ur's last
king to distant Anshan, the expulsion of the Elamites from
Babylonian soil by Ishbi-Erra of Isin—none of this was con-
ducive to peace between the Land of the Two Rivers and the
federated kings of Elam. Ishbi-Erra did try to revive the mari-
tal diplomacy of Ur III, marrying one of his daughters to the
son of Humban-shimiti, who had succeeded Hutran-tempt on
the throne of Simash. Bilalama of Eshnunna, too, a contemporary of Shu-ilishu and Iddin-Dagan of Isin, gave his daughter's hand to the third successor of Humban-shimiti. On the
other hand, Anum-muttabbil of Der, a contemporary of
Bilalama, claims victory over Anshan, Elam, Simash and
Baraḫshi. In general we may suppose, for the Elamite-Babylo-
nian border country, a situation of swiftly changing alliances
and enmities, which was soon to become typical of Babylonia
proper.

But Babylonia had already won a lasting victory in the
Elamite land, where, from the time of its subjection to the
kings of Agade and Ur, written Akkadian was the language
of record, and was to remain so when Elam regained her independence. The rulers and officials of Elam retained Akkadian
through the entire second millennium, preferring it to their
own language for official use. Texts written in Elamite are
extremely rare. In the scribal schools of Susa, Sumerian and
Akkadian literature was studied and cultivated exactly as in
Babylonia itself: we have found, in Susa, nothing less than

fragments of the *Sumerian King List*. Elam could rebel against Babylonian rule, she could invade Babylonian soil, she could be the rival and the terror of Babylonian states, but she could never escape the intellectual influence of Sumer and Akkad.

Conclusion

Once the Sumerians entered the Babylonian plain, in the fourth millennium B.C., they were never again reinforced by new immigration. The Semitic population of the plain, on the other hand, was constantly swollen by the influx of nomadic tribes, sometimes trickling into the country in minimal groups, sometimes flooding it in mass invasions. The proportion between Sumerians and Semites was bound to shift, and did, increasingly in favor of the Semites. With every passing century the Sumerians were subjected to stronger and stronger Semitic influence, ethnically and linguistically; by the beginning of the second millennium, the process reached its destined end. Sumerian, by then, had vanished as a spoken language, and vanished for all time. Sumerian literature became the cultural heritage of Akkadian men of letters—frozen classics in a dead language.

The political picture presents another view when it first meets the eye. Sargon and his successors had subjected Sumer to a great Semitic empire, but, with the advent of the Gutians, central Babylonia and the Akkadian north were more affected by the invaders' rule than was the south: There, in the age of Gudea, Lagash led Sumer to a summit of prosperity. Utuhengal's victory opened the way for the creation, with the Empire of Ur III, of a Sumerian hegemony over most of Mesopotamia. The period between Gudea and Ibbi-Sin has therefore been called a "Sumerian renaissance." But to schematize Babylonian history as an alternation between ages of Sumerian and Akkadian greatness is to oversimplify it. The world-state of the Sargonids owes as much to the achievements of early Sumer as the Empire of Ur III owes to the Empire of

Agade. From the Early Dynastic period on, the relation between Sumerians and Akkadians was not one of alternation,
but of symbiosis.

We have already discussed, in the second chapter of this
book, the presumed conflict between the Sumerian and Akkadian "nations." What we should need to prove it is distinct
evidence of a conscious "national" reaction of one people
against the other, of a glorification, in "national" terms, of
victory or restored independence. Sargon "gained the ascend-
ancy over Uruk in battle and defeated fifty *ensi*'s. . . ." But
this is a typical Early Dynastic struggle of one Babylonian
coalition against another—there happen to be Akkadians on
one side, Sumerians under Lugalzagesi on the other. Yet we
learn from the inscriptions of the kings of Agade that they
use force against *Akkadian* cities that dare to rebel. Sargon
says that he appointed, as *ensi*'s, "sons of Agade." Is this conscious exclusion of Sumerians from power? Or is it a purely
political act, the appointment of men loyally devoted to him
to act as governors of a restive empire, to the exclusion of *all*
others in his dominions? Antagonism between nations, antagonism of long standing, is known in the history of ancient
Western Asia; Elam and Babylonia are the model for it. But it
is precisely this kind of permanent opposition that we cannot
find between Sumerians and Akkadians *in* Babylonia. There
is *one* Sumerian poem that breathes anti-Akkadian sentiment,
the *Curse of Agade*, inspired by the fall of the empire of the
Sargonids. Other than that, nothing.

There is, of course, a certain intellectual snobbery displayed
by the educated Sumerian, above all by the Sumerian scribe,
toward those who do not know his language. Something of
the same kind, a sense of superiority, is perhaps to be seen
in a passing remark of the "Sumerian" King Ibbi-Sin (an
Akkadian name!), baiting his enemy, Ishbi-Erra of Mari, as a
"man of non-Sumerian seed." We should be doing violence
to the facts if we were to share this attitude, if we were to
think of the highly civilized Sumerian in contrast to the raw,
barbaric Akkadian. Akkadian art under the Sargonids is bril-

liant; Akkadian literature, in the classic works of the Old Babylonian period, will bear comparison with the literature of Sumer and fare none the worse for it.

Indeed, rather than collecting contrasts, we should better employ our time in considering, in fact emphasizing, the magnificent collaboration of Sumerians and Akkadians in a work to outlast the ages: the preservation and transmission of the Sumerian language and literature. During the age of Gudea, and in the Empire of Ur III, in other words in the last days of Sumerian as a spoken language, the golden age of Sumerian literature suddenly begins. Not only is the old oral tradition set down in writing, but there are highly successful attempts at original composition. The linguistic form of this late Sumerian, with its slowly rising percentage of "Akkadianisms," shows that both Sumerians and Akkadians had a hand in this, and Akkadians to an ever increasing degree. "Classical Sumerian" held out longest in the scribal schools at Nippur: Sumerian compositions written at Ur and Larsa, in the time of Rim-Sin, abound with difficulties for the modern reader, so widely do they deviate from the classical grammar of that language.

The first kings of Isin consciously act out their role as successors to the Empire of Ur—and yet their dynasty, of purely Semitic descent, is in no way tied by blood to the Sumerian past. We find a strict dependence on the forms of Sumerian civilization, and this is not reactionary archaism by any means. It is a shoring-up of something of value threatened by decline. The acceptance of the Sumerian language as the common cultural possession of Mesopotamia, whose influence was to be felt for millennia to come—this is not something we owe to the Sumerian Empire of Ur III alone. The Semitic Dynasty of Isin played its part in this, and played it consciously and well.

The fall of Ibbi-Sin, then, the destruction of imperial Ur, these did not bring on a break in Babylonian history. The turning point was reached a century later, in the reign of Ur-Ninurta of Isin and Gungunum of Larsa. Sumerian by then is no longer heard on men's lips. The Akkadian language has itself changed, from the Old Akkadian to the Old Babylonian speech and spelling. (Conventionally, an age is thought to have ended with the fall of Ur.) If we have chosen a later date to bring this chapter to a close, during the "Isin-Larsa period" as it is usually called, this is not an attempt to rewrite, but rather to follow, the course of ancient Mesopotamian history.

5

The Old Babylonian Period

Introduction

The time usually allotted to the Old Babylonian period runs from the end of the Empire of Ur III to the year 1594 B.C. In that year the Hittite King Mursilis I struck far into Babylonia in a whirlwind campaign, unseating the First Dynasty of Babylon and leaving behind a vacuum that the Kassites hastened to fill. The period from the fall of Ur to the reign of Lipit-eshtar of Isin (1934–1924 B.C.) we have already treated, in the chapter immediately preceding, as a continuation in other forms of the history of Ur III. With the end of the twentieth century, and during the nineteenth and the beginning of the eighteenth centuries, Babylonia enters a genuinely new age. The political situation is one of a crowd of competing local dynasties, with Isin, Larsa, Babylon, and at times also Uruk and Eshnunna dominating the tumultuous stage, but in no sense filling it. With the end of the nineteenth and beginning of the eighteenth century, a new trend toward the formation of larger states comes into evidence, culminating in the empire of Hammurabi of Babylon (1792–1750 B.C.). It might be said that this empire was the ultimate political expression of the Amorite migration, as the Empire of Agade had been of the influx of Akkadians into Babylonia. It might be said, but it would be wrong. At least it would require a number of qualifications. The Dynasty of Agade had imperial dominion for a century; Hammurabi's house for two decades. The coming of the Amorites did not result in the introduction of a new written language as a medium of cultural expression. Under Hammurabi's immediate successor, Samsu-iluna, the traditional particularism of Mesopotamia was already tearing at the fabric of empire. Added to this, a new danger to Babylon made a sudden appearance in the East—the Kassites, future conquerors of Babylonia and its rulers for four hundred years.

For the period from Lipit-eshtar to 1594 B.C.—for fully three centuries in other words—the sources at our disposal throw open to our examination a far wider area than ever before. For the first time we are able to follow the interaction of events over most of Western Asia, not only in the Fertile Crescent but also in Elam and Anatolia. As usual, however, the sources are richest for Babylonia, and so our vision of the period's history is still basically "Babylocentric," as the very term "Old Babylonian period" implies. This holds true not only for political history, but for our understanding of the cultural and social background of the age. The social order that owed its origin to the Sumerian "temple-state" is dead. We witness now the birth of a society in which the private sector of the economy, with private landownership and private wealth, and with the middle class that these produce, takes its place beside the palace, its economic activities and its official class; as for the temples, they are by and large limited to their functions as centers of the cult of the gods. The position of the ruler is changed almost out of recognition. The idea of the divinized king is foreign to the Amorites, hence to the Amorite usurpers of Mesopotamian thrones and to the dynasties that they founded. Outside of Isin, we find only isolated instances of the divinization of kings, and where we do find it, it seems more an archaizing affectation than a custom felt to be alive. The royal hymn, the poem addressed to the king-as-god, continues on into the First Dynasty of Babylon (Samsu-iluna); but it feeds on the literary clichés of the past, as a weak reflection of the poetry of Sumer.

"Old Babylonian" is not only a historical but also a linguistic term. The Akkadian language has a history, traceable

178

in written documents, of two and a half millennia. We divide this history into several stages. The earliest is the "Old Akkadian," the language of the kings of Agade; it is followed by the "Old Babylonian" stage, beginning at about the fourth generation of the Dynasty of Isin and coming to a close with the beginning of the sixteenth century. These at least are the upper and lower limits; the actual point at which linguistic changes were made varies in different contexts. By analogy with "Old Babylonian" we refer to the Akkadian written in this age in the region of Assur as "Old Assyrian"; "Middle Babylonian" and "Middle Assyrian" take their place in the second half of the second millennium.

The chronology of the Old Babylonian period rests on a framework furnished by king lists for Isin, Larsa and Babylon, and by lists of the date formulae employed by these three dynasties. At Isin, Lipit-eshtar is followed by ten further kings (1923–1794 B.C.). The dynasty of Larsa begins, according to its king list, with Naplanum (2025 B.C.); but the dynasty achieved no significance until Gungunum (1932–1906 B.C.), who was succeeded by a line of nine kings (1905–1763 B.C.). The First Dynasty of Babylon begins with Sumuabum (1894–1881 B.C.) and ends with its eleventh king, Samsu-ditana (1625–1594 B.C.). By means of synchronism, mention of one king in connection with another, we are able to insert into this framework many rulers of other states, although, as with Uruk and Eshnunna, we are so far unable to date events in these states by a local chronology that carries us safely from one decade to another. Shamshi-Adad of Assyria was an older contemporary of Hammurabi, probably dying in Hammurabi's tenth year on the throne (1782 B.C.). But the dates of the older independent rulers of Assur cannot as yet be definitely established. So long as we are unsure of the dates of Ilushuma (see p. 167), those of the dynasty established by his grandfather, Puzur-Asshur, are uncertain. The two decisive dates of the early Old Babylonian period are 1793 B.C., when Larsa, under its King Rim-Sin, broke the power of Isin, and 1762 B.C., when Babylon, under Hammurabi, put an end to the independence of Larsa. But before entering on an examination of this history, there are two other matters that claim our attention.

The first is the relation of the nomads to the settled populations of Mesopotamia. In hardly any other period of the history of this land does the problem of the nomads hold so great a place in the contemporary sources. Secondly, to present the history of each of the local dynasties in a detailed, sometimes inevitably dreary narration would not be enough. If we can attain an overall view of the political situation of Mesopotamia, we shall better be able to make sense of the events. We shall therefore precede the study of those events with an excursus on Old Babylonian liver omens, which vividly reflect the political atmosphere of the age.

The Nomads in the Old Babylonian Period

It is almost impossible to exaggerate the role of the Semitic nomads in the history of Mesopotamia. We have stressed their importance again and again. These nomadic tribes are lumped by the Sumerian sources under the collective term "Martu." "Amurrum" is the corresponding term in the Akkadian texts. Both of these names have to be understood in historical context. They were handed on from one generation to another, which means that we cannot count on either of these terms to signify the same people, the same tribe, the same clan, at different points in time. For example, it may be that the sedentary population originally took the name of a single tribe and applied it to all nomads forever after—there are any number of parallels to this, i.e. to the generalization of originally limited ethnic terms, both in the history of the Near East and of Europe. The French call all Germans *allemands*, after the tribe of Alemanni of the age of the *Völkerwanderung*; the Finns call them *saksa*, after the Saxons who reached them first. The Syriac *tayyāyā* refers to Arabs in general, though originally it was the name of a single Arab tribe.

The first appearance of the word "Martu" in our documents is a curious one. We find it in contracts for the sale of real property in Early Dynastic III, where it is used as a geographical direction: *tum-mar-tu* means "wind [i.e. direction] of the Martu" and signifies the west—or, more precisely, the southwest, for the wind-rose in the valley of the Tigris-Euphrates is not oriented to, but between, the cardinal points of the compass.[74] Shar-kali-sharri of Agade fought the Amurrum in the mountains of Basar, the modern Jebel Bishri extending from Palmyra to the Euphrates. The nomads who played so decisive a part in the fall of the Third Dynasty of Ur are called Martu by the sources. During the early part of the Old Babylonian period we see, everywhere in Mesopotamia, new local dynasties springing up; their founders, to judge by their personal names, are not Akkadians but non-Akkadian Semites: Naplanum of Larsa, Sumuabum of Babylon, Ashduniarim of Kish, Yaḫzir-el of Kazallu, and so on. The *Edict of Ammi-saduqa* of Babylon (1646–1626 B.C.) refers to the population of his state as "Akkadians and Amurrum."

The great question is this: To what extent do these nomads of Mesopotamia, at the end of the third millennium and in the first centuries of the second, form a homogeneous ethnic group? Are they comparable, in other words, to the Akkadians, the Aramaeans and the Arabs, in possessing an identifiable "nationality"? For these, as we have said before (pp. 58 ff.), are the other waves of the periodic Semitic migration into the Tigris-Euphrates basin. Our question is basically a linguistic one: We must see where the language of the Amurrum fits into the general pattern of Semitic tongues. Personal names are all we have to work with, and the few "Amorite" expressions that entered Akkadian in the Old Babylonian period—we have no texts in the nomads' language. For, upon settling down, they adopted Akkadian as their written language; perhaps they soon adopted it as their everyday form of speech. But the personal names give us a point of departure at least. In the more ancient Semitic languages, names in the form of a sentence are common enough ("The God X Has Given His Favor" and the like), and these sentences are usually fairly close to the colloquial speech of the time. We are therefore able to establish that the "Amorite" language is very similar to those called "Canaanite": Hebrew, Phoenician and—the identification is still disputed—Ugaritic. A number of scholars, in fact, refer to the nomads of Mesopotamia in the Old Babylonian period as "Canaanites"; historically this is ambiguous, as its associations with the land of Canaan and its inhabitants are strong, but the term may be applied as long as it is understood in its wider and purely linguistic sense. "Amorite," on the other hand, has a firmer historical basis, as derived from a contemporary name; linguistically, however, it is irrelevant.

The same arguments that serve to identify these Old Babylonian nomads, linguistically, with the "Canaanite" branch of Semitic speech should also hold good for the Martu or Amurrum of the age of Ur III. There is no great agreement on this, as some scholars offer proof that the language of the latter differs from those of the "Canaanite" branch; but a linguistic "branch" always implies a plurality of dialects, which may vary widely from one to another. The best example of this is modern Arabic, in which the remarks of a Moroccan are not entirely intelligible to an Arab from Iraq. By this standard the Amurrum of Ur III can with no real difficulty be thought to belong to a "Canaanite" branch of Semitic. To the language of the nomads of the Agade and the Early Dynastic periods, however, we are entirely deaf, as no personal names are preserved to guide us.

To identify their language does not tell us where these nomads came from. We cannot take the modern situation, with the Arabian peninsula as an inexhaustible reservoir of Bedouins, and transfer it to antiquity. Long-range nomadism could and did not exist before the domestication of the camel, and this took place only toward the end of the second millennium B.C. The earlier nomad, with his herds of sheep and goats, could not move more than one day's march from the nearest watering place; his wanderings were a progress from one well or river to the next. The pastures grazed by the nomads of the third and second millennia were the steppes on the inner edge of the Fertile Crescent, and the semidesert plains of Syria. The Arabian desert was out of bounds to them. Migration normally followed the pattern of the seasons: Regularly the herds and their masters would follow retreating and advancing vegetation, from plain to mountain pastures and back again. Meanwhile, this alternation of pastures, along with regular visits to markets to barter for flour, household utensils and hunting implements, would bring the nomads into recurring contact with the sedentary population of the towns.

Such was the normal pattern. Larger migrations were movements of whole peoples into the zones of sedentary occupation, with intent to stay. Penetration into the interior of Mesopotamia took place, usually, through two points of entry from the western steppes. The Middle Euphrates was one; a point at about the latitude of Sippar, farther south, was another. The northern route, crossing the Euphrates, led on to the region of the Khabur and the southern parts of the "Upper Land" (see p. 130). Mountain ranges effectively blocked nomadic movements to the north and east; to this day, nomads have never invaded the mountain territories of Anatolia and Iran from the plain. Also the hardy inhabitants of the mountains would exert counterpressure, so that some nomadic tribes would be turned back southeastward toward the Diyala region and Babylonia. The southern route also led east: Fording the Euphrates and the Tigris at the latitude of Sippar (where the two rivers run close together), the nomads would reach the territory east of the Tigris and south of the Diyala, called Yamutbal in the second millennium. There, once established, they posed a constant threat to the northeast flank of Babylonia, and to the cities around the Diyala valley as well.

These migrations were not spurred by the search for new pastures alone. True, overpopulation of the steppes, excessive demands on available watering places, the expulsion of weaker by stronger tribes—all of these were and historically have been factors making the acquisition of new pastures imperative. But the raiding and looting of sedentary settlements have been the economic ideal of nomads in all ages. However, land hunger, in the sense of a desire for the possession of the sedentaries' fields and gardens, does not enter into the picture at all at this early stage. Land meant work, and to this the nomads were not accustomed. The transition to a sedentary life is almost always a step taken under economic compulsion. Either hunger drove nomads to take service with the sedentaries as laborers, or the ruler of a settled state would hire them on as mercenaries, to be paid with fiefs in land as well as loot. Sometimes an entire tribe would settle under these conditions; sometimes the tribe would split, one part clinging to the pastoral life, the other going into service with the townsmen.

The Old Babylonian texts not only tell us of nomads in general, they name individual tribes. When we place these names where the documents mention them on a map of Mesopotamia, the result reminds us, by its variety, of maps of the grazing grounds of modern Arab tribes: Branches of the same tribe are to be found scattered all over the land. One of the principal Amorite tribes mentioned in the Mari archive is called Amnanum. These same Amnanum are to be found at the gates of Uruk. King Sin-kashid of Uruk (ca. 1865–1835 B.C.) calls himself "King of Uruk, King of the Amnanum." A letter of Anam of Uruk (ca. 1821–1817 B.C.) mentions that the Amnanum and the Yaḫrurum (who are also named at Mari) camp outside of Uruk. After Hammurabi's time two suburbs of Sippar are named after the Amnanum and the Yaḫrurum.

Amnanum, Yaḫrurum and Ubrabum were branches of the tribal federation of the Maru-Yamina, or Binu-Yamina as they are called in their own language. The name means "Sons of the South" and is linguistically related to the Old Testament tribal name of Benjamin. Another tribal federation, chiefly to be found in the Mari archive, is that of the Ḫanu. The Ḫanu, in contrast to the "Benjaminites," take sides with the sedentaries, so much so that, in the language of the Mari tablets, "Ḫanu" often means any member of the nomadic mercenaries in the service of that city's king. We have as many parallels for this reduction in meaning of an ethnic term (Ḫanu=mercenary) as we have of the opposite process (Amurrum=nomad in general).

The tribal structure of the Amorites corresponds, as far as we can come to know it, rather closely to that of the modern Bedouin tribe. The Amorite chieftain or sheikh is called *abum*, "father" in Akkadian; we also often meet with a word in the nomads' language, *sugagum*. Akkadian texts use the same word for tribal "elders" as for the "elders" of a city. Once a tribe entered into a relationship of dependency with the ruler of a city, its sheikh bore responsibility for the behavior of his followers. The families of the sheikhs had particularly close contacts with the townsmen, storing up experiences that were to be useful in the usurpations of the age. Letters from Mari sometimes show kings treating the sheikhs with the utmost diplomatic delicacy, to head off the possibility of revolt by their tribes.

A letter directed to Zimri-Lim, king of Mari (1782–1759 B.C.), testifies to the importance to the king of the Hanu tribe on the Middle Euphrates: "May my lord preserve his royal dignity. As you are King of the Hanu, so you are also, in the second place, King of the Akkadians. Let my lord not drive with horses, but in a chariot with mules." The Akkadians, now reduced to a minority, are anxious to preserve their civilized customs: or, rather, the Akkadianized nomads are anxious to preserve them, for Zimri-Lim is the son of a house that traced its origin to a nomadic tribe; so, for that matter, was the author of the letter, the palace prefect Bahdi-Lim.

We are so far unable to follow, step by step, the seizure of power in a city by a usurper of nomadic descent, and the foundation of an Amorite dynasty. For this we should have to have more biographical data than we possess for any individual king. All that we find is a new set of date formulae in a city where the ruler has an Amorite name, calling himself "King of [the city of] X" in his building and votive inscriptions. We can presume that a nomad sheikh will not have been able to seize the throne before he had acquired a thorough knowledge of the culture and the way of life of the city. An interesting case in this respect is Kudur-mabuk, who helped his son Warad-Sin to the throne of Larsa in 1834 B.C. Kudur-mabuk has an Elamite name, as did his own father Simti-shilḫak. Yet his title is "Sheikh of Yamutbal, Sheikh of the Amurrum," which tells us that he is not an Elamite at all. His son Warad-Sin, and the latter's brother and successor Rim-Sin, have pure Akkadian names. Kudur-mabuk probably came from a family of chiefs that had spent generations in Yamutbal, and had entered the service of the neighboring Elamites at some point, under circumstances similar to those of the Ḫanu of Mari. When Kudur-Mabuk has his daughter consecrated *en*-priestess of the moon-god at Ur under the Sumerian name of Enanedu, exercising an ancient royal prerogative, he displays more than a passing acquaintance with the refinements of civilization, though he is a descendant of nomads and a chieftain of nomads. The Amorites were already assimilated, at least in part, to the way of life of the cities they proceeded to master one by one.

By the middle of the second millennium, this assimilation was complete. The Amorites had adopted the Akkadian language and Akkadian culture. In the second half of the second millennium a new wave of migrations affected the whole of the Fertile Crescent, with the coming of the Aramaeans. In Syria and Palestine, however, the destiny of the nomads was a different one. There the Canaanites, then the Aramaeans, become the dominant element in the population.

Old Babylonian Omens as a Mirror of the Age

We have already noticed one of the ways in which Akkadian omen texts can prove useful for a reconstruction of Mesopotamia's past: As we saw, in connection with the history of the Empire of Agade (see p. 93), descriptions of peculiar markings or conformations of a sacrificial sheep's liver connect them with some notable event that they "foretold": "If the flesh has grown through the 'gate of the palace' [a technical term for a part of the liver], this is the omen of Shulgi when he took Tappadaraḫ." Several recorded omens suggest that various rulers lost their lives in unnatural ways. Others preserved memories of the fall of Ur under Ibbi-Sin. But even more revealing than statements referring to specific past events are those that refer, in more general terms, to the future. For example: "If [there follows a description of a particular liver omen], then the prince will not return from the campaign on which he departs." We have hundreds of these general predictions. Not all come from liver omens; there are also omens drawn from the behavior of oil dropped in water (lecanomancy) or from the movements of the smoke of incense. These generalized omens give us an extremely vivid picture of the political and economic, and occasionally the social, conditions of this uneasy age. It is just their generality that makes them valuable to us: They show us what was accepted as a matter of course, what was considered as a likely occurrence; we know that they are not reporting special cases, but predicting what were then taken to be probabilities. They often confirm the knowledge we draw from contemporary letters, our best sources for particular events.

Astonishingly frequent in the omens is the theme of the violent death or dethroning of the king. Often enough his kingdom was scarcely as large as an administrative district in the Empire of Ur III, yet many were the men who coveted it. We read that "a dignitary will kill his king" or "the heir of the king will kill his father and take the throne" or "the vizier will sit on the throne of his lord." The "grand vizier" or the "officers of the king" are regarded as potential regicides. Sometimes the king is able to crush his internal enemies in the long run: "The king will be exiled, but he will become strong [again] in a district [of his kingdom]" or "over the land that rebels against its shepherd, the shepherd will retain the advantage." In these surroundings, an omen like "the king will die the death his god has determined for him, and a dignitary will rule the land" is an idyllic exception—*if* it means a natural death. Rebellion is common even at the lower political levels: "The people of a district will expel their mayor." Authority, however, is not always on the defensive: "The king will remove his grand vizier" and, more vividly, "the king will cause the eyes of a man of the palace to be torn out."

External affairs are no more stable; alliances are not firm, loyalties are not dependable, and war is therefore unpredictable: "The Prince will be abandoned by his auxiliaries" or "my ally will turn to the enemy." Treason is universal: "The 'Great One of the Post' will open your city's gate [to the enemy]"; "a spy will go forth"; "one who sits before the king will again and again convey the king's secret to the enemy"; "a dignitary will take flight." For all its melodrama, a war between two such vest-pocket states was basically a small-scale affair: "The enemy will load a boat with barley and carry it away as booty." This is simply nomad-style raiding, though carried on by city dwellers. Nevertheless, it could lead to conquest and a change of rulers—how quickly, we learn from an omen that "the statue that the king had had made will be brought [to the temple, as a votive gift] by another." The usurpation of monuments, by which an interloper attempted to turn the magical efficacy of a votive gift offered by another to his own benefit, was common enough. "The two lands will eat each other up" is one pessimistic prediction of the result of war, but it is also possible that "the opposing kings will make peace and their lands will live in security." Not surprisingly there is a nostalgia for the imperial peace of old: "a king of Sumer will rule" is one hopeful omen, or "a king of the universe will appear in the land."

Instability in high places is not limited to politics, and the omen texts occasionally take on the aspect of a *chronique scandaleuse*: "The *Sangu* priest will repeatedly make love to the *en*-priestess"; "an *en*-priestess will secretly violate the taboo over and over; she will be found out and she will be burned"; "a king's daughter will become a whore."

Natural disasters and prodigies also find their place in the predictions: eclipses of the sun and moon occur, heat, cold (even snow!) put in an appearance; conflagrations, broken dikes, floods and the swarming of locusts afflict the land and

188

take their toll of its economy, resulting in crop failures, starvation, dearth. Omens concerning family life are rare, as are those concerning the individual's dealings with his government: "The man will experience joy on his way to the palace"; "his opponent in the lawsuit will fall in the palace" (in a case under the jurisdiction of a king or a governor); a certain omen is said to signify "for a *mushkenum*: in future the palace will dispose of his house and his effects." *Mushkenum*, in the Old Babylonian period, probably means a dependent tenant of the palace.[75] An "epidemic among the *ḫupshum*" refers to a still-lower social class, the nature of which we have been unable to define in detail. These remnants of a superstitious science, then, have information to give us on social history as well: In their anxiety to learn the lineaments of the future, the Babylonians teach us much about the past.

Larsa, Isin, Uruk, Babylon, and Eshnunna in the Nineteenth Century B.C.

Gungunum (1932–1906 B.C.), as we have seen, is the first real "king" of the Dynasty of Larsa: It was he who took the seaport of Ur, the center of the southern trade, from Lipit-eshtar of Isin (1934–1924 B.C.). As far as we can tell, his relations with Isin nevertheless remained peaceful: Lipit-eshtar had his daughter Enninsunzi elected, by a liver omen, to be the *en*-priestess of Nanna at Ur, a position held by princesses since the time of the Sargonids, and two years later Gungunum installed her in that office. An administrative document from Ur tells us that Ur-Ninurta of Isin, Lipit-eshtar's successor, dedicated a votive gift at Ur, continuing his devotion to the cult of this city, though it was now lost to his state. For nearly a century, until Enlil-bani (1860–1837 B.C.), the kings of Isin uphold, in their titles, the fiction that Ur still remained among their dominions. But, after Lipit-eshtar, Isin had lost its position as the paramount power in Babylonia, and as successor to the Empire of Ur III, for good and all.

Ur-Ninurta was an interloper in the Dynasty of Isin; he had no blood relation to his predecessors. The circumstances of his accession are quite unknown. The name "Ur-Ninurta" is Sumerian, but this tells us nothing of his nationality; for centuries Akkadians in Babylonia had been assuming Sumerian names. We know very little of this king's twenty-eight-year reign. There is a court document, recording a murder trial held before the high court at Nippur in Ur-Ninurta's time, that is important for the history of law. The text is extant in several eighteenth-century copies, indicating that the scribal schools found it of literary interest.

Gungunum of Larsa, on the other hand, left his mark on history: He conducted a campaign against Anshan, resuming the traditional Babylonian policy of expansion in the Elamite east. A tablet from Susa bears the formula of Gungunum's sixteenth year; for at least this year, Susa was under the rule of Larsa. As five of Gungunum's date formulae mention the construction or expansion of canals, it is clear that he was also active at home. His successors also shone in caring for and improving the vital network of canals.

By the eighth year (1898 B.C.) of Abisare of Larsa, hostilities with Isin had broken out, for the following year is named after a victory of Larsa over that city. Bur-Sin of Isin (1895–1874 B.C.) did, on the other hand, manage to regain possession of Ur for a few months in 1895. This would indicate a see-saw of power, but the preponderance of Larsa increased inexorably with time. Under Sumu'el (1894–1866 B.C.) Larsa's dominions sometimes extended to northern Babylonia, bypassing the territory of Isin to be sure. Under Nur-Adad (1865–1850 B.C.), Larsa adopted the use of the royal hymn, which had continued to be cultivated as a literary form under Ur-Ninurta of Isin and his successors. Perhaps this innovation is to be connected with Sumu'el's conquest of Nippur, in the second-to-last year of his reign. For control of Nippur meant control of the cult of the royal god Enlil. Sumu'el is also the first king of Larsa to be divinized, indeed the only king of Larsa until Rim-Sin. Nippur, however, until Rim-Sin's time, went back and forth between Larsa and Isin, forming the bone of contention in their wars.

The position of Larsa was important, but—not even Gungunum's expansion in Elam should deceive us here—it was by no stretch of the imagination imperial. From 1894 on Babylon was an independent state, soon annexing Sippar to the north of it. Kish, nine miles to the northeast, was annexed by Babylon's King Sumula'el (1880–1845 B.C.). Also sovereign states, under independent rulers, were Kazallu, Marad, Malgium (on the Tigris, near the mouth of the Diyala), Kisurra, eighteen miles south of Isin, and several others. Eshnunna dominated the Diyala region, but Tutub (Khafaji D) became independent in the time of Sumula'el. As the nineteenth century continued the map of Babylonia gained in variety. The point was reached where a single state could accomplish nothing, in external affairs, except to raid its neighbors' territory; as in the Early Dynastic age, larger enterprises called for coalitions.

By what means do we judge a state's "independence"? By the dating of documents with its own year formulae, and the appearance in legal documents of the oath sworn by its own ruler. But we also have cases where a legal tablet bears the oath by a local ruler but the date formula of a neighboring state, or where, in addition to a local date formula and oath, another oath is sworn by the name of a "foreign" king. These are probably only semi-independent cities.

From about 1860 B.C. on, Uruk, having seceded from Isin, joins the concert of Babylonian states. Sin-kashid, the "King of the Amnanum nomads," founded a dynasty that lasted down to Irdanene, defeated by Rim-Sin of Larsa in 1809; six years afterward, Uruk fell to Larsa. The territory of Uruk in the Old Babylonian period was of no great size, yet apparently the city was important enough to enjoy an enduring alliance with Babylon. Sumula'el of Babylon married a daughter of Sin-kashid; a letter of Anam of Uruk (ca. 1821–1817 B.C.) to the crown prince of Babylon, Sin-muballit, speaks of the friendship that had obtained between the two states "since the days of Sin-kashid." That Uruk, only eighteen miles northwest of Larsa, could so long retain her independence shows us that the line of Larsa's expansion moved up the Tigris rather than the Euphrates.

Unfortunately we have no clear concept of the river and canal system in the mid-nineteenth century B.C. There are indications of a violent flood in the reign of Nur-Adad of Larsa (1865–1850 B.C.), in which the Tigris shifted its bed. An inscription of that king reads: "When [Nur-Adad] had led Ur to prosperity, eliminating evil and complaints to the sun-god [the god of justice], when he had made firm the foundation of the throne of Larsa and permanently resettled [its] dispersed inhabitants." This exodus of the city's population probably implies a failure of their riverine water supply, forcing them to migrate, perhaps even to relapse into nomadism. A similar passage can be found in the prologue to the *Code of Hammurabi*: the king glories in having "gathered in the dispersed inhabitants of Isin." From the history of Iraq in the nineteenth century A.D., we know of an occasion when the inhabitants of al-Hilla on the Euphrates had to leave their city, the river having changed its course to one north of the town. An exceptionally heavy thaw at the headwaters of the Euphrates or the Tigris can easily cause a flood of such vehemence that one or the other river will shift its bed; the two rivers deposit tons of sediment every year, and the level of the riverbeds is constantly on the rise, so that the established courses are not deep enough to retain their waters during floods or drain them back again when they subside. The Old Babylonian omen texts speak often of dikes ruptured by the rivers in flood.

The reign of Nur-Adad's successor, Sin-iddinam (1849–1843 B.C.), provides us with more definite evidence of a shift in the course of the river. This king's inscription runs: "An and Enlil commissioned me . . . to 'dig' and 'repair' the Tigris." To "dig" the Tigris, which then flowed farther west than it does today, must mean an attempt to redirect the course of the river into its former bed. The date formula of Sin-iddinam's second year confirms the existence of such a project, naming the year "the Tigris was dug out."

A generation before Sin-kashid of Uruk, an Amorite dynasty had established itself at Babylon. Later tradition was to regard Sumula'el (1880–1845 B.C.) as its founder, but in point of fact it was inaugurated by Sumuabum (1894–1881 B.C.). We know nothing of his tribe or place of origin; we know no more of the history of Babylon between Ibbi-Sin's time and his own. Babylon had been, under the Third Dynasty of Ur, important enough to be the seat of an imperial *ensi*. After the fall of Ur it had probably been part of the Kingdom of Isin at first, later perhaps of the state of Kish. Once the Amorites seized the city, the dynasty they established, the First Dynasty of Babylon, retained "Canaanite" names for longer than any other Amorite house ruling in Babylonia: Of eleven kings, only the fourth and fifth (Apil-Sin and Sin-muballit) had Akkadian names. Until Hammurabi's day, Babylon was but one among several northern Babylonian states, and even during the first thirty years of that king's reign, it still had to rely on the traditional policy of alliances to make its weight felt in the land. Babylon, like Isin and Larsa, and unlike Kish, Uruk and Ur, had no storied past behind it. But the kings of Babylon no more transferred their capital to historic Kish, once they acquired that city in Sumula'el's region, than those of Isin and Larsa had transferred their residence to once imperial Ur.

On the Middle Euphrates and in Syria, too, we can assume the existence of a plethora of small kingdoms in the nineteenth century B.C. For Mari, in contrast to Assyria, we have written sources only from the end of the nineteenth century. Yaḫdun-lim (ca. 1825–1810 B.C.) was king of Mari before Shamshi-Adad of Assyria seized the city; he was the father of Zimri-Lim, who was later to drive Shamshi-Adad's son Yasmaḫ-Adad from the city and recover his inheritance. Yaḫdun-Lim's father Yaggid-Lim was the contemporary and sometimes the ally of Shamshi-Adad's father Ila-kabkabuhu. Both the house of Mari and the house of Assur were of Amorite origin. A building inscription of Yaḫdun-Lim's, on the temple of the sun-god Shamash at Mari, reports an expedition to the Mediterranean and the conquest of a country on its shores. The enterprise is reported in ringing phrases, written in rather elegant Old Babylonian, which do not quite conceal its actual purpose: to acquire timber from the Amanus mountains. Here was no conquest, but one of the raids typical of the age. On his way back, Yaḥdun-Lim was waylaid by three "kings" of the nomadic Amurrum (the Urabu, Amnanum and Rabbu tribes), who were joined by the ruler of the city of Yamḥad (the modern Aleppo); Yaḥdun-Lim managed to break through the troops of this coalition. That this raid was, by the way, blown up into a war of conquest on the king's inscription is also typical of the age—the royal inscriptions continually exaggerate, clothing their petty wars in the terminology of the Empire of Agade; one king of Kish, Ashduniarim (probably at the beginning of the nineteenth century B.C.), speaks of an eight-year war he led against "the Four Quarters," then in rebellion against his rule.

Assyria and Asia Minor

Ilushuma of Assur (see p. 167) was the grandson of a certain Puzur-Asshur, and the son of Shalimaḥum. The dynasty of Puzur-Asshur was Akkadian: Shamshi-Adad the Amorite dethroned it one generation before Hammurabi. The great *Assyrian King List* cannot aid us in relating Shamshi-Adad's predecessors to the rulers of Isin and Larsa; the list was compiled in the eighth century B.C., and its rather indistinct picture of the orgins of the independent Kingdom of Assur shows us that the memory of the events that followed the fall of Ur's empire had by then been lost—which is not surprising, after a lapse of what was, after all, thirteen centuries. At the beginning of the list a line of seventeen "kings" is set down, who still "lived in tents"; this might be a remembrance of the original migration of the Amorites; the names, in fact, of the "tent kings" are in part "Canaanite." The immediate predecessors of Puzur-Asshur, however, have non-Semitic names. These are probably leaders of the autochthonous, pre-Semitic population of Assyria, the Subarians—that is, the inhabitants of

194

Subartu. Subartu is the name applied to the Assyrian area in the Babylonian sources. It was indiscriminately used for both the non-Semitic and Semitic (i.e. Assyrian) populations there, and the term was not geographically well defined. These predecessors of Puzur-Asshur are so far attested by no inscriptions of their own. We therefore cannot check the *Assyrian King List*'s reliability on this point. We know that Ishbi-Erra fought an "*ensi* of Subartu," but who that may have been we do not know.

Shamshi-Adad I (1815–1782 B.C.) was the son, as we have said, of one Ila-kabkabuhu: If this name, and a series of "Canaanite" names identifying his ancestors, also appear on the *Assyrian King List*, we must recognize this as the family tree of Shamshi-Adad, inserted into the *King List* as a genealogical digression, not as a line of actual rulers of an Assur they may never have seen—for we know that Ila-kabkabuhu was an insignificant local prince in the vicinity of Mari.

Our contemporary sources for the activities of these early kings are their own inscriptions. We have already met with the inscription of Ilushuma, claiming that the king freed the Akkadians from tribute over an area extending from Ur to Assur (see p. 167). We have building inscriptions from his predecessor Shalim-ahum and from his successors, written in Old Assyrian. Shamshi-Adad, as a non-Assyrian, writes in Old Babylonian.

At the end of the reign of Shamshi-Adad's son Ishme-Dagan, the throne of Assur became the object of a dynastic quarrel. Out of this emerges a King Adasi, whom the later tradition would regard as the ancestor of the Assyrian ruling house.

Far more abundant than the royal inscriptions at Assur are tablets found at the Assyrian mercantile colony of Kanish, in the classical Cappadocia, south of the River Halys (in modern terms, at Kültepe south of the Kizil Irmak, about twelve miles northeast of Kayseri, in east-central Turkey). These archives cover three generations. They begin after the reign of Ilushuma; we find there a copy of an inscription set up at

Assur by that king's successor, Erishum. A tablet containing a decision of a court at Assur, also found at Kanish, gives us a more direct synchronism: It is marked with the seal of Sharrum-ken, grandson of Erishum.

Kanish was the main center of the Assyrian merchants trading into Anatolia. Its archives consist of several thousand clay tablets (business letters, accounts, contracts, court documents) written in Old Assyrian. There were, however, at least nine other Assyrian trading posts, with ten or more subsidiaries, all in central or eastern Asia Minor. The larger of these commercial stations were called *Karum* in Akkadian, a word originally meaning "embankment, quay," then extended to apply to the marketplace on the quayside, then to "the corps of merchants [of a city]." The merchant settlements at these trading posts had their own courts, judging disputes according to Assyrian custom, with a central court at Kanish. Suits between merchants were heard, sometimes also litigation between Assyrians and natives. The Assyrians, however, did not enjoy a preferred political status in Asia Minor. They were liable to pay imposts of many kinds to the native rulers (the Assyrian tablets call them *ruba'um*, "prince"). The excavation of Kanish has shown that the Assyrian settlement was located outside the wall of that city. As the native rulers had a lively interest in the trade, the Assyrians were tolerated, even welcomed, as traders and taxpayers.

Trading colonies were, incidentally, not limited to Asia Minor. The merchants of the northern Babylonian city of Sippar had a post at Mari during the time of Sumuabum and Sumula'el of Babylon. There were probably parallels to be found elsewhere. The peculiarity of the Assyrian settlements is that they were located on non-Mesopotamian soil, close to the source of the desired raw materials.

The principal products brought to Asia Minor by the Assyrians were tin, needed by the natives for the manufacture of bronze, and textiles. Exports to Assyria were largely copper. The Kanish archives—and the minor archives of Boghazköy (the ancient Hattusas) and Alishar (ancient Ankuwa?), about fifty miles southeast of Boghazköy—provide us with extraordinarily important materials for the history of commerce. They show us the organization and methods of the Assyrian traders: transportation, turnover, prices, profits, the organization of private firms and partnerships, accounting procedures, systems of clearing and credit. There are, as we should expect in texts of this kind and in this locality, rather few references to the political situation in Assur: The Assyrian ruler is called *ruba'um*, "prince," while in his inscriptions he assumes the title *isshiakkum*, the equivalent of *ensi*. One of the most important things we can learn from these texts is that the merchants for whom they were written were private entrepreneurs, working on their own account and at their own risk, and not, as is often the case with the Babylonian merchant, on commission for the state.

The Assyrian documents also give us our first real insight into ethnic and political conditions in Anatolia. Until the growth of the first Hittite Empire there were no major states in Asia Minor. The *ruba'um* of Kanish is sometimes called the "great *ruba'um*," perhaps indicating a rank superior to that of other princes, but there are in any case a considerable number of independent native states. These rulers, as well as the rest of the native population, write only in the Assyrian script and language when they write at all; the language of their texts is heavily seasoned with barbarisms. Assyria, then, had a civilizing effect on Asia Minor, as Babylonia had on Elam. The script, of course, could not be transmitted without schools, and there was a scribal school at Kanish; a very few literary texts have been found there. Cuneiform, however, disappeared from Anatolia when the Assyrian trade colonies there came to an end, in the time of Shamshi-Adad. When the Hittites began to write, under Hattusilis I (seventeenth century), they employed a style of cuneiform probably originating in Syria, also serving as a model for the script used by the Hurrians. The Assyrian inheritance had vanished without a trace.

The very little that we know of the peoples among whom the Assyrian colonists lived and moved and made their profits, and of the languages then spoken in Anatolia, we have learned from non-Akkadian personal names that appear in the Assyrian tablets, and from a few loan words from the native languages that occur in these texts. Some of the personal names can be attributed to what we call the "Proto-Hattic" language, represented by passages in liturgical texts from Hittite times at Hattusas. From personal names of another type we can conclude the existence of a second language, provisionally called "Southeast Anatolian."[76] Neither of these languages is related to the Indo-European tongues of later Anatolia or, for that matter, to any Indo-European language; nor are they related to Ḥurrian. Among the personal names, however, we find some Hittite names. These, as well as two Hittite loan words, are our earliest evidence for the presence of the Indo-European tribes that probably migrated into Asia Minor around the end of the third, and the beginning of the second, millennium.[77]

After three generations the activities, and the presence, of the Assyrian colony at Kanish came to an end. We do not know why. Political upheavals in Asia Minor? Disturbances in the mountain lands between Assur and Kanish, so severe as to paralyze caravan traffic? Under Shamshi-Adad another attempt was made to establish an Anatolian colony, but the archive of Alishar that documents it ends within a single generation. From that time on no more permanent colonies of Assyrian merchants were to be found on Anatolian soil, and the history of Asia Minor is once more enveloped in darkness.

Mesopotamia to the Empire of Hammurabi

At the end of the nineteenth century, Mesopotamia began to emerge from the political disruption of the previous generations, and, under Rim-Sin of Larsa, Ipiq-Adad of Eshnunna and Shamshi-Adad of Assur, major kingdoms began to form amid the welter of competing states. For the following fifty years, the history of Mesopotamia was to be characterized by a balance of power between these kingdoms. The reunification of all Babylonia, however, had to wait until the year 1763 B.C., the thirtieth year in the reign of King Hammurabi of Babylon. The empire thus formed was of short duration, but its significance for the later history of Mesopotamia knew no limit in time. Babylon became the metropolis of Sumer and Akkad: The whole country took its name. "Land of Babylon" first appears as a designation for what we now call Babylonia in the Middle Babylonian period, in parallel to "Land of Assur." The Akkadian language is called "Babylonian" in the Hittite archives at Hattusas. Babylon had become the symbol of the Semites of southern Mesopotamia.

As we have seen, the struggles between Isin and Larsa, during the latter half of the nineteenth century B.C., were marked by the constant change of ownership of Nippur. Dated documents show Nippur in the possession of Larsa in 1838, 1835, 1832 and 1828; in the possession of Isin in 1836, 1833, 1830 and, the last occasion, for a few years between 1813 and 1802. In 1835 Larsa itself was conquered by the state of Kazallu (two contracts from Larsa bear date formulae of Kazallu's ruler); thereafter, the house of Kudur-mabuk seized power in Larsa (see pp. 185 ff.). The "Sheikh of Yamutbal," Kudur-mabuk, installed his son Warad-Sin (1834–1823 B.C.) as king; the latter was followed by his brother, Rim-Sin (1822–1763 B.C.), reigning for sixty years. What caused the Amorites of Yamutbal to take Larsa from Kazallu we do not know—possibly an old rivalry with the tribe of Mutiabal, then ruling Kazallu. In any case the seventy-two-year rule of the house of Kudur-mabuk in Larsa gave the state a period of relative quiet and of rich literary productivity. There was an extensive building program, always a sign of strong government in Mesopotamia, and a tremendous application of energy to the canals and irrigation works in Larsa's dominions. Several of the canals built or restored in this period are described as having "led to the sea." This means one of two things: either an attempt to give new outlets to the Tigris and Euphrates and to reduce the danger of excessive floods, or else the exploitation of new agricultural land near the coast. One date formula of Rim-Sin expressly refers to the latter. The need for new land is not the result of overpopulation, but of excessive salinization of the soil in established agricultural areas; the district of Lagash had seen a particularly severe drop in the productivity of its lands. Research carried out in the last ten years has shown us that the settled, agricultural areas in Babylonia shifted time and again, and that the productivity of the soil would drop sharply after a long period of use.[78] The climate necessitated intensive irrigation; constant applications of river water left harmful minerals in the fields; the small amount of rain that fell on Babylonia was insufficient to wash them out. Heavy irrigation also kept the water table rather high, so that the minerals were kept close to the surface, and close to the crops.

In 1793, the thirtieth year of his reign, Rim-Sin conquered Isin, thus eliminating Larsa's ancient rival in central Babylonia. How greatly this event figured in the king's mind is shown by the fact that Rim-Sin named every remaining year of his reign, for thirty years, after the fall of Isin, from "year one: Isin conquered" to "year thirty: Isin conquered," in a chronological era all his own. But in 1803 Rim-Sin had already annexed Uruk, the last independent state of southern Babylonia. This occurred as a result of Rim-Sin's victory over a great coalition, uniting Uruk, Isin, Babylon, Rapiqum (on the Euphrates, north of Sippar) and the Sutu nomads. Isin, under Sin-magir (1827–1817 B.C.) and Damiq-ilishu (1816–1794 B.C.), had tried to escape her cramped position in central Babylonia, where she was surrounded by minor states, by expanding northward. Rim-Sin's victory in 1793 put an end to her attempts, and to her history as an independent power.

In the Diyala region, Ipiq-Adad of Eshnunna took up once more the royal title of his ancestors in 1830, for the first time since Ilshu-iliya, calling himself, after an old Sumerian tradition, "Shepherd of the Black-headed People" (=human beings) and decreeing his own divinization. Ipiq-Adad pushed westward to Rapiqum on the Euphrates, cutting off any northward expansion of Babylon. His son Naram-Sin carried the influence of Eshnunna beyond Assur into the territories of the Upper Khabur; he is identical with the Naram-Sin of Assur, whom the *Assyrian King List* names as second predecessor to Shamshi-Adad. This northward expansion of Eshnunna is, so to speak, the reverse of Ilushuma's southward drive from Assur to Der more than a century before, and was just as ephemeral. The *King List* makes Naram-Sin a son of Puzur-Asshur II, but the compiler is probably simply adhering to an ideology of hereditary succession, according to which he would designate all predecessors as fathers of their successors, unless the contrary was proven.

Naram-Sin's brother Dadusha ruled Eshnunna until shortly after 1790 B.C. It was probably in his reign that the *Code of Eshnunna*, a collection of price regulations and legal rules, was compiled. Two copies of this text were discovered in the small town of Shaduppum east of modern Baghdad. According to one of his date formulae Dadusha won a victory over Ishme-Dagan, the son of Shamshi-Adad, then ruling Ekallatum for his father. Even under Dadusha's successor Ibal-pi'el II, Eshnunna remained an important factor in the political world of Mesopotamia. A victory over "Hana and Subartu" may refer to wars with Zimri-Lim of Mari and Ishme-Dagan of Assur. The usual ally of Eshnunna in its wars was nearby Elam.

Shamshi-Adad, the son of Ila-kabkabuhu of Terqa on the Middle Euphrates, arrived in the northeast as an exile, if we are to believe a note in the *Assyrian King List*. He seized Ekallatum, and from there made himself master of Assur, expelling the last king of the dynasty of Puzur-Asshur. His reign (1815–1782 B.C.) runs more or less parallel to that of Dadusha of Eshnunna. In addition to Assur, Shamshi-Adad had a second capital at Shubat-Enlil, "Residence of Enlil," at the headwaters of the Khabur. This city may be identical with the modern ruins at Chagar-Bazar, where an administrative archive from the time of Shamshi-Adad has been found. Shamshi-Adad's eldest son, Ishme-Dagan, later king of Assyria, at first ruled Ekallatum on the Tigris as subking to his father;

the younger son Yasmah-Adad held the same post at Mari. There the native king, Yahdun-Lim, Zimri-Lim's father, had been murdered, perhaps an act of filial revenge by Shamshi-Adad for his father Ila-kabkabuhu's expulsion from Terqa. Yasmah-Adad proved himself, in his administration of his sub-kingdom, his brother's glaring inferior in energy and acumen. His father's letters to him are filled with anxiety, with parental concern alternating with ironic reproach, and are highly revealing, sometimes amusing human documents.

The personality of Shamshi-Adad bears comparison with that of his younger contemporary, the great Hammurabi. Shamshi-Adad was the first king in northern Mesopotamia to take the Akkadian title *Shar Kisshatim*, "King of the Universe," the more modern version of the Sumerian "King of the Four Quarters." It is probable that this is also a pun on the name of the city of Kish, harking back to the even more ancient title of suzerainty "King of Kish." Shamshi-Adad's letters reveal to us a king who took the responsibilities as well as the powers of his office seriously. He kept an extremely close eye on all branches of the administration, carefully regulated the ever shifting balance between nomads and sedentaries, applied himself to maintaining discipline in the bureaucracy and in the army, and kept himself informed even of the minor details of agriculture and irrigation. In army affairs, for example, he castigated the abuses of officers who had favored themselves, at the expense of their troops, in the division of loot; in agriculture, he pushed the introduction of a new and more practical plow. His correspondence, and indeed the royal correspondence of the eighteenth century in general, is as fascinating as any historical source of any age. The letters are written in the heat of the contemporary situation, in the language and turns of phrase in which they were dictated to the scribes: We hear the authentic voices of ancient kings. They are therefore of far more value to us, and can be utilized with greater assurance, than, for example, the royal correspondence of Ur III, preserved to us only in later copies and formulated in rhetorical terms.

Shamshi-Adad, according to one of his inscriptions, took his arms to the Mediterranean and "erected stelae" on its shores. A king of Carchemish on the Upper Euphrates was his vassal; he allied himself with the king of Qatna, in the neighborhood of the modern Homs, by marrying the feckless Yasmaḥ-Adad to the former's daughter. In short his power and influence extended well into northern Syria; to the east, it extended into the foothills of the Iranian mountains. In the area south of Lake Urmiah the probably Hurrian Turukka tribe was a dangerous enemy. To the south, the area under Assyrian influence marched with the states of Eshnunna and Babylon. A document from Sippar is confirmed by an oath between the two parties, sworn in the names of Hammurabi and Shamshi-Adad. Either the two men were subjects of different kings, or Sippar, part of Hammurabi's state, had temporarily come under the suzerainty of Shamshi-Adad—we have no way of choosing the correct alternative.

According to the Assyrian usage, documents written by or under Shamshi-Adad were dated by the names of eponymous officials (see note 2), not, as in the Babylonian states and Mari, by date formulae. Since we do not yet know in what order to arrange these names, the chronology of events during Shamshi-Adad's reign remains unsure. We must not entertain, from the evidence given here of Shamshi-Adad's expansion, the idea of a consolidated empire enduring for several decades. Indeed we must not picture any of these ephemerally expanded kingdoms of the Old Babylonian period, before Hammurabi, as highly organized empires after the manner of Ur III. Shamshi-Adad's kingdom, and many another of the age, was the product of its founder's personality, and disappeared with it. With Shamshi-Adad dead, Zimri-Lim, returning from exile in Syrian Yamḥad, seized it from his inept hands and made himself king of his native city, reigning there from 1782 to 1759, when Hammurabi seized it in turn. Ishme-Dagan succeeded his father on the throne of Assur, but his power extended over Assyria alone.

The decisive dates for the rise of Babylon under Hammurabi are these: fortification of several cities of northern Babylonia in the years 1776–1768 B.C.; victory over a coalition of Elam, "Subartu," the "Gutians," Eshnunna and Malgium in 1764. ("Subartu" means Assyria under Ishme-Dagan; the "Gutians" would be mountain peoples in the region between the modern Hamadan and Lake Urmiah, in western Iran; we cannot be quite sure whether the descendants of the conquerors of Agade are meant, or whether this is a historical use of the name, applied to peoples now living in the Gutians' former home.) In 1763, after a siege of several months, Rim-Sin was defeated and Larsa added to the kingdom of Babylon. At the same time Hammurabi records that he took possession of the banks of the Tigris "into Subartu"; he had probably definitely added Ekallatum to the area under his rule. Mari and Malgium were overrun in 1759. In 1757 and 1755 battles with Subartu are again reported. This is the history as we know it from the date formulae. If this were all we had, we should think of Hammurabi's rise as a single-handed military triumph. But Babylon's allies remain unnamed; we know that the play of shifting coalitions was the determining factor in the politics of the age; the king's success was a function of the king's skill in maneuvering the counters of this dangerous game. Babylon, in other words, did not stand alone against the rest of Mesopotamia. The situation cannot be better described than it was in a letter of Zimri-Lim of Mari: "There is no king who can be mighty alone. Behind Hammurabi, the Man of Babylon, march ten, fifteen kings; as many march behind Rim-Sin, the Man of Larsa, Ibal-pi'el, the Man of Eshnunna, Amut-pi'el, the Man of Qatunum [=Qatna], and behind Yarim-Lim, the Man of Yamḫad, march twenty kings." The Mari letters show us specifically and distinctly that, at first, the "Man of Babylon" was but one among many. A letter dating from shortly before the war on Larsa implies that Hammurabi had to come to an understanding with Eshnunna before he could venture to attack Rim-Sin.

In the date formula for his thirtieth year Hammurabi first, and finally, expresses the idea of his rule over all Babylonia. Borrowing a phrase from Sumerian royal hymnology, he says that he "established the foundations" of Sumer and Akkad. In the prologe to his *Code*, Hammurabi lists the great cities subject to him in the last years of his reign, along with their principal sanctuaries. In Babylonia, reading from south to north, they are: Eridu, Ur, Lagash, Girsu, Zabalam, Larsa, Uruk, Adab, Isin, Nippur, Keshi, Dilbat, Borsippa, Babylon, Kish, Malgium, Mashkanshapir, Kutha, Sippar. In the Diyala region, Eshnunna; on the Middle Euphrates, Mari and Tuttul (on the lower course of the River Balikh); on the Middle Tigris, Assur and Nineveh. With the exception of Elam, then, the empire of Hammurabi was roughly the same as that ruled by the Third Dynasty of Ur, in terms of space. In terms of time, it was far more limited. The date formulae mentioning battles against "Subartu" tell us that Assur and Nineveh can have been under Babylon's control only a very few years. Babylonia itself continued to be torn by its age-old particularism and dissension. By the second decade of Hammurabi's successor, Samsu-iluna, the south of Babylonia had broken away from the dynasty.

Before turning to examine the administration of this empire, the *Code of Hammurabi* and the social structure of Babylonia in the Old Babylonian period, we must complete our survey of the political history of Western Asia with a sketch of events in Mari, in Syria and in Elam.

Western Asia Viewed from Mari— The Hurrians

The palace archive of Mari covers the period from about 1810 to about 1760. So far 1,600 texts have been published, the bulk of them from the period of Yasmah-Adad's rule as subking and from the reign of Zimri-Lim. Aside from letters, we have, in published form, over a hundred legal documents and about a thousand administrative texts. The letters are partly addressed to the palace at Mari and partly copies of letters sent from the palace.

Mari's importance was based on its location on the main

trade routes between Syria and Babylonia. It was a way station for caravan and boat traffic along and on the Euphrates, the principal link between the Mediterranean and the Persian Gulf; a secondary route, running from Syrian Qatna through the oasis of Palmyra to the Euphrates, ended at Mari. The territory of Mari was probably never very extensive; this was also true of the cities farther north. Under Zimri-Lim, Mari controlled the Euphrates valley from the mouth of the Balikh south to about the modern town of Hit; the lands along the lower course of the Khabur were added to this. Terqa, thirty-six miles upriver from Mari, was independent under Ila-kabkabuhu, Shamshi-Adad's father, at the time of Yaḥdun-Lim. Under Zimri-Lim it was a possession of Mari, and his governor there, Kibri-Dagan, had a voluminous correspondence with the king and the palace at the capital.

The revenues from the traffic that passed through Mari made its rulers rich. In turn, they endowed their city with temples. The greatest monument to their wealth, however, is the palace of the Old Babylonian period, the largest palace of the time of which we know: over 260 courts and chambers, covering an area of about two and a half acres. The king of Yamḥad wrote a letter to Zimri-Lim that implies that the palace of Mari was no ordinary appurtenance of kings, but famed far and wide; it passes on a request from the king of Ugarit to visit the palace at Mari. Aside from its size, the splendid frescoes that decorated its walls must have made an extraordinary impression on the visitor. This palace housed the great archive that has proved so priceless to us, in terms of the light it sheds on Old Babylonian history and humanity. It is the largest archive known from the Old Babylonian period, but there must have been similar archives in many capitals; Mari was but one of the cities involved in the daily exchange of couriers and envoys, and everything written was deposited in an archive on principle.

The Mari palace archive records a world that extends to Crete in the west, Hattusas in Asia Minor on the northwest, "Gutium" on the east, Susa, Larsa and Tilmun to the south-

1. The great stone tower, part of the defenses of Neolithic Jericho, c. 7000 B.C.

2. Neolithic portrait head, modeled in plaster on a human skull, Jericho, c. 6800 B.C.

3-4. Male and female terracotta figurines, from Eridu and Ur, Ubaid culture

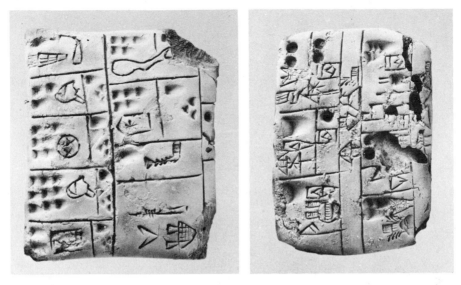

5-6. Clay tablets showing archaic Sumerian script, from Uruk IVa (Proto-literate period)

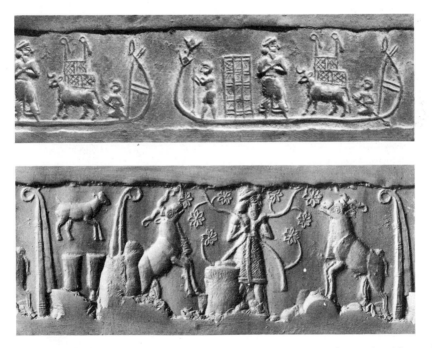

7-8. Early Sumerian cylinder-seal impressions: boat carrying cult objects and men, and "the man in the net skirt"

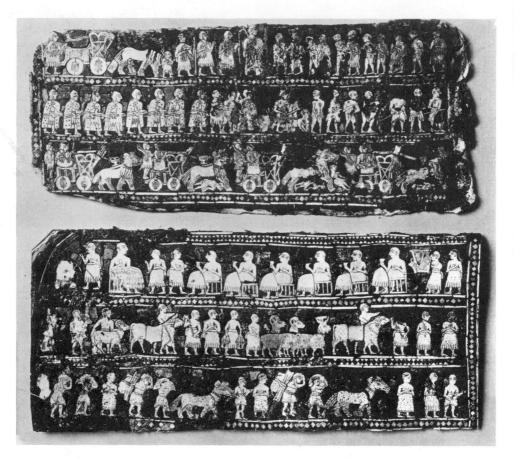

9. The so-called "standard of Ur" showing "war" (*above*) and "peace" (*below*), Early Dynastic period

10. The storm-god Imdugud, emblem of Ningursu, god of Lagash. Copper relief from a temple at Al Ubaid, Early Dynastic period

11. Phalanx, detail from the "Vulture Stele" of King Eanatum of Lagash, Early Dynastic period

12. Name and head in relief of Enanatum, *ensi* or governor of Lagash. Part of a votive plaque, Early Dynastic period

13. Stele of Ur-Nanshe of Lagash, Early Dynastic period. The king carries a basket as symbol of his prerogative as temple builder

14. "Worshiper" statues from Tell Asmar in the Diyala region, Early Dynastic period

15. Ebihil, superintendent of the Ishtar temple at Mari, Early Dynastic period

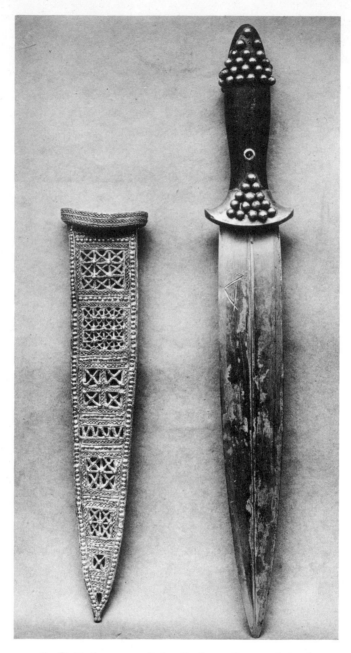

16. Gold dagger and sheath from the royal tombs
of Ur, Early Dynastic period

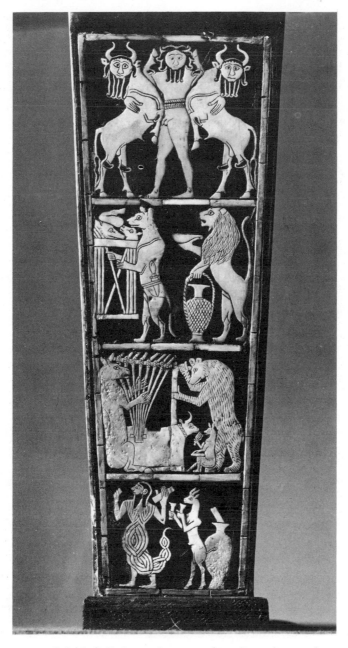

17. Inlaid shell decoration on a lyre from the royal
tombs at Ur, Early Dynastic period

18. Bull's head in gold and lapis lazuli on a lyre from the royal tombs of Ur, Early Dynastic period

19. Stele of Naram-Sin, King of Agade

20. Cylinder of Gudea of Lagash, the oldest surviving Sumerian text of any length

21. Gudea of Lagash

22. Nin-gal, consort of the Sumerian moon god

23. Ziqqurrat of Ur-Nammu in Ur, after restoration

24. Stele of Hammurabi, with his law code

25-26. Both sides of an ivory knife handle from Jebel el Arak, designed to hold a flint knife. Egyptian, Predynastic period

27. Two flint knives, Egyptian, Predynastic period

28. Painted pottery from Predynastic Egypt, showing ships, men and animals

29-30. The palette of King Nar-mer. The king wears the crown of Upper Egypt on one side and of Lower Egypt on the other

31. Stele of the "Serpent King." *Above* A falcon, symbol of Horus. *Below*
A palace with three towers. Egyptian, Thinite period

32. The Step Pyramid of King Djoser at Sakkara, with entrance gate (restored),
Third Dynasty

33. Wooden panel with portrait of the royal scribe, Hesire, from his tomb at Sakkara, Third Dynasty

34. The Great Pyramids of Gizeh, Fourth Dynasty

35. King Chephren, Fourth Dynasty

36. Egyptian scribe with his writing materials, from Sakkara, Fifth Dynasty

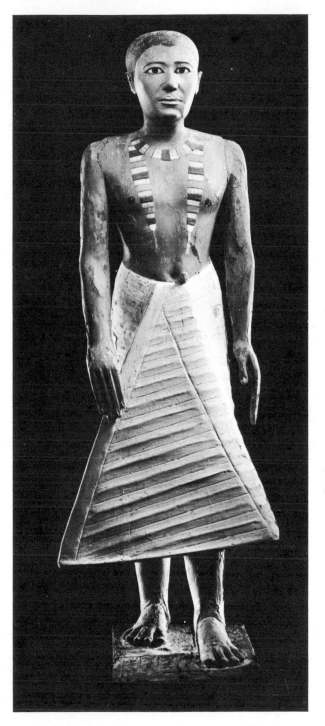

37. Painted wooden portrait statue of Methe-
thy, Sixth Dynasty

38. Scribes recording tax delinquencies. Tomb of Mereruka, Sakkara, Sixth Dynasty

39. Wooden tomb model of a granary. Tomb of Meket-Re, Thebes, Eleventh Dynasty

40. Tomb model of a boat used for fishing and fowling. Tomb of Meket-Re, Thebes, Eleventh Dynasty

41. A slaughterhouse, wooden tomb model, Eleventh Dynasty

42. Servants carrying offerings, wooden tomb model from tomb of Meket-Re,
Thebes, Eleventh Dynasty

43. King Mentuhotep III, stone relief, Twelfth Dynasty

44. Portrait head of King Sen-Wosret III, the Sesostris of legend, Twelfth Dynasty

45. Amenemhet III (son of Sen-Wosret
III), Twelfth Dynasty

46. Hieroglyphic inscription of King Amenemhet III, from the temple of Sobk in Croco-dilopolis, Twelfth Dynasty

47. Servant carrying ducks, wall painting from a tomb near Sakkara, Seventeenth Dynasty

east, and, to the southwest, to Ḥazor in Galilee. Some of these places appear as correspondents of the king, some as the sources of imported goods. Gifts from Crete are mentioned in a letter from Zimri-Lim to Hammurabi; the economic documents mention copper from Cyprus. The "Land of the Gutians" is represented by the queen of Nawar, of whom it is said that at one time she mustered 10,000 men as her contribution to a coalition. A Ḥurrian city, Shusharra, in the valley of the Dokan River near the modern Rania, finds mention in the archive. An embassy from Elam stops over at Mari on its way to Qatna; Elam appears frequently in the diplomatic correspondence, as an ally of Eshnunna. Hammurabi and Rim-Sin are the king of Mari's principal correspondents in Babylonia, and they are the subjects of many letters from others, reporting their activities. What is strange, however, is the entire absence of any reference to Egypt. At the time of the Mari archive, it would seem, the spheres of influence of Egypt and of the Mesopotamian states did not touch.

The language of the Mari letters is Akkadian—Old Babylonian, to be precise. Letters from Ḥurrian areas show barbarisms based on Ḥurrian forms, and in general the quality of the letters depends on the degree to which the sender, and the scribe who takes down his dictation, have mastered the language. Nevertheless, they are clear enough to be understood. Akkadian, then, is the diplomatic language, but its use by non-Semites is not limited to international correspondence: In Elam, legal and administrative documents are composed in Akkadian, as are the texts in the archives at Ḥurrian Shusharra.

The Mari correspondence covers every subject under the Mesopotamian sun: the internal affairs of the subkingdom (under Yasmaḫ-Adad) or independent state (under Zimri-Lim) of Mari, its relations with the nomadic tribes, agriculture, irrigation, the administration of the palace, court intrigues, legal problems, and international affairs. The arrival or departure of embassies is regularly mentioned, either accredited to Mari or stopping over on their way elsewhere.

Some states kept permanent "legations" at foreign courts, to keep themselves informed of their rulers' plans; by this means it was possible to react quickly to distant events and prepare in time against surprise attacks. Allies also kept each other informed of their plans, by personal letters between kings. The best way to gain information on the enemy's plans was to intercept his courier and read the tablets he carried. Diplomatic letters mention armies gathered by the coalitions that number in the tens of thousands. We have no reason to be skeptical of these figures, as we usually, and advisedly, are of all ancient statistics. These are first-hand sources, not subject to the creative imagination or tendentiousness of the ancient historiographer. Troop movements on so great a scale must have been an enormous burden on the economies of the states that mounted them, requiring a highly efficient administrative machine, and a highly productive agriculture and industry, to equip and feed so many men.

The forms of address employed in these letters have some interest for us. Rulers of equal status address each other as "brother"; "father" and "son" mark the relationship of overlord and vassal. Immediate subordinates of a king will call him "lord," themselves "slaves." The internal administrative correspondence is concise, objective in tone; the international correspondence tends to a more long-winded rhetoric, seeking to present even unwelcome information in as agreeable a form as the circumstances permit. It was impolite to employ direct address in the second person: The ruler will repeatedly be called "my lord" or "my brother," and he is referred to in the third person even in letters addressed to himself.

Syria in the eighteenth century, as we learn from the Mari archive, was, exactly like pre-Hammurabic Mesopotamia, a checkerboard of independent kingdoms and their vassal states. Yamḥad was the most powerful of these states, with its capital at Ḥalab (i.e. Aleppo); the prince of Alalaḫ on the Orontes was its vassal. Northeast of Yamḥad was Carchemish on the Euphrates, a thriving commercial center on the caravan route leading from Mesopotamia northward into the Taurus range

and on to the Anatolian plateau. King Aplaḫanda of Carchemish was vassal to Shamshi-Adad of Assur; his son Yatar-
ammi, who, unlike his father, had a Semitic, "Canaanite"
name, allied himself to Zimri-Lim of Mari. To the north of
Carchemish lay a series of Ḫurrian states, Urshu and Ḫasshum
among others. Ugarit on the Mediterranean, Qatna on the
Orontes plain near the modern Homs, and Byblos on the coast
were Semitic states. Qatna had political relations with Babylon,
Larsa, Eshnunna, Susa and Arrapḫa near Kirkuk. Syria, in
other words was fully involved in the international affairs of
Western Asia in the eighteenth century B.C.

In the Ur III period the Ḫurrians were still settled in the
territories east of the Tigris only; in the Old Babylonian period
they expanded westward, even crossing the Euphrates. Northern Mesopotamia presents a picture of mixed Semitic and
Ḫurrian elements, with the Ḫurrian side coming increasingly
to the fore. A third of the personal names found at Chagar
Bazar are Ḫurrian, and are therefore more numerous than
"Canaanite" names (Akkadians are in the majority). In an
area with a thoroughly mixed population, we must be cautious
in evaluating such statistics, but we must not by any means
underestimate the Ḫurrian percentage of the population of
northern Mesopotamia and northern Syria. There is already a
high percentage of Ḫurrian names in the Old Babylonian texts
of Alalaḫ, although the local dynasty is Amorite. By the fifteenth century, Alalaḫ was largely Ḫurrianized. Our knowledge of the Ḫurrians, however, is not limited to personal
names: At Mari six literary texts in Ḫurrian were found,
excerpts from ritual manuals. The Ḫurrians had adapted cuneiform to the writing of their own language as early as the end
of the Agade period. The Ḫurrian religion is further documented in, for example, a treaty concluded between Abba-El
of Yamḫad and Yarim-Lim of Alalaḫ, in which the Ḫurrian
sun-goddess Ḫepat is invoked. The Ḫurrian language is agglutinative; it is related to Urartian, which we meet in sources
of the ninth to the seventh centuries B.C. found in what was
later to be Armenia; no other link between Ḫurrian and the

other languages of the ancient Near East can be established.

From the last entries of the Mari archive to the beginning of the fifteenth century B.C., we have very few cuneiform sources that throw any light on the history of Syria and of the regions of northern Mesopotamia to the west of Assyria. The Hittite King Hattusilis I extinguished the feudal kingdom of Yamḫad and destroyed Alalaḫ. When, after the middle of the second millennium, our sources begin once more to speak freely of events in this area, they show us a completely changed conformation of the land. From the Mediterranean east to Nuzi everything is embraced in a single state, the Empire of Mitanni, in which an Indo-European upper class rules over a predominantly Hurrian population.[79]

Elam in the Old Babylonian Period

For the Early Dynastic period, the age of Agade and the Empire of Ur III, we have only sparse and scattered information on Elam and her neighbors; for the Old Babylonian period, we have sources in quantity. Royal inscriptions in Akkadian have come down to us, along with a quantity of legal and economic texts (more than 800 from Susa, and further tablets from the modern Malamir). Elam was a confederation, with three rulers of unequal rank: (1) the *sukkalmaḫ* as the supreme ruler, residing at Susa (under the kings of Ur III this title was that of the "grand vizier" of that empire); (2) the "*sukkal* of Elam and Simash," usually the younger brother of the reigning *sukkal-maḫ*; (3) the *sukkal* of Susa, usually the *sukkal-maḫ*'s son, acting as subking of the province of Susa. On the death of a *sukkal-maḫ* his brother, the *sukkal* of Elam and Simash, would succeed him on the throne. This fraternal succession accorded with the fratriarchal structure of the Elamite family.

The Dynasty of Simash (see p. 128), which ruled at Susa until the middle of the nineteenth century B.C., was superseded by a king named Eparti; he assumed the title of "King of

Anshan and Susa." We know nothing of his background or of his relation to the previous house. In a date formula written in Sumerian, his name is given with the determinative for "god"; this is the only known case of divinization among the kings of Elam. Eparti's successor, Shilḫak, ruled jointly with his sister, who exercised the functions of *sukkal* of Susa. She was revered as the ancestress of the following royal generations, who called themselves "sons of the sister of Shilḫak."

Elam often entered the game of coalition politics in Mesopotamia, usually as the ally of Eshnunna. We learn this from Hammurabi's date formulae, and again from the diplomatic correspondence at Mari. Her diplomatic relations reached as far as Syria; her influence on Mesopotamian power politics was not eliminated until the creation of Hammurabi's empire. And even then, according to historical records of the New Assyrian period, the Elamite Kutir-naḫḫunte I, a contemporary of Samsu-iluna, attacked Babylonia. To this day, we know nothing of this from contemporary sources, but the Assyrian king Asshurbanipal (668–626 B.C.) reports that he brought back to Uruk a statue of the goddess Nanaya (one of the forms of Ishtar) that the Elamites had carried off 1,635 years before. This number is unreliable, and the raid, if it occurred, may have taken place in the reign of Samsu-iluna.

Elam, however, never exerted a lasting influence on Mesopotamia. Quite the contrary, as we have pointed out again and again, the cultural debt ran the other way round. Between 2250 and 1250 B.C. we have only one authenticated inscription in the Elamite language. Otherwise everything is in Akkadian —contracts, administrative documents, royal inscriptions. Elamite texts in quantity do not appear before the end of the second millennium. Elam adopted the Akkadian language along with the cuneiform script, when her own "Proto-Elamite" script was dropped in favor of it, perhaps because Akkadian provided her rulers with an extensive, ready-made thesaurus of juridical and administrative terms. A general Akkadian influence is also to be seen in the adoption of Akkadian personal names. Legal forms at Susa generally correspond to Akkadian models, although they do show certain features of their own—sanctions for breach of contract, for example, or the regulation of inheritance, which reflect the custom of the country.

We cannot yet tell whether, and in what way, the migration of the Kassites affected Elam, those mountain barbarians who were to sweep over Babylonia and rule it for four centuries. The few Kassite personal names we find in Elam are probably, as in Babylonia before 1594, those of individual immigrants who have taken service as laborers, and not seized power as conquerors. At the end of the seventeenth century our sources at Susa run out, and the Old Elamite period in the history of Elam comes to a close.

Old Babylonian Society; Palace and Temple; the Code of Hammurabi

Our sources for the administration, law and social structure of the Empire of Hammurabi, or, for that matter, of any other Old Babylonian state in Mesopotamia, are as informative as those for the Empire of Ur III, but of an entirely different nature. From Ur III we have nearly 20,000 administrative documents, displaying for our amazement a highly centralized state machine, organized down to the most minute detail in a rigid bureaucratic structure, manned by an endless hierarchy of clerks and officials with, at the peak of the pyramid, an absolute and divinized king, one of whose main concerns is still providing for the temples of his gods. For the Old Babylonian period administrative documents are rare, compared with other, nonliterary records: private contracts, court protocols, accounting records and, above all, letters, partly palace correspondence, partly private correspondence, and all in the Akkadian language. The difference in the nature of the sources is by no means an accident of excavation; it is a result of, as well as a clue to, changes in the nature of Babylonian society. A large class of free persons has sprung up who are attached neither to the temple nor the palace, as well as a class of royal tenants, who hold land of the crown but are only loosely dependent on it. The private sector of the economy has now come to the fore, based on extensive ownership of agricultural land and on the employment of slave or hired labor. The accounting methods developed in Ur III are, as public documents show us, continued in the administration of the palace and its possessions, with the same meticulousness as before; but private persons, too, now employed them, where the size of an enterprise required written records of income and expenditure that could be reviewed at any time.

The system of using subordinate *ensi*'s in the local administration of the country, employed in the empires of Agade and Ur III, while still continued in the state of Isin down to, let us say, Lipit-eshtar, has been abandoned in the Old Babylonian period. The word *ensi*, or rather its Akkadian equivalent *isshiukkum*, now means an independent city prince (at Eshnunna, at Assur, and at Larsa during a six months' interregum preceding the conquest by Kazallu); from Hammurabi on, however, we find it applied to a certain class of feudal tenant. In other words, it has been devaluated. The *ensi* system had been rendered worthless by the division of the land into many states, which, if not city-states in the most literal sense, controlled only a few cities each, and those mostly rural towns. Local administration in these states therefore required nothing in the way of a provincial governor; the frequent conquests simply meant that the cities would be given new local chiefs. At the head of a city was a *rabianum* ("mayor"; as in romance languages the title is connected with the word "great," Akk. *rabum*), or a *ḫazannum* (roughly, "headman"). Both offices are documented in the Empire of Ur III, where they were subordinate to the *ensi*. The *shagin* (Akk. *shakkanakkum*) also reappears in the Old Babylonian period. There are also a number of new Akkadian titles for administrative officers. The royal title has been brought very low; in Babylonia (although not in the Diyala region), rulers of quite tiny territories lay claim to it. The Mari letters show that a "king" may even be vassal to another king.

The limitations on the authority of the highest officials probably varied, in accordance with the size of the state and the personality of its ruler. Sin-iddinam, installed by Hammurabi as governor of Larsa after his conquest of that city, often consults his king on questions of even minor importance, as we know from copies of his letters. Problems of irrigation or disputed land allotments waited on the king's reply; it is evident that the governor did not have the authority to make decisions on his own. We do not know whether this pertains to the nature of his office, or simply to the interest of this particular king in the details of the administration of his empire and his lively participation in every aspect of it. Next to skill in diplomacy, in the making and timely unmaking of alliances, and to military success, a ruler's administrative competence was decisive for the health and growth of his possessions. Shamshi-Adad of Assur is another example of a ruler of this kind (see p. 195), who made the welfare of his subjects his daily care. Hammurabi himself seems to have convinced his people of his passion for a just administration, for petitions and complaints of every kind were laid before the king directly, often initiating a strict investigation of the facts. Seeing to it that "the strong do not oppress the weak" is more than a literary commonplace, at least where Hammurabi and Shamshi-Adad are concerned.

Although there are now lands in private hands, the palace is still a great landowner. And it can still call up certain segments of the population for compulsory public service. The ruler still considers as his immediate responsibility the construction and repair of city walls, temples, irrigation works. Prisoners of war and palace slaves are of course employed on these works—the question is, who else? If the term *mushkenum* is correctly translated as "dependent tenant of the palace,"[80] this class probably provided one contingent. The *Code of Hammurabi* distinguishes between three classes in the population to whom its regulations apply: The *awilum* (the general meaning of the word is "man," and its social meaning is "gentleman") is a free citizen of the upper class; the *mushkenum* we have already encountered; the *wardum* is a slave. But the *Code* does not take into account, as Ammi-saduqa's edict

214

will (see pp. 225 ff.), the distinction between Akkadians and Amorites. We do not know what proportion of the population was made up of *mushkenum*. We do know that, whoever was held liable for compulsory labor, this liability was bounded by very precise rules: We have a letter to Hammurabi complaining that an individual has illegally been set to work; the king frees the writer and directs that a substitute be found who is unequivocally subject to this service.

We are not sure whether settled Amorites could be called up for compulsory labor as well as military service. One of the official posts mentioned in the sources (originally only at Babylon, but also in the south after the annexation of Larsa) is the *wakil amurrim*, "Overseer of the Amurrum." This officer was at first leader of the Amorite contingents in the army, in charge also of the fields allotted to individual Amorites as payment for military service; the title then becomes a military rank, whether the troops under its incumbent are Amorites or not. There are two categories of soldier, mentioned in the *Code of Hammurabi* and other documents of the time, who hold lands from the crown on military tenures, i.e. in return for service in war on "the King's campaign": *redum*, conventionally translated "gendarme," and *ba'irum*, literally "catcher." The military fiefs consisted of house, fields and garden. They were not private property, and were therefore not hereditary in law, but it was customary to allow a son to take up his deceased father's tenure, and the widow of a soldier killed in war could manage the fief for the benefit of her minor children, until one was sufficiently grown to fulfill the military duties that were the price of the land.

Also entirely changed, in the Old Babylonian social order, is the position of the temple. This change is visible in two ways. The palace now has authority to use and dispose of temple property, and the relation of citizen to temple is now placed on an individual basis. The identity of temple and state has entirely vanished; the temple is now only one of many institutions in the city or state. Beside it stands the palace, and the private properties and enterprises of the free middle class.

The temple and its priesthood now become closely involved with private interests and private rights.[81]

Encroachments by the palace on the possessions of the temple are, it is true, no novelty in Babylonia. Urukagina of Lagash denounced them in his reform texts, Ibbi-Sin of Ur had had to fall back on the temple treasures in order to alleviate his city's needs in a time of crisis. But the latter is an exception in the history of Ur III. The palace archive of Uruk in the nineteenth century, on the other hand, shows the ruler making use of temple property normally and not by necessity, partly to invest it in trade ventures, partly to furnish the needs of the palace. It is significant that a large inventory of the possessions of the Nanaya temple of Uruk was kept in the palace. Undoubtedly the reason for this was the inability of relatively small states such as Uruk to finance the royal budget from taxation and tribute alone, and from the profits of the lands belonging to the palace. An Old Babylonian omen does indeed denounce such encroachments, predicting that "the king will take property of the house of the gods to the palace; but Shamash will see it" (the sun god was the guardian of law and right); but this is an idealizing, moralizing view of recognized and common practice. As usual, the omen puts into a general formula the ordinary probabilities of the age.

We may not, of course, interpret this development as a downgrading of the temple to the status of a mere source of revenue. Down to the last ruler of the First Dynasty of Babylon, we observe donations to the temples by the kings. Also the temples continue to carry out their economic enterprises independently; they are under no obligation to render accounts to the palace. We have a considerable number of loan contracts, recording the borrowing of barley or silver "from Shamash" or "from Sin." There is also a "dividend of the sun god," i.e. the rate of interest set by the temple of Shamash. The temple functions as a kind of bank, in other words. It also functions as a charitable institution, issuing interest-free loans to the needy, and the *Code of Hammurabi* provides for prisoners-of-war who could not be ransomed by their city or by the palace, requiring the temple of their native city to buy their freedom.

The secularization of temple property has another aspect: Prebends, i.e. lands whose income is devoted to the support of certain priestly offices, are now in private hands as heritable property. From the beginning of the First Dynasty of Babylon on we have contracts of sale or donation of temple prebends by private persons; prebends are also mentioned in the division of inheritance. In Ur III the king or his *ensi* could grant temple prebends to private individuals as a source of income, but the lands did not thereby become their property. How the transition to outright ownership was made is difficult to reconstruct. Perhaps it developed as a customary right, from a renewal of the grant of a life interest in the land's income for one generation after another.

An example of the manner in which priestly service and private economic interests could become entangled is the position of the *naditum* priestesses[82] of Shamash at Sippar. These were women under an obligation of celibacy, without exception drawn from wealthy families. There are hundreds of documents that mention them, distributed over almost the entire period of the First Dynasty of Babylon. Nearly all of these tablets are loan contracts or contracts for the lease of agricultural land, in which the *naditum* appears as creditor or lessor. As there were always several dozen *naditum* at any one time, they must have played a significant role in the economic life of Old Babylonian Sippar. As moneylenders they are, as it were, the feminine counterpart of the Old Babylonian "merchant" (*tamkarum*), whose business activities also involved lending on a large scale.[83]

By far the most important written document that has come down to us from the Old Babylonian period is the *Code of Hammurabi*. While we have only copies made in the scribal schools of the codes of Ur-Nammu, Lipit-eshtar and Eshnunna, written on clay tablets, from other texts we know that legal promulgations, including codes, were first "published" on stone stelae. The original stele of the *Code of Hammurabi* was discovered in Susa, one of the many monuments removed by the Elamite King Shutur-naḫḫunte in the course of a raid on Babylonia about the beginning of the twelfth century B.C. and brought back to grace his capital. The publication of the *Code* in modern times has had a profound effect on the history of law and raised endless questions, many of which still lack a satisfactory answer. But the *Code of Hammurabi* is also our longest coherent text in the Old Babylonian language, and is therefore our standard for the "classical" language of that period. Like the Ur-Nammu and Lipit-eshtar codes, the *Code of Hammurabi* has a prologue and an epilogue, with a series of legal rules in between. The rules are couched in legal formulae, naturally, but the prologue and epilogue are written in an elaborate, sometimes archaizing style.

The *Code of Hammurabi* is divided, or rather its legal content is divided, into 282 "paragraphs." This division, and the designation "code," are not ancient but were imposed by the *Code*'s first modern editor. We do not find here a strict systematic structure, corresponding to that of modern codes. Nevertheless the *Code* does treat similar legal topics more or less together, and it is in this respect at least more systematic than the *Code of Eshnunna*.[83a] The *Code of Hammurabi* covers civil, criminal, and administrative law, of course without separating them distinctly, as we can hardly expect a work of the eighteenth century B.C. to conform to modern notions of the divisions of law. The summary that follows will not attempt to do so either. Another way in which Hammurabi's and the other codes differ from modern legal texts is that they do not try to cover all possible legal situations. The *Code of Hammurabi* ignores parricide, for example. A superficial comparison of the *Code* with our enormous store of Old Babylonian contracts and court documents is enough to establish the "incompleteness" of the *Code of Hammurabi*.

The following subjects, however, *are* treated in the *Code* (this list does not follow strictly the order of its paragraphs): slander, corruption of justice, theft of various sorts, receipt of stolen goods, looting, breaking and entering, murder, accidental homicide, bodily injury, and kidnapping. The legal situation of crown tenants is explored: liability for agricultural damage caused by negligence, damage to crops by grazing herds, unauthorized felling of palm trees. Commercial law refers largely to the relationship between the merchant and his traveling agent: embezzlement of trade goods, deposit, loans and interest. Regulations for "alewives," women keeping taverns, also find their place in the code. Slavery and redemption from slavery, debt enslavement, runaway slaves, purchase of slaves and claims of title to slaves, and suits for recovery of free status appear; hire of persons, animals or boats (with legal rates of hire), and responsibility for offenses of hired persons and for damage caused by goring oxen are covered. In the domain of family law: bride price, dowry, wife's property, principal wives and concubines, legal status of the latter's children, divorce, adoption, wet-nursing contracts, and regulation of inheritance. The legal status of certain priestesses is also treated.

The *Code of Eshnunna*, older by only a few decades, is less extensive by far (sixty paragraphs). It deals mainly with price fixing; with hire of persons, animals, boats and wagons; with trade partnerships and deposits; with breaking and entering, theft, illegal use of persons as collateral for loans, bride price, betrothal, marriage, divorce; with defloration of slave girls, runaway slaves, legal capacity of slaves to engage in business; with foster parentage; with bodily injury, goring oxen and biting dogs, and accidental death by collapse of walls.

The discussion of the purpose of the *Code of Hammurabi*, and of its role in the legal practice of the day, is apparently without end. Expressions such as "legal reform" and "codification" have been freely aired, without the possibility of justifying them by proof. Hammurabi himself, in the epilogue to the *Code*, describes it as *dinat misharim*, "laws of justice."[84] He also says, again in the epilogue: "Let any oppressed man who has a case go before the statue of myself, the King of Justice, read my inscribed stele and heed my precious words; let my stele clarify his case to him, so that he may see his rights."

By which the king makes perfectly clear what in his opinion the code is: It is a source of information for the subject seeking justice. But what, in turn, is the source of the *Code*? For this there is no clear answer. In one place we might suppose we are dealing with the fixing of customary law in written form, in another with the recording of outstanding precedents, and often we will assume that what we have are legal innovations, in other words legislation by the king. Theory, too, is involved, provision for possible legal contingencies by drawing analogies from those experienced in the past. The number of paragraphs that are foreshadowed in the Sumerian *Code of Lipit-eshtar* is rather small; if more of the missing sections of that code turn up, we may expect it to be larger. The fact that a copy of the *Code of Lipit-eshtar* was found at Kish may indicate, as we have pointed out, an influence on the compiler of the *Code of Hammurabi* in nearby Babylon. It would, however, be a notable error to suppose that the *Code of Hammurabi* was nothing but an outgrowth of the *Code of Lipit-eshtar*. For Hammurabi's code differs in several fundamental ways from its Sumerian predecessors. What is new is, for one thing, the extreme harshness of the punishments prescribed: frequent capital punishment, by execution with weapons, by drowning, by burning, by impaling, and frequent and ingenious mutilations. Another novelty is the principle of talion, retaliation in kind for bodily injury or accidental homicide. We may, perhaps, doubt that in actual practice everyone who "purchased or received on deposit, without witness and without a contract, silver or gold or a male slave or a female slave or an ox or a sheep or an ass or anything else from the hand of a relation of an *awilum* or a slave" was instantly regarded as a thief and put to death, as paragraph seven of the *Code* prescribes. We must also not assume that these innovations are exclusive with the *Code of Hammurabi*. As early as a century before the lawgiver's reign, we find contracts with a penalty clause that lays down corporal punishment for breach of contract. Violent penalty clauses and talion are a trait of Old Babylonian law that is clearly contrary to Sumerian practice, and the Sumerian tradition in the *Code of Lipit-eshtar*. We need have no cause to doubt the origin of these innovations. They are to be ascribed to the customs of the "Canaanites."

What effect did Hammurabi's code have on the legal practice of his day, and on that of the reigns of his successors? That is an extremely difficult question to answer. That it was universally followed, or that it was valid for any length of time, has been denied or doubted. We do have one contract from Ur, dated in the fifth year of Samsu-iluna, for the cultivation of land. The penalty clause provides that, in case of breach of contract, the cultivator shall be treated "according to the wording of the stele." The stele meant by this is probably Hammurabi's. Astonishingly enough, in the sea of tablets that we have for the Old Babylonian period after Hammurabi, amid all the contracts and court documents available for our inspection, there is not a single other certain case[85] of men employing, or appealing to, the "law" in Hammurabi's code.[86]

Whatever its legal validity, as a work of literature the *Code* was so admired that it was recopied in the scribal schools well into the first millennium. Several tablets containing excerpts from the *Code of Hammurabi* were found in the library of Asshurbanipal. Hammurabi was one of the few Mesopotamian kings who knew how to write his country's script: in his code, he left in words a memorial to his name as grand as any monument in Western Asia—and more enduring.

The Successors of Hammurabi and the Coming of the Kassites

In the reign of Samsu-iluna (1749–1712 B.C.), the empire acquired with infinite patience by his father, Hammurabi, was placed in jeopardy. Danger appeared in two quarters: the first, central and southern Babylonia, which broke into rebellion; the second, the eastern borderlands, where the Kassites began an invasion *en masse*. At Larsa and Ur, a man with the nostalgic name of Rim-Sin (II), probably a descendant of the house of Kudur-mabuk, set up a short-lived independent state. Samsu-iluna's eleventh and fourteenth years are named after the dismantling of the city walls of Ur and Uruk (year eleven) and of Isin (year fourteen); this tells us that Samsu-iluna had to crush the rebels by force. The king's twentieth year is named after a victory over Eshnunna. But, toward the end of the reign, documents from Nippur are dated after a King Ili-man. So far they are our only authenticated proof for the existence of a southern Babylonian dynasty that later tradition will call the Dynasty of the "Sealand." According to the *Babylonian Chronicle*, Samsu-iluna's successor Abi-eshuh fought against this Ili-man. Where this new king's capital was, we do not know. Central and southern Babylonia, then, were no longer permanent possessions of the kings of Babylon after Hammurabi, although Abi-eshuh regained temporary control of Ur, and Ammi-saduqa, the next-to-last king of the First Dynasty of Babylon, was to name Uruk and Kisurra on the list of territories given in his edict (see pp. 225 ff.).

More pregnant with consequences for the future was another event: the invasion, from the East, of a new barbarian people, the Kassites (Akk. *Kasshu*). We first hear of them in the date formula for the nineteenth year of Samsu-iluna, which we know only in an abbreviated form: "Year: the army of the Kassites." Probably a victory over the invaders is implied. In the twenty-fourth year of Samsu-iluna a fortress bearing the king's name was constructed, Dur-Samsu-iluna, in the Diyala region near the Diyala's confluence with the Tigris, at roughly the same latitude where Shu-Sin had built his wall against the Amorites. Samsu-iluna succeeded in beating back the attackers; up until the reign of Samsu-ditana, whenever we find Kassites in the Old Babylonian texts, they are laborers who have entered the country peacefully looking for work and sustenance.

As is always the case with migrants from the east, we know nothing about the place of origin of the Kassites, nor can we tell what route they traveled to arrive in Mesopotamia. It does seem probable that the name of the modern region Khuzistan, in Iran, can be traced back to the ethnic name "Kassite"; Greek authors name an Iranian mountain tribe *Kossaioi*, i.e. Cossaeans. From this it would appear that a part of the Kassite nation stayed behind in Iran. Whatever their origin, the Kassites did not reach the Iranian-Mesopotamian border area until the second millennium B.C.; in the Ur III period, they were nowhere near Mesopotamia—at least no Kassite names appear among the many names of persons hailing from Iran mentioned in the Ur III messenger texts. We have a New Assyrian copy of a long inscription of the Kassite King Agum II; its authenticity is still in doubt, but it does mention, for what it is worth, among the titles of the king "King of Alman and Padan." Alman, or Ḥalman, is the modern Iranian district of Holwan in the region of Sar-i-Pul on the pass route to Kermanshah. We may have here a hint at the migration route of the Kassites. They crossed the Zagros considerably farther south than the Ḥurrians, probably following the course of the Diyala in their descent to the Mesopotamian plains.

We have only the vaguest of ideas on the nature of the Kassite language. We know the names of persons, of horses and of a few Kassite gods; we can also identify some Kassite loan words in Akkadian. Scribes made some attempts to translate compositional elements of certain Kassite names into Akkadian. From this material we can elicit only a negative result: The language of the Kassites was non-Semitic, non-Indo-European, and had nothing to do with Sumerian, Elamite or Ḥurrian. On settling in Babylonia the Kassites adopted the Akkadian language, and, as far as we now know, made no attempt at any time to write their own language in cuneiform; in this they differed from the Ḥurrians, as we have seen. The consequences of their willingness to adapt was that the rule of the Kassites in Babylonia was never regarded as foreign oppression, as that of the Gutians had been in the past.

The defensive measures of Samsu-iluna and Abi-eshuḥ succeeded in forcing the Kassites into a temporary retreat toward the northwest. They settled in the Euphrates Valley north of the district of Suḥum, in the land of Ḥana that included Mari

223

and Terqa. From the period of Abi-eshuḫ's successors we have several contracts from Terqa bearing the date formulae of the kings of Ḫana. These kings have "Canaanite" names except for one, Kashtiliashu, whose name is Kassite. But no Kassites appear among parties or witnesses to the contracts. An Old Babylonian letter of the end of the First Dynasty of Babylon (the names of the sender and addressee are not preserved) reports an embassy from the ruler of Ḫalab (Aleppo) to Babylon that stopped over in "the houses of Agum." Agum's title is *bukashum*, meaning something along the lines of "duke."[87] In two other sources "houses" of the Kassites find mention; these are, perhaps, a kind of military camp.

Agum and Kashtiliashu are the names given for the second and third Kassite kings in the *Babylonian King List* and in the *Synchronistic Chronicle*, a work placing Babylonian and Assyrian kings in chronological relation to each other. Two questions are raised by this: Are the Agum and Kashtiliashu of the Old Babylonian documents the same as the Kassite kings of Babylon? If so, the later lists would, as in the case of the *Assyrian King List*, have inserted into the line of kings of Babylon ancestors who had never lived in the city. Or, if they are not identical, does the line of Kassite monarchs in Babylon, the first of whom was Gandash (or Gandish), begin only after the invasion of Mursilis the Hittite? Our inability to give concrete answers to these questions is one of the reasons for the "chronological dark ages" of the mid-second millennium, which make the whole previous chronology of Mesopotamian history an exercise in speculation.

Whoever their leader was at the time, the Kassites came to power in Babylonia as a result, direct or indirect, of the raid of King Mursilis on Babylon. A raid it was, the Hittites withdrawing to Anatolia on its conclusion, so that the event had no historical consequences as far as the relation between Babylonians and Hittites was concerned. The interesting question is whether Mursilis had come to an understanding with the Kassites before he descended on the plain. The Kassites in Ḫana were in a position to strike at his flank as he came down the Euphrates; did he buy their neutrality with concessions that led to their rule of Babylonia? The whole course of events is wrapped in darkness.

The final period of the First Dynasty of Babylon produced a legal document of the first importance, an edict of the king Ammi-saduqa (1646–1626 B.C.), issued in the first year of his reign. It contains, insofar as we can complete the gaps in the text, regulations on a variety of subjects, but all with a common end: remission of private debts, in silver or in barley, originating in actual loans (i.e. not sums owed as a result of other business transactions); remission of arrears in taxes owed by certain functionaries to the palace; waiver by the king of arrears in barley from the district of Suhum and of arrears in silver and barley owed by alewives in the countryside; waiver of alewives' claims to collect on small loans of beer and barley; reduction of rents on crown lands for the *redum* and *ba'irum* (see p. 215); redemption of members of debtors' families left, as pledges or otherwise, in the hands of creditors (the ruling did not apply to slaves); prohibition, on pain of death, of high officials' coercing holders of crown lands into harvest or other labor on the basis of prepaid wages.

A number of these regulations are presented with the formula "because the king has established justice in the land." The *Edict of Ammi-saduqa*, by showing us what the connotations of this phrase are, is the key document for our understanding of the many earlier royal edicts, Sumerian or Akkadian, that are mentioned in terms of the king's desire to "establish justice in the land" but whose actual contents are unknown to us. The king's intervention in the country's economy, annulling private debts and rescinding certain taxes (both are temporary and not permanent measures), has a twofold aim: to prevent the collapse of the economy under too great a weight of private indebtedness (the normal interest rate for barley was 33⅓ %, for silver 20%); and to prevent excessive accumulation of private wealth in too few hands. The royal codes, as we have seen, raise every kind of question as to their universality of application, their validity as operative law; the edicts, however, leave no doubt that they are binding on the people of the realm and enforceable in the courts. We find many references to the edicts in legal documents of the Old Babylonian period.

The *Edict of Ammi-saduqa* is of value to us in another manner. We can deduce, from the cities and districts mentioned in it, what territories the First Dynasty of Babylon ruled in the mid-seventeenth century B.C., toward the close of its allotted span. Babylon, Borsippa, Larsa, Uruk, Isin, Kisurra, and Malgium are the cities whose names are given; larger territories are Emutbal (=Yamutbal) and two other provinces, probably also east of the Tigris, plus the district of Suhum on the Euphrates. The date formulae of Babylon, in this last century of the dynasty, no longer refer, insofar as we have knowledge of them, to military campaigns. (An apparent, but unclear, exception is the date for the seventeenth year of Ammi-ditana.) We receive the impression of a period of peace and security. The Kassite danger seems to have been averted, the threat from the "Sealand" is a threat no longer. But, as all of our documents come from Sippar and its environs, this picture may be deceptive. For a proper knowledge of the history of Mesopotamia at the end of the Old Babylonian period, we shall have to await the discovery of new sources. And, above all, we shall have to find some means of illuminating the "dark ages" that lie between the year 1594 and the fifteenth century B.C.

Literature and Intellectual Endeavor in the Old Babylonian Period

What we have of Sumerian and Akkadian literature comes to us, in large part, from two great sources: the royal libraries of Assur and Nineveh (twelfth to seventh centuries B.C.) and the Babylonian scribal schools of the nineteenth, eighteenth and seventeenth centuries B.C. For Sumerian literature, the great majority of our texts, whether compositions of the period or copies of earlier texts, come from the Old Babylonian age.

We still have relatively few Sumerian works from the period before Ur III, from Ur III itself, and from the twentieth century. Most of our texts are therefore later copies, but the copies seem perfectly reliable. Our longest literary text before Ur III is the temple-building hymn of Gudea of Lagash. The very earliest texts that can be identified as literary are from the archives of Shuruppak (twenty-sixth century B.C.). Literary catalogues of the Old Babylonian period show us that we possess only a fraction of Sumerian literature, that much of it still awaits discovery. These catalogues list works by their first lines: "From the great above to the great below," for example, is the opening line, and therefore the Sumerian "title," of the myth we call, conventionally, *Inanna's Descent to the Nether World*.

This vast activity of copying and cataloguing, in the Old Babylonian period, was carried out by Akkadian scribes. The zeal they displayed in preserving the literature of a language not their own was a fruit of the symbiosis of the two peoples of Babylonia, the reciprocal exchange of influences between Sumerian and Akkadian that went back to the Early Dynastic period. The Akkadians took over a troop of deities from the Sumerian pantheon, or identified their own gods with the Sumerian immortals (Ishtar with Inanna, Adad with the weather-god Ishkur, Su'en or Sin with the moon-god Nanna, and so on). From this arose the common interest in Sumerian myths. Gilgamesh of Uruk became the national hero not only of the Sumerians, but of all the inhabitants of Babylonia. Indeed, his fascination was felt by Hurrians and Hittites, too, who adapted the Gilgamesh story in their own languages. Sumer, then, represented the common past of all Babylonians, but in addition to this the Sumerian language had all the prestige of the medium of a high and older culture. This the Akkadians acknowledged quite ungrudgingly. During the Old Babylonian period, written Akkadian was well established as the language of correspondence and increasingly established as the language of law and administration. The reason for this was simple—Sumerian had died out as a spoken language—and it was irreversible. And nevertheless, time and again, any number of

Akkadian kings attempted to compose their building and votive inscriptions in Sumerian. True, the language was less well written as time went on, its grammar, with its categories so foreign to the Semitic mind, less understood. From about 1850 B.C. on the quality of Sumerian texts declined, and the "modernization" of traditional texts by Akkadian scribes produced some curious vagaries. But the threat of the disappearance of Sumerian was keenly felt, and the attempt to preserve a proper understanding of it was energetically undertaken. A bilingual literature arose.[88] It began with Akkadian glosses of individual Sumerian words and ended in complete bilingual texts. In most cases Akkadian translations are interlinear; very occasionally they appear on the reverse of a tablet with Sumerian text. Aside from literature, a number of royal inscriptions of Hammurabi and Samsu-iluna are bilingual, although the Sumerian and Akkadian versions are on separate tablets. Date formulae, too, were issued in both languages in the period after Samsu-iluna (no earlier examples are documented); in actual practice, the Sumerian version was in general use, often in abbreviated form.

The greatest of the achievements of the Old Babylonian period along these lines was the Sumerian-Akkadian word list. The Sumerian word list is as old as the Sumerian script itself. It was a product of the scribal schools. Its purpose was, in part, educational, helping the student to master the hundreds of cuneiform signs and the thousands of combinations of them. But the word list is something more than a student's primer. The fully trained scribe would utilize the word list as a means to help him comprehend and order the world around him in terms of names, of concepts. Thus we find lists of animals, plants, and stones, or of names of gods, of classes of men, and so on. The bilingual list places a second column beside the first, giving the Akkadian equivalents of the Sumerian words. As long as cuneiform was written these lists continued to be copied. Let it be understood that we are not dealing here with genuine dictionaries. They lack any clear order; one term leads on to the next by mere association, often without any logical connection. The system, however, was so successful that it spread; after 1500 B.C., Sumerian-Akkadian-Hittite word lists were worked out, and we even have, from Ugarit, a quadri-lingual list for Sumerian, Akkadian, Hurrian and Ugaritic. Although many of the equivalents given in the bilingual and multilingual lists are simply incorrect, their value for the ancient student of Sumerian must have been high, and their value for the modern student of Sumerian continues undiminished.

A new, and Akkadian, literary genre, appearing for the first time in the Old Babylonian period, is the omen text. Its significance as a historical source has already been examined here (see pp. 186 ff.). Divination by animal viscera can be shown to have been a Sumerian practice, but the writing down of their appearance and of their interpretation is an Akkadian invention of the Old Babylonian age. As the "philology" of the age did not go beyond the word list, so the "science" of divination never went beyond the collection of individual omens to arrive at a general statement of principles, at the presentation of a system. Throughout Old Babylonian science, the universal statement, the abstraction from individual observations, is conspicuous by its absence. Naturally we may not for this reason condemn the intellectual achievement of the Old Babylonian period—reproach the Sumerians and Akkadians, as it were, for not having been Greek. They were what they were. Mathematics, for instance, they developed to an extraordinary degree, and yet they have no formulae at all. We see, if we read between the lines, that they have some knowledge of quadratic equations, of calculating with unknowns, of Euclid's theorem; and yet nowhere do they expressly formulate a single theorem.

The Sumerians had developed a rich variety of literary genres: epic and didactic poetry, disputation, elegy, hymn to the gods, to the divinized king, to the temple, the incantation and the anthology of proverbs, to name only the more important types. Side by side with this an Akkadian literature was born, grew and, in the Old Babylonian period, entered on its prime. The Empire of Agade had fostered the establishment of Akkadian as a written language. In the Old Babylonian period it became a literary language as well. And it produced works of literature that allowed it to stand beside Sumerian on equal terms of quality and depth. Many of the Sumerian genres were taken over—myths, epics, and hymns to the divinities, and the hymnlike prologue and epilogue to the legal codes; some were dropped (the hymn to the divinized king); some, as we have said, were invented (omen literature). But in dealing with the Akkadian debt to Sumerian literature, we must distinguish between texts based on the oral tradition of the Akkadians, adaptations from Sumerian models, and straight translations from the Sumerian. The best example of a new creation on a Sumerian model is the great Akkadian *Epic of Gilgamesh*. The Sumerians had a series of independent poems revolving around the demigod of Uruk; *Gilgamesh and Ḫuwawa* (the expedition to the Land of the Cedar Mountain, the slaying of the monster Ḫuwawa, the felling of the cedar sacred to Enlil); *Gilgamesh, Enkidu and the Nether World* (the king confronted with the fact of death); *Gilgamesh and the Bull of Heaven*; the warrior tale of *Gilgamesh and King Aka of Kish*. The Akkadians, in writing their own poems about Gilgamesh, centered them on a new conception, the theme of one man's search for eternal life. In the Old Babylonian period we still know only of individual parts of the cycle; the middle Babylonian period would weave them into the masterpiece that is the *Epic of Gilgamesh*.[89]

As with the political, so with the literary history of Babylonia: The century after Samsu-ditana of Babylon is totally obscure to us. Between the Old Babylonian literary tradition and the literature of the second half of the second millennium, the "dark ages" draw an impenetrable veil.

Prospect

Once that veil is lifted, once the "dark ages" come to an end, the view that meets our eyes, in the fifteenth and the following centuries, differs from that of the Old Babylonian period so greatly that we have to posit a series of revolutionary changes—changes, in the political and intellectual life of Babylonia, as profound at least as those caused by the arrival of the Amorites. The object of the next volume in this series will be to describe those changes. For the present, and as a last word, we should like to give one point final emphasis: The interplay of political forces over the entire Fertile Crescent, as we have seen it in operation through the letters of the Mari archive, is to determine the entire history of the second half of the second millennium. Babylonia, Elam, Assyria, the Ḫurrian states, the Hittite Empire—all play their part on a truly international stage. And, for the first time, and with immeasurable consequences, Egypt is drawn into the history of Western Asia. For the Early Dynastic period, the age of Agade, the Empire of Ur III and the Old Babylonian era, the historian is bound by a "Babylocentric" view. From now on, his vision expands as though he had reached a mountain peak, to take in an entire world—the world of the ancient Near East.

6

The Origins of Egypt

From the Lower Palaeolithic to the End of the Predynastic Age,
±8000–±3000 B.C.

When, at the end of the fourth or the beginning of the third
millennium B.C., Egypt presents us with her first written records, she already appears to be everything she will remain for
three millennia more. All of the constituents of her civilization
are already there. One can imagine, then, the importance to
the historian of the preceding period; it was in these prehistoric
centuries that the language, the script, the religion, the institutions and the art of Egypt were formed, and that the political
unity of the Nile valley was prepared.

Unfortunately its importance is more than matched by its
obscurity. We can barely trace the main outlines of the development of prehistoric Egypt. We do have two kinds of sources
that throw some light on the period toward its end: above all,
archaeological sources, the fruit of excavations in the valley of
the Nile, and also texts copied and collected by the Egyptians
themselves, at a point in time long after the events, at about
2300 B.C.

For the earlier stages of prehistory, we must rely on archaeology alone, and on the speculative inferences that can be
drawn from it.

In the light of this evidence, we are able to divide our study
of the origins of Egypt into three main periods: the late Palae-

olithic age and the Mesolithic age (± 8000–± 5000 B.C), the Neolithic age (± 5000–± 3800 B.C.), and the Predynastic period (± 3800–± 3000 B.C.).

Egypt in the Late Palaeolithic and the Mesolithic Ages

The very early prehistory of Egypt is treated elsewhere in this series (Vol. I, Chapter III); we shall pass over it briefly here. For it is possible that there was a hiatus in the occupation of the Nile valley by human beings, between the Palaeolithic age and the appearance of Neolithic man. It is clear that what marks the beginnings of civilization in Egypt is the human use of that valley for agriculture, and it is known that Neolithic tribesmen first began to put it to that use. With their primitive societies, then, begins the true history of Ancient Egypt: the rest is prologue.

In Egypt we are able to distinguish several phases of the Palaeolithic age, as they have been defined by the archaeology of Europe. Thus, on the high terraces left by the Nile on its former banks, lower and middle Palaeolithic levels can be recognized in Upper Egypt, particularly in the region around Thebes; in the Delta, notably at its southern angle in the thick, rich strata of the Abbassiyeh, near Cairo; and in the oases of the Western Desert, as at Khargeh. There have been found, in the Nile valley, Pre-Chellean, Chellean and Acheulian tools from the Lower Palaeolithic age, as well as Levalloisian (formerly designated as Mousterian) implements of the middle Palaeolithic. These different "industries" cover a fantastic period of time, as do their European counterparts, although the Egyptian remains of each kind may not be strictly contemporary with those of Europe.

The various levels of the upper Palaeolithic (the last phase of the Paleolithic age) are all attested in Egypt, in the upper valley, in the Fayum and in the southern Delta, both the older (Aterian and Sebilian) and the more recent levels (the

233

Aurignacian, Solutrean, and Magdalenian of Europe, which appear to correspond with Sebilian II and the Capsian in Egypt). The Helwan industry follows, extending into the beginnings of the Mesolithic age. At this point, the climate of the Nile valley begins a slow, inexorable trend toward desiccation. And the stoneworking techniques, until now identical with those of Europe, begin to diverge in Africa; Kom Ombo, in Upper Egypt, has furnished a fine series of Sebilian II implements that, like those of the industry of Helwan near Cairo, show definitely exotic features, although in the main they closely resemble the contemporary industries of Europe. In other words men in Egypt are beginning to evolve something like a culture of their own.

If this is indeed so, nearly three millennia separate the end of the upper Palaeolithic and the beginning of the Neolithic in Egypt. The Mesolithic age would occupy these 3,000 years, but its implements are little known in Egypt (deposits at Kom Ombo, Helwan and Wadi Angabiyeh). Possibly this poverty of Mesolithic sites is the result of archaeological chance. Recently, in fact, it has been discovered that men with a Mesolithic industry dwelt at the Second Cataract of the Nile around 7500 B.C. (O. H. Myers). If this particular region, so difficult of access, was inhabited, we have a very good chance of finding, some day, traces of their contemporaries who must have occupied the more approachable banks of the Lower Nile.

Most of what we know about Palaeolithic man in Egypt comes, to be sure, from his stone artifacts—fist axes, knives, scrapers, awls. These tools are exceptionally handsome, thanks to the fine quality of the flint from which they are made, the Egyptian silex that can be found in abundance in the limestone cliffs of the Libyan mountain chain. But traces of Palaeolithic camps have also been found and studied. "Kitchen middens" show us, for instance, that the then inhabitants of Egypt lived largely on shellfish, fish and game. If they did not yet cultivate the land, they did gather certain wild grains for food, cereals among them, for they possessed and used querns to grind them. They knew the use of the bow, for they left behind a great quantity of arrowheads. This was progress; a leap into the future was to follow.

Neolithic Egypt

With the Neolithic age, in the fifth millennium B.C., important changes take place in the valley of the Nile. Its climate, growing drier and drier with the passage of the centuries, nears its present state of almost total desiccation. Its inhabitants take up, as their means of sustenance, agriculture and stock-raising, without entirely giving over the activities of their ancestors—hunting and fishing implements continue to be found at their sites, alongside the sickle and the hoe. Finally, men discover pottery making and weaving. Here is the beginning of a development that, step by step, will lead Egypt from a society of tiny human clans on the shores of Lake Fayum, on the banks of the Nile and in the oases, leading an existence more hunted than hunting, to a great centralized monarchy capable of creating the pyramids. Certainly the "Neolithic revolution" in Egypt differs in no way from that which affected all humanity, but, once its results were achieved, around 4500 B.C., there is no break whatever in the evolution of Egyptian society from that point on. The first king of the Thinite dynasty was as much the descendant of the chieftains of these Neolithic tribes as the great Theban Pharaohs were of the Memphite kings.

To the Neolithic age, too, go back the first efforts to control the Nile for the benefit of man. These were continued through the entire Predynastic and Protodynastic period; surely it was this that turned the tribes of the late Mesolithic and early Neolithic ages into a united, well-ordered society. In point of fact, agriculture in the lands of the valley could be pursued only on two conditions: The marshlands on the river's banks must be dried up, which meant that the soil must be leveled so that water would drain freely from it at the end of the annual flood, rather than remain behind; and, this accomplished, the newly won land must be irrigated. For Egypt is situated in a

235

desert zone. The annual precipitation is quite close to zero, and agriculture can only exist by the utilization of the Nile floods. But the Nile, left to itself, irrigates only a niggardly portion of its valley. If these first farmers were able, and were forced, to limit themselves to these bands of soil close to the riverbed, their fields were soon unable to support an increased population. From this crisis begins, and develops more and more, the system of retaining dikes and barrages, basins and canals, which transformed Egypt into an immense, fertile oasis. This, too, seems to have had its first beginnings in the Neolithic age. It is thus impossible to overestimate the importance of this period for Egypt and its history.

The Neolithic culture of Egypt is known only from a very small number of archaeological sites, which are scattered very loosely over the entire length of the country, and are not even contemporary with each other. The oldest of these sites seem to be those on the ancient bank of the Fayum depression, to the west of Middle Egypt. There, several feet above the level of the present-day lake, a series of human settlements have been found that, archaeologically, make up the Fayum A culture, to distinguish it from Fayum B at a lower level, nearer the modern lakeshore.

We turn to the western part of the Delta to find another Neolithic culture, the Merimde-Beni-Salameh. At the southern point of the Delta, not far from Cairo and near Mesolithic Helwan, is the Neolithic site of El Omari. The Neolithic in Upper Egypt is known almost entirely from the great center at Deir Tasa, and by the smaller sites at Wadi-es-Sheikh, Tûkh and Armant-Gebelein (a little south of Luxor). Much farther to the south, near Khartoum, a whole series of Neolithic sites has been discovered. They belong to a culture called Shaheinab, after the only site that has been thoroughly excavated so far (A. J. Arkell).

From these few sites we have been able to establish a chronology of sorts, thanks to the technique of carbon-14 (radio-carbon) dating (see note 4). The resulting scheme is rough and sometimes questionable, but it is the best we can do for Neolithic Egypt so far. The Fayum A sites are the oldest and date from 4400 ±180 B.C. Merimde-Beni-Salameh seems to be slightly later. There follows Shaheinab (3490 ±380 B.C.), then El Omari (3300 ±230 B.C.), and the Tasa center a bit later than that. Fayum B begins where Neolithic occupation in Tasa ends, but most of its remains come from the Predynastic period.

Taking into account the uncertainty inherent in radio-carbon dating (a margin for error of 150 to 400 years on either side is always involved), the Neolithic age in Egypt can be thought to have lasted from 4500 to about 3500 B.C., i.e. about one millennium. This is confirmed by the thickness of silt deposits from this period (ten meters in Upper Egypt, thirty in the Delta). But, as the known sites are thinly scattered, both geographically and chronologically, we can gain only a schematic notion of the evolution of Egypt during these 1,000 years.

The human groups of Fayum A and those of Merimde-Beni-Salameh were engaged in agriculture and stock-raising in a major way. We have found sickles made of flint, their cutting edges polished by use. We have found silos dug into the ground, filled with winnowing baskets lined with clay, some of them still containing grains: here, in the earliest levels of the Egyptian Neolithic, men already knew wheat, barley, buck-wheat and flax, indicating a previous (i.e. pre-Neolithic) experience of agriculture. The remains of stock-raising are many: bones of cattle, goats, sheep and pigs as well as dogs have been found on the sites. Weaving was known, as we can see from the clay spindle whorls, and even shreds of woven cloth, found at Fayum and at Merimde-Beni-Salameh. Leather-working, too, has left its evidence behind, in the form of scraping tools, etc. Pottery is still crude, but its use is common.

Supplementing the fruits of agriculture are the old, Meso-lithic means of subsistence: Bone harpoon heads attest to fishing, flint arrowheads to hunting, both found in the huts of which these settlements were formed. These huts, dwelling places of the men and women who made and used the objects we have described, were round in shape or oval, sometimes partly sunk into the ground, and made of mud. They were grouped together in villages. At Merimde-Beni-Salameh, as in the villages of Fayum A, the dead were buried within the villages, as if the deceased were thought of as still taking part in the activities of the living groups; grain, left near their heads, shows a belief in some sort of life beyond the doors of death.

We would give much to be able to follow closely the progress of these tribesmen. But at this time the level of the Nile began to rise above its usual limits; silt bit by bit covered the lower lands of the valley, until thick alluvial layers now hide the Neolithic sites that must have been located on low hilltops near the river. It is rarely that any of them can be discovered. Those that can belong chiefly to the very end of the Neolithic age and clearly demonstrate that there are already, as there would be throughout prehistory, two centers of culture in Egypt, one in the south, the other in the north.

The majority of these late Neolithic sites are in Upper Egypt. Deir Tasa is the most characteristic of them, and the culture that is found in them is called Tasian. The north at about the same time shows what appears to be a different culture, for which we have only a single site, El Omari; this is often called the Helwan culture, after the modern village where the latest finds have been made. To avoid confusion with the Mesolithic culture of Helwan, we prefer the designation El Omari–Helwan.

The cultures of Tasa and of El Omari–Helwan show considerable changes from the state of things in early Neolithic Egypt. At Deir Tasa, the dead are no longer buried within the villages, but in necropolises at the edge of the desert. It is these burials that give us our best information on the life of the period. The body is laid at the bottom of an oval pit, in a crouched, embryonic position. Sometimes it is covered with an animal skin or mat and surrounded with the objects that the dead used in this world or might have use for in the next. It would seem, from this, that by this time there was not

238

only a belief in survival after death, but also well-established funerary rites. In the northern part of the country we find the same line of development, but slower progress along it. As at Merimde-Beni-Salameh, the men of El Omari–Helwan continue to bury their dead in the village itself, to begin with— even under the floors of their houses. But soon there are separate cemeteries, at some distance from the settlements. There the dead are laid on their left sides, in the flexed position, their heads to the south and faces to the west. Again, some idea of an afterworld and the existence of regular burial rites are indicated, and confirmed by the grave furnishings that have been found.

From the point of view of technology, the northern culture, El Omari–Helwan, seems to be ahead of the southern, at least on certain points. The stone utensils are better made; the flint spearheads (in the form of a laurel leaf) are real masterpieces. Artisans are trying out the techniques for making stone vessels, launching what was to be one of the typical industries of pharaonic Egypt; the south knows no such accomplishment. The herdsmen of the north are raising pigs, which do not appear in the upper valley. Perhaps, too, the houses are better grouped in the villages of the El Omari–Helwan culture, for the south sets up its dwellings on a more scattered plan.

In ceramics, however, the south unquestionably has the lead. There is a greater variety of forms in the north, but the south simply knows how to make better pottery. Already it produces black pots with white incrustations, and above all an admirable black-topped red ware, which will remain the characteristic pottery of the Predynastic age. The only thing that comes out of the north is uniformly black or red pottery.

While it is clear that the El Omari–Helwan culture is the direct descendant of early Neolithic Fayum and Merimde, it is not at all clear from what source the southern culture springs. It has, it would seem, much in common with the Neolithic Shaheinab culture, especially the handsome red "rippled ware" and the stone palettes used for grinding cosmetics. As Shaheinab is located far to the south, near Khartoum, we may wonder whether, around 3500 B.C., there was not one great culture covering the entire upper valley of the Nile, from Middle Egypt up to the Sixth Cataract and, perhaps, beyond.

Predynastic Egypt

The Predynastic age in Egypt covers a period of time often called the aeneolithic or chalcolithic era. These are borrowed terms, borrowed from European prehistory, and they tend, for Egypt at least, to give a false impression: namely, that the introduction of metal was a major break in history. There is no break, none whatever, between the Neolithic and aeneolithic ages in Egypt. To the contrary, there is a clear continuity in development. It is for this reason that we prefer to drop this borrowed plumage, in favor of the simpler "Predynastic."

We have seen that in both early and late Neolithic Egypt there are pronounced differences between north and south, and this continues in the Predynastic age. The southern Tasian culture is succeeded by the Badarian and the Amratian; the El Omari–Helwan, in the north, by three successive cultures, Fayum B, the Gerzean and the Meadian. The two areas developed along parallel lines, with some points of contact with each other; then, in the mid-Predynastic period, they blended together to give Egypt a single material civilization, prelude to a united nation.

We are still not well enough informed about Egypt in the Predynastic age. And we are unevenly informed: We have a better idea of what is taking place in the upper valley than we have for Lower Egypt. Anywhere south of the Fayum the desert plateau can easily be reached from the villages in the valley, and, being out of reach of the annual flood, it is an ideal location for cemeteries. In Lower Egypt, except for the edges and the southern point of the Delta, Predynastic sites and cemeteries are either buried under sizable deposits of silt, or covered by present-day villages. They therefore remain little known, and are likely to continue so.

We can divide the Predynastic period into four stages, which helps us to trace the evolution of Egypt in this obscure age: primitive, early, middle and late Predynastic.

In the south, the primitive Predynastic culture is that known as Badarian, from El Badari, the most important site (others were found at Hemamiyeh and in Nubia). In the north, it is Fayum B (sites at Demeh, Kasr Karum, Khasmet-ed-Dib). The Badarian culture is still so close to its Neolithic predecessors that it has been suggested that we are dealing, here, not with a new culture but with a local variant of Tasian. (This is proof enough that the introduction of metal brought no great break in the continuity of Egypt.)

Egyptians still lived in oval mud huts, but they were beginning to enjoy some degree of comfort—woven mats, leather cushions and even wooden beds were now at their disposal. Physically, the Badarians were quite close to the average Egyptian now living in the same area. The cult of the dead was still developing: The body is, as before, laid in an oval trench, but an animal skin is no longer sufficient protection for it; often a wooden partition separates it from the earth walls of its tomb. The usual objects and offerings of food are buried by its side. And, it would seem, there now appears that cult of animals that was to strike Greek travelers so strongly, three long millennia later on.

Metal was known, but nevertheless the greater part of the tools found are still made of the native flint. Copper is rare, and when it occurs it is wrought (i.e. simply hammered into shape) and never cast. Badarian man still knows how to weave; he grows and spins flax as did his Neolithic ancestors, although he continues to retain leather for all sorts of uses. The hides for this he acquires as much from the hunt as from the herd, for hunting is still much in vogue. Pottery is still the same as late Tasian ware: red with black tops, or a finely polished solid red.

Personal adornments now begin to appear in the archaeological record. Beads covered with a colored glaze are often found, the first sign of a characteristic Egyptian technique, the production of the vitrified enamel miscalled "faïence." These beads are entirely made of opaque glaze—in other words of *glass*, which Egypt can therefore justly claim to have invented. Cosmetic palettes, already known in the Neolithic age, are carved from now on out of schist, down into the first dynasties of the Egyptian monarchy.

Art is not limited to personal decoration, however. The Badarian artist knows how to carve ivory or mold clay into statuettes of women in a naturalistic style. He decorates with animal carvings the odd ivory combs, or the handles of perfume ladles, found in the tombs of his people.

When we speak, however, of the "Badarian culture," this is not to imply that we are dealing with an independent civilization, but rather with a stage in the origin and development of Egyptian civilization as a whole. Nothing would be further from the truth than to imagine that these cultures, which we call Tasian, Badarian and Amratian, are ways of life sufficient to themselves, receiving nothing from the past and leaving nothing for the future. On the contrary, they are but links in a continuous chain; each inherits a tradition established by its predecessors, to be enriched by itself and then passed on.

The Badarian culture covered a considerable part of Egypt. Its northern boundary is Middle Egypt, and its traces can be found, to the south, not only in Upper Egypt but in Nubia as well.

Meanwhile, to the north, in Lower Egypt, development continues along lines independent of the south in the primitive Predynastic period. Here we have a straightforward continuation of the northern Neolithic cultures. Its traces have been found on the shores of Lake Fayum: Fayum B is its designation, to distinguish it from the earlier culture near the same site.

The men of Fayum B, like the Badarians, continue to use flint more than metal for their tools. Their pottery shows greater variety of form and less technical skill in manufacture, as we have said. On the other hand, stonecutters continue the tradition begun by Merimde-Beni-Salameh, producing quite beautiful stone bowls and vases. It seems entirely likely that the Fayum B culture was that of the whole Delta as well, although no site has ever been found there to confirm it.

In both north and south, then, the cultures of the primitive Predynastic period are rather close to their Neolithic forerunners. The early Predynastic period presents quite another picture. Unfortunately, it is not a complete one. There are a good many sites in Upper and Middle Egypt, but none for Lower Egypt at all so far. At the present time, then, everything we know about the period refers to the culture called Amratian, after the site of El Amrah near Abydos, at the border between Upper and Middle Egypt.

In former years what we now call the Amratian culture was designated as Nagada I, or the first Predynastic culture, Nagada being the first site where its artifacts were identified. It was there that Flinders Petrie worked out the dating system known as the Sequence Dates (abbreviated S.D.), based on the evolution of pottery forms and of certain elements of pottery decoration. Thanks to this system Petrie was able to draw up a scheme of relative chronology, i.e. to decide which groups of tombs came before or after others. He left the S.D. categories one to thirty blank, to provide for the discovery of Predynastic cultures earlier than Nagada. Once Badarian was discovered, the major divisions of the relative chronology of the Predynastic period remained these:

S.D. 21–29: Badarian
S.D. 30–39: Amratian (Petrie's Nagada I)
S.D. 40–62: Middle Predynastic or Gerzean (=Nagada II)
S.D. 63–76: Late Predynastic or late Gerzean
S.D. 77–   : Beginning of the historic period

This purely relative, and therefore imperfect, chronology turned out to be of the greatest value when it was found possible to attach it, at a number of points, to the absolute (more or less) chronology provided by carbon-14 dating, and particularly when carbon-14 dating itself became more exact.

The Amratian culture is in direct line of continuity with

its predecessor, the Badarian: In some places, the lowest Amratian level has been found right on top of the highest Badarian. Again, there is no break. The same black-topped red ware is used by both cultures, but the Amartian also introduces innovations of its own: Along with monochrome or two-colored ware, decorated pottery makes its first appearance. Some pots are covered with geometric or naturalistic figures painted in dull white on a red or red-brown ground; others, more rare, are black, with an elaborate incised decoration filled in with white. The creativity of Egyptian artists in this period extended to the invention of new pottery shapes as well —vases in the form of animals, for example, or a cup to which the artist has given, perhaps humorously, a pair of human feet. There are, among the naturalistic scenes, a great many devoted to themes of hunting, particularly the hunt for the Behemoth of the Nile, the hippopotamus. For during the Amratian period the Egytians still depended for their food, to a large extent, on fishing and the hunt; the reclamation of the Nile valley by drainage and irrigation was still incomplete. Even classical Egypt would retain these hunting themes in its funerary art (especially that of the hippopotamus hunt), giving them a religious meaning. It is not impossible that they had a similar meaning for the Amratians, when they first appeared.

The ancient Egyptians used a green or gray eye make-up with a mineral base (malachite or galena), and the stone palettes that we have already seen in the Badarian culture were used to grind its ingredients together. These continue to be used in the Amratian period; but by the end of the next period, the palettes will bear a new and significant kind of decoration: the first, primitive hieroglyphic signs. For, from this and other indications, we infer that the first steps toward the hieroglyphic script may have been taken in the Amratian age. The typical weapon of the period, for example, is a mace with a head in the form of a truncated cone. Now this particular type of mace went out of use entirely after the Amratian period, yet it lives on as a phonetic sign in the later hieroglyphic script.

There is no change, however, in the continued use of flint more than metal, and the Amratian culture produced some beautiful, meticulously flaked stone knives. There is also an occasional obsidian object—and, as this volcanic glass is not to be found in Egypt, its presence there shows some sort of trade relations with distant lands, probably with the Mediterranean world (A. Lucas), possibly with the region to the south of the Upper Nile.

Egyptian art continued its evolution in this period. One class of works that appear now are the statuettes of bearded men wearing phallic sheaths; these are characteristics of the Libyans of historical times.

There are a number of sites where the Amratian culture appears: Nagada, Ballas, Huh, Abydos, Mahashna, Hemamiyeh, etc. These are centered around the middle part of Upper Egypt; therefore the Amratian culture covers less of the Egyptian ground than the Badarian had.

Regrettable in itself is the absence of evidence for this period from Lower Egypt, but the more so since there appears to have been some contact just now between north and south; in Amratian grave furnishings, for instance, we find certain objects typical of the north, such as stone vessels.

The Middle Predynastic Period (Gerzean)

After a century, perhaps less, the Amratian culture seems to have been absorbed into a new complex, a mixture of developments from the Amratian itself and of influences drawn from the north. At S.D. 40, then, begins the middle Predynastic period (Nagada II or second Predynastic culture, in the older terminology), which is nowadays being called the Gerzean culture after a site in Lower Egypt (Gerzeh) near the Fayum.

Here we are able once more to observe both north and south. What we know about the north, which is now to play an important role in the development of Predynastic Egypt, comes not from the Delta, whose remains are still inaccessible to us, but from the region around the Fayum and Memphis (the present-day Cairo). It is here that the Gerzean culture can be studied in its pure form; *a* Gerzean culture is later to spread over all Egypt (Late Gerzean), *the* Gerzean culture is represented by these northern sites. It is these we shall examine to begin with.

The Gerzean remains give us an unusual opportunity to watch funerary customs change before our eyes. Tombs slowly cease to be dug in oval form; they grow closer and closer to the rectangular (almost certainly following a change in the domestic architecture of the living), and they now consist of several chambers. The position of the dead changes too, the result of new religious beliefs, perhaps: The head is now laid toward the north, the face turned toward the east and no longer to the west.

The differences between Amratian and Gerzean are best seen in their pottery. Amratian pottery employs for the most part two ground colors, red and black, to which dull-white decoration will be added; Gerzean pottery is made with a more easily worked material, taken not from the Nile mud but from a marly clay that gives the ceramics of the period their characteristic hue: a light gray verging on buff. Decorations are naturalistic and not geometric, but very much different from those of the Amratians. They are drawn with a rather dark red ochre: highly stylized representations of mountains, ibexes, flamingoes, aloes, and, above all, boats—boats carrying at their high point a staff or "standard," which in turn is capped by the figure of an animal, an object or a plant. These figures could be related to what we know, later on, as the symbols of the Egyptian nomes or provinces. However stimulating to the mind this hypothesis might be—since it would trace back the political organization of Egypt to the Gerzean period— it is, unhappily, so far impossible to prove, or disprove, any link between the "standards" depicted on the Gerzean pottery and the nome symbols of later date.

Sometimes we also find Gerzean pottery covered with painted lines that imitate the surface grain of stone vessels. Stone vessels themselves are in this period remarkable both for their material and their form. Craftsmen are carving them out of the hardest stones available to them—breccia, basalt, diorite, serpentine, and so on. The typical weapon left by these people is a mace with a pear-shaped stone head; this, too, will figure in the hieroglyphic script.

So much for the differences between Amratian and Gerzean. The similarities are also to be noted: The two cultures use similar objects, cosmetic palettes in particular, and flint and bone implements are unchanged.

Jewelry, however, is now richer than ever before. For one thing, much more precious materials are employed—chalcedony, carnelian, turquoise, agate, lapis lazuli, copper and ivory. Gold appears more frequently, too—metallurgy in general is making progress; there are many more copper objects found in the tombs than had been buried before: harpoon heads, daggers, chisels especially, for it was metal chisels that made the production of hard-stone vessels possible. And they, too, account for the beginnings of stone sculpture at this time, which in turn throws light on the beginnings of Egyptian religion: It is difficult not to see, in the statuette of a falcon, Horus, the earliest of the known Egyptian gods; or in a cow's head, the first known representation of his consort, Hathor, the goddess of fertility and of love.

It is clear that the Gerzean culture was in contact with its neighbors. We have certain jars at Gerzeh of a style also found in Palestine; the lapis lazuli used must have come from abroad. Obsidian objects continue to point to foreign trade—we cannot be sure in which direction; a southern one is not altogether excluded.

The Late Predynastic Period (Late Gerzean, or Semainian)

While the Gerzean culture developed in the north, at the same time it was making its influence felt in the south, where we see the Amratian culture slowly disappear, to be replaced by a mixture of northern and southern traits, i.e. of Gerzean and Amratian. The Egyptians of the Upper Nile give up their two-colored pottery to adopt the more complex ceramics of their northern neighbors. This is a slow process, indicating that there was no sudden substitution of cultures. Infiltration and interchange seem better to describe what actually occurred, and we see this not only in pottery but also, for example, in weaponry, with the northern pear-shaped mace head replacing, slowly and gradually, the traditional truncated cone of Upper Egypt.

We have now reached the point where written sources, for the first time, can fill just a few of the gaps left by the archaeological record. Just a few, and these texts must be read with caution, for they were composed at a period very much later indeed than the events to which they refer. Nevertheless, they allow us to make some guesses as to the political condition of Egypt at the beginning of the late Gerzean period—as long as we remember they are guesses.

According to the texts, it would seem that at the very beginning of the late Predynastic, or perhaps already at the end of the middle Predynastic age, the most powerful town in the south was Ambos (Nubet, in Egyptian), near Nagada—that is, in the very heart of the Amratian culture as we know it from the archaeological record. The god of this place was Seth. This god (again according to the texts) found himself involved in a struggle against Horus, the falcon-god worshiped in the north at Behedet, which must have been located in the Delta— i.e., in the heart of the Gerzean culture. At the end of the Amratian period, then, Egypt is divided into two zones (just as archaeology tells us), the one dominated by Ombos in the south and its god, Seth, and the other in the north, where Horus rules from Behedet.

Now it has been proposed, on the basis of various scraps of information from the texts, that the war between Seth and Horus, between Ombos and Behedet, can be thought to have ended in a victory of the north; as a result of this the first unified Kingdom of Egypt would have come into being, with its capital at Heliopolis near Cairo. Translated into archaeological terms, this would correspond to the spread of Gerzean artifacts, pottery in particular, into formerly Amratian territory. But if this kingdom was established it was of short duration. The south would have regained its independence, and, having assimilated the culture of its northern enemy, would have turned on it with (northern-style) arms in its hands. We assume this, because precisely this struggle was to occupy the rest of the Predynastic period.

There now occurs a change in the leadership of these two kingdoms (or confederations, since that is all they may have been). The northern capital appears to have shifted to Buto, in the western Delta, the southern to El Kab. And at this point we detect the beginnings of the traditional pharaonic royalty: In the great age of Egyptian civilization the pharaohs still retained, among their titles, that of "The Two Goddesses" (i.e. the deities who then dominated Egypt, the cobra-goddess of Buto, Wadjyt, and the vulture-goddess Nekhabit of El Kab), of whom the Pharaohs thought themselves the legitimate heirs.

One later Egyptian monument would tell us much that we should like to know about this period, if only we had it entire— as it is, we have but five frustrating fragments of it. It is known as the *Palermo Stone* (after the largest fragment, now at the Palermo museum in Sicily) or the *Old Kingdom Annals*. On a tablet of black diorite are engraved the annals of the kings of Egypt. They were inscribed there under the Fifth Dynasty, i.e. about seven centuries after the founding of the united monarchy. Before the list of the rulers of unified Egypt come names marked with two series of human figures, the one wearing red crowns, the other wearing white crowns. In the classical age, these crowns symbolize Lower and Upper Egypt respectively. The compilers of the *Old Kingdom Annals*, then, knew, around 2500 B.C., the names of the rulers of the two kingdoms in the late Predynastic age. As ill luck would have it, the part of the monument that bore these names has been badly shattered: Of the names of the sovereigns of Lower Egypt, only seven have been preserved on a line that originally

249

must have recorded fifteen; for Upper Egypt, we have only five. But where did the annalists of the Fifth Dynasty get their information on the Predynastic kings? From an old oral tradition, perhaps; or, perhaps again, from a king list or annals older than their own. This could imply that writing was in existence from the beginning of the late Predynastic period on—which is not *a priori* out of the question.

In this late Predynastic period, Egypt, although politically divided, manifestly enjoys a unified culture, not only materially but also spiritually; the god Horus is worshiped on both sides of the frontier, and the kings of both north and south regard themselves as his "servants" or "followers" (*Shemsu Hor*).

There is hardly any change in material life between the middle and the late Predynastic ages, but there is progress in the arts and in technology. The human figure, previously a timid intruder, becomes a frequent artistic theme. Wall painting makes its first appearance at Hieraconpolis; the cosmetic palettes of schist are decorated from now on. The technique of relief engraving also appears, apparently developing out of the art of carving in ivory, already being attempted by the Badarians. The material culture of the late Predynastic is, then, fairly well known; but we know neither the duration nor the course of the war between north and south that overshadowed its history. Of its outcome, the victory of the south, we do know, from a series of documents that have reached us from the end of the late Predynastic age.

The End of the Late Predynastic Age and the Unification of Egypt (Pre-Thinite Period)

We have not yet been able to establish the chronology of the late Predynastic age. The period between its end and the beginning of historical times has been estimated to be 50 to 200 years. The only site for a contemporary culture in the north is Meadi, a little to the south of Cairo. The Meadian culture, to our surprise, differs noticeably from the late Predynastic, then continuing in the south. In particular the pottery no longer bears the typical marks of Gerzean ware. In fact, what we have is clearly a retrogression from the progress of the previous centuries.

It is difficult enough to fix that point in time by which Amratian and Gerzean elements had blended into the late Predynastic culture (ca. 3400 B.C.?); it is no easier to find a date for the end of the conflict between north and south. The southern victory is known only from a few monuments, all found in the south. These are historical scenes engraved on huge schist palettes or on oversized pear-shaped mace heads. Their size, and their discovery in temple ruins, shows that they are meant not for use but as gifts to the gods. It is impossible to date these objects with any precision. They must go back to the very last years of the late Predynastic period, i.e. the years just before the foundation of the First Thinite Dynasty, for which reason this is sometimes called the pre-Thinite period.

Both palettes and mace heads were found in the earliest temple at Hieraconpolis, which would indicate that the capital of the south, just before the unification, had been transferred there from nearby El Kab on the opposite bank of the Nile. Hieraconpolis (Nekhen in Egyptian) is known in classical texts as the place of origin of the "Souls of Nekhen," which are nothing other than the divinized kings of Upper Egypt, those of the north being called "Souls of Pê" (Pê=Buto). This last, by the way, would indicate that the northern capital remained at Buto. The name Hieraconpolis comes from the Greeks, *hierakon* being Greek for "falcon," i.e. Horus, the falcon-god of Nekhen.

There, in the temple of Nekhen, one of the most important documents found was a pear-shaped mace head, with carvings representing a king, wearing the crown of Upper Egypt, engaged in a foundation rite (breaking ground for a city, a canal, or something of the kind). Above this scene are ranged a series of gallows, as it were, topped by symbols representing the nomes, i.e. the provinces of his kingdom. From these gallows hang objects, sometimes birds (lapwings), sometimes bows. We therefore conclude that this mace head commemorates a victory of the nomes of the south over a coalition of Egyptians and foreigners, represented by the objects hanging abjectly from the gallows (bows are symbols for barbarians in later Egypt, and lapwings for a part of the indigenous population). The south had been led to victory by the king pictured on the mace head; we do not know how to pronounce his name, but it is *written* on the stone with a drawing of a scorpion.

The victory of King Scorpion, as we consequently call him, over his Egyptian enemies (who can be no one but northerners) is confirmed by another monument found at Hieraconpolis: a magnificent palette of schist on which a king, Nar-mer by name (for here at last we have readable hieroglyphic signs), wearing the crown of Upper Egypt on one side of the palette and of Lower Egypt on the other, is pictured striking northern enemies dead, then inspecting their decapitated corpses.

By following these two monuments, the scorpion mace head and the Nar-mer palette, it would seem simple to reconstruct the events: The next-to-the-last southern ruler of the Predynastic age, King Scorpion, began the conquest of the Kingdom of Buto, but did not complete it. His successor, Nar-mer, finished the job and assumed the double crown of north and south, marking the end of Egyptian prehistory.

A very recent discovery upsets this neat edifice. A. J. Arkell, while studying the objects from Hieraconpolis at London, found and published (*Antiquity*, 37 [1963], pp. 31–35) a fragment of a votive mace head that pictures King Scorpion wearing the crown of *Lower* Egypt, which means that the south's claim to, perhaps conquest of, Lower Egypt can no longer be attributed to Nar-mer alone. It may be, it is even probable, that the *permanent* conquest of the north could not be carried out in a single reign; we must remember that the *Palermo Stone* pictures, among its representations of northern and southern Predynastic kings, the occasional figure wearing the double crown of a united Egypt. Are Nar-mer and Scorpion *both* to be placed among these merely temporary unifiers of their country? There is one conclusion that fits all the facts: We must not attempt to fix a single date for the end of the Predynastic period, i.e. for the union of Egypt, for this surely took several generations to accomplish for all time.

The Origins of Egypt: Conclusion

To what other conclusions can we come?

From the end of the Upper Palaeolithic period, stoneworking in Egypt visibly departs from the line followed by contemporary Europeans. With the Mesolithic age (Helwan industry) there already seem to be two centers of culture in the valley of the Nile, the northern and the southern. This seems to be confirmed in the Neolithic age, and is undeniable fact by primitive Predynastic times. From that point on, the two areas develop in parallel until, in the middle Predynastic age, a single civilization involves all Egypt, which is politically divided, however, into two states. At the end of late Predynastic times the south carries the day and unifies the whole country under its rule. In barely 1,500 years, counting from the beginning of the Neolithic period, Egypt has thus gone forward from a society of primitive huntsmen, stripping wild grasses for food in their spare time, to a centralized monarchical state.

This speed, this rapidity of development, almost breakneck from the middle Predynastic on, has inspired several historians to "explain" the birth of civilization in Egypt by the arrival of outsiders in the valley of the Nile. Foreigners, at one point or another, must have brought into Egypt a superior technology and culture. I do not happen to believe in these explanations. I must, however, point out that this is a personal point of view, and that, as the evidence for the study of these early ages is entirely insufficient, theories that resort to invasions to explain the flowering of Egyptian civilization cannot be ruled out.

According to some of these, even Neolithic culture was imported into Egypt from Asia. In point of fact the Helwan industry of the Mesolithic age shows parallels to Natufian implements of Palestine; certain grains found at Mesolithic Egyptian sites come from Asia, as well as some of the domestic animals, especially the sheep. To this theory of an Asian invasion A. J. Arkell has opposed the idea of an African origin of the Egyptian Neolithic, and indeed Neolithic remains at Shaheinab in the Sudan can be compared to those at Fayum. We must simply admit that the Neolithic age in Egypt poses problems that we cannot resolve in the present state of our knowledge. For my part, I should wonder whether the mere geographical position of Egypt, at the crossroads of Asia and Africa, would not result in a mixed Neolithic culture, where Asian elements blend into an African complex. This would explain the appearance of grains and animals of eastern origin, side by side with artifacts influenced by African techniques.

The appearance of metal at the beginning of the Predynastic age sets us no new problems: The art of metallurgy certainly was not born in Egypt, where metal plays a secondary role, at least down to the middle and late Predynastic age. (Thereafter, a greater use of stone vessels and the introduction of sculpture make metal tools, if not indispensable, at least more convenient.) And in any case there is no metal ore to be found in the Nile valley proper. Where did the early Egyptians get their metals, then? The Sinai peninsula was long thought to be their only source of copper—recent finds in Sudanese Nubia show that the south must not be set aside *a priori*. An analysis of scraps of wood found on the sites has shown that the Lebanon furnished timber from the early Predynastic period on—for usable trees, too, are a rarity in Egypt. Obsidian, finally, first appears in the Amratian culture, and this too is absent in Egypt, as we have seen. The source of Egyptian obsidian has been located, but unfortunately in several different places: in the isles of Greece (notably Melos), or in Armenia (A. Lucas), in any case someplace in Europe or in Asia. But it has been forgotten that obsidian can also be found in Ethiopia, and, even closer to Egypt, in the Sudanese Darfur and in the Red Sea Hills. Here, too, then, a southern origin need not be excluded. The point is that where each of these importations has been taken as a sign of Asian influence, or of trade routes that might have carried Asian influence, there is nothing to prevent the evidence from applying to Africa as well.

Far more productive of imagined invasions are the middle and late Predynastic periods (Gerzean and late Gerzean), where their inventors require them to explain what they suppose to be the facts: the development of a culture, "hardly advanced beyond the Neolithic stage," into an ordered society organized in two centralized monarchies. These invasions, or *an* invasion, would have come from Asia, from Mesopotamia to be exact, either through Palestine and the Delta or through the Red Sea, via the Wadi Hammamat and Coptos. The Mesopotamian invaders, along with an advanced art and architecture, would have brought to Egypt the art of writing. This theory rests on four pieces of evidence: (1) In the Egyptian necropolises at the beginning of the Gerzean culture, among the ordinarily long-headed (dolichocephalic) skulls, one finds round-headed (brachycephalic) ones as well. The latter must be the remains of a new, conquering "dynastic race" (Derry). (2) The carved ivory handle of a Predynastic flint knife (Jebel el-Arak knife handle) reproduces objects (boats), scenes (facing animals) and persons (a turbaned, bearded figure) that are "typically Mesopotamian." (3) Buildings of sun-dried brick erected at the end of the late Predynastic period must have been inspired by contemporary Sumerian monuments, for they use the same principles of construction and the same decoration. (4) Finally, the appearance of writing in Egypt at the same time as the above can only be explained as an imitation of the already existing Sumerian script, for both systems are based on the same principles, and combine elements of the same type.

This is not the place to make a critical review of these scraps of evidence and the conclusions drawn from them; they are in any case of very unequal worth. But the one, the essential objection to these theories is that they do not give enough weight to the *continuity* of development of the Predynastic cultures. In the south, Tasian gives way to Badarian, which in turn gives way to Amratian, to Gerzean-Amratian and finally to late Gerzean, without a genuine break at any point in the line. What has been called the "Gerzean revolution" (which means, in fact, simply the sudden introduction of buff pottery with red decoration) makes no interruption in the internal development of the Amratian culture; and if it strikes us as revolutionary, this is probably because we know no northern sites for the period preceding it (i.e. contemporary with the southern Amratian), where evolutionary stages leading up to it might be observed. If we did, we might be able to state (what we are now in any event free to guess) that the decorations typical of Gerzean ware began in the north at the time when decorated pottery began in the south. Is it absolutely necessary to see in this the result of a foreign invasion? Particularly when the Meadian culture in the Delta, the best place geographically to retain traces of an irruption from the East, retains none. In reality, everything we know about this period will fit into a scheme where the flowering of Egyptian civilization is the result of a confrontation between northern Gerzean and southern Amratian, one supplying as much as the other to a common creation.

That there never was a violent invasion does not mean that Egypt lived in a closed corner. There are any number of proofs to the contrary: the importation of food, metal, obsidian, even of manufactured objects such as certain Palestinian ceramics, or of Mesopotamian cylinder seals from the Jemdet Nasr period (corresponding to the late Predynastic, perhaps). During the exchanges with distant peoples that this trade implies, ideas and techniques could have, and would have, entered and spread abroad in the valley of the Nile. For one thing, the climate was not yet as dry as it is today, in the greater part of the Predynastic age: The Eastern and Western Deserts were still habitable, and the presence of settlements there would have made a chain of cultural exchanges reaching Asia perfectly possible. Let us recall what has been pointed out before, in connection with the Neolithic age in Egypt: That country's very geographical situation, touching as it does both Asia and Africa, put it in a perfect position to profit from the inventions of both. In addition, Egypt's strong political organization, the result of the requirements of agriculture in her valley, made her capable of perfecting the discoveries of others, and of making a host of discoveries of her own. Finally, there is such a thing as the phenomenon of convergence; that the Sumerians knew writing a little before the Egyptians did—and even here the chronology is uncertain—is no sure proof that Egypt borrowed the principles of the art from them. On the contrary, the evidences we have noted for the early evolution of hieroglyphics (see p. 244) point to another conclusion: that writing was discovered independently by both.

At the close, then, of the late Predynastic epoch, King Scorpion's mace head and the Nar-mer palette show us Egypt already in possession of a workable script, and of a solid political organization. The permanent unification of the Nile valley marks the end of prehistoric times, and the beginning of the Ancient Egyptian *history* that will be our subject from now on.

7

Archaic Egypt

First and Second Thinite Dynasties

With Nar-mer's reign, the long formative period of Egyptian civilization came to an end. From now on Egypt had her language, her script, which was to remain precisely the same for 3,500 years, and her well-organized, centralized monarchy. In the next two centuries two dynasties successively occupied the Egyptian throne, both stemming from the south, from the town of Thinis near Abydos. They, and the period that they dominate, are therefore called Thinite. Their administrative capital was, however, soon to be Memphis, at the southern angle of the Delta, from which they could oversee both north and south, for the only political unity that Egypt as yet had was the person of her king, and it was rightly felt to be a precarious bond.

Sources and Chronology

From the beginning of the Thinite period our sources for Egyptian history become much more abundant than those we have had to work with up to now. Archaeology remains important, but literary sources complement it from this time forward. Certain temples maintain royal annals, where outstanding events of the king's reign are recorded year by year. Only one of these annals is known to us, the *Palermo Stone* (see pp. 249 ff.), but its existence suffices to establish that of the entire class. Scribes of later ages were able to use them to compile king lists, tables of dead sovereigns to whom a funerary cult was still offered, at certain sanctuaries and at certain times of year; the lists were painted or carved on the walls of those shrines. Presently known are the following lists: The *Karnak Table* numbers sixty-two pharaohs from the First Dynasty to Thutmose II in the Eighteenth; it was compiled around 1500 B.C. The *Abydos Table*, dating from ca. 1300 B.C., names seventy-six kings from the First to the Nineteenth Dynasty; the *Sakkara Table*, of ca. 1250 B.C., gives us forty-seven royal names, from the sixth king of the First Dynasty to Ramses II in the Nineteenth.

To these we can add the *Turin Papyrus*, which preserves a king list different from those inscribed on sanctuary walls. First of all it sets down, at the beginning, the dynasties of gods who were supposed to have ruled Egypt before the first human kings; then, too, it gives for each king the length of his reign in years, months and days. It originally included the name of every Egyptian king from the First Dynasty to the Nineteenth, under which last it was composed at some time between 1300 and 1200 B.C. It was found intact in a tomb at the beginning of the nineteenth century A.D., but was so mishandled by its first owner that it crumbled into numberless fragments, and we have never been able to rearrange them all in their proper place. There are therefore important gaps in the text that we do not know how to fill.

Sometimes, however, we can fill these, and gaps in the king lists, from the work of Manetho, an Egyptian priest who lived at Heliopolis in the third century B.C. At the request of Ptolemy II, he wrote a history of Egypt, in all probability making use of documents of the type of the *Palermo Stone* and the *Turin Papyrus*. This work, the *Aegyptiaca*, was unfortunately destroyed at the burning of the Library of Alexandria. It is only known to us by extracts made in early Christian chronological works, chiefly those of Julius Africanus and Eusebius, written in the third and fourth centuries A.D. Among these extracts, luckily, is Manetho's list of the kings of Egypt, giving the length of each reign, a list that he divides into the thirty-one dynasties that have been adopted as the framework for all modern versions of Egyptian history.

The result of all this is that we now have the names of all the kings of the First and Second Dynasties, and we can put them in chronological order. Archaeology has furnished us with inscriptions for each reign. The only problem is to match the names given by these later lists with those inscribed on the monuments of the time. For, beginning with the Thinite period, every Egyptian pharaoh had several names at once, which, taken together, were his official titulature. And, for reasons entirely unknown, the lists of the New Kingdom did not designate the pharaohs by the names they had used on their own monuments. Modern historians have therefore been obliged to play a very difficult matching game, the results of which are not always sure.

The names, then, are not certain, and neither for that matter is the chronology of the Egyptian kings. Absolute chronology presents definite problems. We have from Manetho a relative chronology, arrived at by adding up the lengths of reigns that he provides. This reckoning gives us a total of 253–252 years for the First Dynasty and 302–297 for the Second (the different sources that cite Manetho give varying figures for individual reigns, hence the discrepancy in the totals). This results in 555 or 549 years for the Thinite period as a whole. Now the *Palermo Stone*, in spite of its gaps, allows us to estimate about 450 years for the length of the Thinite period. This figure might be taken as preferable to Manetho's, being the earlier, but even 450 years has seemed to historians too long to fit into what we know of the overall chronology of Egypt; usually it is brought down to two centuries. To turn this relative chronology, uncertain as it is, into absolute dates is no easy task. The first careful attempt set the beginnings of the Thinite monarchy at 3200 B.C. (E. Meyer). For various reasons the present tendency is to bring this date down by at least two centuries. The first pharaoh would have begun to rule a united Egypt, then, at about 3000 B.C., or even, according to some

authors,. around 2850 (A. Scharff and A. Moortgat, 1950).
On the other hand it has been suggested that this lapse of time
is nowhere near long enough to account for known facts,
notably the total ruin of the royal tombs of the First Dynasty
even before the end of the Second (W. B. Emery, 1963). One
can see that there is nothing definite about the chronology of
the Thinite period.

Menes, and the Problem of the First Pharaoh

No more definite is our knowledge of the identity of the
founder of the First Dynasty, and therefore of the entire
Egyptian state. Manetho, the *Turin Papyrus* and the *Table of
Abydos* all agree, to be sure, that his name was Menes. But
there is not a single document of the period that bears anything we can reliably identify as this name. Until recently it
was supposed, on the basis of the scenes pictured on the Nar-
mer palette, that it was Nar-mer who first wore both crowns
and founded the united monarchy. But in this case we have
two names for him, one of which (Nar-mer) is attested on his
own monuments, the other (Menes) on lists at least 1,700
years younger than his time. This has been explained in various
ways: Like every pharaoh, the first one had several names,
Nar-mer and Menes being two of them, and they are one and
the same man (most recently, Grdseloff, 1944, and Gardiner,
1961); or, Nar-mer must be the predecessor of Menes, in
which case the latter would be identifiable with King Aha
(W. B. Emery, 1963); or, Nar-mer was indeed Menes, and
also took the name of Aha after his victory over the north
(J. Vandier, 1962).

All of this has been shaken by the discovery that King
Scorpion, too, wore the double crown of Upper and Lower
Egypt (see p. 252). Does that mean that King Scorpion was
Menes (A. J. Arkell)? This would force us to bring the First
Dynasty up to nine kings, where Manetho knows but eight,
i.e. it does not remove but adds a difficulty.

The problem can be attacked from another angle. Herodotus

(II, 99) and Manetho both report that the first pharaoh founded the city of Memphis as his capital. It has been proposed that this is precisely what King Scorpion is doing in the foundation rite pictured on his mace head (see p. 252), which would confirm his identification with Menes (A. J. Arkell). On the other hand it has been pointed out that the oldest architectural monument *in* Memphis, the necropolis at Sakkara, goes back to King Aha, which would tip the balance toward him (W. B. Emery).

The only thing that is clear about this problem is that it has no clear solution. All things taken into consideration, the identification of Nar-mer as Menes is still the best of the possibilities, but none of the others may lightly be disregarded.

If we do not know for certain who united Egypt's first ruler was, we are no more sure where he ruled it from. Manetho calls the first two dynasties "Thinite." We can take this in two ways: Either both ruling families came originally from the district of Abydos, or Thinis was their administrative capital. On the one hand, undoubtedly royal tombs have been found in a great necropolis of the Archaic age at Abydos; on the other, W. B. Emery has discovered at Sakkara, near Memphis, a series of magnificent tombs of the same period, beginning in the reign of King Aha. The ancient Egyptians invariably buried their kings near the residence from which they had ruled in life. This is the dilemma. If the royal tombs are those at Abydos, then the royal capital is nearby; but then what are those enormous tombs at Sakkara? The burial places of high officials, perhaps; but then that would mean that high officials received more magnificent burial than kings in Thinite Egypt. But if the royal tombs are really those at Sakkara, then the capital was at Memphis, and we do know that Memphis was extremely important at this time for *some* reason, as the rich private burials recently found at Sakkara and Helwan attest. But then what are those royal tombs doing at Abydos? The suggestion has been made that, since the king was king of Upper and of Lower Egypt at one and the same time, he required one tomb for each, i.e. he had to have a tomb in both of his kingdoms. One of these tombs, then, would be a symbolic one, an empty cenotaph. It ought to be easy to establish which, except that both the Sakkara and the Abydos burials were thoroughly and professionally looted at some point in the past 5,000 years. One significant find, however, was made in an Abydos tomb, namely a mummified arm, and as a great many royal stelae were discovered in that city, it might perhaps be taken as the real burial place of the kings, with their permanent capital nearby. But here too there is no clear solution, and the question must remain an open one. The only thing we know for certain, then, is that at the beginning of the First Dynasty Egypt was ruled by one king. Who? Where? For the time being, that is asking too much.

The First Dynasty

To help us reconstruct the history of the First Dynasty, we have Manetho's list with his occasional comments on the one hand, and on the other inscriptions found in the necropolises of Abydos and Sakkara, especially a series of little labels made of ivory and ebony. The latter, attached to grave offerings and furnishings, date the time at which these were deposited in the tomb by picturing the most striking event of the year. Thanks to these two types of sources, we can establish the succession of kings and form some idea of the events that marked their reigns.

These kings we shall name according to the names used on contemporary inscriptions, rather than those employed by Manetho and the king lists. They are, in order of succession:

1. Nar-mer (=Menes?)
2. Aha
3. Djer (or Khent)
4. Meryt-Neit (queen)
5. Wadjy (or Djet)
6. Udimu (or Den)
7. Adjib-Miebis
8. Semerkhet
9. Ka

Nar-mer (if that is who Menes really was) founded Memphis, but with the exception of a few objects found at Abydos everything connected with him comes from Hieraconpolis. According to Manetho, Menes reigned sixty-two years and was killed by a hippopotamus. Aha is much better known: There are many inscriptions for him, alluding to victories over Nubians, Libyans and perhaps northern Egyptians, which would indicate that the unification was not yet secure. From the same sources we hear of many religious festivals, and the foundation of a temple at Saïs, in the Delta, for the goddess Neith. According to Manetho, Menes' son reigned forty-seven years, and built the royal palace at Memphis, which may be confirmed by the monuments, contemporary with his reign, found at Sakkara. Aha is supposed to have been a physician and to have written medical books.

A tomb at Abydos has revealed many objects, notably a bracelet made of multicolored beads of turquoise, amethyst and lapis lazuli, as well as amulets bearing the name of *Djer* (or *Khent*). A label from Abydos with his name may refer to the heliacal rising of the Sothis star (see p. 000). If it does, then the solar calendar came into use under Djer, and by astronomical calculation the years 2785–2782 B.C. must have fallen in his reign. Manetho gives him a reign of thirty-one years. It has been thought that a queen, *Meryt-Neit*, succeeded Djer (W. B. Emery, 1963), but Manetho makes no mention of her, passing directly from Djer to *Wadjy* (or *Djet*), also known as the Serpent-King. Like Djer, he led expeditions outside Egypt, and we have found traces of his passage in the Arabian Desert (i.e. the Egyptian desert east of the Nile), on the route leading to the Red Sea. The sources quoting Manetho give him twenty-three, or forty-two, years on the throne (depending on which source one reads) and add that a great famine raged in Egypt in his time; also, that he built "the pyramids near Kokome," which has been identified with Sakkara.

Udimu, or *Den* (the reading "Udimu" is not certain), was his successor; he is known by a good many objects found in his tomb at Abydos. One of the most important of these is a label that portrays the king celebrating the rites of the Sed

festival, whose main object was to repeat the king's enthronement rites and thereby magically renew his powers, and his
efficacy for the land as a whole. Like his predecessors, Udimu
was active on the field of war: Another label shows him in the
act of striking eastern enemies. The *Palermo Stone* mentions
a general census in his reign, and many religious festivals. He
had reigned twenty years when *Adjib-Miebis* succeeded him.
The latter is assigned a twenty-six-year reign by Manetho. His
name was often erased from contemporary monuments, a sign
of political troubles in or after his reign. The *Palermo Stone*
mentions a military expedition against nomads, and the foundation of cities. It was probably his successor, *Semerkhet*, who
was responsible for the suppression of Adjib-Miebis' name,
which leads us to suspect Semerkhet as a usurper; this might
explain Manetho's enigmatic report: "In his reign, there were
many prodigies and a great calamity befell Egypt." He reigned
but eighteen years, and was followed by *Ka*, last king of the
dynasty. Ka treated Semerkhet's name as the latter had treated
Adjib's. We know nothing about his reign except that he, too,
celebrated the Sed festival.

With Ka, the First Dynasty, to which Manetho assigns two
and a half centuries, came to an end. Why? We do not know
at all, and cannot speculate.

The Second Dynasty

With the next dynasty, we are on somewhat firmer ground.
The capital of Egypt is now definitely to be located at Memphis: There are no more royal tombs at Abydos. This, at least,
tells us that Manetho's information on a change of dynasty
is not entirely imaginary. Again according to Manetho, there
are nine kings in the new royal line, but we have so far confirmation from contemporary monuments for only seven, possibly
eight; the list follows:

1. Hotepsekhemui
2. Nebre (or Raneb)

265

3. Nineter (or Neterimu)
4. Uneg
5. Senedj
6. Sekhemib-Peribsen
7. Khasekhem
8. Khasekhemui

Hotepsekhemui is the first of the line; his name, which means "the double power is pacified," seems to refer to troubles between south and north that were quieted by his accession to the throne. Unfortunately from his reign onward the "labels" employed under the First Dynasty go out of use in burials; they are replaced by the imprints of cylinder seals, which give us the names of officials and provide us with information about the royal administration, but leave us in the dark where political and religious events are concerned. As if that were not enough, the *Palermo Stone* is full of gaps for this period. We therefore have very little on which to base a history of the Second Dynasty, except for a knowledge of the order of succession of its first five kings. Manetho tells us that in the reign of Hotepsekhemui "a crevasse opened in the ground at Bubastis and many people died." After a reign of thirty-eight years, Hotepsekhemui was succeeded by *Nebre*, who ruled for thirty-nine. We learn from Manetho that in his reign "the Apis bull at Memphis, the Mnevis bull at Heliopolis and the goat of Mendes were worshiped as gods." In point of fact, these cults (at least that of Apis) went back to the beginning of the First Dynasty. *Nineter* (or *Neterimu*) succeeded Nebre; the *Palermo Stone* records, in his time, religious festivals and another census. He is assigned forty-seven years by Manetho, who notes that in this reign "it was decided that women could exercise the royal power." This is all very slender fare for the historian, but for the following reigns he must make do with even less: *Uneg*'s name is found only on some vases unearthed at the Step Pyramid of Sakkara; he reigned seventeen years, if, that is, he is to be identified with Manetho's Tlas; *Senedj*, Manetho's Sthenes, succeeded him and reigned (so Manetho) forty-one years.

In addition to this, our knowledge of the Second Dynasty includes indications of some sort of political, perhaps also religious, struggle. From the time before the land's unification, kings were under the patronage of the falcon-god Horus, to the point where one of the titles of the king was "*The Horus* Aha," or whatever the name might be. Upper Egypt, it appears, had forgotten the importance formerly assigned there to Seth, god of the southern capital of Ombos in the Amratian age. However, the successor of Senedj, after mounting the throne under the name of "*Horus* Sekhemib," later changed this to "*Seth* Peribsen." We are not at all sure what his reasons were: A revolt of the north against the south is the explanation often proposed. In fact, the "Seth Peribsen" seems to have abandoned Memphis as his capital—his burial, at least, took place at Abydos. After his reign, the national unity seems to have been reestablished quickly enough, and the dynasty ends with two kings, whose names so closely resemble each other that we may wonder whether they are not the same (i.e. variations of the name of one ruler). *Khasekhem* is the first; we know this name only by monuments found at Hieraconpolis. It would be he who restored unity to Egypt, by a conquest starting from the south. With this victory, Khasekhem may have taken the name of *Khasekhemui*. There is nothing sure about this, of course, and some authors prefer to see here two different kings.

So ends the Second Dynasty, in a manner still unintelligible to our eyes, and with it ends the Thinite period.

Archaic Egypt—Conclusions

The essential characteristics of Egyptian civilization were, as we have seen, already formed by the end of the late Predynastic period. The Thinite period was to refine and develop them. The national unity, for example, was as yet precarious and had to be made firm. To this end the Thinite kings appear to have employed two means: force, i.e. armed suppression of revolt, and marriage, i.e. diplomatic marriages, which we seem to be able to discern through the names of the queens of the First Dynasty—Her-Neit, Meryt-Neit, Neit-Hotep, all of these are formations with the name of the goddess Neith, patroness of the city of Saïs and of Lower Egypt in general. We seem to make out here a series of marriage alliances with powerful families of the north. In addition to which, the Horus Aha builds or rebuilds the temple of Neith, and Djer visits the sanctuaries of Buto and of Saïs; Memphis is made the administrative capital of all Egypt, and Memphis at that time was part of Lower Egypt (which then extended south to the Fayum). The last queen of the Thinite period is named Nimaat-Apis, and Apis is the most popular god of Memphis; the kings of the Second Dynasty are following the example of the First. There is a deliberate policy, then, of conciliation of Lower Egypt; linked with the application, when necessary, of force, it was an unquestionable success, for the unity of the Egyptian state survived the crisis of Peribsen's time, and was easily restored by the last of the Thinite kings.

For the most part, then, these kings enjoyed internal peace, and they took advantage of this to wage external war. Djer penetrates into Nubia, as far as the Second Cataract at least, where a relief celebrating a victory over southern tribes bears his name. Aha and Djer do battle with the nomads of the nearby deserts, gravitating toward the riches of the valley of the Nile, in particular with the Libyans. Udimu throws back the Bedouins of the East, and Adjib-Miebis recounts a victory over the *Iuntiu*—that is, over the nomads, generally speaking, of the southern, southeastern and eastern deserts. The pharaohs of the Second Dynasty are preoccupied by internal disorder, or so it seems, for they do not send any expeditions abroad—none, at least, of which we have any trace.

In the south, the rulers of the First Dynasty made sizable advances, but elsewhere Thinite military policy seems to have been defensive more than offensive. It was a matter of discouraging Bedouin greed, perhaps of punishing those, like the Libyans, who seem to have been allied with northern rebels.

Besides, relations with the outside world were not always war-like. Since Predynastic times Egypt had been exchanging goods with her neighbors, particularly with Palestine. With the Thinite period, these exchanges increase. Makers of jewelry and stone vessels utilize materials drawn from desert quarries that are often far to the east, west and south of the Nile valley. Wood is imported from the Syro-Palestinian coast: Nar-mer's name has been found there on a potsherd. In Egypt has been found pottery that must come from Syria and Palestine; Egyptian pottery appears in Palestine and Byblos (on the Phoenician coast). The name of Wadjy has been found in the desert east of the Nile, on the route that cuts through the coastal hills to link the river with the Red Sea; the name of Nebre appears on a trade route in the Western Desert. Ivory, ebony, perhaps obsidian come to Egypt from the far south, through the upper valley of the Nile.

Unity required a centralized monarchy, and therefore a centralized administration. This is slowly organized and elaborated throughout the Thinite period. Egypt is a union around the person of the king, and all officials are therefore directly responsible to him. Among the most important officers are those who supervise public works, especially the *adj-mer* (literally, "canal digger"), who is later to become the provincial governor or nomarch. It is not certain (but it is possible) that there is already a chief minister, a vizier. The chancellor, one of the highest officials in the land, is in charge of the biennial census, which is mainly concerned with cattle, it would seem, but also covers lands and movables to some degree. Taxation, in kind, is presumably based on this census. These goods move to the royal granaries, which form part of the national treasury and part of the national resources as well, as one of the monarchy's main duties is to provide against famine seasons (too low or too high Nile floods) and feed its subjects in time of dearth; for this reason, too, there is a water administration (*per mu*), charged no doubt with reporting to the king on the level of the Nile and the resulting prospects for the harvest. The Thinite system of administration, then, is based on the profits of the country's agriculture, which in turn depend on the efficient management of its irrigation works. That this system, aided by the spread of the art of writing, was successful is shown by the new towns that were founded, the vineyards that were established, the lands that were wrested for human use from the desert and the marshes. All of these were paid for by the abundant harvests of the valley of the Nile, administered as a single agricultural unit. Memphis was, and remained for many centuries to come, headquarters for the entire elaborate machine, which in the interest of the state ensured the prosperity of the people of all Egypt.

The monarchy itself now establishes its special ideology of kingship; enthronement ceremonies become fixed; the Sed festival, closely linked to the ideology of royal power, takes place more and more regularly; a court, with its titles and prerequisites, comes into being around the person of the king. Pharaoh, representative and descendant of the god Horus, himself tends to be spoken of as a god.

One of the results of this elaboration of the Thinite administration was the rapid development of the Egyptian script, the basis for which had already been established by the end of the late Gerzean period, as we can see in the Nar-mer palette. This script was fundamentally pictographic, i.e. each of its signs originally gave a pictorial representation of the thing it signified. This was, of course, the system employed in any number of ancient scripts. But, where in China and Mesopotamia, for example, the original pictographic characters soon developed into more abstract signs, Egypt remained faithful to her ancient system of writing down to the very end of antiquity.

Every object and every being that could possibly be pictured was employed as a pictographic sign in the Egyptian script. To write "dagger," "duck," "bed" and so on, the scribe had but to make a drawing of a dagger, a duck or a bed. (These are word-signs, where one sign stands for an entire word.) This principle remained in force down to the end of Egyptian civilization. As Egypt came into contact with new objects and new animals, new word-signs would appear in her script; the chariot, the horse, the sickle-sword made their way into hieroglyphic writing in this manner.

Up to a certain point, actions, too, could be conveyed by pictorial representations. To write the verb "to run" the scribe would draw a running man; "to swim" could be signified by a picture of a swimmer; "to fly" by a picture of a flying bird. Even the verb "to give" could be pictured in the form of an extended arm, "giving" a loaf of bread that lay on the palm of its hand.

But for all its ingenuity the pictographic system was quite incapable of conveying the sense of more abstract words, such as "remember," "love," "become," "die." To overcome this handicap Egyptian writing had to go beyond pictography pure and simple. It did so by employing two additional principles: homophony and ideography. The result, exceedingly frustrating to the first modern decipherers of hieroglyphics, was that certain signs were to be read as part of the text and others were not, the latter serving as footnotes, so to speak, to aid the reader in determining the meaning of the text before his eyes.

The principle of homophony was a simple one: In spoken Egyptian the word for "chessboard," for example, was pronounced *men*; the pictographic sign for a chessboard was therefore used by the scribes either to denote the object itself or to write, *phonetically*, every other word that was pronounced *men*, e.g. the word for "to be stable"; similarly the sign for "hoe," pronounced *mer*, could be used for the verb "to love," which was also pronounced *mer*. In such cases the original word-signs were now employed as sound-signs. But, as the number of homophones—words that, like "chessboard" and "to be stable," had the same pronunciation—was relatively small in the ancient Egyptian language, these innovations would have represented only a limited gain had the principle of homophony not been extended to complex words. To write, for instance, the word "to establish," pronounced *semen* and having no homophone in a word that could be drawn pictographically, the Egyptian scribe would employ two word-signs:

s(e), a folded piece of textile, and *men*, the chessboard; set side by side these signs would be read, phonetically, as sound-signs: *s(e)* + *men* = *semen*.

At this point the Egyptian script could transcribe phonetically any word in the language, no matter how complex: All that was needed was to find, for each sound, a word-sign that had approximately the same pronunciation. In the Thinite period this was the stage that the script had already attained, and for the most part this was the stage at which it remained, under the first two dynasties. But the system thus developed had two defects: It employed a very large number of signs, which sometimes left the reader in some confusion as to just which sound the scribe had meant to indicate, and, further, there was no way of telling whether a particular sign was being used as a word-sign or as a sound-sign.

The first of these difficulties the Egyptians solved by developing bit by bit a system of phonetic complements. Twenty-four of the word-signs in the script stood for words of one syllable having one consonant only. They are therefore called uniliteral signs, for they can be used as sound-signs indicating a single consonant each. And, as time went on, they were employed in just this way, to clarify the reading of polysyllabic word-signs. For example, the sign picturing a mat with a loaf of bread on it was to be read, phonetically, *hetep*, and to ensure that the reader understood this the scribe would write, immediately after the word, the uniliteral signs *t* and *p*; the reader was therefore guided step by step through the interpretation of the written text. It will be obvious that these twenty-four uniliteral signs were letters, and that herein lay the germ of the invention of an alphabet; the uniliteral signs expressed all the consonants current in the Egyptian language, and as for vowels, ancient Egyptian, like Hebrew and Arabic, made no use of them in its written form. There was therefore nothing that could not be written in uniliteral signs alone. A single step —the writing of texts exclusively in uniliteral signs, abandoning all others as superfluous—would have brought Egypt to an alphabetic script not unlike our own. This was a step the

272

ancient Egyptians never took; they kept their complicated system of writing to the last.

The second of the defects mentioned above, that of determining whether a particular character was to be read as a word-sign or a sound-sign, was overcome by a twofold refinement of the script: The scribes would place, after a word-sign, a vertical tick that would indicate to the reader that the character was indeed being used as a word-sign; further, the general meaning of words written with sound-signs would be indicated by adding to them ideographic signs, i.e. those representing no longer a thing or a sound but an abstract idea, in fact a category. With the help of these the reader could immediately determine to what class of things or notions his word belonged, and could therefore distinguish it from words of similar sound but different meaning. Verbs of motion, for example, had as their determinative (the name we give such signs) two legs in the act of walking; nouns denoting wooden objects were followed by the drawing of a tree branch; abstractions, by a drawing of a sealed papyrus roll.

With its word-signs, its sound-signs, its phonetic complements and determinatives, the Egyptian script is nothing if not complex in form. The astonishing thing, however, is that it is relatively simple to read. In spite of the thousands of possible signs he might encounter, the reader is always guided by the phonetic complements and by the determinatives in such a way that he need rarely hesitate over the meaning of a word.

To make clear the general organization of the Egyptian script we reproduce here an Egyptian sentence. The signs that are to be read as part of the actual text are marked with a dot, the rest are either phonetic complements or determinatives.

He says: he has come in peace, he has crossed the heavens,
it is Re.

The greatest inconvenience of the hieroglyphic system is the number of signs it requires. It is curious that the Egyptians were never moved to lighten their burden in this respect. Quite the contrary, the longer the script was in use the more its complement of signs was increased: Thinite and Old Kingdom texts are much more sparing in signs than those of the latest periods of ancient Egyptian history.

This applies to the hieroglyphic script properly so-called, i.e. to the formal script used for monumental inscriptions and for the older literary compositions; but it also applies to cursive adaptations of the script, such as hieratic (almost coeval with hieroglyphs) and demotic (first found in texts of the seventh century B.C.); in these scripts the forms of the hieroglyphic signs were simplified for rapid writing of documents and letters on papyrus, but the number of signs employed was in no way reduced.

The Thinite age is similarly an era of accomplishment in the aesthetic sphere. The arts of Predynastic Egypt are improved under the first two dynasties. This is the great age for the making of stone vessels, and in consequence decorated pottery slowly goes out of vogue. The very hardest stone is now raw material for sculpture, which produces the first masterpieces of Egyptian art—the stele of the Serpent-King (Wadjy), for example, and the statue of Khasekhem. Carved funerary stelae appear in the tombs. Metalworkers now know the art of making copper statues; lapidaries can make admirable jewelry, like that found in the tomb of King Djer. The techniques of architecture do not lag behind: Tombs become larger and larger, more and more complex. They are made entirely of sun-dried brick at the beginning of the First Dynasty, but first the corbel arch, then dressed stone and wood come increasingly into use.

We are very ill informed about Thinite religion. Only a single sanctuary from this period has been found, at Abydos. Still, the *Palermo Stone* and the inscriptions tell us that temples were built or rebuilt by the kings of the first two dynasties, and that the great gods were worshiped in them: Horus, Re,

Osiris, Isis, Min, Anubis, Neith, Sokaris. The cult of the sacred animals already plays an important role. Tombs are thought of as the permanent homes of the dead; food, furniture, every kind of object are buried there for their convenience. Servants, too, are buried around the tomb, and it has been thought that they were sacrificed at the death of the sovereign, to assure him of service through eternity (W. B. Emery). This practice, if ever it existed, ceased entirely toward the end of the First Dynasty. It appears, too, that there was already a belief in the survival of the soul after death in the heavens, in the company of the sun; there are boats buried near the tombs, perhaps to permit the dead to follow the bark of the sun-god on its daily round, or to travel about at will.

What, then, had the Thinite period accomplished by its end? The solid establishment of the pharaonic monarchy; the creation of a highly centralized, already hierarchical admin istration under the direction of the king; the efficient irrigation and therefore the prosperity of the Egyptian land; the refine- ment of techniques, in the arts and crafts, that were soon to produce works destined for the admiration of the ages.

8

Egypt Under the Old Kingdom

With the Third Dynasty begins what is known as the Old Kingdom of Egypt, which is to last from about 2700 to 2300 B.C.
The land of Egypt stretches from the First Cataract to the
Mediterranean, a single nation, though its rulers continue to
call themselves "Kings of Upper and Lower Egypt." Its institutions are solidly established, based on the idea of a monarchy
by divine right. Its agricultural territory has reached what was
to remain, for thousands of years, its full extent; the main lines
of its religious beliefs are already drawn. The techniques of
art, architecture, and writing are already fully worked out:
Egyptian civilization has been born.

Before proceeding with its history, we ought to consider
what the permanent factors of this civilization were, i.e. the
limitations imposed on it, and the challenges presented to it,
by nature.

Physical Background

Egyptian civilization owes much to the natural conditions
of the land. It existed only as a by-blow of the Nile, and the
history of this river had immense influence on the history of
those who were to settle on its banks. Toward the end of the
Tertiary period, some 12,000,000 years ago (to begin at the
beginning), the lower valley of the Nile sank beneath the sea,
becoming a gulf stretching into the far south of Egypt, to

the vicinity of El-Kab. During all of the Pliocene age (i.e. from about 12,000,000 to about 1,000,000 years ago), huge deposits of limestone filled up this gulf by degress; then a general uplifting of the land carried this limestone to levels 590 to 685 feet above that of the sea. The Nile had to cut its way anew through these deposits. A much larger river than it is today, it was able to carve out a wide valley, which was progressively filled up by its own silt until the volume of the river began to diminish. This silt or mud made the valley's fortune as an agricultural area; the limestone cliffs at its edge put an endless supply of flint, and of first-class building stone, into the hands of its human settlers.

Geographically, Egypt divides into two entirely different parts. The Delta is one, a very wide alluvial plain. From the Fayum southward, this narrows into the tight corridor of arable land pinched, so to speak, between two deserts, which is Upper Egypt. The Said, as it is called in modern times, is poorer and dryer than the Delta; the only link between the two is the Nile.

Since Herodotus it has been a commonplace to speak of Egypt as "the gift of the Nile," but to do so is to speak the simple truth. The Egyptian climate is almost bone-dry. Annual precipitation is nearly nil. If not for the Nile, Egypt would be a desert like the Sahara or the interior of Arabia, for it is situated at the same latitude. And, if the river did not behave in a manner peculiar to itself, only the land directly bordering on its waters could yield up food for man. For what makes Egypt eternally rich is not so much the Nile as its yearly floods, which bring her the water and the mud without which she would starve.

The flooding of the Nile is a highly complicated matter. The main element involved is the monsoon rains that, in spring, break against the Ethiopian mountains, slowly flooding the eastern tributaries of the Nile, the Blue Nile and the Atbara. From the beginning of August to the end of October, Egypt is covered by these waters. Her lands drink up their humidity and receive the silt torn from the volcanic hillsides and pla-

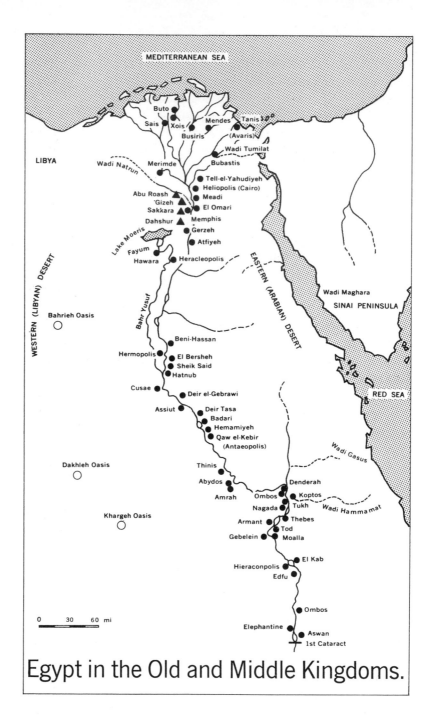

Egypt in the Old and Middle Kingdoms.

teaus of Abyssinia. But if the flood is beneficial to Egypt, it can also be catastrophic: The rise of the Nile is sudden, sharp; left to itself, the towering current would uproot everything in its path. And, most important of all, the flood is entirely undependable; true, it arrives every year, but hardly three times out of ten does it deliver the amount of water proper for cultivation—the other seven, it brings either too little or too much.

The origin of Egyptian civilization, then, is to be dated at the point where man mastered the flood. He used several means. First of all he raised dikes along the river's banks, to keep it within bounds. Then a complex system of canals and retaining walls was built, to bring the flood under human control. The Nile, from now on forced to pass through one basin after another from Aswan to the Delta, had the violence of its current broken and left its waters behind, to moisten the fields and deposit the silt suspended in them, until such time as men saw fit to release them. Finally, by a careful planing-down of the valley floor, and the cutting of a network of irrigation canals, bit by bit the Egyptians succeeded in bringing water to lands normally beyond the reach of the flood. The Nile and its flood may be miracles of nature, but Egypt was the creation of man.

To bring about this extraordinary result, a rigorous organization of the available human resources was required. This more than anything else explains the speed with which Egyptian civilization was developed. The importance given, in Thinite administration, to the cutting of canals and the supervision of waters (see p. 269), shows that is was in this period that the organization of the country was completed.

Further, to make up for the unpredictability of the Nile's gifts, systematic provision was made for reserves to be laid up in the years of good floods, to be shared out in times of bad ones. The "royal treasury" is essentially a granary; there is one in every province. Good administration consists of keeping dikes and canals in optimum condition and keeping granaries full. These were necessities of life in the Nile valley and must have contributed heavily to the formation of a centralized, authoritarian regime and to the development of an effective administration.

Natural conditions, then, require the presence of a centralized authority; geographical ones tend toward its dismemberment. Egypt is thirty-five times longer than it is wide. Wherever it might set itself up, the central power would always be far from the little administrative headquarters that are strung out along the whole length of the Nile, in little pockets of arable land. There is thus always a temptation for these provincial capitals to set up tiny independent principalities, whenever the royal power is weakened or whenever it makes the mistake of giving them too much freedom of action. The history of Egypt consequently alternates between periods of strong centralization (Old Kingdom, Middle Kingdom, New Kingdom) and periods of disunity (First and Second Intermediate Periods). These last are, of course, also ages of famine and social disturbance, for the maintenance of the system of river control was so imperative that the slightest weakening of the central power, which kept the whole elaborate mechanism in tune, brought on economic collapse. This, in its turn, made for the eventual, and popular, restoration of central control.

Chronology

To the annual flooding of the Nile the Egyptians owed not only their prosperity, but also their possession of the best calendar of all the peoples of the ancient world. Originally, as the needs of agriculture required, their year was divided into three seasons: *Akhet*, during which the fields were covered by the waters of the inundation; *Peret*, covering the sowing, growth and maturation of the crops; and *Shemu*, which saw their harvesting and storage.

The year, then, begins with the flood, and for long the New Year was dated by the beginning of the Nile's rise. Eventually the Egyptians observed that this phenomenon coincided with the appearance on the horizon of the star Sothis (Egyptian *Sepedet*), our Sirius, just before sunrise. This heliacal rising of Sothis must have seemed to them the very cause of the flood; they dated their New Year by it from then on. The Egyptian year was now divided into three seasons lasting four months, each with thirty days, for a total of 360, to which they added five supplementary days (which the Greeks called *epagomenal*). The result is a 365-day solar year, far superior to those based on the phases of the moon, but not yet perfect. The true solar year runs about 365¼ days, so that every four years the official Egyptian year moved a day behind the astronomical year, every 120 years a month, every five centuries over four months; only after 1,460 years would the calendar and the seasons be back in step. This last stretch of time is called a Sothiac period. The Egyptians, of course, were not slow to realize that the real planting season was occurring in the middle of the official harvest season, for example, and they made note of it: So the third-century-A.D. Latin author Censorinus preserves the memory of a coincidence of the Egyptian New Year with the heliacal rising of Sothis in 139 A.D. This has allowed modern astronomers to calculate that the same coincidence would have occurred in 2773 B.C. and in 1317 B.C. Now we have hieroglyphic inscriptions that report the heliacal rising of Sothis at various times: the twenty-eighth day of the third month of the season *Shemu*, under Thutmose III; the ninth day of the same month in the year nine of Amenhotep I; the sixteenth day of the fourth month of *Peret* in the year seven of Sesostris III. This means that we can fix solidly three base dates in Egyptian chronology: the seventh year of Sesostris III fell in 1877 B.C., plus or minus two years; the ninth year of Amenhotep I fell in 1536 B.C.; and one of the years of Thutmose III's reign coincides with 1469 B.C.

Working forward and backward from these dates, by using the length of reigns given by Manetho and the *Turin Papyrus*, and the year numbers of the monuments (for, as we have just seen, the Egyptians numbered the years of each king's reign and used these as chronological guideposts), we have been able to fix a chronology of the sovereigns of Egypt that, while not faultless, nevertheless satisfies our needs. There is, however, something lacking: We have no Sothiac date for any of the reigns before that of Sesostris III, which means that the chronology for all the preceding ages is a bit unsure. But we do know that the adoption of this calendar must have taken place at the beginning of a Sothiac period, which means either in 2773 or 4233. It was for long believed that the date must have been 4233; carbon-14 dating has shown us that this fell right in the middle of Egypt's Neolithic period. We therefore now consider that the solar calendar was put into effect about 2773. Possibly this date falls in the reign of Djer, but it is just as likely that it falls in that of Djoser, first king of the Third Dynasty, with whom begins the history of the Old Kingdom.

The Third Dynasty

Why Manetho chose to begin his Third Dynasty after the death of Khasekhemui, we do not know. One thing only is clear: Djoser (also written Zoser), whose figure dominates the history of the whole dynasty, was related to Khasekhemui through his mother, Nimaat-Apis, who was the earlier king's wife. It has been suggested that this queen was a secondary wife of the king; the principal wife, perhaps, had borne only daughters, or no children at all, so that the son of a queen of the second rank had to succeed to the throne.

The history of this Third Dynasty, then, begins with an enigma, and it continues to supply us with them as it unfolds. Neither the number nor the order of succession of its kings is particularly well established. It was believed for some time that Djoser, as a son of Khasekhemui, must have been the new dynasty's first king. Recent finds have made it clear that his reign was preceded by that of the Horus *Sanakht*, in all probability his brother. Of this Sanakht we know precisely nothing, except that his funerary monument may have served as the starting point for the Step Pyramid associated with the next king.

The name of this successor, *Djoser*, is attested only on later monuments. Under the Third Dynasty, the pharaohs continue to use a special "Horus-name" on their monuments; as a result the only name found in the Step Pyramid is that of *Neterykhet*, and it is only from graffiti of the New Kingdom, and inscriptions of still later times, that we know that Neterykhet and Djoser are the same monarch.

The outstanding fact of Djoser's reign was the construction of the great architectural ensemble that we call the Step Pyramid. This rose at the edge of the desert, at Sakkara, a little to the south of the later Great Pyramids. The whole was the work of Imhotep, architect, physician, priest, magician and minister to Djoser. It is the first complete stone construction that Egyptian civilization has left us, and it won Imhotep such renown that he was later made a god. The Greeks were to identify him with Asclepius, their god of medicine, and worship him under the name of Imouthes.

The Step Pyramid proper, six levels rising to 206 feet and dominating the plateau and the valley, is but part of the great complex planned and constructed by Imhotep. Part of this ensemble, at least, the funerary temple, has been thought to be a copy in stone of the brick royal palace Djoser had built at Memphis. The pyramid proper, in its present state, is the result of a long series of modifications in plan made as construction progressed. It began as a simple mastaba (perhaps Sanakht's tomb)—that is, a long rectangular construction with sloping sides, of the type of the royal and private tombs of the first two dynasties. It grew, in the architect's mind and in execution, into a great six-storied tower. Its massive masonry covers a network of underground chambers and corridors, carved out of living rock and comprising no less than eleven tombs, which are believed to have been destined for Djoser's family. At the pyramid's northern face a temple was raised where funerary cult was to be offered the dead king; there, a life-sized statue of Djoser himself was found by modern excavators.

But it is to the south of the pyramid that the most remarkable constructions are to be found. An enormous rectangular court is flanked to the south and east by chapels and side chambers, among which two great pavilions seem to symbolize the kingdoms of north and south, and thirteen smaller buildings housed, perhaps, the gods of various nomes. It is believed that this court and its buildings were provided for the celebration of the Sed festival.

The Sakkara complex is surrounded by an immense enclosure wall, with modular recesses and buttresses, which surrounds an area more than 650 yards long by more than 325 yards wide, and imitates, in dressed stone, the regularly recessed facades of the tombs and palaces of the Thinite age. This is one of the characteristics of the Step Pyramid complex: the scrupulous imitation in stone of an architecture of brick and wood. The gates of the sanctuaries, for example, are of carefully worked stone set in a half-opened position and carved with bolts, hinges, panels, beams, bars all faithfully copied, in fine white limestone, from their wooden originals. Imhotep uses columns for the first time, but does not dare to leave them freestanding; they are still engaged in the walls. The stone column in the form of a giant bundle of papyrus reeds makes its first appearance, and, finally, the first fluted column. In the underground chambers (some of which are covered in decorated blue enamel tiles, or limestone panels carved in delicate relief), several *thousand* plates and vessels of alabaster, schist, porphyry, breccia, quartz, rock crystal and serpentine (among other things) have been found. On some are carved the names of kings of the First and Second Dynasties.

The recent discovery of an unfinished step pyramid has given us the name of Djoser's successor, *Sekhemkhet*. He may have reigned only six years, which would explain the fact that his pyramid, standing near Djoser's, remained unfinished. There are 132 storerooms under it, and, in the tomb chamber, a sarcophagus, carved out of a single piece of alabaster, unfortunately empty.

The finding of Sekhemkhet's step pyramid has enabled us, by comparison, to attribute to the Third Dynasty another step pyramid, also unfinished, that of Zawiyet el-Aryan, south of Gizeh. Its date is uncertain. It seems likely, however, to come from the reign of Khaba, which would give us enough evidence to establish the order of succession of the kings of the Third Dynasty, as follows:

1. Horus Sanakht (perhaps the Nebka of the *Westcar Papyrus*)
2. Horus Neterykhet = Djoser, builder of the Step Pyramid
3. Horus Sekhemkhet = Djoser-Teti (?), builder of the unfinished pyramid of Sakkara
4. Horus Khaba, builder of the unfinished pyramid of Sawiyet el-Aryan
5. Horus X, perhaps the Nebkare of the Sakkara king list (Černy, 1958)
6. Horus Huni, builder of the step pyramid of Meidum

Khaba is attested only by a few stone cups inscribed with his name. He must have reigned only a few months; his successor would be *Nebkare*, of whom we know only that his reign was the next-to-last of the dynasty. The last king, *Huni*, known from a scrap of granite found at Elephantine, is thought to have begun the pyramid at Meidum, completed by Snefru, first king of the Fourth Dynasty.

It can be seen that the Third Dynasty's history is an obscure one. Only six of its kings are known with any certainty; Manetho lists nine, giving them a total of 214 years on the throne. But the discovery of Sekhemkhet's name on his pyramid was totally unexpected; excavation may yet present us with more surprises.

Three of these kings' names—Sanakht, Djoser, and Sekhemkhet—have been found in the Wadi Maghara, which means that to this period belong the first Egyptian military expeditions to the Sinai peninsula, no doubt for the purpose of bringing back turquoise. Huni is thought to have fortified Elephantine; on the basis of a very much later document, from the Ptolemaic age in fact, Djoser is believed to have annexed to Egypt the southern territory lying between Aswan and Takompso (Kasr Ibrim), all of Lower Nubia in a word. This is as it may be. Indisputable is the fact that the Step Pyramid complex at Sakkara is still our best basis for judging the achievement of the Third Dynasty. It shows us the importance of religious rites in the enthronement of the king; it shows us Egyptian art in full enjoyment of its capabilities. It shows us the fantastic wealth of the kingdom: 30,000 vases in the underground chambers attest to it. So, indeed, do the tombs that private persons are now able to construct, such as that of Hesire, Djoser's contemporary, whose wood panels, carved in relief, are among the masterworks of Egyptian art. But all of the achievements of the Third Dynasty can be summed up in one: It prepared the way for what some have considered to be, and with good reason, the high point of Egyptian civilization; it prepared the way for the Pyramid Age.

The Fourth Dynasty

No monument erected by the hand of man is better or more universally known than the Great Pyramids at Gizeh; and yet their builders are obscure to us. The number and, even more, the order of succession of the Fourth Dynasty kings is not entirely clear. Manetho gives us the order of the first four pharaohs: Snefru, Cheops, Chephren, Mycerinus. But older sources, such as the *Turin Papyrus*, slip Dedefre or Radjedef between Cheops and Chephren, and either one or two kings between Chephren and Mycerinus. After Mycerinus, Manetho lists four pharaohs, while the *Turin Papyrus* offers only two. The same disagreement applies to the length of reigns: Manetho reports sixty-three years each for Cheops and Mycerinus, but the *Turin Papyrus* gives them twenty-three and eighteen years respectively. Archaeological sources have so far proved of little help here.

We do have private monuments that throw light on Egyptian

daily life under the Fourth Dynasty—our first information on the subject—but the royal monuments tell us hardly anything, the Great Pyramids particularly having furnished us with hardly a word on the men who raised them. Still, had the Fourth Dynasty left us literally nothing but the perfection of its sculpture and its architecture, it would nevertheless merit a place among the golden ages of human history.

Our outline for the history of the dynasty is the order of the pharaohs, insofar as we have been able to establish it from the monuments:

1. Snefru (twenty-four years, according to the *Turin Papyrus*)
2. Cheops = Khufu (twenty-three years, according to the *Turin Papyrus*)
3. Dedefre = Radjedef: eight years
4. Chephren = Khaefre: length of reign unknown
5. Mycerinus = Menkaure: eighteen years
6. Shepsekaf (omitted from the *Turin Papyrus*)

In the absence of reliable documents, we cannot fix the dates for each reign; the dynasty as a whole controlled Egypt between ca. 2700 and ca. 2500 B.C.

Snefru. As is often the case with Manetho's dynasties, there is no evident break between the Third and the Fourth that might explain the change. Snefru was probably a son of Huni. But, as son by a secondary wife (Meresankh), he appears to have strengthened his claim to the succession by marrying, while his father was still alive, his half sister Hetepheres, Huni's heiress in the direct line. This was to happen often in Egyptian history.

Snefru's reign, thanks to the *Palermo Stone*, is the best known in the dynasty. He led his troops into Nubia, returning with 7,000 prisoners and 200,000 head of cattle; if these figures are correct, he must have struck far into the Sudan. He turned next against the Libyans, overcoming them and bringing back 11,000 men, 131,000 animals. Reliefs at Wadi Maghara show us that he sent several expeditions into Sinai.

The *Palermo Stone* records a very great number of temples, palaces and fortresses raised by Snefru in every part of Egypt; this would explain why he sent expeditions by sea to Lebanon (one numbered forty ships) to bring back cedar and pine for his constructions.

Snefru completed his father's pyramid at Meidum, and then built two pyramids of his own at Dahshur, some four miles south of Sakkara. One is known as the Bent Pyramid, for its sides were built with a broken slope; the other, square in plan, 305 feet high, is the first true pyramid in Egypt; it was this that was to be imitated by the other pharaohs of the dynasty.

Royal tombs follow a well-established plan from the time of Snefru on. The pyramid is but one part of a larger complex. In the valley nearby, there is always a small temple, with a canal leading to the river for easy access; the funerary boat is laid up there after the burial of the king. Egyptologists call this the valley chapel. A ramp or causeway leads from this to the funerary temple proper, built at the eastern edge of the pyramid. There the cult of the dead king is celebrated. The faces of the pyramid are oriented according to the cardinal points of the compass. The tomb chamber is cut into the rock beneath it (Cheops alone set his tomb in the middle of the pyramid itself). An enclosure wall surrounds the pyramid; in the space inside it oblong trenches are dug out, in which boats for the dead king's employment are laid. All pyramids from now on retain these four elements; only the decoration varies from one dynasty to another.

Cheops (Egyptian Khufu) was the son of Snefru and Hetepheres. He succeeded his father without incident. As the *Palermo Stone* breaks off after Snefru, we know nothing of the events of Cheops' reign. Even its length is uncertain: twenty-three years according to the *Turin Papyrus*, sixty-three according to Manetho. And yet this almost entirely unknown king is responsible for the largest edifice ever built by human hands. One can form no idea of the grandeur of the Great Pyramid of Gizeh, built by Cheops near present-day Cairo, without recourse to comparisons. We can read that, in its original state, it rose to a height of 471 feet (presently 452), that its base, a nearly perfect square, measured about 745 feet to a side, enclosing an area of over thirteen acres. All of which tells us nothing in immediate terms. But if we calculate that the monument swallowed 2,300,000 blocks of limestone before it was completed, at two and three-quarters tons' weight for the average block (some weighing sixteen and a half tons); or, that one could fit the cathedrals of Florence and Milan, St. Peter's at Rome, St. Paul's at London *and* Westminster Abbey side by side into the area covered by its base; or, that this mountain of stone would, if cut into foot-square blocks laid end to end, reach two-thirds of the way around this planet at the equator—if one makes this kind of comparison one can begin to understand the simply staggering size of the Great Pyramid of Cheops, one of the Seven Wonders of the ancient world.

Yet its size is as nothing compared to the perfection of its construction. Its sides are oriented toward the four cardinal points, not roughly, but *precisely*, with a deviation of hardly more than five seconds of arc. Its corners form practically perfect ninety-degree angles. The blocks of each course are laid on top of each other with no mortar, and yet it is quite impossible to slip a knifeblade between them, so perfectly have their surfaces been planed to the same level.

If, as seems probable, Cheops reigned no more than twenty-three years, in order to complete his pyramid before his death the laborers, quarrymen, craftsmen and masons of Egypt would have had to carve out of the cliffs, dress, transport and set in place over 300 blocks of limestone every single day of his reign, i.e. about 800 tons of stone daily, which would have occupied a working force of about 100,000 men. This, for the pyramid alone: But simultaneously were built the funerary temple with its basalt paving and its granite columns, the processional causeway, the valley chapel, and five 140-foot trenches dug into solid rock for the death boats of the king.

And, as Herodotus pointed out, Cheops did not limit himself merely to the construction of the largest monument in the world. He built and restored temples all over Egypt, in his spare time, as it were. This stupendous building program stands as proof of the efficiency of the country's administration, and, more important, of the economic prosperity of the entire land of Egypt.

Dedefre (Radjedef). The dazzling reign of Cheops was followed by that of Dedefre, about whom we know very little indeed. For his pyramid, Dedefre chose the site of Abu Roash, northwest of Gizeh. His name has been found inscribed on the flagstones covering the trench where, in 1954, one of the boats of his father, Cheops, was found. His pyramid, still incomplete, seems to show that Dedefre reigned no great length of time, which would agree with the eight years ascribed to him by the *Turin Papyrus*.

Chephren (Egyptian Khaefre). Dedefre's reign had been obscure; that of his younger brother, Chephren, was to make up for it. Manetho records sixty-three years for his reign. This is definitely too long; Chephren must have reigned about twenty-five years, long enough to build his pyramid at Gizeh side by side with that of Cheops.

The Pyramid of Chephren is slightly smaller than its colossal neighbor, but, built on a spur of the desert plateau, it appears to the naked eye at least as large if not larger than the Great Pyramid. The funerary complex is much better preserved. The valley chapel in particular, built of massive blocks of granite, is one of the masterpieces of Egyptian architecture. It was here that was found the famous diorite statue of Chephren, one of the treasures of the Cairo Museum. Beside this sanctuary stood a limestone bluff, which Chephren's architects carved into the shape of a sphinx, a lion with a human countenance. The Great Sphinx of Gizeh, its face carved in Chephren's image, became as celebrated as the Great Pyramids. The generations that followed the Old Kingdom in Egypt saw in it a god, "Horus of the Horizon" (the Greek transcription is Harmachis), and set up at its feet a crowd of votive stelae that excavation has recently brought to light. Two hundred and forty feet long, sixty-six feet high at its head, the Great Sphinx, despite the clumsy restorations of later ages, remains one of the most astonishing creations of ancient art.

The succession to Chephren raises a problem. Just after his name there is a gap in the *Turin Papyrus,* long enough to allow at least one name to come between his and that of Mycerinus, builder of the third of the Great Pyramids. Rather recently (Debono, 1949), a Middle Kingdom inscription has been found on a block of stone in the Wadi Hammamat, giving us a king list composed of Cheops, Dedefre, Chephren, Hordjedef and Bauefre; the last two names are known, from other sources, as sons of Cheops like Dedefre and Chephren. The inscription of the Wadi Hammamat would permit us to guess that they actually reigned over Egypt, and at least one of these names must have figured on the *Turin Papyrus.* Whatever the truth may be, Hordjedef and Bauefre can only have reigned, if at all, a few months each, and therefore need not concern us.

Mycerinus (Egyptian Menkaure). Chephren's son Mycerinus married, according to the Egyptian custom, his elder sister. The eldest son of this union appears to have died before the close of his father's reign.

Mycerinus raised his pyramid next to Cheops' and Chephren's. His was the smallest of the three, but it would have been their equal in beauty had Mycerinus been able to carry out his plan of covering it entirely in blocks of red granite. The work was left incomplete by his death. His funerary temple has furnished a great many statues and statuettes of schist, representing the king alone, or in company with his queen or one of the goddesses of the nomes.

Shepseskaf follows Mycerinus, whose son he probably was, although not by the principal queen; to confirm his right to the throne, he seems to have married his half sister, a legitimate heiress.

With his reign, the dynasty's decline becomes plain to see. Shepseskaf cannot complete his father's funerary monument in stone, but does so in brick; he builds no pyramid for himself. His tomb, south of Sakkara, is built in the form of a giant sarcophagus; the Arabs call it the *Mastabat Fara'un.* Its workmanship is still excellent, but it is a far cry from the engineering miracles of his predecessors. Shepseskaf's reign was a short one, no longer than seven years in all probability.

The history of the end of the dynasty is unclear. Manetho lists four kings after Mycerinus; the third, Sebercheres, would be Shepseskaf; he is followed by one Thampthis, who is supposed to have reigned nine years. But the monuments bear no trace of these Manethonian rulers, and we may well wonder whether Thampthis ever reigned, or even existed. The son of Shepseskaf and Queen Baunefer did not even bear the titles of a prince; power passed to a new dynasty.

We therefore know really very little about whatever events may have filled the two centuries, more or less, presided over by the Fourth Dynasty. Recent discoveries in Sudanese Nubia (1962) show us that Snefru's immediate successors inherited his interest in the far south. They occupied Buhen, near present-day Wadi Halfa. It seems likely that they also preserved an interest in Asia, for they had greater need than Snefru for the construction timber that came from that continent. At least a part of the wood used in building the great bark of Cheops (discovered in 1954) was cedar from Lebanon. The Sinai peninsula, the deserts of both east and west would have been regularly invaded by expeditions in search of raw materials, metallic ores and stones for the royal workshops. The seated statue of Chephren at Cairo, for example, was carved from a block of gneiss diorite that came from a quarry in the Libyan Desert, some thirty-nine miles northwest of Abu Simbel. What was the dynasty's attitude toward the Libyans? We do not know, but it is likely that it knew how to contain them within, if not to control, their own territories.

There are two essential movements that distinguish the Fourth Dynasty: a development and perfecting of the royal administration, and a tremendous progress in the arts. Alongside the great royal monuments we have already discussed appear private monuments of lesser size but of equal technical accomplishment: statues of princes, princesses or high officials, reliefs and paintings in private tombs. The latter are usually limited to representations of offerings and of the funerary meal, but the scenes of daily life that will enrich the mastabas of the Fifth Dynasty now begin to appear. And the minor arts, as revealed to us by the tomb furnishings of Queen Hetepheres, the wife of Snefru and mother of Cheops, witness to a perfection in taste and in technique which would in future be equaled, perhaps, but never exceeded.

The Fifth Dynasty

The dynasty of the pyramid builders has left us no clear picture of the number or the identity of its members, the length or the order of their reigns, and a good many other matters on which we might wish to be better informed. The nine rulers of the Fifth Dynasty are better served; their names and their years of reign are thoroughly known to us:

RULER	TURIN PAPYRUS	MANETHO
1. Userkaf	7 years	28 years
2. Sahure	12–14 years	13 years
3. Neferirkare-Kakai	over 10 years	20 years
4. Shepseskare-Isi	7 years	7 years
5. Neferefre-Raneferre	over 1 year	20 years
6. Niuserre-Ini	11 years	44 years
7. Menkauhor	8 years	9 years
8. Djedkare-Isesi	28 or 39 years	44 years
9. Unas	30 years	33 years
	116 years	248 years

Manetho's figures appear to be a bit too high, compared with those of the *Turin Papyrus* and with the earlier dates attested by monuments. Bearing in mind that two of the figures on the *Turin Papyrus* have dropped out and that some of the reigns given by that document are clearly too short, we can estimate, for the duration of the dynasty, about 130 years, dating about 2480–2350 B.C.

Following the sources and monuments available to us, there was no break between the Fourth and Fifth Dynasties. Indeed it seems that Userkaf, first king of the Fifth, was a descendant of a younger branch of the family of Cheops, i.e. a grandson of Dedefre. He, too, confirmed his right to the throne by marrying a representative of the elder house, a daughter of Mycerinus. The Fifth Dynasty then follows the Fourth in a manner little different from that in which the Fourth followed the Third. And nevertheless a folktale of the late Middle Kingdom (the *Westcar Papyrus*) pictures the change of dynasties in an entirely different fashion: In the reign of Cheops the god Re in person fathered the first three kings of the Fifth Dynasty. Their mother was Redjedet, wife of a priest of Re at Heliopolis. The story is a fabrication, but an interesting one: It takes account of the distinguishing mark of the dynasty—the importance of the sun-god Re of Heliopolis and of his daughter Hathor, and perhaps also of their clergy. With the Fifth Dynasty begins the regular appearance in the royal titulature of the title: "Son of Re." Our folktale, then, is simply interpreting in its own fashion the origin of this designation of kings. The *Palermo Stone* lists the many temples and pious donations of the dynasty, and Herodotus, too, knows of a tradition of the religious dedication of its kings.

Userkaf raised up his pyramid at Sakkara, near the Step Pyramid. An admirable royal head has been found there, at one time part of a colossus. This pyramid, like all those of his dynasty, is far less impressive than those at Gizeh; its core is merely a "fill" of loose masonry, covered over with dressed blocks. The result is that few of the Fifth Dynasty pyramids (for all followed the low standard set by Userkaf) have resisted the ravages of time, and today have nothing but formless piles of stone to show for their builders' pains. But if Userkaf and his successors down to Isesi devoted less of their resources to the erection of these tomb-mountains, each of them set up a temple of his own to the sun-god Re, their father. We have yet to find a satisfactory reason for this, i.e. we do not know why each king felt he had to build a temple in his own name. In any case, they ceased to do so before the end of the dynasty, for Ddjedkare-Isesi and Unas both broke the tradition.

Although the texts tell us there were six royal temples of Re, only two have been found and excavated, those of Userkaf and Niuserre. They contain an obelisk set up in a large open court and built on a wide base in the form of a truncated pyramid, no doubt as a symbol of the primeval hill that arose out of chaos at the creation of the world by the sun-god. In front of this is a very large altar for sacrifice. A paved causeway led down to the valley. All around the central court stood minor buildings for the preparation of sacrifices and for the lodging of the god's priests. Beyond the wall, on the southern side, a gigantic bark was built, representing the solar bark in which the god made his daily circuit of the heavens. The walls of the temple buildings were decorated with reliefs, hymns in stone in honor of the deity. The seasons are pictured there, and the flora and fauna created by the father of all living things.

Of Userkaf's actual reign we know only that, perhaps in reaction to the autocracy of the great Fourth Dynasty pharaohs, perhaps for other reasons as yet little known, the leading families in the provinces began to acquire more power. His reign, in any case, lasted only seven years, according to the *Turin Papyrus*.

Sahure succeeded Userkaf in the direct line. He is only allowed twelve years on the Egyptian throne by the *Turin Papyrus*, but he was more likely to have had fourteen, if we follow the *Palermo Stone*. He founded the royal necropolis at Abusir, slightly north of Sakkara, which would be used by the rest of the dynasty as a burial place. From this point on, the walls of all funerary temples are decorated with reliefs, and it is to these that we owe what definite information we have on the reign of Sahure.

We know, for instance, that he set on foot campaigns against the Libyans—he took prisoner the wife and children of their king—and against the Bedouins of the northeast. One wall of his temple bears a representation of Syrian bears; we have also a relief showing seagoing Egyptian vessels, with bearded foreigners being held on board. Sahure, then, continuing in the tradition of the Fourth Dynasty, has contacts with the Syro-Palestinian coast. The *Palermo Stone* informs us that he even sent an expedition to the distant land of Punt, near the Somali coast, and a stele with his name demonstrates that he, too, used the gneiss diorite quarry northwest of Abu Simbel, which implies control of Lower Nubia at least, perhaps of Upper Nubia as well.

Kakai (Neferirkare) was Sahure's brother. His reign lasted at least ten years, so the *Palermo Stone* informs us, and Manetho is willing to grant him twenty. Yet Kakai had not the time to bring his pyramid and his temples to completion; his successors had to finish the job. It was no doubt in his reign that the *Palermo Stone* was inscribed, and we have papyrus archives, written toward the end of the dynasty, concerning the management of his funerary temple.

The immediate successors of Neferirkare-Kakai, *Shepseskare-Isi* and *Neferefre* (Raneferre), have left us hardly anything but the memory of their names and the number of the years of their reigns, seven for the first and twenty (according to Manetho) for the second. *Niuserre-Ini* succeeds these almost invisible kings, and he is slightly better known, thanks to the ruins of his funerary complex at Abusir. He reigned something like thirty years, we may believe, and his monuments declare that, like Sahure, he sent his troops abroad and notably to Sinai.

For the seventh king of the dynasty, *Menkauhor*, we have his name, carved on a rock in the Sinai desert, and nothing else whatever. But his successor, *Djedkare-Isesi*, had the longest reign of the dynasty. The archives of the temple of Kakai, which go back to his reign, mention a twentieth cattle census. As this census was taken every two years, Isesi must have stayed on the throne at least thirty-nine years. Traces of his expeditions are to be found in Sinai, in the Wadi Hammamat, in the quarries near Abu Simbel. One of his officials tells us that he brought back to Egypt a dwarf from the land of Punt.

And objects with Isesi's name have been found in Phoenician Byblos.

Unas is the last king of the Fifth Dynasty. His, too, was a long reign, of thirty years at least (*Turin Papyrus*). He is the first of the pharaohs to inscribe, on the walls of the underground chambers of his pyramid, extensive religious texts. These are the *Pyramid Texts*, which give us our best information on the royal funerary religion of the most ancient times. For the texts are compilations of sources already extremely old in the reign of Unas; sometimes they throw light on conditions of the Predynastic age. Notable also are the reliefs carved on the walls of the causeway leading to Unas' funerary shrine: a giraffe is pictured, Asians on a seagoing ship, a battle between Egyptians and outlanders, and Egyptians, reduced to skin and bones by famine. These scenes, remarkable for their artistic quality, do not tell us nearly as much about the reign of Unas as we might hope, for the accompanying texts are all destroyed. But at least they show that Unas had an active foreign policy, and actively carried it out.

This much remains to be said of the Fifth Dynasty, as it comes to an end. It left behind it fewer royal monuments than the Fourth had, to be sure; but, under its rule, private persons had little by little taken up the custom of decorating their tombs (mastabas, from an Arabic word for "bench," alluding to their shape) with scenes taken from daily life. Here the artists of Old Kingdom Egypt have given free reign to their vitality and their creative imagination. They have also given us a matchless source for a study of the civilization of Egypt in their age. But we must take note that the richness of these tombs is in itself a sign of the decay of royal power. The psychological distance between Cheops, spending a luxurious eternity under his incomparable monument, a structure out of all proportion to the tombs of his officials that crowd around it, and Unas, with nothing but a midget pyramid to mark off his tomb from those of his own officers of state, is as significant as it is immense. The decorations of the private tombs of Fifth

Dynasty Egypt, the tomb of Ti, for instance, or of Mereruka or Ptah-hotep, can bear comparison with the reliefs on the causeways of the royal pyramids. This diminution of the royal power is to increase in the next dynasty, until the very face of Egyptian civilization is changed. Before observing that alteration, we must learn to know its original features, as they existed under the Old Kingdom at its height.

Egyptian Civilization in the Old Kingdom

It was during the Old Kingdom that Egypt became one of the great civilizations of antiquity. Her pharaohs ruled a territory that stretched from at least the Second Cataract to the shores of the Mediterranean. Egypt was therefore, by its extent, one of the most powerful states, if not *the* most powerful, in the world as it then existed. How was this impressive empire governed?

1. Political and Administrative Organization

As we have seen (pp. 279 ff.), the precondition of prosperity in Egypt was the proper management of its irrigation works: Everything must be made ready in time for the yearly flood, everywhere in the land. In the Old Kingdom, then, as in the Thinite period, the *adj-mer*, "officer in charge of cutting canals," is head of the administration of each province, or nome. He is directly under the royal authority. He now adds new titles to his former designation: "Master of the Castle," "Director of the Land." He is the local officer in charge of the biennial census, and he gives justice to the provincials. In fact, it appears that he unites in his person, and exercises in his province, all the powers that the king holds for the country as a whole. He is, in short, what the Greeks meant by their title for him, nomarch: ruler of the province.

Possibly this very great authority of the nomarch was tem-

298

pered by some form of control by the central administration. Our only source for these matters is the lists of titles carved onto the walls of the officials' tombs. Some of these titles are purely honorific, and therefore tell us nothing useful: outdated court offices of the Archaic age, such as "Unique Companion," "King's Acquaintance," "Overseer of Hieraconpolis" and the like. Some are forged titles, invented to gratify the vanity of the deceased, e.g. those preceded by the phrase "Master of the Secrets": "Master of the Secrets of the Things That Only One Man Sees," "Master of the Secrets of the King in Every Place," and so on. Titles indicating personal service to the king probably have more real content. Certain officials are set over sections of the royal wardrobe (keepers of loincloths, of wigs, of crowns, of sandals), or over units of the household staff, such as the launderers. Doctors belonged to this class of officials, and probably also the chief craftsmen of the royal workshops for weaving, metallurgy, carpentry, and the like, which supplied the court and the royal domain with all the manufactured articles indispensable to daily life. Also mentioned on the lists of titles are many priesthoods attached to the cult, either of the gods in their temples or of the dead pharaohs in their funerary shrines. This is, by the way, no specialized clergy: Priestly titles are very often borne by members of the civil administration.

Whatever authority these titles imply, every scrap of it comes from the king, who is the real head of the administration of the entire country. If we were to take the epithets applied to him at face value, we should see in him a veritable god on earth: "Son of Re," descendant of Horus, he is the *neter nefer*, the "good god," on whom the whole universal order depends. The cord of "cartouche" that surrounds the royal name first appears under the Old Kingdom; it symbolizes, perhaps, the daily course of the sun around the earth. Like the sun itself, the pharaoh is the master of the universe—in theory. The reality is rather more modest, and G. Posener has shown us that the pharaoh, far from being all-powerful, had no hesitation in calling on physicians to tend to his servants' ills. The king is not a "god" in our sense of the word; but he nevertheless partakes of the nature of divinity. According to the popular belief, the god Re in person united with a mortal woman to father the first kings of the Fifth Dynasty (see p. 294). The royal power, then, is of divine origin, and this accounts for the importance, in the transmission of that power, of the royal blood. Every change of dynasty reveals it: Under the Old Kingdom, the first ruler of a new house always comes from a younger branch of the preceding royal family, and often confirms his position by marrying into the direct line.

The king, then, is monarch by divine right. He holds every power in his hands: administrative, judicial, military and religious. To be sure, he cannot exercise them personally everywhere at once, so he acquires assistants. In the Archaic age, and again under the Third Dynasty, the chancellor of Lower Egypt appears to be in charge of the central administration. With Snefru and the Fourth Dynasty, this supervisory power passes to a vizier (*taty*). It is not unlikely that this office already existed under the Third Dynasty. Imhotep, for example (see p. 283), had the powers of a vizier, but the title itself is not attested until the Fourth. At the same time, the title of "Chancellor of Lower Egypt" drops out of sight, to be replaced by "Chancellor of the God," the god in this case being the reigning king. The "Chancellors of the God" are very often charged with leading expeditions to the mines, or to the quarries or to lands abroad.

The vizier is veritable alter ego to the king, and for this reason appears usually to belong to the royal family. Nefermaat, the first known vizier, seems to be a son of Huni, and therefore half brother or brother to Snefru the king. The same applies to the viziers of Cheops and of Chephren. Among the many duties of the vizier is the administration of justice. He is chief justice of the "Six Tribunals," and, from the Fifth Dynasty on, he is also priest of Maat, goddess of truth, justice and the order of the universe. The vizier, in fact, supervises the entire administration, the treasury, the arsenal, public and agricultural works and the services of the court. He is assisted by

"Heads of Mission," and we may suppose that these assure liaison with, and central control of, the provincial governments.

Among the departments of the royal administration, the treasury is of capital importance. In the beginning, it is composed of a "White House" and a "Red House," but in the Old Kingdom it is united under the name of "The Double White House." To this department comes the grain, the flax, the hides, the papyrus rope that make up the royal taxation. They are stored in the "Double Granary," directed by an "Overseer." Each nome has its double granary, which pays out the salaries of the administrative personnel of the province, and the expenses of the public works (dikes, canals, etc.). These payments are all in kind, for Egypt knew nothing of coined money until the very end of her independent history. High officials received grants of royal land for their support, but lesser bureaucrats and workmen received bread, beer, and clothing from the treasury's storehouses. The old title *imakhu* (literally, "he who is fed") refers to this system, where the servants and officials of the king live by eating of his bounty.

To function properly, this system required an extreme decentralization of the royal wealth. The treasury had to be able to pay out its reserves to men in every part of the Egyptian territory. The central treasury in the capital would therefore retain only as much of these reserves as would be indispensable to the court and the royal officials who crowded it, the rest being shared out among the provincial granaries. But for the effective administration of the country the central treasury would have to know the state of the reserves in every provincial storehouse: This created a sizable administrative correspondence. Therefore one of the essential tasks of the vizier would be to keep the royal archives, where royal decrees, title deeds to property, contracts and wills would be preserved, as well as the tax documentation needed by the treasury, to ensure the collection of all that was its due.

It can therefore clearly be seen that the entire administrative organization rests upon the scribe. It is he who, on the provincial level, keeps the inventories and checks the receipts, and at the capital, classifies and files the provincial reports, reports on which the vizier and his assistants will base their administrative decisions. Egypt can be ruled as a unit only because she possesses enough men who know how to write.

From the First Dynasty at least, the Egyptian scribes have at their disposal a writing material that is ideal for their needs: papyrus. Made from the internal fibers of the stalk of the plant *Cyperus papyrus*, the papyrus rolls were light, flexible and easy to handle, in contrast to the clay tablets used in Mesopotamia. They enabled the scribes to accomplish easily all the tasks indispensable to a bureaucracy: drawing up inventories of personnel and material, keeping accounts, maintaining land registers, registering decrees and judgments, and so on without end. The only drawback of papyrus is its susceptibility to damp and fire (clay tablets are immune to these); the result, crippling for the historian, is the very nearly total loss, with very rare exceptions, of the archival materials that would have allowed us to study in detail the administration of Old Kingdom Egypt. These had already disappeared long ages ago.

One of the common motifs of Old Kingdom sculpture is the representation of the scribe: sitting crosslegged on a mat, with his head raised, a papyrus roll in his left hand, with the portion he is working on unrolled on a board between his knees, he seems forever poised, ready to write at his superior's dictation, or to reread the last sentence that he has just traced with his stylus, a slip of reed with a frayed end. He is the mainspring of the Egyptian state machine, and we might wish to know better how he was trained to carry out his tasks. Every Egyptian town, at a later age, seems to have had its "House of Life" (*Per-Ankh*) for the education of scribes. It is not impossible that the Old Kingdom had something similar.

New scribes were no doubt recruited from the sons of officials. But Old Kingdom Egypt had no castes, and it appears that there was nothing impossible about a peasant's son becoming a scribe: All subjects were equal before the king. Still, it is probable that influence or luck played as much of a part in the advancement of an official as capacity or application.

The army, in principle led by the king, does not seem to have had a special organization under the Old Kingdom. There was no standing army. In case of need the nomes were required to furnish levies of young men drawn from a certain age group. The pharaoh would then name the "Chiefs of Mission" who were to take command of these levies and, for this occasion, granted them a military title, which we may translate "Head of the Troop" or "General." This rank was simply added on to their civil titles. The organizational unit of the army often seems to have been the "boat," after the vessels that would transport it to its campaign base.

2. Economic Life

The economic existence of Egypt rested entirely on agriculture; the living cell of the Egyptian organism is the agricultural estate. But we are far from sure who owned these estates; the nature of landed property in Egypt is still a subject for debate. On the basis of conditions in Ptolemaic Egypt, it was long agreed that the king was sole proprietor of all the land in Egypt. But there are many facts that contradict this (J. Pirenne); Meten, a high official at the end of the Third Dynasty and the beginning of the Fourth, bought lands and owned them in his own right, and we know of bills of sale for landed property. Land can be bought and sold, and can be burdened with permanent charges by the mere will of its proprietor, the prime example of which is the relegation of the income from certain estates to the perpetual upkeep of the owner's funerary cult. Finally, land can be divided equally among an owner's children after his death. Property in land does not, then, seem to be the exclusive privilege of the king. But we must note that private property in Egypt is not a matter of vast estates: Meten, whom we may consider a great landowner, owns no more than 250 acres (150 in his own name, 100 attached to his office by way of salary), which are scattered in different nomes.

Side by side with these private lands are royal domains, the *khetiu-she*, which are rented out to special officials. Many of them seem to be located on the edge of the desert, i.e. they are lands reclaimed from the waste by irrigation, and suitable for truck gardening or pasture. The rents from these lands are often granted by the pharaoh to temples or to individuals, in the latter case usually to establish a perpetual income for their funerary cult.

The rhythm of agricultural life in Egypt is set by the Nile; the runoff of the waters of the inundation is its downbeat. From the end of September the peasant takes advantage of the still-moist—indeed semiliquid—soil that has emerged from the flood to sow his crop in it; a herd of animals driven across the ground is enough to tamp down the seed. But if the land has not received enough water, or has already dried out, he sows his seed broadcast on the ground and then digs it under with the aid of a hoe or a wooden plow.

The two main crops are durum wheat, or spelt, and flax; the peasant also plants oats and millet. Wheat is the mainstay of the Egyptian diet. Transformed into bread, and from bread into beer, it is so much the staff of life that the expression "a bread-beer" is a synonym for a meal. Once the fields are sown the peasant gives a great part of his time to garden cultivation: onions, cucumbers, garlic, lettuce, and leeks are some of the things he grows to vary his diet. While flax and grains seem to thrive on the water deposited in the soil by the flood, and require little or no additional water as they grow, the garden vegetables die off without regular watering. And, since the Old Kingdom does not seem to have known the shaduf, the counterweighted sweep by which the modern fellahin still draw water from the Nile, their ancestors of the third millennium B.C. had to draw water by hand—from the Nile, if their fields were on its banks, or from the basin prepared in every garden for that purpose.

Four or five months after the beginning of the sowing season (*peret*), the harvest, which occupied the greater part of *shemu,* was begun. Grain was reaped halfway up the stalk with a sickle; flax was torn from the ground and then husked. The grain would next be threshed by the feet of farm animals driven over a circular threshing floor, then winnowed, then stored in cylindrical silos, under the attentive eye of the scribes, who counted every sack as the peasant emptied it into his store. After which, there was nothing to be done but wait through June and July for the next inundation, which, in the season *akhet*, would come once more to cover the fields parched by the sun.

But Old Kingdom Egypt did not live by bread alone. Stock-raising, hunting and fishing still played a great part in the economic life of the country. We know that during the Pre-dynastic and Archaic ages the Egyptians tried out many experiments in domestication. They attempted, for example, to turn into a sort of hunting dog, and a source of butcher's meat, no less an animal than the hyena. These experiments continued in the Old Kingdom. Certain antelopes, the oryx notably, were still raised in herds for their meat. Domesticated fowl included many species of duck and goose, but cranes and pelicans too were kept in barnyards on the estates.

Stock-raising must have occupied the energies of a large part of the population. It had its own rhythm, with two seasons. In the first, the herd lived at complete liberty in the natural open pastures left by the Nile, i.e. in parts of the valley near the river that were not yet fully dried out. The herdsmen lived with their animals and followed them where they led. They milked the cows, delivered the calves, and took care of the young when the herd crossed a watercourse or a difficult marsh. In the second season the herdsmen cut out certain animals who were transferred to cattlefarms, where they were tethered in thick meadows and force-fed. These animals were destined for the king's table, and for the altars of the gods. A special official, the *Heri-udjeb*, supervised their fattening. As work animals, the peasants of the Old Kingdom used the ass during the harvest, especially to tread out and to transport the grain; it was probably only rarely that an ox was used to draw the plow. The horse does not put in an appearance until about 1700 B.C.; the camel, later still.

Barnyard fowl also lived a rhythm of their own, again in

two sessions. In the first they were left free in a huge yard provided with a basin and a plentiful supply of grain. Then the geese or cranes were force-fed with pellets of feed, until they were ready for the spit. There were special poultry-fattening farms, and special scribes to supervise them.

The high officials of the Old Kingdom loved to have themselves pictured at the hunt, in the desert or in the marshes of the Nile. The desert hunt had, it would seem, a double aim. For one thing it furnished fresh meat, as well as new subjects for experiments in domestication; this is why huntsmen are pictured with the lasso as well as the bow in hand, for they sometimes take their prey alive. The hunters were accompanied by saluki hounds, identifiable on the reliefs. But there was another side to the chase, and that a religious one. The animals dwelling in the desert were by that very token evil, for they were creatures of the god Seth, brother and enemy of Osiris: The religious man would help to root them out. He would do the same in the marshes and on the river, where the hippopotamus hunt seems also to have been a pious sport. (It may have been so since Predynastic times: see p. 244.) The hunt is not only a pastime of the rich, it is also the profession of a corps of specialists, the *nuu*-hunters who also serve as a kind of frontier patrol.

From the marshes ancient Egypt draws no negligible part of her wealth: papyrus for writing materials, for ropes and rigging, and for the light fishing and hunting vessels that are made by binding its stalks into thick bundles that float through the marshes with ease. Fishing is one of the basic sources of the Egyptian's food. Any method will do, and all are employed: seine fishing, which calls for a sizable troop of men; fishing with nets of various sizes; with hook and line; and, where necessary, with harpoons. Fish are prepared where they are caught, split in two and set out to dry. In the marshes, too, can be found wild migratory birds, which the Egyptians catch to replenish their poultry-yards; immense nets are spread out on the water, which at a signal from a watcher close upon their prey.

306

With her peasants tilling her fields of grain and gardens, her stockmen who increase her flocks and herds, her huntsmen and her fishermen in the marshes, Egypt can boast an economy nearly self-sufficient, the more so as the craftsmen in her workshops prepare the tools needed for the exploitation of her resources and transform her raw materials into articles of use.

We only know the landed estates of Egypt from the depictions of them on mastaba walls. But it is evident that, along with private holdings, there were also royal and temple lands. Every class of land, private and ecclesiastical, is subject to taxation in kind. But in the Fifth Dynasty begins the practice of grants of immunity by the king, to temples and to individuals, or of the income from parts of the royal domain to both— to individuals, to allow them to establish foundations for the celebration of their funerary cult, to temples, to support the daily offerings to the gods. This was to lead to an impoverishment of the state's resources and was one of the causes of the fall of the Old Kingdom.

We have said that Egypt was nearly self-sufficient; it is clear that she was not entirely so. Materials indispensable to her civilization were not to be found in the Egyptian land. Timber, for one, as we have seen, was lacking, and in a country where all heavy transport was by water, shipyard timber was a vital need. Neither temples nor palaces could be built without it. There are no metalliferous ores in the valley of the Nile; mines are all located on the periphery, especially in the hills of the Arabian desert and often at a considerable distance from the river. Yet the development of her economy forced Egypt to seek metal in increasing quantities. Wood and copper, then, were her necessary imports, and the rare or semiprecious stones that were raw material for her jewelers and her vase makers, as well as incense for the daily service of her gods.

It does not seem that there were, in the Old Kingdom and during the centuries preceding it, private merchants or traders who would go abroad to exchange Egyptian products for materials lacking in the homeland. Trading expeditions were essentially the king's business. They could be rather impressive affairs: Snefru, as we have seen, sent a veritable fleet of forty ships to the coast of Syria-Palestine, and Sahure sent a mission to the Somali Coast (if not beyond) to purchase incense. The Sinai peninsula was regularly visited by Egyptians, in search of turquoise and perhaps of copper. Copper was sought out in the eastern desert, perhaps also in Nubia. The amount of copper drawn out of these mines was sizable: Sahure could have made, for his pyramid, a copper drainpipe stretching the length of the causeway, a distance of close to 1,000 feet. Gold came from mines to the east and was common enough to serve as a standard of relative values in trade (we shall see in a moment how this worked). Many were the royal expeditions sent out to the quarries, in the deserts to the east, west and south of Egypt, to return with stone for the country's architects and sculptors, and for its makers of stone bowls.

Foreign trade was the king's province; local trade and retail commerce was no one's in particular. No special class of the population seems to have been devoted to it. Services were paid in kind, and the ordinary Egyptian of the lower class got along well enough, as it appears, by bartering his surplus against some one else's to fill his needs. The occasional tomb relief has come down to us of a gardener exchanging vegetables for a fan, or a peasant a liquid (beer?) for a pair of sandals. The gold standard facilitated exchanges: Onions could be bartered against ornaments because both had been given values in terms of weight of gold; the unit of value was the *shat*, a weight of about seven grams, in this case of the precious metal. No gold changed hands, but an official, for instance, traded a house for furniture valued at ten *shats* of gold. To simplify their accounts, the Fifth Dynasty scribes translated various commodities the treasury received in taxes into so many *shats* per item. At no point, it must be stressed, does this gold standard lead to a gold coinage. There is no money in the Egypt of the Pharaohs. The individual Egyptian's economic status depends entirely on his social one. His wealth is determined by whether he is an official of the king, a peasant

308

or a craftsman on an estate, or the heir of a family able to leave him lands enough to live on.

3. The Social Order

At the top of the social ladder there is the king, and the royal family. This can be rather a sizable one, for the sovereign, unlike his subjects as it seems, can have several legitimate wives at once; his first wife always remains the country's queen. Other than the royal family, there seems to be no hereditary nobility at all. The court is formed entirely of the high officials and personal servitors of the king. However, the requirements of funerary cult tend to make offices hereditary, in a manner to be described below (see p. 314). Under the Old Kingdom a hereditary ruling class is therefore being formed, but the process is not not yet completed.

Officials are essentially scribes. To know how to read, write and count is the sufficient but indispensable condition for a career in the king's service. One of the favorite themes of Egyptian literature, from the Old Kingdom onward, is the contrast between the easy, pleasant life of a scribe and the hard labor of other classes. There is, as we have said, no closed caste of scribes, but the profession is usually entered by the sons of officials—i.e. of scribes.

Public office, on the higher levels, is a source of wealth; high officials use it to buy land, acquired as private property that they can leave to their children. It is therefore possible that the Old Kingdom also saw the beginning of a class of *rentiers*, living off the revenues of their estates. But the growth of such a class was strongly held in check, by the Egyptian custom of dividing family property equally among all the children on the owner's death. An exception was made for the lands entailed by the owner to the support of his funerary cult. One result of this was that private property tended, over the generations, to be transformed into estates devoted to the dead.

Below the scribes are the peasants and the craftsmen. A

309

rather developed specialization of labor may be seen on the estates: The peasant in the strict sense of the term devotes himself to raising the staple crops, grain and flax; herdsmen are specialists in stock-raising alone; fishermen and huntsmen are grouped in teams that are not interchangeable. The same applies to all the craftsmen; joiners, carpenters, potters, stone-cutters, quarrymen, foundrymen and goldsmiths stick to their trades. Public works are performed by *corvée* labor, probably drafted for the most part from the peasantry; once the harvest is in, a part at least of the summer season (*shemu*) is free time for the peasants, which the government turns to public uses by calling them up to put the dikes and canals in order, against the coming of the next inundation. This, when it occurs, putting Egypt under water for three months, again frees a large part of the labor force, and it is probably then that the pyramids are constructed, and other monuments located in the desert, which is the only part of the country beyond the reach of the flood. At the same time, the Nile in flood is ideal for transportation by boat, for there is that much less land across which men must drag limestone, for example, from the river. The pyramids, too, are in a certain sense a gift of the Nile.

We cannot form a clear picture of the legal status of the various classes; we lack the documents for it. The peasant, however, would probably have been more or less bound to the land, although certain hiring contracts point to the existence of free rural labor independent of the estates. On the other hand, slaves, as the word was to be understood in classical antiquity, simply do not exist: If we have, in a few legal documents, mention of lands transferred along with the peasants who till them, not a single example of the wills (*imyt-per*) that we possess leaves a servant of any kind to the heirs. Besides, our ideas of freedom and servitude simply will not apply to Egyptian society, where a man, in order to live, must be attached to an office or an estate, which alone can provide him with his food and clothing. He has no other way to acquire them; there is no medium of exchange. He either serves or starves; in Egypt, all men serve.

4. Religion

Herodotus believed that "the Egyptians are the most religious of all men," and there is some truth to his opinion. The place of religion in Egyptian life was measureless. To understand it, let us divide it. Egyptian religion can be thought of as having two aspects, ordinary religion and funerary religion, the cult of the temple and the cult of the tomb. From the beginning of the Old Kingdom, the latter takes on more and more importance, until it forms a body of belief and practice distinct, in a way, from that of ordinary religion, although the same gods will be found in both. While the ordinary religion is local, every nome having its own principal divinity and subsidiary gods, the funerary religion is universal: The gods who preside over the cult of the dead are the same for all Egypt, and the burial rites are exactly the same (at least in historical times) from the First Cataract to the Mediterranean.

We have few temples from the Old Kingdom, other than the solar temples of Re of the Fifth Dynasty (see pp. 294 ff.). Most of the sanctuaries of this age were destroyed during the First Intermediary Period, or had already fallen in ruins by that time. It is therefore very difficult to study the cults of the provinces, for which these temples would have been our only evidence. But we do know that the more important centers of local religion were the scenes of great activity. It was here that the great mythological narratives that explained the creation of the world were worked out. There were almost as many of these creation myths as there were major cities in Egypt. The priests of Heliopolis, Hermopolis and Memphis, for example, pictured the creation as a process of generation, in which successive divine couples are born and generate others in their turn, each deity representing one of the features of the universe or one of the forces of nature. The names and numbers of these deities varied according to place. This was scholastic religion, the religion of the learned priesthoods in the great temples. Popular religion, insofar as we can know anything about it, favors the cult of the sacred animals, known since Predynastic times: The Apis bull, one of the most popular, is mentioned under the First Dynasty. Particular beasts bearing some special marking as a sign of divine presence are worshiped, and not entire species. From popular devotion, too, it seems, come the legends of the gods, which we know only from late versions; the cycle of the sun-god and the cycle of Osiris are the main branches of this stream of religious folklore: They are picturesque, sometimes grotesque, in their details.

The great gods of the Old Kingdom are these: Atum-Re of Heliopolis, Ptah at Memphis, Thoth at Hermopolis and Min at Coptos (one of the oldest known Egyptian gods). Osiris, originally worshiped in the Delta (his existence is attested in the Archaic age), takes on greater and greater importance and attaches to his legend very old gods such as Horus, the falcon-god worshiped in several places, and Anubis, the dog-god of Assiut. Among the goddesses, we note Hathor, goddess of Denderah; Isis, a native of the Delta like Osiris and early taken to be his wife; Neith of Saïs and Nekhbet, the vulture-goddess of El Kab. Each of these major divinities, and many of the other gods of Egypt, were the patrons of, and objects of special worship in, one or several nomes, where he or she was associated with other deities to form divine families. The picture is complicated by the syncretisms of the temple theologians. Those of Heliopolis assimilate nearly all of the nome gods to Re; those of Memphis identify the great gods with Ptah. This is a tendency that will grow with the centuries, to reach its high point in the Ptolemaic age.

The funerary religion is the most peculiarly Egyptian aspect of the national beliefs. As its origins were various, its nature was complex. There is an afterworld, to be sure, but where is it located? Underground, to begin with, a tradition that goes back to the very earliest times, for Neolithic and Predynastic Egyptians believed that the dead continued to live in the ground, where they were buried with their arms and food beside them. In the stars, in the second place, an idea that first seems to have been developed during the Predynastic age, when a certain part of the Egyptian people believed that the soul, leaving the body, rose up to its heavenly rest among the constellations of the northern sky. With the sun, finally, an afterlife reserved for deceased kings, who would fly (sail, climb) to the solar bark, and spend eternity in the sun-god's company. Toward the end of the Old Kingdom these three afterworlds tended to melt into one, and a contradictory one as a result. The souls of the dead live on in a subterranean world ruled by Osiris; but at the same time, thanks to magical arts, they can accompany the sun on its cosmic round by day and night, or take their ease in celestial fields of stars. Yet essential to the eternity of the spirit is the availability of a body equally eternal, where the soul (or souls; each individual has several) of the dead may take on a material form at will. Best for this purpose is, of course, one's own former body, which is why in the Old Kingdom the complicated half medical, half magical process of mummification first appears, with the aim of rendering the body incorruptible. But bodies despite all precautions may disappear, which is why statues of the dead are placed in tombs as surrogates in case of need. To this belief our museums owe their wealth of Egyptian sculptures.

The burial practices of the Egyptians developed with the same complexity. The oval trench of primitive times becomes a tomb of more and more chambers with the late Predynastic age; in the first two dynasties this becomes, for kings, a palace, in the fourth and fifth a pyramid. In the Old Kingdom private persons, however, had "castles of eternity," the mastabas with their many statues and their increasingly elaborate wall decorations. The scenes depicted there, by retracing all the steps in the production of food and of manufactured necessities, the grain harvest or the storing of beer and wine, for instance, assure the lucky owner of such a tomb an eternal supply of the goods of this world.

It was the need to assure just such a supply, the need to support the funerary cult, that brought on the decadence of the Old Kingdom. To survive after death the deceased require material offerings, food and drink, which are provided in one of two ways: either by the filial piety of their sons, who begin to demand the inheritance of offices and functions, and of the lands attached to them, to enable them to support their fathers in the style to which they were accustomed during life; or by the revenues of lands deliberately and perpetually reserved to this use. The Memphite monarchy is slowly impoverished by its generosity in supplying such lands, and its piety in reserving them to the use of its own dead kings.

The greater part of what we know about religion, particularly the funerary religion of the Old Kingdom, is drawn from what are called the *Pyramid Texts*. These are an anthology of magical formulae intended to give the dead power to resolve any of the difficulties they might encounter in the afterworld. Or, rather, the royal dead, for that is whom the *Pyramid Texts* were written for, but they reflect beliefs that had already spread among the population at large. They appear for the first time on the walls of the pyramid of King Unas, and they are to be found on every pyramid of the Sixth Dynasty thereafter— hence their name. These formulae are of very different ages, some of them unquestionably going back to Predynastic times, for they sometimes make reference to political events of that age. One finds two funerary traditions in the *Pyramid Texts*: one must have originated with the temple clergy of Heliopolis, as the sun-god Re plays the principal part in it; the other gives first place to the subterranean god Osiris. Many of the formulae of the *Pyramid Texts* were to be taken over by the *Coffin Texts* of the Middle Kingdom, to be passed on in the New Kingdom to what we know as *The Book of the Dead*.

5. Art

From many points of view the art of the Old Kingdom may be considered the finest in all the long history of Egyptian civilization; the artists of the Saïte renaissance were to take its masterpieces as their models. By the Third Dynasty, Egyptian architecture had taken the decisive step: Sun-dried brick had been abandoned, at least in the construction of major monuments, for stone, often the limestone of Tura, a quarry to the south of Cairo. Stone was at first cut and laid in place in quite small blocks, as if in imitation of brick construction, but architects were quick to sense the possibilities of their new material and soon used larger and larger masonry.

The construction of the pyramids, and of the whole complex that surrounded them (see pp. 283 ff.), was a matchless technical education for the architects and their aides. As a new funerary complex was called for by each reign, the experience so acquired could not be lost. Often it was the same craftsmen who finished the monument of one king and began that of another. This is sufficient explanation for the extraordinarily rapid progress of the art of construction, from the reign of King Djoser onward.

The buildings of the Step Pyramid, for example, have columns that are still engaged into the walls; in the next dynasty architects use free-standing square pillars, and also probably polygonal or round columns, to bear the weight of roofs and architraves. The pillared court becomes one of the typical elements in the repertoire of Egyptian architecture. Architects also learn how to ease the weight of the enormous mass of masonry pressing down on the tomb chambers under the pyramids by roofing these chambers and the passages that connect them with the corbel arch.

Architectural decoration advances with the same speed as the techniques of construction. Imhotep already sets up, at Sakkara, fluted or ribbed columns, with floral capitals imitating the lily or papyrus. The Fourth Dynasty seems to prefer the sober, straight lines of the square pillar; the Fifth Dynasty restores the floral capital, which is to outlast the pharaohs in Egypt.

Refinement of forms is matched increasingly by richness of materials. Granite, which had been used to pave the royal tomb chambers of the Second Dynasty, in the Fourth and Fifth becomes part of the standing structures of the monuments. The Valley Chapel of Chephren owes much of its distinction to the use of monolithic blocks of red granite for the walls, as well as for the architraves and pillars. Alabaster, too, is no longer limited to sarcophagi; temples are paved with it.

Sculpture and painting develop their own masters, their own masterpieces. These arts are exercised both at the command of the king or the royal family and on private commission. Chephren's funerary temple alone contains no less than seventeen statues of the king, all over life-size; Mycerinus' must have had as many sculpture groups of the king accompanied by a nome deity as there were provinces in Egypt at the time—something around forty. For the making of these royal statues the hardest stones were often used, and the diorite statue of Chephren at the Cairo Museum shows that this was no impediment to the artist. Statues of private persons, smaller though they are and of less challenging materials, are no lesser testimony to the stature of the Old Kingdom sculptors. I need call no other witness than the *Kneeling Scribe* of the Louvre, or the *Sheikh el-Beled* at Cairo. An ability just as striking is displayed in the art of carving in relief. In the Fourth Dynasty, but above all in the Fifth, the tombs of private men, the causeways of the pyramids and the walls of the sun-temples of Re, were decorated with scenes in bas-relief that are as remarkable for their style as they are valuable for their subject matter.

Both statues and bas-reliefs were painted in lively but harmonious colors. The painter was the helpmate of the architect and the sculptor, but he was more than that in his own right. The Egyptian wall paintings are the equal of the best work of the Egyptian sculptors. Unfortunately the painters worked in a medium more perishable. Frescoes are more subject to the ravages of time than sculptures even in wood. Painting of the period is therefore known to us only by rare examples. The famous, extraordinarily realistic *Geese of Meidum*, painted in the time of Snefru, show us what the world's art has lost by the disappearance of Old Kingdom painting.

The minor arts are just as little attested. The looting of the Old Kingdom tombs spared very few of the objects whose manufacture is pictured on mastaba walls. The articles found in the tomb of Hetepheres, mother of Cheops, show that lapidaries and workers in ebony had a taste as developed as that of any of the other artists of the age.

Among these were practitioners of an art of which we have nothing; we have no examples of metal sculptures before the Sixth Dynasty. But the texts inform us that there were men who knew how to cast them, or how to hammer them. A gold falcon head from Hieraconpolis hints at what we have lost.

Despite the loss of innumerable objects, despite the passage of four and a half millennia, the works of art that have reached us from Old Kingdom Egypt have a perfection so timeless and an impact so immediate that they have attained, in their own right, the end to which they were originally but the means: immortality.

6. Literature

Aside from the *Pyramid Texts*, the literature of the period from the Third to the Fifth Dynasty is represented only by short autobiographical texts, and by a fragment of *The Instruction of Prince Hordjedef*. For longer Old Kingdom texts one must wait until the Sixth Dynasty. The *Pyramid Texts* themselves, compiled probably between the Second and the Fifth Dynasties, are enough, however, to give us an idea of the literature of this age. The Egyptians there already display their taste for parallelism, for balanced phrases the second half of which repeat the ideas expressed in the first, but in different words.

From a later period we have two pieces of "Wisdom Literature" bearing the names of notables of the Old Kingdom, *The Instruction of Kagemni* and *The Instruction of Ptah-hotep*, that probably preserve many authentic maxims and proverbs of this age. Kagemni lived under King Huni of the Third Dynasty, Ptah-hotep was vizier to Isesi in the Fifth. Both texts are collections of advice to young men on how to achieve "success." They are counsels of prudence rather than of morality. Essentially they recommend the following course: in society, silence and good manners; toward inferiors, integrity and benevolence; toward superiors, and parents, obedience.

7. *Science and Technology*

When an Egyptian published a didactic work, in later ages, he would declare, to increase its authority, that he had copied it from a manuscript going back to one of the Memphite pharaohs, Snefru in particular, or Isesi. Was there any truth at all to this? We cannot know; not a single scientific work of the Old Kingdom has come down to us. Still, it has been rightly pointed out that the language of the *Smith Papyrus*, the best Egyptian medical treatise we have, dates in certain prescriptions back to the Old Kingdom. If we remember that Imhotep, among others, was accounted a skilled physician, it seems possible that scientific texts did exist at the time. The monuments that the Old Kingdom erected, particularly under the Fourth Dynasty, show that Egyptian mathematical knowledge in this period was at least equal to that of the Middle Kingdom, when the great *Rhind Mathematical Papyrus* was composed (see p. 382).

The state of technology is better known to us: It is one of progress from the Third Dynasty on. We have already noticed the ability of sculptors to master stones as hard as diorite. This ability has led certain authors to suppose that the Egyptians already knew the use not only of iron, but of steel. Others have imagined that artisans then knew how to harden copper, by processes lost to modern metallurgy. All of this is fantasy. It has recently been proved that the sculptors used no metal tools at all on the hard stones. Stone chisels were all that they employed. Copper chisels were used only for carving wood and ivory, and softer stones like schist and limestone.

The smiths of the Old Kingdom did know how to cast and weld their metals, as well as how to forge, chase, rivet and engrave them. Joiners and carpenters could, with mortise, tenon and dovetail, put together perfectly seaworthy ships, almost without employing a single nail. Enamelers maintained and improved the art of making the vitreous enamel improperly known under the name of "Egyptian faïence." One of the underground chambers of Djoser's Step Pyramid was entirely lined with blue enameled tiles, their design imitating a reed wall mat and creating a truly astonishing effect.

Astonishing, indeed, is the word we must apply to the degree of civilization attained by Egypt in the Third, Fourth and Fifth Dynasties of her history. But words will not serve the purpose. A visit to the great European or American museums, or to the Cairo Museum itself, will better convey the nobility, and the grandeur, of the civilization of Old Kingdom Egypt.

9

The Fall of the Old Kingdom and the First Intermediate Period

When the pharaohs of the Sixth Dynasty succeeded those of the Fifth on the Egyptian throne, the monarchy of the Old Kingdom was at its peak. Its strength, its stability, had never been greater. Yet four reigns were enough to reduce Egypt to total anarchy. The Egyptians themselves were to feel that the advent of the Sixth Dynasty was a "turning-point of history"; the *Turin Papyrus*, when it reaches the reign of Unas, the last of the Fifth Dynasty kings, pauses to count up all the reigns from Menes to him, as if his passing marked the end of an epoch.

The Sixth Dynasty

However, as is so often the case, there is no particular break between the reign of Unas and that of Teti, the first king of the Sixth Dynasty. The same officials pass from the service of Unas to that of Teti, notably the celebrated Kagemni (see p. 317). One of Teti's wives, Iput, mother of the future Pepi I, may have been a daughter of Unas—in which case we should have, again, one of those changes of dynasty based on the failure of legitimate male heirs, with the king's eldest daughter passing on the royal power to her husband, founder of a new line.

There are six, perhaps seven reigns in the Sixth Dynasty, of very unequal length and importance. They lasted, all told, a little more than a century and a half, i.e. from about 2420 to about 2260 B.C., but the reign of Pepi II alone occupies two-thirds of the entire period. A list follows:

1. Teti (Seheteptawi)
2. Userkare
3. Pepi I
4. Merenre I
5. Pepi II
6. Merenre II (Antyemsaf)
7. Nitocris

Teti reigned approximately a dozen years. According to Manetho, he was assassinated by his bodyguards, but in fact we have very little in the way of contemporary evidence for his history. His name has been found on pottery at Byblos, and he may have sent an expedition into Nubia. One of the rare documents of his reign that has come down to us is a decree granting exemption from taxes to lands belonging to the temple of Abydos. This is symptomatic. It was this practice of generosity at the expense of the royal treasury that was to sap the monarchy's powers.

Userkare had the briefest of reigns. We know of him only from the king lists; the contemporary monuments do not seem to have taken any notice of him. It has been speculated that he may merely have aided the Queen Iput to exercise the regency at the beginning of the reign of Pepi I, who was still very young at Teti's death.

Pepi I reigned at least forty years, perhaps forty-nine. Resuming the policy of previous dynasties, he sent expeditions to Asia and to Nubia. He celebrated a Sed festival. The outstanding fact of his reign (because of its implications) was his marriage to two daughters of a provincial nobleman, Khui, who were to be the mothers of the following two kings. These marriages were a sign of the importance that the great families of the nomes were in the process of acquiring, to the detriment of the already weakening monarchy. Pepi I raised his pyramid slightly to the south of Isesi's. It is thought that the name of this monument, Men-nefer, was the origin of the later Hellenized name of the Egyptian capital, Memphis.

Merenre I, Pepi I's eldest son, reigned only a short time; it is possible that he was coregent with his father for about nine years, and reigned alone only five. Perhaps under his mother's influence, or to follow his father's policy, or out of necessity, he appears to have favored the provincial nobility: He installed Ibi, son of his maternal uncle, as governor of the twelfth nome of Upper Egypt. This was the beginning of a great line of feudal princes whose tombs, carved into the cliff of Deir-el-Gebrawi, have furnished any number of documents for the history of the end of the Old Kingdom.

Pepi II, also a son of Pepi I, succeeded his brother (and cousin, as Merenre was the son of his mother's sister) on the throne, where he was to enjoy the longest reign in Egyptian and no doubt in world history. According to Manetho, he was but six years old at Merenre's death and lived to be a hundred, ruling for all of the ninety-four-year interval. The highest year date for his reign attested by a contemporary document is for his year sixty-five; we are therefore unable to verify Manetho directly on this. But that he had a very long reign indeed is beyond any doubt: He celebrated *two* Sed festivals (normally held after about thirty years of a king's reign), and the *Turin Papyrus* gives him a reign of ninety years and perhaps more (the end of the number is lost). During his minority, the country was under the regency of Meryreankhnes, the king's mother, and her brother Djau, the nomarch of Thinis. Djau was to remain the king's vizier when he reached his majority. At least four successive queens shared the throne with Pepi II during his long reign; he seems even to have survived most of his children.

The Abydos list tells us that Pepi II's successor was *Merenre II–Antyemsaf*. According to the *Turin Papyrus*, he reigned only a year. That may be so, but what we can be sure of is that, with the death of Pepi II, a period of extreme obscurity begins; we are, in fact, already in that time of troubles for

Egypt that historians call the First Intermediate Period. Our literary sources, notably the *Turin Papyrus*, still have two reigns to record for the Sixth Dynasty, the last that of a Queen *Nitocris*. Not a single contemporary document confirms her existence, which is a pity, as Manetho calls her "the noblest and most beautiful of women." Herodotus has picked up a story that she committed suicide after avenging the murder of her brother Merenre II, but we do not know what his source was. Still his report would fit, disturbingly well, the one fact that we are sure of: Something, whether in the form of dynastic troubles or in some other shape, went drastically wrong almost immediately after the death of the aged Pepi II.

1. Political Development of Egypt Under the Sixth Dynasty

Very great changes in the organization of the Egyptian state had taken place in the preceding century and a half. From the Third to the Fifth Dynasty, power had become more centralized with every reign; with the Sixth Dynasty, the process was reversed. Power is slowly but steadily decentralized, with no halt short of actual anarchy.

The reason for this is easy to explain. For one thing, the royal fortunes were progressively dissipated in donations to temples and to noblemen. The practice of grants of income from land, begun in the Fourth Dynasty, was already appreciable in the Fifth Dynasty, and by the Sixth had got out of hand, so much so that the king was no longer the only power in Egypt; the great temples, above all the great families of the nomes, began to rival him in wealth and influence.

It was the provincial nobility that had benefited most from the largesse of the king. For this the causes were, first, the need, in order to assure the efficient administration of the state, for a royal representative with extensive powers in every province (see p. 301); second, the tendency, prompted by the fundamental religious beliefs of the Egyptian people, for every official to ask and obtain the transfer of his office to his eldest son, whose duty it was to offer him funerary cult. Heredity of office was the source, at worst, of minor inconvenience when applied to subordinate posts. The same would not hold for provincial governorships. A provincial governor who had inherited his office was guaranteed that office for life, so he could pass it on to his son in turn. The governor, as representative of the king, held all or nearly all powers in his hands: He levied troops, directed public works, had the responsibility for the royal granaries, dispensed justice, and had the surveillance, more or less, of the temples of his nome and their estates. The only way the king might limit these powers was by still respecting the nomarch's right to office, but regularly changing the province in which he exercised it. Merenre appears to have attempted this, but the experiment was not repeated. By leaving individuals, then families, permanently at the head of the same nomes, the Sixth Dynasty kings were architects of the Old Kingdom's destruction.

This was a gradual process, accelerating in the very long reign of Pepi II. For all its growing weakness, the monarchy was still strong enough to maintain the unity of the land down to about 2260 B.C. Teti and Pepi I may be numbered among the great pharaohs of Egypt; many are the temples and monuments they left behind; the accomplishments of the Sixth Dynasty were far from negligible. It would even seem that, in the beginning, the provincial nobility's power was applied to the national benefit: Djau, nomarch of Thinis, uncle of Pepi II, contributed to the country's stability in the boy-king's minority, and the governors of Elephantine played a major role in the external affairs of Egypt.

Egyptian expansion in Nubia and Asia, in fact, is the distinguishing mark of the dynasty. For the first time, the Egyptians move on neighboring lands in force. They establish commercial contacts, direct or indirect, with Asia, Arabia (Punt), distant parts of Africa, perhaps even with Crete. A whole series of texts illuminates this Egyptian expansion for us. The most valuable are autobiographical inscriptions from the reigns of Pepi I, Merenre and Pepi II. The oldest are the work of Uni, who lived under Teti, Pepi I and Merenre and whose autobiography, inscribed on his mastaba at Abydos, is now preserved at the Cairo Museum; Hirkhuf, whom we know from an inscription on his tomb at Aswan and who lived under Merenre and Pepi II; and Pepinakht, a contemporary of Pepi II, whose tomb and its inscription were also found at Aswan.

Uni's autobiography is full enough to give us valuable details of the royal administration under the Sixth Dynasty. A minor official under Teti, it was the favor of Pepi I that made of him a great officer of state. For reasons that he does not explain, Uni was called upon to try a case of conspiracy in the royal harem; it was the beginning of his rise to power. Pepi I made him his special envoy to the army in Asia, then engaged in a campaign in, probably, southern Palestine. In the Egyptian force were levies from the nomes, and mercenaries from Nubia and Libya. Uni's task seems to have been to assure good relations between the chiefs of the various contingents and to see to it that the army committed no exactions: "no one took so much as a sandal from a traveler, no one stole so much as a loaf of bread in any city." On the expedition's return from Asia—it had carried out more of a raid than a conquest, as the Egyptians returned home after having destroyed some strongholds and "cut the fig trees and the vines" —Uni was sent out on five campaigns of the same kind. These raids, it is generally agreed, penetrated as far as Mount Carmel in Palestine.

Uni continued his career under Merenre, who named him "Governor of the South," from the First Cataract to the Fayum. Perhaps we should see in this office an attempt by the central government to control the nomarchs, becoming ever more independent. Uni, in fact, supervised the "allotted taxes"—those allotted to the court, that is, which implies that the king now collected only a part of the revenues, but enough to give his representative an excuse to keep an eye on the internal administration of the individual nome. Uni was also charged with organizing quarrying expeditions for the royal building program, the pyramids and temples to the gods or departed spirits that were still being raised. He goes, for instance, to Aswan and returns with granite blocks for the

325

sarcophagus of Merenre, or to the eastern desert, to Hatnub, to bring back alabaster. In the course of these commissions he has to shoot the rapids at the First Cataract five times, to procure wood in the south for the royal workshops.

Hirkhuf, prince of Elephantine, was a member of the generation after Uni's. For the greater part of his career he was in the service of Pepi II. He was one of the agents of the Sixth Dynasty's foreign policy in the south. Already in his father's time he had taken part in a seven-month campaign south of the Second Cataract. On his own, he set out on an exploratory journey in the desert of eight months' duration, again to the south of the Second Cataract. A third and a fourth expedition took him deep into the southwestern desert and brought him back via the Nile, laden with incense, ebony, panther skins, ivory, and a dwarf, perhaps a pygmy, at whose presence the still very young king was overjoyed. This Egyptian penetration of Africa, at the end of the reign of Merenre and the beginning of the reign of Pepi II, is still a peaceful one. Hirkhuf, perhaps himself half Nubian, spoke the language of the chieftains whose lands he explored.

With the expeditions of Pepinakht, who also lived under Pepi II but later in his reign, we are in a different atmosphere. Pepinakht makes war on Lower Nubia, in his first expedition, and massacres her people, so it seems; from his second, he returns with hostages, chiefs and sons of chiefs, and with herds of cattle. The situation is no more peaceful in the east, where Pepinakht, on his return from the south, leads a punitive raid against the desert Bedouins, destroying one or several bands: War now mars all the borders of Egypt.

Things seems to have improved not at at all by the end of the reign, when a fourth official from Aswan, Sebni, holding Uni's old post of "Governor of the South," goes below the border to retrieve the body of his father, killed in Upper Nubia during a previous campaign. He returns with the body, leaving the land pacified. His reward from the king, aside from gifts in kind, included thirty "arouras" of land, i.e. about twenty acres, scattered in the north and south of Egypt. It was in this way that noble estates were founded and increased. This nobility of Aswan is matched elsewhere in Egypt: Ibi, named governor of the "Gazelle" nome, was able, thanks to royal gifts, to set up an endowment for his funerary rites, to which the revenues of eleven villages and localities were devoted.

2. The Sixth Dynasty—Conclusion

All of the above information is drawn from the autobiographical inscriptions of Sixth Dynasty officials. Their very number is a sign of how far the political situation in Egypt had deteriorated in that age.

Under the Fourth and the Fifth Dynasties, everything had been concentrated around the person of the king, including the afterlife, for the only important private cemeteries are those that surround the royal pyramids, whose funerary offerings they may share. With the Sixth Dynasty, this condition is reversed. The provinces take on as much importance as the capital. The titles of the central administration proliferate in an alarming manner—there are several viziers at once, it seems. This indicates a certain weakening in the vigor of the central administration. Worse is the growth of a vigorous, hereditary provincial nobility of nomarchs now only nominally representatives of the king. These princes are in fact independent. Inheritance of office, at first requested as a religious favor, is now assumed as a political right. When the death of Pepi II precipitated a dynastic crisis, for reasons that escape our understanding, the central administration at Memphis collapsed, apparently under the onslaught of social revolution. So began, for Egypt, the darkest age of her history: the First Intermediate Period.

The First Intermediate Period

These centuries between the Old and the Middle Kingdoms are dark to us also, one of the most confusing and obscure chapters in the whole record of Egypt. The age lasts from about 2260 to about 2040 B.C.; the Seventh to the Tenth

Dynasties are included in it, and part of the Eleventh. We may, for our purposes, divide it into three different periods. The first period sees the swift decay of what was left of the Old Kingdom, marked by social disturbances and foreign invasion. In this period the Sixth and Seventh Dynasties rule, after a fashion, from Memphis; it lasts no more than about forty years.

During a second period the princes of Heracleopolis succeed, at least partially, in consolidating power over Egypt. There is a short stretch of calm under the Ninth Dynasty, but under the Tenth internal warfare breaks out again. Part of the land is occupied by foreigners; in the rest, the independent nomes war with one another, some recognizing the authority of Thebes, others of Heracleopolis.

The third and last of these periods, which some see as already part of the Middle Kingdom, witnesses the victory of Thebes and the establishment of a new dynasty, the Eleventh, which, after ruling the southern half of the country, takes over the rule of all Egypt, with the capital of its native province as the new capital of the nation.

1. The Seventh and Eighth Dynasties and the Social Revolution

Here, in the first part of the Intermediate Period, we are in almost absolute darkness, and specialists are still far from agreement as to the course of events and their duration. Forty or fifty years is what was lately thought to be the total time involved; recently it has been proposed to reduce this to twenty-one (W. C. Hayes). Dynastic anarchy is the essential attribute of the time.

The Seventh Dynasty succeeds the Sixth, and still includes, perhaps, some kings related to the earlier royal line—Neferkare II, for example, whose name is found on a stele near the tombs of the Sixth Dynasty queens. He seems to have been the son of the fourth and last wife of Pepi II, Pepiankhenes. The history of this dynasty is so muddled that Manetho mentions seventy kings, who reigned . . . seventy days. The dynasty as a whole was long thought to be fictitious. According to the latest study (W. C. Hayes), it produced nine kings, but did not rule Egypt for more than eight years, an average of about ten months for the reign of each pharaoh.

It was undoubtedly in this disturbed time that revolutionary upheavals broke out, appearing to call into question the very principle of monarchy. Unfortunately these events are reported by a single text only. We should be justified, as critical historians, in ignoring this text, were its contents not of supreme importance for an understanding of the First Intermediate Period.

This text, on a papyrus now at Leyden, still bears the name given to it by its first editor (A. H. Gardiner): *Admonitions of an Egyptian Sage*. It is in a fairly bad state of preservation, and is a late (Nineteenth Dynasty) copy of an older original. Like many Egyptian texts it seems to follow no logical order in the narration of the events that form its subject. Still, the information it provides can be divided into that concerning the situation outside Egypt, and that referring to internal conditions, the latter being given far more place.

Remarks about external affairs are vague, but they nevertheless allow us to glimpse Asian nomads infiltrating Egypt and occupying the Delta by force. The policy of Egyptian expansion in Asia, and no doubt in Africa as well, had to be abandoned. "No one raises sail for Byblos today; what shall we do to replace the cedars for our dead? Gold is lacking." The central power seems no longer able to send abroad the expeditions indispensable to the nation's prosperity.

This rupture of trade relations is the result of internal conditions described at length and with feeling by the *Admonitions*. Dominating the condition of Egypt is a collapse or overthrow of the social order. "The gatekeeper says: let us go out and loot. The poor have become proprietors of good things. . . . He who could not even get himself a pair of sandals is now the possessor of great riches. . . . Every city says: let us put down the powerful ones among us. . . . Gates, columns, and walls are in flames. . . . Gold and lapis lazuli, silver and turquoise, carnelian and bronze adorn the necks of servants while the mistresses of the house [say]: ah, if only we had something to eat."

The *Admonitions* repeatedly stress and illustrate this social upheaval, but are less explicit as to its causes. The text does describe the breakdown of the administrative system: "The hall of judgment, its archives are carried off, the public offices are violated, and the census lists torn up . . . the officials are murdered and their papers seized." But political information is ambiguous. From some passages it would seem that hands were laid on the pharaoh himself: "The king has been removed by the populace . . . a handful of lawless men has succeeded in stripping the land of royalty . . . The royal residence is overthrown in an instant." In other passages the king appears to be still in place, for the author criticizes him: "Justice is with you, but what you spread abroad in the land, with the grumbling of revolt, is confusion." And finally the king is admonished: "Give order that an accounting be made unto you."

To explain this contradiction, the monarchy destroyed but the king in power, it has been supposed that the legitimate king was overthrown and then replaced by a reformer, an idealist, a new king who sought (in vain) to restore order by his mildness (J. Spiegel, 1960). The text, after having described the fall of the monarchy, would show the anarchy resulting from the rule of a well-meaning but weak pharaoh. This extremely attractive explanation is, unfortunately, founded on a single source, whose interpretation is full of pitfalls. Spiegel supposes that the dethroned king is Merenre II, and his weak successor an Eighth Dynasty pharaoh, the Seventh Dynasty being fictitious, or corresponding to a period when power was in the hands of an oligarchy (i.e. the no doubt brief period of confusion and anarchy that would have followed on the fall of the king, and that the *Admonitions* describe). But we have just seen that, disturbed though its rule undoubtedly was, the Seventh Dynasty really existed.

The text of the *Admonitions* was found at Sakkara and seems to be of Memphite origin, and it is generally believed that the events it describes were limited to the capital and its environs. The monarchy maintained itself, more or less, and the Eighth Dynasty, succeeding the Seventh, remained at Memphis, although it has sometimes been believed that it transferred its seat to Coptos (K. Sethe). The pyramid of a king of this dynasty was found near that of Pepi II.

The ever increasing weakness of the Memphite monarchy is displayed in a series of royal decrees that have been found carved on the walls of the temple of Coptos. Issued by the last kings of the Eighth Dynasty, these decrees clearly intend to ensure the pharaoh the alliance of a certain Shemay and of his son Idi, who were in turn nomarchs of Coptos, governors of Upper Egypt and viziers. Here is proof that, by the Eighth Dynasty, the drift that took the post of nomarch from a revocable royal office to a quasi-feudal fief, handed on from father to son, had reached its goal. In seeking the alliance of such princes, the king was but recognizing facts. The Old Kingdom monarchy was dead. Egypt now returned to what she had been before Menes—a congeries of warring states.

2. The Ninth (Heracleopolitan) Dynasty
(c. 2160–2130 B.C.)

Insofar as the rare sources allow us to observe them, the last kings of the Eighth Dynasty retain only the most limited sort of power: The Delta, occupied by nomads, was out of their control; in the south, the Thinite nome, with its nationally important religious center of Abydos, was independent, as was the nome of Elephantine, the gateway to Nubia; both recognized, but seldom obeyed, the royal authority. The pharaoh had nothing left but a precarious rule over the region around Memphis, and the costly allegiance of the Coptite nome.

These shreds of power were torn from Demdj-ib-Tawy, the last king of the dynasty, by a revolt of the prince of Heracleopolis. The latter, in point of fact, occupied a key position:

His capital, Nen-nesut (the present Ahnas-el-Medineh), was located in the heart of one of the richest provinces of Middle Egypt, at the latitude of the Fayum; he was capable of completely cutting off the king at Memphis from his ally at Coptos to the south. Around 2160 B.C., Meribre-Kheti openly revolted against his suzerain, and assumed the complete titulature of king of Upper and Lower Egypt. This is the Kheti I of modern historians, the Achthoes of the Greek authors.

The capital of the new pharaoh, and of the new dynasty he founded, "Herakleopolis" to the Greeks, was already an important center in the Predynastic period. The *Palermo Stone* associates it with royalty by reason of its name: Nen-nesut, in Egyptian, means "the royal child." The Egyptians worshiped there a ram-god, Harsaphes (Egyptian *Horshefi*, literally "He Who Is on His Lake"), whose cult is attested from the Thinite period on. The nomarch could therefore profit from both the political and the religious prestige of his capital. From the strategic point of view as well, the position of the ruler of Nen-nesut was excellent: At the outlet of Lake Fayum he held one of the richest agricultural areas of Egypt; he was near Memphis but had a safe distance between his lands and the Asian invaders of the Delta; finally, he was far enough from the south to have no fear, at least in about 2160, of the warlike nomarchs of Thebes and Elephantine.

The history of the Ninth Dynasty is poorly known to us. It left few monuments behind it, and the principal sources remain Manetho and the *Turin Papyrus*; but of its thirteen kings, only four names have reached us unmutilated:

> 1. Meribre-Kheti I
> 2. (Name lost)
> 3. Neferkare
> 4. Nebkaure-Kheti II
> 5. Setut
> 6–13. (Names lost or incomplete)

Names such as Neferkare and Nebkaure demonstrate that the dynasty intended to hark back to the traditions of Memphite royalty. And, although Heracleopolis was the royal residence, the administrative center of the kingdom seems to have remained at Memphis.

The founder of the dynasty, Kheti I, is the best known of its kings, although in fact very little indeed is known about him. Manetho reports that "he behaved more cruelly than his predecessors"; Eusebius relates that he went mad and was slain by a crocodile. One thing we may take as fact: His power appears to have been recognized by all of independent Egypt, from Aswan to a point north of Memphis; our sources do not tell us what went on farther north, where Asians ruled the Delta.

The national unity, partially reestablished, was rapidly negated or at least disturbed by the rivalry of nome against nome. Texts contemporary with the Ninth Dynasty speak of wars and famines from the reign of Neferkare on. The dynasty's end is completely hidden from us; it is thought that it may have lost its power after a Theban revolt.

3. The Tenth Dynasty (2130–2040 B.C.) and the Struggle with Thebes (Beginning of the Eleventh Dynasty)

With the advent of the Tenth Dynasty we are on somewhat firmer ground. Our knowledge is far from satisfactory, but at least the names of its kings have been preserved to us. From the end of the Ninth Dynasty, Thebes was ruled by princes bearing the name of *Antef*. Thebes had become one of the most powerful states in the south. At first, the Theban princes recognized the suzerainty of the Heracleopolitan pharaoh, but shortly before 2130 B.C. they rose against him and took the title of "King of Upper and Lower Egypt," so that for a fairly long time Egypt had two pharaonic dynasties at once, the Tenth Heracleopolitan Dynasty ruling in the north, the Eleventh Theban Dynasty in the south. The following chronology is after W. C. Hayes and J. Vandier:

TENTH DYNASTY (2130–2040)	ELEVENTH DYNASTY (2133–2040)
Meryt-Hathor ⎱ (2130–2120) Neferkare II ⎰ Wahkare-Kheti III (2120– 2070) Merikare (2070–ca. 2040) X (a few months)	Sehertawy-Antef I (2133– 2118) Wahankh-Antef II (2117– 2068) Nakhtnebtepnefer-Antef III (2068–2060) Seankhibtawy-Mentuhotep (2060–2040) (Thereafter the Eleventh Dynasty continues as sole rulers of Egypt)

We are not quite sure who should be considered the founder of the Eleventh Dynasty: either Sehertawy-Antef, or his immediate predecessor Mentuhotep, whom some authors take to be the dynasty's first king under the name of Tepy(a) Mentuhotep I (W. C. Hayes). In either case, we have here the appearance of an entirely new force on the Egyptian historical stage: Thebes.

Under the Old Kingdom, in fact, Thebes was no more than two little villages on the right bank of the Nile joined together, one the modern Luxor, the other Karnak. The capital of the nome in which Thebes was located was then Armant, the Greek Hermonthis, Iun-Resyt in Egyptian (Armant is the Arabic name). There stood the main temple of the nome god, Montu, who was also the god of early Thebes. For it was not until after 2130 that the name of Amun, destined to become one of the greatest gods of Egypt, is attested at Thebes; he did not become its principal god until the Twelfth Dynasty.

Under the rule of the Ninth Dynasty, the princes of Thebes had little by little established themselves as a major power. The situation in which they found themselves was this: Under the Eighth Dynasty, if not under the Seventh, all provincial governors had, as we have seen, become de facto independent of the crown. These rulers had their own armies and their own treasuries, and many of them, even though they might recognize the suzerainty of the king at Memphis, dated their documents and monuments according to the year of their own rule. Among the more powerful of these prince-nomarchs we may note, in Middle Egypt, those of Coptos, long the allies of the pharaohs themselves (see p. 331); those of Assiut, who also bore the name of Kheti, and supported the Heracleopolitan kings, to whom they were perhaps related; those of Khmunu (the Greek Hermopolis, today's Ashmunein), who were buried at Sheikh Said and El Bersheh; and those of the "Oryx" nome, whose tombs were found at Beni Hassan. These nomes of Middle Egypt often joined, now on one side, now on the other, in the warfare that sprang up between the Heracleopolitan and Theban states.

In southern Egypt the situation was much the same: Under the Ninth Dynasty Thebes succeeded in making herself capital of the fourth nome of Upper Egypt; Armant, the former capital, was thus hostile to her. The nome of Hieraconpolis (Edfu), as a great religious center, had played a major role in the affairs of the south; much the same applied to the Thinite nome, where Abydos, center of the cult of Osiris, was growing in importance. These provinces no doubt watched the growth of Theban power with misgivings. Thebes, then, before making her bid for national power, had first to submit to her authority the hostile nomes of the south, led by Hieraconpolis.

The tomb of a Hieraconpolitan nomarch, Ankhtifi, was found at Moalla; the texts carved there retrace the earlier steps on Thebes' road to power (J. Vandier). Just before the reign of Sehertawy-Antef, Hieraconpolis was still faithful to the Heracleopolitan kings, and by its position to the south of Thebes was able to menace that state's security; at this point, Ankhtifi joined the nomarch of Elephantine to come to the aid of Armant, then besieged by Thebes, by invading the Theban territory. But this opposition was unsuccessful in the long run; Thebes eventually reduced the southern nomes to obedience, and became the mistress of the "Head of the South" from Elephantine to Thinis.

335

Around 2120, then, the southern nomes up to Thinis obeyed Thebes, while those of Middle Egypt generally followed Heracleopolis. North of Memphis we cannot be sure of anything; we cannot know what sort of relations obtained between the Egyptian nomarchs and the invaders who occupied the Delta.

The reigns of the first kings of both the northern Tenth and the southern Eleventh Dynasties were devoted to a battle for the hegemony of Egypt. Eventually the frontier between the two confederations established itself near Abydos; Wahkare-Kheti III of Heracleopolis was able to seize the city at one point, but soon had to abandon it. Heracleopolis then seems to have given up the idea of a military reconquest of the south and to have accepted the division of the land into two independent kingdoms. This we know from a remarkable text, the *Instruction for Merikare*, the political testament, as it were, of King Kheti III to his son, the next-to-last ruler of the Heracleopolitan house.

The text has come down to us on a papyrus of the Eighteenth Dynasty. Along with general counsels on the arts of politics and administration, it contains clear allusions to contemporary events: "Be on good terms with the south. . . . Do not destroy the monuments of another. . . . If you follow these counsels and continue what I have done, you will have no enemies within your borders." This advice is accompanied, perhaps by way of consolation, by suggestions on the proper policy to follow in the north: Kheti alludes to his position in the Delta, where he had reestablished Egyptian authority up to its eastern frontier, the Pelusiac branch of the Nile. But he concludes by once more adjuring his son to follow his established policy, i.e. to remain at peace with Thebes.

Our sources do not permit us to know whether Merikare followed this advice. In any event, if there was a *de facto* truce between north and south it was a short one; on the death of Merikare or shortly before, the king of Thebes once more took the offensive. The last king of Heracleopolis, whose name we do not even know, lost his throne in defeat and cannot have reigned more than a few months.

So ended the struggle for the rule of all Egypt, some time around 2040 B.C., with the victory of Seankhibtawy-Mentuhotep of Thebes. We have some details of that struggle, but it is difficult to know where to place them in time; they do, however, help us to understand its general characteristics.

Our sources are the numerous autobiographical texts found in the tombs of Middle and Upper Egypt. Warfare between one nome and another was, first of all, absorbed into the struggle between the great confederations. The membership of these must have varied greatly at first according to the sympathies and interests of individual nomarchs; we have seen that certain southern nomes did not hesitate to support Heracleopolis, the better to oppose the Theban power; others, more prudent, were careful not to take sides, and were rewarded after the Theban victory by a recognition of their feudal rights. The texts reflect this political instability quite clearly: "I armed my bands of recruits and went into combat accompanied by my city, it was I who formed the rear guard at Shedyetsha [place-name]. There was no one else with me but my own troops, while the Medjays and the men of Wawat, Nubians and Asiatics, Upper and Lower Egypt were united against me. I returned in triumph, my whole city with me, with no losses." This prince then had to fight both the north, i.e. the Heracleopolitan alliance, and the south, i.e. the Thebans. It will be noticed that his enemies use mercenaries. The Medjays and the people of Wawat are tribes of Lower Nubia, and the often reproduced "models" of Assiut show us a troop of these Nubians armed with the bow and arrow; the same class of soldiers is represented in a battle scene at Beni Hassan, riddling a fortress, defended by Egyptians, with their arrows.

The long series of internecine struggles that disfigured the years 2130–2040 B.C. can only have wearied the feudal princes themselves; as for the people, the political anarchy brought on such a disruption of the economy that there can be no question as to their distress. The texts of this period make endless allusion to the scarcities and famines that were the product of civil war. Ankhtifi of Hieraconpolis informs us

337

of a horrible famine raging in Upper Egypt in his time, so bitter that, according to his inscription, cases of cannibalism were known. A number of other texts report famines just as severe. All Egypt must have been profoundly weary of war, which cannot but have aided the Theban drive toward unity.

In that unification Thebes indeed played the principal part, but the Heracleopolitans made no small contribution to it: It was they, it seems, who restored the nomes of the Delta to Egyptian rule. The difficulty of the text of the *Instruction for Merikare* does not hide the fact; Kheti III declares: "I pacified all the west [Libya], up to the neighborhood of the Lake. In the east too everything was going badly: [it] was divided into districts and cities, and the authority that ought to belong to one only was in the hands of tens. But now these same lands bring their taxes, tribute is paid and you [his son] receive the products of the Delta. On the frontier . . . cities have been established and filled with inhabitants from the best of the whole land, to be able to repel the Asiatics. . . . I have caused the Delta to strike them, I have captured their people, plundered their cattle. [Now] you need no more worry about the Asiatic . . . he can still raid an isolated post, he can do nothing now against populous cities."

It was, then, thanks to the work of the rulers of the Tenth Dynasty in the north that Seankhibtawy-Mentuhotep, by seizing the Heracleopolitan state, could extend his power to the Mediterranean at a single stroke. What the situation was in the far south we are not sure; before the reunification, Lower Nubia must have been more or less under the control of the nomes of the southern confederation; Ankhtifi, for instance, says that he sent grain as far as Nubia. Shortly before the fall of Heracleopolis, Thebes definitely controlled Lower Nubia; one of her generals in fact affirms that he conquered the land of Wawat, and we have seen the Theban army using Nubian troops. By 2040 B.C., then, a united Egypt extended from Lower Nubia to the northern sea. Libyans, Nubians and Asiatics were held in check; the country would be allowed to recover from the long generations of dissension and danger.

338

The pharaohs of the Eleventh Dynasty were to consolidate what they had won, and, in so doing, inaugurate the Middle Kingdom.

The Civilization of the Sixth Dynasty and the First Intermediate Period

Under the Sixth Dynasty, Egyptian civilization retains all of the qualities that gave the Old Kingdom its greatness. Fifth Dynasty artistic traditions are continued by the artists of the Sixth. Yet there are differences, which show the path of political development.

Memphis remains the artistic capital of the land for the first half of the dynasty's rule, but, where the Old Kingdom's royal monuments were incomparably superior to those of private men, with the reign of Teti the latter begin to come within range. With the reign of Merenre, Memphis loses its superiority too: Provincial cities have their own necropolises from now on, where the tombs are covered with decorations. The style of these works is far below the perfection of the art of the Fifth Dynasty, but the loss in quality is often balanced by a gain in picturesqueness. Among the Sixth Dynasty works that have come down to us we may cite a charming alabaster statuette of the boy Pepi II, and especially the great copper statue of Pepi I. The latter, found at Hieraconpolis, was hammered out over a wooden core, and decorated with precious materials; the loincloth is of gold, the wig of lapis lazuli.

The "provincialization" of art, begun under Merenre, continues to develop through the First Intermediate Period. Every important nome now has its individual school or style of art. The artists and artisans trained in these little provincial courts are utterly without the virtuosity of the great Memphite masters, but their works, above all their paintings, which survive in certain tombs (the cemeteries of Sheikh-Said, Deir-el-Gebrawi, Deshasheh, Beni Hassan, El Bersheh, Moalla, Thebes, Aswan and Siut), have in spite of their clumsiness a

339

spontaneity too often missing from Old Kingdom art. This is folk art, to be sure, but it has its charm.

The First Intermediate Period has left us very few royal monuments, but, thanks to a new funerary custom, has given us instead a host of human and animal figurines that are bursting with life. These little objects are replacements for the scenes of daily life that used to cover the mastaba walls; the substitution begins toward the end of the Old Kingdom and becomes general in the First Intermediate Period. The statuettes or "models" are made of stone (alabaster and limestone) or, more often, of stuccoed and painted wood. Like the reliefs and frescoes they replace they are intended to provide the dead, magically, with all the goods necessary to, or merely agreeable in, the afterlife. This is why we find, in the main, servants grinding grain and preparing beer, butchers slaughtering animals, carpenters, weavers, and women bearing offerings. The political instability of Egypt is mirrored in the afterworld: Here are soldiers for the soul's protection, infantry armed with javelin and shield, archers with their bows and arrows. Usually these figurines have nothing to be said in their favor, aesthetically, other than how well they catch the attitudes of men in action, but sometimes they are also true works of art—the *Offering-bearer* of the Louvre, for example, found in a tomb at Assiut. Egyptians who could not afford these little models had painted on the inside of their coffins (the rectangular wooden sarcophagi that would be used from now on) the various objects for which they might find use beyond the grave. These "object friezes" are often painted with considerable style.

In the south, another novelty appears in the First Intermediate Period: carved and painted stelae. Like the wall reliefs and frescoes of the mastabas, like the tomb "models," too, the stele has the purpose of assuring the necessities of life to the dead. The deceased is found depicted, often with astounding clumsiness, seated at a table groaning with every kind of offering.

The few portrait sculptures from this period that we have

are in wood, and usually of modest size. The artist gives all his effort to catching the expression of the face; the body remains stiff.

The end of the Old Kingdom and the First Intermediate Period, then, witness a decline of the visual arts; but they also see an outburst of literary activity, forerunner of the golden age of Egyptian literature that was to be the Middle Kingdom's glory.

The *Instruction of Hordjedef* and the *Instruction of Ptah-hotep* go back at least in part, as we have seen, to the Fifth Dynasty; but the *Admonitions of an Egyptian Sage* and the *Tale of the Eloquent Peasant*, as well as the *Instruction for Merikare*, are unquestionably the work of the First Intermediate Period, and it is likely that another famous text, the *Dialogue of a Desperate Man with His Soul*, dates from the same age.

Our manuscript of the *Admonitions* is in too poor a state of preservation to allow us to judge its literary worth. This is not the case with the *Tale of the Eloquent Peasant*, for which we have several manuscripts of a much more complete text. From this we are able to gain an impression of the literary taste of the Egyptians who lived under the Heracleopolitan dynasties. The theme is simple: A peasant of the Wadi Natrun "goes down" into Egypt proper to sell the produce of his oasis; near Heracleopolis, his little caravan of donkeys and their burdens excite the greed of the overseer of a great estate, who seizes them by trickery. The unfortunate peasant lays his protest before various officials, finally before the king himself. The subject allows the author to exercise his rhetoric; it may be that he has put into his rustic hero's mouth a series of malapropisms, or a pseudo-elegance of expression, but we do not know the language well enough to detect this sort of verbal humor, if indeed it is there; for the most part, then, these long harangues strike us as so much stylistic calisthenics. And something more, for the author uses them to hold up to criticism the corruption and injustice then prevailing in the land of Egypt.

The value of the *Instruction for Merikare* for political history we have already seen; its value for the history of literature is no less. The text stresses the importance of literary training for both man and king: "Be dexterous in speech so that you may prevail. For language is the power of a man. A speech is more powerful than any battle." It is regrettable that the manuscripts of this text, too, are corrupt.

The *Dialogue of a Desperate Man with His Soul* has a place all its own in Egyptian literature; it is philosophical fiction. Its hero is the thoroughly disillusioned man, tempted to put an end to a life he has learned to detest. His soul, in a moving colloquy, at first revolts against this decision, then consents to it. There is a melancholy beauty that shines through the difficulty of the text:

> To whom shall I speak today? No one remembers
>   the past,
> No one today returns good to him who has been
>   good to him.
> To whom shall I speak today? There are no more
>   righteous men, the earth is given to those who do evil. . . .
> To whom shall I speak today? I am bowed down by
>   anguish,
> I have no friend in whom I might confide. . . .
> Death is before me today, like a sick man's recovery,
> Like walking on the road after an illness,
> Death is before me today, like the odor of incense,
> Like the way one feels at the boat's tiller when
>   the wind is good. . . .
> Death is before me today, like a brightening
>   of the sky,
> Like a man longing for his own home after a captivity
>   of many years.

The fall of the Old Kingdom had extraordinarily important repercussions on religion. The greatest was what has been called the "democratization" of funerary religion. The *Pyramid Texts* in reality are concerned solely with the king; we have nothing to indicate that any other individual could hope for an afterlife in the company of the god Re. In the First Intermediate Period we can see private persons little by little taking over the royal prerogatives in the afterworld, and there becoming kings in all but name. The very *Pyramid Texts* are now inscribed on the inner walls of wooden coffins. And in these *Coffin Texts* the Osirian religion plays a larger and larger part.

A second consequence of the united monarchy's disappearance was a return to the old provincial cults. This explains the sudden, unexpected prominence of gods who were obscure or minor deities in the Old Kingdom—Wepwawet of Assiut, for instance, or Khnum of Elephantine, and above all Montu of Thebes who, with the victory of his city over Heracleopolis, became one of Egypt's great gods. Montu, a falcon-god, became more or less assimilated to Re; he himself was basically a warrior-god.

One god more than any other came, in the First Intermediate Period, to national prominence, and this was no minor local deity, but Osiris, the King of the Underworld.

The cult of Osiris in Egypt is attested from the Archaic age onward, and in the elaborate cosmogonies of the Old Kingdom, Osiris figures, with Isis, among the divine couples born at the world's beginning. A divinized hero, his tragic death and happy resurrection in the underworld had made of him the god of the dead *par excellence*. As such, he has no negligible place in the *Pyramid Texts*. Still, in the eyes of the theologians of Memphis and Heliopolis, his importance was by no means on a par with that of Re. With the end of the Heracleopolitan age Osiris is already on the way to becoming, little by little, "the great god," and pilgrimages no more take their way to Heliopolis but to Abydos, where Osiris was believed to have his principal tomb. Now every Egyptian longed to be buried near the god's temple or, if that wish could not be granted, to leave behind at least some trace of his presence at Abydos. Countless, therefore, are the stelae found within the sacred precincts. Abydos now became the greatest religious center in Egypt, which explains the savagery with which Heracleopolitans and Thebans battled for its possession.

The place of Osiris in Egyptian religion was now the highest imaginable, but it would not have been had it not been paralleled by a change in Egyptian moral ideas. As the Osirian religion spread there spread with it ideas of justice and mercy and, for the first time, precarious and mixed with magic though it was, the idea that our actions on earth will be judged after death. The judgment of the dead king, of course, already exists in the *Pyramid Texts*. The king, to gain admission to the solar bark, must be pure—that is to say he must have undergone all the magical rites of purification; he must be just, but the word is taken in its juridicial rather than in its moral sense; finally, he must be perfect, which is to say his body must be intact. A "passer," charged with transporting souls over the lake at the entrance to the afterworld, puts questions to the king on his justice, his purity and his integrity. The king cannot pass over, in theory, unless his answers are correct.

With the First Intermediate Period it is no longer the king alone who will be judged—all men must answer before the bar. This belief crystallized slowly until Egyptian theology had created a "tribunal of the dead," with Osiris as judge and the nome gods as assessors; the deceased, called before the court, had his heart placed upon one side of a balance, the other bearing a feather, symbol of the goddess of truth, justice, and cosmic order, Maat. Thoth, the god of writing, was secretary of the court; he, and Horus and Anubis, Osiris' coadjutors in the legend of the god, made sure that the weight was just and that the scales were balanced. If the weights were equal, the deceased was declared "justified"; if not, he was handed over to "The Great Devourer," a hideous monster with the head of a crocodile and the body of a hippopotamus, whom the illuminators of the funerary papyri of the New Kingdom show poised beside the scales, jaws agape for the destruction of the unjust.

The Osirian epithet "justified," which follows the name of the donor on the stelae, does not appear until the middle of the Eleventh Dynasty, after the fall of Heracleopolis. But there is no question that the ideas that led to this remarkable claim crystallized between the end of the Sixth and the end of the

Tenth Dynasty. To be "just," the Egyptian must above all practice charity; hence the affirmations repeated over and over on the stelae, to the eventual boredom of the modern reader: "I gave bread to him who was hungry, water to him who was thirsty, clothing to him who was naked, I protected the widow and the orphan." This attitude of responsibility toward one's neighbor is echoed in the *Instruction for Merikare*: "Do not be wicked, it is good to be benevolent. Let your memory endure thanks to the love that you inspire. . . . Do justice as long as you are on earth. Console the afflicted, oppress not the widow, do not take from a man the property of his father." The formulae of the stelae are these counsels further developed. These formulae become general at the end of the Eleventh and under the Twelfth Dynasty, but the ideas of justice and humanity they embody are already and everywhere present in the texts of the First Intermediate Period. Ankhtifi of Hieraconpolis boasts that, in time of famine, he fed not only the people of his own nome but those of the neighboring nomes as well; Kheti advises his son to practice justice in more places than we have quoted above.

This refinement of the moral sense, a matter in which Egypt was far ahead of the other civilizations of the age, is the direct result of the Egyptian devotion to the gods. The *Instruction for Merikare*, once more, shows us the reality and intensity of the religious sentiment in Egypt: "Raise up monuments to the gods. They ensure the survival of his name to him who builds for them. A man must do that which profits his soul. . . . Go to the temples, fulfill the mysteries, enter the sanctuaries. . . . Be pious, make sure the offerings are made. . . . God knows the man who acts for him."

Egypt's reunification by Thebes is comparable to the original unification of the valley by the Thinite kings. And yet there are real differences. The Old Kingdom had left behind the memory of an age of order and greatness to which the Egyptians loved to allude; it was held up as a model for all future generations. The Theban supremacy, however, had been forged by violence. The Theban kings had often been obliged to come to terms with the provincial princes, and in many cases the nomarchs retained, under the Eleventh Dynasty, the powers they had acquired after the end of the Sixth. It was not until the mid-Twelfth Dynasty that the monarchy was able to regain all its authority over the nomes.

Lastly, the army, which up to now had played only the most subordinate role in Egyptian life, became one of the principal concerns of the state. Here again our best source is Kheti's advice to Merikare: "Foster the young troops . . . see to it that you have a numerous following. . . . The younger generation is happy to follow its inclination [the text breaks off here, but the inclinations of youth are clearly toward action and violence] . . . Increase therefore the number of your loyal young men . . . give them fields, reward them by giving them cattle."

Each nome had such "age-classes," well-trained in the arts of combat by the wars of the late First Intermediate Period. To this highly experienced militia, add mercenary bands of Libyans and Nubians, and the armed might available to a king of reunified Egypt can be seen. The rulers of the Eleventh and Twelfth Dynasties, as we shall see, were not slow to put it to use.

Thus Egypt emerged, with the reunification of 2040 B.C., from an age of anarchy and despair, but she emerged transformed. The Theban pharaohs now possessed a political and military power that would allow them first to solidify their control over Egypt, then to extend their country's rule over surrounding lands.

10

Egypt in the Middle Kingdom

Later Eleventh Dynasty and Twelfth Dynasty

A Nineteenth Dynasty inscription associates the names of Menes, Nebhepetre and Ahmose. The reason is not far to seek: To the Egyptians, these would be crucial figures in their history. For Menes, first king of the First Dynasty, was considered the founder of the Old Kingdom; Ahmose, first pharaoh of the Eighteenth Dynasty, inaugurated the New Kingdom. We can therefore deduce that the Egyptians themselves thought of the reign of Nebhepetre–Mentuhotep as the beginning of what we call the Middle Kingdom.

If we follow them in this, we begin our history of the Middle Kingdom in some confusion. It is only recently that the succession and chronology of the Eleventh Dynasty kings has been established, not yet to the satisfaction of some. The task had been complicated by the fact that the founder of the Middle Kingdom took, successively, three different Horus names (see p. 348), which long led us to suppose that we had to do with three different kings. In older works one can therefore still find five pharaohs, all named Mentuhotep, assigned to the latter half of the Eleventh Dynasty and the beginning of the Middle Kingdom. We have now sufficiently disentangled all this to conclude that, after the reign of Antef III, only three kings of the Eleventh Dynasty ruled a united Egypt; the architect of that unity, the Nebhepetre just mentioned, was none other than Seankhibtawy–Mentuhotep, conqueror of Heracleopolis. A revised list follows:

Mentuhotep I (2060–2010) (=Nebhetpetre), ruled under the following successive Horus-names:
    2060–2040, Seankhibtawy
    2040–? (ca. 2025?), Neteryhedjet
    ?–2010, Sematawy
Mentuhotep II–Seankhtawyef (2009–1998)
Mentuhotep III–Nebtawy (1997–1991)

It must be noted that in some works (W. C. Hayes) the name Mentuhotep is given to the very first of the Theban kings (i.e. the first pharaoh of the Eleventh Dynasty), who ruled only the south of Egypt. His Horus-name was Tepya. Mentuhotep–Nebhetpetre is therefore counted, by these authors, as Mentuhotep II, and so on for his two successors.

Mentuhotep I (2060–2010 B.C.)

The changing Horus-names of Mentuhotep I are commentaries on the different stages of his reign. On the death of his father, Antef III, he took as his Horus-name Seankhibtawy, "He Who Causes to Live the Heart of the Two Lands." Under this name he led his troops to the conquest of northern Egypt, a conquest not yet permanent. In the fourteenth year of his reign (about 2046), the supporters of the Heracleopolitan kings succeeded in throwing off Theban rule, retaking Thinis. This sparked a new, mercifully brief, war between south and north, resulting in the final and definitive defeat of Heracleopolis. To mark this victory, which gave him the rule of all Egypt, Mentuhotep took in about 2040 the Horus-name Neteryhedjet, "Lord of the White Crown."

There were, in all probability, sporadic battles still to be fought in the nomes of northern Egypt, before the country was entirely pacified. When this had been accomplished, Mentuhotep I took his last Horus-name, Sematawy: "He Who Unites the Two Lands."

We do not know how Mentuhotep I went about his task of pacification. By force, to some degree, we may suppose, since he had at his disposal the victorious army; by diplomacy as well, for the nomarchs, especially those of Middle Egypt, were still powerful enough to make it wise to win their support with concessions. We may have some traces of both these methods in the documentary sources; the nomarch of Assiut was simply deposed, but those of Beni Hassan and Hermopolis retained their privileges. To restore the authority of the central administration Mentuhotep I seems to have employed a simple means: Thebes was still his capital, so he appointed as his chief officials Thebans loyal to the dynasty. The three viziers who served him, one after the other, were Thebans, as were the four "chancellors," a new and important function then created. The "Governor of Lower Egypt" was also a Theban, and the inspector of the thirteenth nome of Lower Egypt and the nomarch of Heracleopolis were Thebans as well. In creating new offices, Mentuhotep created new means of restoring order to a country shattered by civil war; by filling them with men loyal to the crown, he created a counterweight to the feudal rulers of the nomes. To have tried to supplant the latter entirely might have spurred new outbreaks of rebellion; the time was not yet ripe.

The effects of Mentuhotep's policies were soon visible within and without Egypt's boundaries. One of the results of the First Intermediate Period had been an interruption of Egypt's contacts with the outside world. Mentuhotep restored these as soon as the pacification of the country was complete. In the year thirty-nine of his reign (i.e. about 2020), near the time when the end of internal war was celebrated by his last name change, Mentuhotep sent out an expedition to Wawat (Lower Nubia); it was but the first of many in the same direction. These may have been raids in retaliation for Nubian service with the Heracleopolitan forces, but they were forerunners of a policy of expansion to the south to be carried on by the Twelfth Dynasty. Such expansion was a necessity for Egypt. Lower Nubia, profiting by the distraction of Egypt in the First Intermediate Period, had organized itself in an independent kingdom, whose rulers left inscriptions between Umbarakab and Abu Simbel

349

(W. C. Hayes); they presented no great threat to Egypt, but disturbed its commerce to the south. Mentuhotep I and his successors therefore undertook the conquest of the southern borderlands. Under Mentuhotep I, Wawat (Lower Nubia) was not entirely occupied by Egypt, but already paid tribute, gave free passage to Egyptian expeditions, and furnished mercenaries for the Theban army.

Even earlier, Egypt had resumed her activities in the Arabian desert to the east of the valley. Mentuhotep sent an expedition to the Wadi Hammamat in the second year of his reign. We have no inscription of his time in the Sinai peninsula, but Sesostris I's dedication of a statue to Mentuhotep I at Serabit-el-Khadim suggests that it was the latter who reopened the road to the Sinai turquoise mines; this is confirmed by an inscription of an official of Mentuhotep, Akhtoy, who declares he has "sealed the treasures in the mountain called Temple of Horus of the Turquoise Terraces," which can only mean a place in Sinai. If the mines were reopened, Egypt must have been in control of the nomad tribes of the peninsula; there are even certain indications that Egyptian troops may have marched farther, into Asia, although they will not have gone as far as their Sixth Dynasty predecessors.

To Libya, Mentuhotep sends forces whose purpose, it appears, is to hold in check these neighbors who have been menacing Egypt since the time of the Old Kingdom. On one of these campaigns a chief of the Libyan Tehenu is killed. The oases of the Libyan desert west of the Nile are also visited by Mentuhotep's troops, and the king takes steps to control the southwestern and southeastern deserts, on either side of Lower Nubia, where the Medjay rove, warrior nomads whom he boasts of having defeated.

Egypt, prosperous at home and powerful abroad, once more becomes a favored home of the arts. Mentuhotep himself concentrates on construction in Upper Egypt, where he expands the temples of Elephantine, El Kab, Tôd, Denderah and Abydos. At Thebes he builds, for his own funerary cult, a majestic monument, the first important royal tomb since Pepi

350

II. For this tomb, he chooses the magnificent site of Deir-el-Bahri, and adopts the design of a pyramid on a pedestal, surrounded by a colonnaded portico. Leading up to the whole is an alley of painted sandstone statues of the king himself, seated and wearing the ornaments of the Sed festival. Around his tomb were buried his queens, to the north of it the high officials of his court.

Mentuhotep II–Horus Seankhtawyef (2009–1998 B.C.)

Mentuhotep I's eldest son, Intef, died before his father; a younger son therefore succeeded the great king. Already at least fifty years old on his accession, his reign was to be short.

Nevertheless it was filled with construction. Many are the temples of Upper Egypt that preserve reliefs from this reign, in a style notable for its dignity. For reasons unknown, this great builder left his own tomb and funerary temple unfinished.

The best-known figure of this reign is a high official, who had already served under Mentuhotep I. Henenu, high steward of the king, in the eighth year of the reign organized an expedition of 3,000 men who, striking out from Coptos, crossed the eastern deserts to the Red Sea and reached the land of Punt, on the Arabian coast. An inscription carved on the rocks of the Wadi Hammamat gives us a report of this mission. Henenu's troops began by clearing the route of the king's enemies; nomad scouts covered the operation and brought in intelligence. Each man was issued a leather waterskin; daily rations were two jars of water and twenty pieces of bread; donkeys carried the supplies. Henenu, on his way to the Red Sea, had twelve wells dug out or cleared of sand. On reaching the coast, he had his men "build" boats. As the Red Sea coast, at the eastern end of the Wadi Hammamat route, is desert land, this must mean that the army had carried with it knocked-down boats to be reconstructed at the shore; a detachment would then cross over to the expedition's goal. Egyptian seagoing

351

boats, held together mainly by mortise and tenon and ropes, were easily dismantled, and therefore easily transported overland when there was need of it.

While the ships sailed in search of the incense of Punt, the men remaining in the Wadi were sent to quarrying blocks of green breccia for temple statues. Henenu brought men, stone and incense back to Coptos without incident. This reopening of the quarries of the eastern desert was matched by a flurry of activity in the Sinai mines.

Daily life in Egypt under Mentuhotep II is known to us through papyrus documents, carelessly scattered and miraculously preserved in a Theban tomb. These are the correspondence of one Hekanakht, addressed, during a trip to the south, to his eldest son. Hekanakht was a funerary priest at the tomb of a vizier of Mentuhotep I, and he owned a farm. In his absence his son had to fulfill his father's duties at the tomb as well as look after the family's land. Before leaving, Hekanakht leaves his son an inventory of the produce of the farm for the present year; in transit, he writes him two long letters containing orders for work to be done and food to be distributed to different members of the family, with quantities rigidly specified. Hekanakht's farm is made up partly of his own property and partly of rented land, for which he pays in grain and cloth. The letters offer many, and acid, counsels on how to behave toward the family and the servants. One of them reports a famine south of Thebes where (so says Hekanakht) "they are starting to eat people!"

Mentuhotep III and the End of the Eleventh Dynasty (1997–1991 B.C.)

The *Turin Papyrus* ends the Eleventh Dynasty with the reign of Mentuhotep II, but in a note its compiler indicates that there was a gap in the document from which he was copying the list at this point, and that there was a period of seven years between the end of Mentuhotep II's reign and the beginning of Amenemhet I's. This period coincides with the reign of Mentuhotep III, the Horus Nebtawy. If, as is extremely likely, his absence from the *Turin Papyrus* is simply the result of a lacuna in its author's sources, it is useless to suppose he was a usurper.

His reign was short, to be sure; the latest date we have from it is the year two (at Dadi-el-Hudi). Most of our information on it comes from inscriptions in the Wadi Hammamat, where he sent a vizier, Amenemhet, with a force of 10,000 men from "the nomes of the south, of Middle Egypt and of Oxyrhynchus" (the sixteenth nome of Lower Egypt, with Mendes as its capital), in a word from all Egypt. The object of the expedition was to bring back a block of stone for the royal sarcophagus; it returned with its prize, and, as Amenemhet states: "My men came back with no losses, not one donkey perished, not one patrol was lost, not one craftsman even fell ill." But what is really interesting for us is the expedition's leader; he modestly lists his titles: "The Hereditary Prince, the Count, Governor of Thebes and Vizier; Chief of all the Nobles, Inspector of all that heaven gives, earth creates and the Nile brings, Inspector of everything in this entire land, Amenemhet."

This expedition seems to have played an extremely important part in the life of the vizier Amenemhet. He devotes four different inscriptions to it, reporting that "the animals of the desert came to him, among them a gazelle ready to drop her young. Walking toward the men, she did not run away and when she came to the block for the cover of the [king's] sarcophagus, she delivered her fawn [there] while the army looked on." A miracle, soon to be followed by another: "While they were at work at that mountain on the block for the sarcophagus, a miracle occurred: It rained, the god appeared, his glory was manifested to men, the desert became a lake and the water rose to the level of the rock. Then, a well was found in the middle of the valley, twelve cubits by twelve [i.e. nearly twenty-one feet on a side], filled to the brim with fresh, pure water, protected from animals and hidden from nomads."

Where we see coincidence, it may be that the Egyptians saw

a manifestation of the divine will. The inscription informs us: "Those who where in Egypt heard of it. From the south to the north they prostrated themselves and celebrated the virtue of His Majesty forever, forever!" If, in the text, it is the king who benefits from the intervention of the gods, it is not unlikely that the head of the expedition also profited to a very great degree. Would it be too bold to see in this one of the reasons, perhaps the overriding reason, for Amenemhet's seizure of power some five years later? We do not think so; however, as the instrument of god's will, Amenemhet could have been chosen for this very reason by Mentuhotep himself to be his successor. This would explain why we find, on a schist bowl, the royal cartouches of Mentuhotep II and Amenemhet I written together.

Whatever the truth of the matter, the end of the third Mentuhotep's reign, the end of the Eleventh Dynasty, is hidden in the most absolute darkness. In the present state of our knowledge, there is no reason whatever for believing that the *coup d'etat* (if there was one) that put Amenemhet I on the throne was a violent one. We do not know that the new king employed violence; we do know that he aroused it, both at the beginning and the end of his reign.

Amenemhet I and the Beginning of the Twelfth Dynasty

About 1990 B.C. (1991 according to Hayes), the vizier Amenemhet ascended the throne under the Horus-name Sehetepibre; this is Amenemhet I of the Twelfth Dynasty, Manetho's Amenemmes. The circumstances of his accession are unknown. What is clear is that it was strongly opposed after the fact, perhaps to the point of civil war. This was because the vizier was not of the blood royal, although it is not impossible that he was related to Mentuhotep III, whose mother, too, it seems, was not from the royal line. It must be borne in mind that, under the Old Kingdom, the vizier was

354

very often a relation of the king's; this might have been the case with Amenemhet, which would explain both the favor he enjoyed from the last Mentuhotep, and the boldness with which he seized his throne.

In any case we may be sure that Amenemhet was not descended in the direct line from the pharaohs of the Eleventh Dynasty. This is to be seen in a text written, apparently, at his behest, that gives us information on the king's origin and family. This is the *Prophecy of Neferty* (in fact a "prophecy" written after the event it "foretells"), a text that was to become exceedingly popular in Egypt, for we know two copies of the Eighteenth Dynasty and eighteen of the Ramesside period (Twentieth). To give his composition more authority, the author, a Lower Egyptian, presents his prophet Neferty as a priest of Bubastis living in the reign of Snefru, first king of the Fourth Dynasty, and addressing this report of his vision to the king.

In a first prophecy, Neferty describes the evils that are to descend on Egypt; this occupies more than half the text. The resemblance to the "pessimistic" literature of the First Intermediate Period (e.g. the *Admonitions of an Egyptian Sage*) is striking. In his second prophecy Neferty then announces that a king from the south would restore order and prosperity. He is even able to foretell this pharaoh's name: Ameny, a simple abbreviation of Amenemhet, certainly referring to the first sovereign of that name. In his description of the situation preceding "Ameny," Neferty refers to an invasion of the Delta by Asiatics; he then describes civil disturbances: "The land will live in disorder. I show you a son for an enemy, a brother for an adversary, a man slaying his father. . . . The land is poverty-stricken but its leaders are many." All of which so resembles the *Admonitions* that it has sometimes been thought that the two texts must refer to the same events. But the second prophecy removes all doubt. Neferty continues: "But behold, a king will come from the south, named Ameny. He is the son of a woman from Ta-seti [nome of Elephantine]. He is a child of Upper Egypt, he shall take the White Crown, he shall wear the Red Crown . . . justice will return to its place, iniquity having been driven away."

The author, then, makes no attempt to hide the nonroyal origins of his royal hero; on the contrary he seems to dwell on them. And he stresses that this king puts an end to a period of troubles. Obviously he draws for his description of this period on earlier texts. But that does not mean that there *were* no troubles preceding Amenemhet's accession. It has been pointed out, in fact (G. Posener), that other texts of the Eleventh Dynasty allude to the same dissensions. It would seem that the author of the prophecy has consciously confounded the events of the end of the Eleventh Dynasty and those of the First Intermediate Period, to heighten the importance of Ameny–Amenemhet's role. This text tells us nothing about the manner in which Amenemhet acquired his throne, but it does confirm the existence of a disturbed period, which could have begun not long after the second year of Mentuhotep III, and which resulted in the disappearance of the Eleventh Dynasty. It also confirms the nonroyal origin of the founder of the Twelfth Dynasty, whose father seems to have been a certain Sen-Wosret; at least the Egyptians of the New Kingdom considered him to be that dynasty's ancestor.

Amenemhet reorganized Egypt after the upheavals that marked the end of Mentuhotep III's reign. First of all, as a text at Beni Hassan expressly tells us, he reestablished the boundaries of the nomes: "he caused one city to know its frontiers with another, so that their good frontiers would be as solidly established as the sky." He then restored Memphis as administrative capital of the country. His reasons for this were no doubt complicated. It is probable, for one thing, that the family of Mentuhotep, deprived of national power, was nevertheless still locally powerful in Thebes, and, although Amenemhet took pains to present himself as the legitimate successor of Mentuhotep III, Thebes was probably not enthusiastically loyal to the new king. Then, too, Thebes, in the heart of Upper Egypt, was not too well placed to be capital of the whole kingdom; Memphis, at the angle of the Delta, was more centrally located. Thebes, finally, had been a capital for only a very brief time, whereas Memphis had a tradition of administration already nearly a thousand years old, preserved by the scribes who made it their home. For these and probably for other and unknown reasons Amenemhet moved the capital from Thebes to Ittawi, near Memphis. The name of the new capital is indicative of the king's aims: "[City] that conquers the Two Lands." Amenemhet could keep an eye on both parts of his kingdom from the new residence and, when necessary, rapidly recall them to obedience by force.

Texts of the First Intermediate Period inform us that the whole administrative apparatus of the Old Kingdom had been destroyed (*Admonitions of an Egyptian Sage*: see pp. 329 ff.). Central storehouses, courts, land registers, laws written and customary had disappeared, and the officials had scattered to their homes. We have seen that Mentuhotep I restored some degree of central administration, but much remained to be done, and little of it was done by his successors, as far as we can tell. Amenemhet I, on the other hand, seems to have decided to restore the full table of organization of the old administration. His choice of Ittawi as a capital was of considerable help. Near Memphis, the Old Kingdom's administrative headquarters, it was also near enough to Heracleopolis, capital for the Ninth and Tenth Dynasties. The few officials who had survived the general collapse were therefore likely to be found in the neighborhood. Kheti III had known of them; in the *Instruction for Merikare* he speaks of the Sakkara-Memphis area: "There are officials there from the time of the Royal Residence."

But the Heracleopolitan monarchy was over half a century dead by Amenemhet's time; its surviving, and experienced, officials would have been too few for all the tasks of a fully restored bureaucracy. Amenemhet I therefore had recourse to a full-scale propaganda campaign, with the object of interesting young men in an official career (G. Posener). We have two works written in his reign for just this purpose. *Kemyt* was written at the beginning of the reign by the same author as

357

the *Prophecy of Neferty*. It includes practical aids for the inexperienced scribe (epistolary formulae, ready-made phrases in officialese for use in administrative correspondence) and general exhortations: counsels of "wisdom," the advantages of study, etc. It closes with a sentence that betrays its purpose: "As for the scribe, in no matter which of his labors for the Residence, he is not unhappy." The second work, which has been named the *Satire on Trades*, is even clearer in its intentions. The writer is supposed to be advising his son, but is in fact addressing (over his head, as it were) all future officials, trained, so he tells us, in a special school opened at the capital. In a general way he glorifies the studies and duties of an official, and then, comparing the various trades and professions in Egypt, he shows how superior is that of scribe to all the others, including the priesthood; for the priest in spite of his cloth can be called up for *corvées*, while the scribe alone is immune. It is unfortunate that the text is often faulty, for in the process of praising his profession the author lets drop a good deal of valuable information on the civilization and social conditions of Twelfth Dynasty Egypt.

Amenemhet I had not only to restore the royal administration, he had also to restore the royal prestige, the image of kingship in the eyes of the Egyptian people. This had suffered disastrously in the First Intermediate Period, where the kings of the Seventh, Eighth, Ninth and Tenth Dynasties were no more powerful than the nomarchs, their vassals in principle, their rivals in reality. This depreciation of the public value of royalty was not simply a political matter, it was a spiritual one as well. In the Old Kingdom the king had been thought of as partaking in the nature of divinity; even if this idea is not to be understood literally (see pp. 299 ff.), it is clear that the sovereign is something very different from his subjects. In the First Intermediate Period, however, the authors of folktales do not hesitate to place the king in positions of the most humiliating kind. So in the *Tale of Neferkare and General Sisene* (G. Posener), which takes place either at the very end of the Sixth Dynasty or during the Eighth, the author presents the king as combining secretly with a general and certain high officials against a "litigant of Memphis." The Memphite sets spies on his sovereign, and discovers that the relations between the Son of Re and his general are of rather a special nature: "The king arrived at the house of General Sisene. He threw a brick and kicked [the door] with his foot. Upon which a ladder was let down to him. He climbed up. . . . After His Majesty had done what he wanted with him [the general], he went toward his palace. So . . . he had spent four hours in the house of General Sisene." The rest of the story is lost, but what we have is quite enough: The expression "to do what one wants with someone" has a precise sexual sense in ancient Egyptian. One can see in what direction the prestige of Egyptian royalty has gone.

There are other tales from the earliest years of the Middle Kingdom that are not as scabrous as this, but that display certain pharaohs of the Old Kingdom in a highly disagreeable, not to say odious, light. Everything tends to show that there was, at the time, a current of opinion unfavorable to royalty itself (G. Posener). It was against this that Amenemhet I set his stable of writers to work. Through them, he sought to connect himself to the early kings of the Old Kingdom, Snefru in particular, as the latter still retained the prestige that his more authoritarian successors had lost. Also, possibly under the influence of Osirian religion and morality, he seems to have tried to make royalty more humane. His son was to put these words into his mouth: "I gave to the poor and fed the orphan. I enabled the man of no account to make his way as well as the man of substance."

We have no way of really knowing whether these efforts of Amenemhet I met with success. Still, it is to be noted that, from his reign on, there are no more even veiled attacks on the persons of kings in the literary texts. There was, however, one more thing needed to restore completely the royal prestige— to bring the provincial princes under the direct and absolute authority of the sovereign. But the political situation was still too unstable, the princes still too powerful, for such a program to be carried out; indeed it was not until the reign of Sen-

Wosret III (formerly written Sen-Usert) that the power of the monarchy was restored in the image of the Old Kingdom.

Amenemhet I therefore made no change in the organization of the nomes and respected the hereditary rights of the nomarchs. However, he did attempt to supervise the administration of the provinces and to prevent civil dissension at the delicate moment of the succession, i.e. to assure the continuity of royal power in his line. These were the measures he adopted: first, to install royal overseers in every nome; second, to make the eldest of the royal heirs his coregent on the throne during his own lifetime.

Royal supervision in the provinces was exercised mainly in regard to the taxation the nomes paid to the crown. The proper administration of the country required an exact knowledge of the economic situation of Egypt by the central government. It was not indispensable that all the royal revenues be brought to the capital, but it *was* necessary that the precise extent of the royal resources all over the country be known, in order to dispose of them in the general interest. Therefore, at least in the earlier half of the Twelfth Dynasty, a *de facto* collaboration between the royal and princely administrations arose, although we cannot be sure that this was Amenemhet's design. We do have some indications (very few) of how royal officials and nomarchs jointly managed the royal revenues and the resources of the royal estates. Our best source comes from the reign of Sen-Wosret I, but we have every reason to suppose that the conditions it describes obtained also under Amenemhet I. "All of the taxes due to the king passed through my hands" (the speaker is a nomarch). "The chief overseers of the royal cattle lands sent me 3,000 draft oxen . . . and I paid regularly the profits of their hire, and there were never any arrears in my accounts in any royal office."

It was through the treasury, then, that Amenemhet I reestablished, slowly but surely, a degree of royal control over the provincial administration, while leaving their hereditary governors a great deal of authority and freedom of action. The settlement of the frontiers and the restoration of the land register (in the second year of the reign, according to the papyrus

"Day-book" of an employee of the central registry) already meant a degree of royal interference in local administration. Year by year this increased, by an increasing supervision of the personnel, lands and herds attached to the royal patrimony in the various nomes.

The royal treasury was therefore one of the essential instruments of power in the Twelfth Dynasty's hands. It had its own fleet of transports, and was completely managed by high officials at the king's court, who were therefore independent of the nomarchs.

The real danger from the nomarchs was to be expected in those moments of temporary weakness for the monarchy when the crown changed hands; it was then that rebellious alliances among the nomes could be expected to recur, with the object of influencing the succession; something of the kind seems to have sprung up on the death of Mentuhotep III. Amenemhet therefore set about removing temptation by assuring the transfer of power before his death. A stele of Abydos, from the twentieth year of his reign, tells us that he granted his son, Sen-Wosret I, equal royal status with himself, while he was still on the throne. His son (also known by the Greek version of his name, Sesostris, and appearing in older Egyptological works as Sen-Usert), being already a king, would after the father's death be better able to resist the claims of pretenders to the throne. A wise precaution, as we shall see, for Sen-Wosret's succession was not an easy one.

Sen-Wosret's coregency coincides with a flurry of Egyptian military activity abroad, as if the king, too old to lead his armies beyond the borders, had placed their leadership in younger hands.

If we follow the *Prophecy of Neferty*, Amenemhet, in the first half of his reign, limited his military efforts to the expulsion of those foreigners who had swept into the Delta during the troubles that marked the end of the Eleventh Dynasty. To prevent the return of such intruders, he constructed fortifications on the Delta's frontiers: To the east, where Asiatics posed the greater danger, he built the "Princes' Wall"; to the west, a fortress to contain the Libyans. The Princes' Wall, despite its name, was not a continuous "Great Wall" such as the Chinese and the Romans were to build, but rather a series of forts commanding the strategic passages leading to Egypt. The celebrated *Story of Sinuhe* confirms this; the hero, fleeing Egypt, anxious to avoid arrest at the Princes' Wall, describes his actions: "I crouched in a bush, for fear that the watchman on duty on the wall that day might look in my direction." A key position was fortified, in other words, but not walled across, as when night fell he easily passed through unobserved. This fortress, in all probability located at the entrance of the Wadi Tumilat, has not been found.

In the first half of his reign, then, Amenemhet's military policy was essentially a defensive one. With the coregency of Sen-Wosret, this changed abruptly. In Amenemhet's twenty-fourth year, the fourth year of the coregency, the Egyptian army seems to have struck into Palestine (stele of Nesumontu). In the south, again Egypt takes the offensive: Sen-Wosret founds the fortress of Buhen in Nubia in his father's twenty-fifth year, and Amenemhet glories in having "subdued the inhabitants of the land of Wawat and . . . taken the Medjays prisoner" (*Instruction of Amenemhet I*). In the twenty-ninth year, a new Egyptian force descended on Nubia, and, in the same period, the Egyptian army is extremely active in the eastern, southeastern and southwestern deserts.

There is still argument over how far into Nubia Egypt then expanded. At Kerma, south of the Third Cataract, two large buildings of sun-dried brick have been found, with a cemetery nearby with mounded tombs. In one of these, the statues of a certain Hapydjefa and his wife were discovered. Hapydjefa, nomarch of Assiut, was a contemporary of Sen-Wosret I. From this find it has been concluded that Hapydjefa was Egyptian governor of the Sudan and had been buried in his province (Reisner). This has been energetically opposed (Junker, Säve-Söderbergh) on the grounds that, first, the Egyptians thought it an abomination to be buried outside Egypt, and, second, Hapydjefa is all the less likely to have resigned himself to his ill fortune since we have found a tomb at least prepared for him at Assiut. In addition to which, the Kerma necropolis has produced any number of objects later than the Twelfth Dynasty, and nowadays the opinion is being put forward that the site is likelier to belong to the Thirteenth (Säve-Söderbergh, Hintze); the earlier objects found there, particularly those of the late Old Kingdom, would be the result of looting during the wars of the Second Intermediate Period, in which the Sudanese took part extensively.

If this is the case, then in Amenemhet I's reign only the area stretching from Aswan to the northern end of the Second Cataract was conquered by Egypt. Sen-Wosret I, when he held the throne alone, was to push Egypt's boundary much farther south into the Sudan.

In the Old Kingdom, Egypt's principal enemy was Libya, the land of the Tehenu. In the Sixth Dynasty there appears, in the same region, the Temehu; the two peoples will often be confused with each other in subsequent Egyptian texts. In the Middle Kingdom, the Libyans still represented a danger to Egypt, and Amenemhet built a fortress at the Wadi Natrun to block them. In his thirtieth year, with Lower Nubia subjected, Sen-Wosret I turned toward the territory of the Temehu. His campaign brought victory, but he returned to tragedy. For, before he reached the capital, a palace revolution broke out in Ittawi, and Amenemhet I was assassinated. The *Story of Sinuhe* tells us that this took place in "the year thirty, the third month of the inundation, the seventh day," i.e. possibly February 15, 1962 B.C. (W. C. Hayes). Sen-Wosret had been coregent a little more than nine years.

The scene that closed the remarkable career of Amenemhet I is known to us by a very strange text: the *Instruction of Amenemhet I*. Strange, for in this document the dead king addresses his son Sen-Wosret I from the next world, and tells his son of the manner in which he was forced to quit this one:

It was after supper, night had come, I had retired and was stretched on my bed. I was weary and had sunk into slumber. [Suddenly] it was as if I heard a [distant] noise of clashing arms and men calling out my name. I was awakened then by the sound of fighting. I was alone, I saw the guards were fighting each other. Had I applied myself [immediately] with arms in hand, I could have put the

cowards to flight, but no man is brave by night, no man can fight
alone, no man can conquer without allies. Alas, the attack was
made when I was without you . . .

For Sen-Wosret, at the time, had barely crossed the border
into Egypt; what happened when he heard the news, still in
the far western Delta, we learn from the *Story of Sinuhe*: "The
friends of the palace sent messengers . . . to make known to
the king's son the events that had occurred at the court. The
messengers found him on the road; they reached him as night
was falling. He did not hesitate an instant. The Falcon [i.e.,
metaphorically, the new pharaoh] took wing with his attend-
ants without letting his army know of it."

For the secrecy and speed of Sen-Wosret's departure we
have Sinuhe's own explanation: "[But] the royal children who
were following him in that army had [also] been sought out,
and an appeal had been made to one of them . . ." For the
assassination plot had been hatched in the old king's own en-
tourage, as the *Instruction of Amenemhet* informs us: "I had
foreseen nothing, I had not been wary. . . . But had women
ever taken up arms? Had traitors ever been bred up in the very
heart of the palace?" And, in another passage: "He who ate
my bread enrolled the plotters, he to whom I had given my
arm raised a revolt." In other words, in spite of Amenemhet's
precaution in naming Sen-Wosret coregent, there was every
possibility of a dynastic struggle, and the situation was so
uncertain that Sinuhe fled to Asia, for fear of being himself
implicated (as an official of the harem, perhaps he had good
grounds): "I did not propose to return to this court, where I
thought there might be fighting."

Sen-Wosret (Sesostris) I (1971–1928 B.C.)

We do not know how Sen-Wosret I overcame this conspiracy. We do know that he did, and reigned for thirty-eight years
more in his own right. It was not until two years before his

death that he associated his son Amenemhet II in the royal title. The dynastic crisis of 1962 B.C. does not seem to have long or seriously disturbed the public order, and Sen-Wosret's reign was one of very great accomplishment both internally and externally.

The conquest of Nubia had already gotten well under way by the beginning of the reign, thanks to Sen-Wosret's campaigns as coregent. As sole king, Sen-Wosret left these expeditions to the nomarchs; they were charged with maintaining the Egyptian presence in Nubia and continuing its expansion. In the year eighteen, around 1954 B.C., the kingdom of Kush was reached. If the latter, as everything leads us to suspect, was really located a little to the south of Semneh, the armies of Egypt had overcome the obstacles of the Second Cataract. It is possible that, in order to consolidate his conquests, the king had a chain of fortresses constructed along the Nile, as his father had on the eastern and western borders. The present all-out archaeological campaign in Nubia (1964 A.D.) may make it possible to know whether the great fortifications erected by Sen-Wosret III were preceded by others built by Sen-Wosret I. This is definite for Buhen, and there is no reason to suppose this was an isolated case.

Under the Old Kingdom, Egyptian policy toward Nubia was determined primarily by the needs of defense, secondarily by those of trade. With the Middle Kingdom a new motif appears: gold. In Sen-Wosret's reign Egypt's gold begins to be drawn from Sudanese mines; as time went on, gold mining was to become the principal resource of Nubia.

In Asia, a softer climate seems to prevail: Sen-Wosret I maintains almost an *entente cordiale* with the rulers of the lands to the northeast. This can be seen both by the Sinai inscriptions and by the *Story of Sinuhe*.

Since the beginning of the Old Kingdom, Egyptian expeditions had set out for Sinai to return with turquoise and, probably, copper. After Pepi II, these expeditions cease. They do not begin again until the early Twelfth Dynasty. Under the Old Kingdom, the relations between Egyptians and the natives of the peninsula had been difficult; scenes of warfare are carved on the rocks of the peninsula in great number. With the Twelfth Dynasty, these relations are on a different footing: "The inscriptions contain not even one allusion to enemies, quite the contrary, the Asiatics of Sinai and of the adjacent regions often, if not regularly, accompany the Egyptian expeditions" (J. Cerny, 1955). In fact, one can find, fairly often, inscriptions carved by Asiatics side by side with those of the Egyptians.

This atmosphere of peace is confirmed, for territories further north, by the *Story of Sinuhe*. As we have seen, the harem official Sinuhe fled to Asia during the dynastic struggle of 1962 B.C.; he was to remain there for over twenty years. Now throughout his narrative of these years, in other words during the greater part of Sen-Wosret I's reign as sole king, in the first place there is never a mention of any war between Egypt and an Asiatic state, and, in the second place, all of these principalities appear to be independent of Egypt, with whom they are all on excellent terms. Egyptians, like Sinuhe, live in Syria-Palestine, and the pharaoh's messengers travel everywhere without being troubled in any way. After the campaign some six years before Amenemhet I's death, and all through Sen-Wosret I's reign, there is no further Egyptian military action in Asia. And the campaign just referred too, in the fourth year of the coregency of Amenemhet I and Sen-Wosret I, was in itself a limited one, having penetrated no farther than the southernmost towns of Palestine, on the border of the desert of Suez.

In the course of excavations in Palestine and Syria, many Egyptian objects of the Middle Kingdom have been brought to light. The texts preclude the possibility that these are the remains of war and conquest; they must have reached their destinations by peaceful means. Either they are the result of trade between Egypt and Asia, or they are testimony to a systematic policy on the part of Egypt's king. We do know, from the New Kingdom diplomatic correspondence at Tell-el-Amarna, that the Egyptian court was then in the habit of making gifts to the kings and princelings of Asia in return for their alliance; we have every ground for supposing that this was already the custom under Sen-Wosret I. At Ugarit (modern Ras Shamra), a necklace of amulets and pearls has been found bearing the cartouche of Sen-Wosret I, and many scarabs with the same name engraved have been discovered in Palestine (Gaza, Lachish, Gezer, Beisan, Megiddo). Besides, there is a passage in the *Tale of Sinuhe* that seems to refer to this very policy: Sinuhe has received an invitation from the king to return to Egypt, and this is how he describes it: "Then His Majesty sent me envoys with royal gifts, he gladdened the heart of this humble servant like [i.e. as if I had been] a ruler of some foreign country."

This "gift policy," begun by Sen-Wosret I, was continued by his successors, and to it we owe the Middle Kingdom sculptures found not only in Asia but also in Nubia, and even Crete. The presence of Egyptian objects in Crete has led historians to assume direct relations between the two countries from the reign of Mentuhotep II on. This opinion is founded, aside from the archaeological evidence, on a mistranslation of the Egyptian word *Hau-nebut*, which, it was thought, meant the peoples of the Pre-Hellenic Aegean. I have shown (1953) that this is an error. The Egyptian name of Crete is *Keftiu*; direct relations between these two civilizations do not really begin until the Eighteenth Dynasty. Still, there is no question that *indirect* relations date back to the Middle Kingdom. The ancient seamen were not yet as bold as has been supposed; the trade route passed through the ports of Syria and Cyprus. Ugarit, to which Sen-Wosret had sent gifts, was a great commercial center to which objects from the Aegean were drawn in quantity (C. F. A. Schaeffer); from there, they would be reexported to Egypt. In the same way and by the same indirect route Egyptian wares, found in great number in Palestine and on the Syrian coast, would reach Crete.

Nubia and Asia were not the only lands to feel, in one form or another, the influence of Egypt. The military campaigns in the south, under the coregency, had been preceded by a sweep through the eastern and western deserts. This effort was not relaxed in Sen-Usert's reign as sole king: The documents tell us that Egyptians went as far as the great western oases, in expeditions setting out from Thebes. "I reached the western oases," writes one commander. "I explored all the routes leading to them, and I brought back the fugitives I found there. My army remained safe and without loss" (Stele of Kai, at Kamula). In Libya proper, to the northwest of Egypt, the campaign shortly before the assassination of Amenemhet I seems to have assured tranquillity in this direction, for there is no further mention of the Temehu in the texts of Sen-Wosret I's time.

When that king's reign reached its end, Lower Nubia, from the First Cataract to a point south of the Second, was under Egyptian control: Asia was open to peaceful Egyptian influence; the eastern and western deserts were familiar to Egyptian mining expeditions; the Libyans, crushed, were no more a danger to the valley of the Nile. This expansion and influence of Egypt beyond her borders were a direct result of her internal strength.

To turn, then, to internal affairs, Sen-Wosret I does not seem to have changed in any way his father's policy toward the nomarchs. They were, in his reign, for the most part sons of those who had ruled under Amenemhet I. They gave Egypt continuity in the administration of the provinces without abusing, it would seem, the independence that their hereditary right and personal wealth gave them. They remained loyal to Sen-Wosret after the assassination of his predecessor, and furnished him with the contingents of which the royal army was composed.

The policy of the "revaluation" of royalty, if we may call it so, which Amenemhet I had set in motion, now began to bear fruit. We have but to read the eulogy of Sen-Wosret I in the *Story of Sinuhe* to recognize it: "He is surely a god, who has not his peer, before whom no other [like him] has existed. He is a master of wisdom with perfect plans, with excellent commandments . . ." The text of Sinuhe always employs the term "god" to designate the king, but attributes to him human

368

qualities: loyalty, wisdom, courage, good will. We see by this how far the concept of royalty has come since the Fourth Dynasty. The king is still the *neter nefer*, the "good god," but he is more a superman than a god, and the human character of his authority, perhaps the result of Osirian influence, makes the strongest possible contrast with the inhuman authority of the Old Kingdom pharaohs.

Sen-Wosret made his son Amenemhet coregent but, perhaps learning by his own experience the dangers of too long a coregency, did not give the prince royal rank until late in his reign; their joint rule lasted only two years, from the forty-second to the forty-fourth year of Sen-Wosret I. To aid him in the administration of the country, Sen-Wosret made use of a vizier. Either because Amenemhet I had been wary (again learning by his own experience) of placing too great power in the hands of a vizier, or because by chance we have no text referring to the role of the vizier in his reign, viziers seem to have played only a secondary role in the affairs of Egypt in the very early Twelfth Dynasty. Under Sen-Wosret, at least five viziers succeeded one another, and we may wonder whether the king, following his father's policy, did not seek to reduce the dangers of usurpation by dividing the vizier's functions in two: There would then have been two viziers, one for the north, the other for the south.

Whatever the geographical extent of his power, the vizier, under Sen-Wosret I, was the head of the courts and of the administration in general. It was he who promulgated the laws and kept the archives. His titles of chief of royal works and treasurer-in-chief made him the arbitrator of the country's economy. He had, then, all powers in theory, aside from the army and the police.

With the assistance of the hereditary nomarchs and the viziers, Sen-Wosret I carried on the administrative reorganization begun by his father. This, too, soon bore fruit, and the reign of Sen-Wosret I was a period of great economic development in Egypt. The provincial cemeteries throughout the country display the very great wealth of the nomes at this time. And the first Twelfth Dynasty kings were not satisfied to restore the abundance that Egypt had known in the Old Kingdom, they also set about the deliberate creation of new resources; in the Fayum, for example, a whole new province was opened up to agriculture. The name of Amenemhet III is connected with this great work, but it is the lineal descendant of programs set in motion by Sen-Wosret I.

Moving upstream from the Delta the Nile is a succession of small pockets of arable land, pinched between the Libyan and Arabian escarpments. None of these pockets is of any great size, except the Fayum, where there was in Neolithic times a large lake, fed by an arm of the Nile. This arm seems subsequently to have silted up, and the lake consequently dropped below sea level. One of the aims of the Twelfth Dynasty was to resupply it with water, by restoring its connection with the river; the former lake bottom was rich land, and could be expected to produce superbly if only it could be brought into contact with the annual inundation. The proximity of the Fayum to Memphis was an added inducement; the new fields might supply the needs of the capital. They did, and more. Thanks to the work of the Twelfth Dynasty, the Fayum became one of the richest provinces in Egypt.

Our best proof of Egypt's economic improvement in this reign is still the number of monuments that Sen-Wosret I was able to build and restore in his forty-four years on the throne. At least thirty-five sites have revealed architectural ruins of Sen-Wosret's time; from Alexandria to Aswan there is no important site where he has not left his trace. This presupposes an economy so flourishing that it could supply the labor needed to maintain the daily life of the people, and still have hands left over for the construction program of the king. No doubt the most important undertaking of the reign was the restoration of the temple of Heliopolis. This had both political and religious ends in vew. Religious: Heliopolis, *Iunu* in Egyptian, capital of the thirteenth nome of Lower Egypt, was the home of the sun-god Re, one of the oldest gods of Egypt; the dynasty had an interest in reviving the influence of a cult and priesthood acceptable to the whole country, for that influence could be turned to its own uses. Which brings us to the political aspect: The god of Heliopolis was the great protector of the pharaohs of the Old Kingdom, who had indeed taken the title of "Son of Re"; in restoring the earthly residence of this god, Sen-Wosret would be, in the popular mind, connected with the traditions of the Old Kingdom and ratified as the legitimate successor of its great kings. Finally, Heliopolis lies at the entrance to the Delta, and its temple was one of the great centers of pilgrimage for all the residents of Lower Egypt; as Sen-Wosret had beautified it, so he would win the esteem of all these pilgrims, a considerable gain for a king who had all his local roots in the south. In this light the restored temple of Heliopolis can be seen as a pledge of the reconciliation of north and south, a gift by a southern king to his northern subjects, marking an end to the lingering bitterness left by fratricidal war.

The reign of Sen-Wosret I had begun in shadow, but it went on to become one of the most glorious in Egyptian history. Egypt had recovered all of its old power, her royalty had recovered all of its old prestige. It is therefore no great wonder that Sen-Wosret was made a god after his death, and that the Sesostris legend of classical antiquity (best seen in Diodorus Siculus) retained, after two thousands years, an echo of his accomplishments.

The Successors of Sen-Wosret I—Amenemhet II and Sen-Wosret II (1929–1878 B.C.)

Those accomplishments go far toward explaining the reigns of his immediate successors: They had but to maintain what had already been established.

Amenemhet II (1929–1895 B.C.) had been, as we have seen, coregent with his father for a little over two years. He followed his policies with regard to the nomarchs, whose hereditary right to office he confirmed (tomb text of Khnumhotep II, at Beni Hassan). Egypt's position abroad was now so strong that he had no need to reaffirm it by arms; we have not a single text referring to a military campaign under Amenemhet II. Nubia was regularly visited by the treasurers of the king; Asia remained open to Egyptian influence, as is shown by the number of objects found there with this pharaoh's name, or those of members of the royal family (a sphinx at Qatna, a statue at Ugarit). The Sinai mines were regularly worked and new veins opened up. A treasure discovered in the foundations of the temple of Tôd in Upper Egypt shows that Amenemhet brought to his gods gifts originally procured in Asia. Four bronze coffers marked with his cartouche contain gold jewelry and utensils, gold and silver ingots, Babylonian cylinder seals, cups, lapis lazuli. We have no grounds for imagining that this treasure represents booty gained in war; it could easily have been amassed by exchanges with Asiatic rulers.

Commercial relations were also maintained with the southeast. A Red Sea port was established at Sau, at the mouth of the Wadi Gasus, and, by at least the twenty-eighth year of the reign, a fleet returned there from a voyage to the land of Punt. These expeditions to Punt are always a sign of prosperity in Egypt, and this was clearly the case under Amenemhet II, to judge by the richness of the provincial tombs, the impressiveness of his pyramid built in stone at Dashur, and the splendor of the grave furnishings in the neighboring tombs of the king's family. The jewelry found there is among the most beautiful productions of the art of ancient Egypt.

Sen-Wosret II (1897–1878 B.C.), son of Amenemhet II, was named coregent in 1897; he shared the throne for three years with his father, who died in 1895. He continued his predecessors' policies completely. There was no interference with the nomarchs' hereditary rights. He appears to have waged war neither in Africa nor in Asia. His only known military activity is a tour of inspection of the Nubian fortresses. The exploitation of the mines and quarries of Sinai and of the Wadi Hammamat was actively continued. This is one evidence of the country's prosperity under his rule; another is the size of the king's building program. Like his father and grandfather before him, Sen-Wosret II took a particular interest in the development of the Fayum.

With the death of Sen-Wosret II, around 1878 B.C., a remarkable period of Egyptian history comes to a close. The first four pharaohs of the Twelfth Dynasty, having reunified and pacified Egypt and having restored the royal authority, set out to revitalize the Egyptian economy and succeeded in their task. Avoiding, as much as possible, the burdens of foreign war, they nevertheless extended Egypt's influence far beyond her boundaries. Within those boundaries they were able to uphold the authority of the crown, without destroying the rights of the nobility. Much of this was to change with the reign of Sen-Wosret III.

Sen-Wosret III (1878–1843 B.C.)

In all the two-hundred-year record of the Twelfth Dynasty, no reign is half so famous as that of Sen-Wosret III. The face of the king, as conceived by his portrait sculptors, is forceful, peremptory, stern—or so it has been interpreted in modern times. It is as if the powerful personality of this monarch had eclipsed, in human memories, those of the other rulers of his line—unjustly, as it appears, for nothing indicates that an Amenemhet I or a Sen-Wosret I was his inferior. In fact the reality behind the Sesostris legend belies it: Many of the traits that adorn the ideal pharaoh of its Hellenistic authors are borrowed, not only from Ramses II, but also from Sen-Wosret I, even Amenemhet I, as well as from Sen-Wosret III himself. And yet his reputation rests ultimately on a basis of solid fact: Under his reign, the Middle Kingdom reached its height.

The first pharaohs of the dynasty had come to power with the aid of the feudal princes; they left their prerogatives untouched. On the contrary, one of the first official acts of Khakaure–Sen-Wosret III was to abolish the very office of nomarch. We do not know his reasons. Had the princes tried to revolt on his accession? Or was it simply that the new king's authoritarian character could no longer support the independence of his nobles? Our sources tell us nothing. We only know that from about 1860 B.C., toward the middle of the reign, the texts speak no more of nomarchs. The little local dynasties of haughty barons, who dated events by the years of their own reign and not the king's, who had consecrated in the temples colossal statues in their own image as large as any of the king's, these were no more; they disappear from the Egyptian scene. All of the provinces from now on are directly administered from the royal residence by three government departments (*waret* in Egyptian), one for the north (*waret* of the north), one for Middle Egypt (*waret* of the south), one for Upper Egypt (*waret* of the head of the south). A great official directs each of these departments, with the aid of an assistant, a council (*djadjat*), and a horde of minor bureaucrats. The whole apparatus is under the direction of the vizier.

It may be that the eviction of the nomarchs was a gradual process; it may even be that it was not universal, but was directed mainly at the powerful princes of Middle Egypt, those of the "Oryx" and the "Hare" nomes in particular, for we know that the nome of Antaeopolis (the modern Qaw-el-Kebir, the tenth nome of Upper Egypt) retained its nomarch in the reign of Amenemhet III. It is nevertheless perfectly clear that, by this measure, Sen-Wosret III had returned to a highly centralized brand of administration quite close to that of the Old Kingdom. It is therefore no particular surprise to see, in his reign, the first appearance of a new social level that one may call a "middle class" (W. C. Hayes): officials of middling rank, artisans, small landowners, who apply their new riches to the erection of stelae in their name, or statuettes in their image, in the sanctuary of Osiris at Abydos.

Sen-Wosret III's second departure from the tradition of his dynasty was an all-out attack on Upper Nubia. Here too we have no idea what his reasons were. Nubia does not seem to have been particularly restive in the reign of Sen-Wosret II, nor does she seem to have become suddenly menacing, but we must remember that we are very ill informed indeed about events from 1930 to 1880 B.C. Whoever visits the network of fortresses erected during the Middle Kingdom at the Second Cataract, from Semneh in the south to Buhen in the north, cannot fail to be impressed by their number and their complexity as well as by their strength. They can only be explained by the assumption that the Egyptians faced, in this area, an enemy at once powerful, organized and aggressive. They would not have been justified against occasional nomad raids out of the eastern deserts. They were, in fact, Egypt's answer to the problem of Kerma.

From the beginning of the second millennium B.C. we have every indication that Upper Nubia had entered on a phase of accelerated development. Possibly this was because the country had been invaded by pastoral peoples from the south or the southwest. Recent archaeological work in Sudanese Nubia (1961–1966) has given us more information on a population, designated as the "C" group, occupying in this period all the region from Aswan in the north to the first rapids of the Second Cataract in the south. Still farther south appear peoples connected with what is called the Kerma culture.

The peoples of the "C" group were, it appears, African whites, Hamites; cousins german, that is, to the southern Egyptians, and related to the present-day Berbers of northern Africa. They were therefore not Negroes, although no doubt they were dark enough in skin color, and Negroid physical characteristics would from time to time appear among them as a result of contacts with the peoples of the distant south. They were a sedentary people, settled on the banks of the Nile, but devoting a good deal of their energies still to stock-raising, especially cattle. Their pottery is very handsome, red with black borders, after the manner of Predynastic Egyptian ware, or black with incised white or (sometimes) polychrome decoration. At least a part of the Nubian mercenary forces who fought for one side or another in the wars of the First Intermediary Period were drawn from the peoples of the "C" group. It is often proposed that they entered Nubia from some area outside the valley of the Nile; but it is just as possible to see in them descendants of the earlier indigenous "A" and "B" groups who, in the First Intermediate Period, perhaps under Egyptian influence, had made rapid strides in cultural evolution, their population expanding to the point where new lands became a necessity. This development, whatever its cause, affected Lower Nubia to a degree that called forth the conquest by Mentuhotep I and Åmenemhet I of Wawat at the very beginning of the Middle Kingdom. But the general cultural advance seems to have affected the region between the Second and Fourth Cataracts to the south as well.

One of the political centers of the new Nubian power was Kerma, just south of the Third Cataract. The possibility of an Egyptian seizure of Kerma at the beginning of the Twelfth Dynasty now seems to be ruled out; it is likely that the relations between Egypt and the Nubians of Kerma were not yet basically hostile. Egypt limited herself to probing the periphery of the new state, which in any case was as yet, in all probability, not unified. Still, that Sen-Wosret I already felt the need of fortifying the Second Cataract shows, in our opinion, that Egypt was well aware of the potential danger. What came next? Did the neighborly relations between Egypt and Kerma vanish as a result of the acts of one side or the other? We are absolutely in the dark. All we know is that Sen-Wosret III intervened with characteristic energy. He led no less than four campaigns southward, to face these newest enemies of Egypt.

The king began by assuring his lines of communication, improving or clearing the channels through which Egyptian boats crossed the rapids of the First Cataract. One of the channels when completed was over eighty yards long, ten yards wide, and twenty-six feet deep. In the eighth year of the reign these engineering works had been accomplished, and the king set out "to overthrow Kush the contemptible." The campaign did not fulfill his hopes, for three more were to follow it, in his tenth, sixteenth and nineteenth years. In the campaign of the year sixteen the king seems to have pushed deep into enemy territory, where he ravaged the villages, appropriated the women, destroyed the wells and burned the fields of his too stubborn

376

enemy. The expedition of his nineteenth year left at high Nile, when the rapids could most easily be traversed, i.e. in late September or the beginning of October, and did not return to Egypt until low Nile, in April or May. In other words he spent seven or eight months in enemy territory, in his fourth and final attempt to crush the Nubians.

Without success. The peoples of the south remained a source of danger. Sen-Wosret III therefore took measures to fortify the frontier at its most easily defended point, i.e. between Semneh and Buhen. In addition to this he issued strict regulations for the prevention of any infiltration of Nubians into Egypt. The stele of the eighth year of his reign, found in Semneh, is an example of the thoroughness of the king: "Southern border fortified in the year eight under the majesty of the King of Upper and Lower Egypt Khakaure [=Sen-Wosret III] . . . to prevent any Nehesy [i.e. Nubian] from crossing over when he comes downriver by land or boat, or any horde of Nehesiu, excepting a Nehesy who comes to carry on trade in Iken or on an official mission . . ." (Berlin stele 14935, after a translation from the Egyptian by G. Posener).

We have certain dispatches sent home by commandants of these forts. They show that these regulations were still carried out to the letter by the successors of Sen-Wosret III. Nubian war parties were therefore prevented from passing the Second Cataract. The king had not succeeded in annihilating the Nubian power, but he had at least contained it. Egypt was protected from its threat. This explains why, in the neighborhood of the cataract, Sen-Wosret III was honored as a god. In the New Kingdom, the fort at Semneh still celebrated his cult.

In Asia, too, Sen-Wosret III broke with the policy of his predecessors. The peaceful coexistence of Egyptians and Asiatics in the Sinai peninsula ends abruptly; the mining expeditions from now on must be protected by the army. At the beginning of the reign an army led by the king in person enters Asia and marches as far as *Sekmem* in Palestine (probably the Biblical Shechem). We have no other direct evidence for

Sen-Wosret III's campaigns in Asia. There are, however, the "Execration Texts," found on potsherds in Upper Egypt and in Mirgissa, giving a list of Asiatic princes and peoples who are to be broken magically when the pottery is dashed to the ground. The texts show a very close knowledge by the Egyptians of the political situation in Syria-Palestine; they also show that all these little states and tribes were considered enemies of Egypt—else why use magic to render them harmless? The king, in short, had been active in Asia, bringing not gifts but destruction: Greek legend was to invent conquests stretching to the Black Sea and the borders of India.

When Sen-Wosret III departed a world he had so thoroughly stirred up, the power of the Egyptian monarchy was at its peak. Egypt was protected against incursions from the south and east; the abolition of the office of nomarch had left all power in the hands of the king; the economy of the country was flourishing, as is now for the first time attested not only by royal monuments, but also by the statues of the middle class. Such was the condition of Egypt on the death of Sen-Wosret III. In two generations, the Dark Ages were to begin again.

Amenemhet III (1842–1797 B.C.)

So great were the accomplishments of Sen-Wosret III, at home and abroad, that his son and successor Amenemhet III seems to have been able to rest on his father's laurels through a long and uneventful reign. Sen-Wosret III had ruled for thirty-five years; his son was therefore quite mature on his accession, and reigned for forty-five years more. This long reign was devoted to the economic development of Egypt.

Our evidence for this is the intensive exploitation of the mineral resources of the Sinai peninsula that then took place; no less than fifty-nine inscriptions from Amenemhet III's reign have been counted there. The mining installations were improved, and the temple of Hathor considerably enlarged. The other mining regions, in the Wadi Hammamat to the south, seem to have been the scene of similar activity. But the fame of Amenemhet III was to be assured above all by his work in the reclamation of the Fayum. The Greeks (who knew the area as Lake Moeris) attributed the entire work of restoring the Fayum to him alone, although, as we have seen, the project had been begun under Sen-Wosret II, if not before. Amenemhet III, however, was certainly responsible for the system of barrages and canals that, by regularizing and controlling the flow of Nile waters through the Bahr Yusuf, allowed a very great area in the Fayum depression to be opened to agriculture—the modern estimate is an area of more than 17,000 acres.

The riches of Egypt in his reign were translated by Amenemhet III into buildings. The Greeks considered the "labyrinth" to be, in Herodotus' phrase, "beyond speech." Now this monument is simply Amenemhet III's funerary temple at Hawara—perhaps also his palace and administrative center as well. Unfortunately, it is completely destroyed, and we cannot therefore form any idea of its appearance and extent. Herodotus says that it surpassed, in beauty, the Great Pyramids themselves.

King Hor and Amenemhet IV (1798–1790 B.C.)

At the death of Amenemhet III, Egypt had been ruled for a century by just two sovereigns, Sen-Wosret III and Amenemhet III; it was therefore inevitable that their successor would be already advanced in years. It is possible that one of the sons of Amenemhet III, after several years of coregency with his father, predeceased him. This, at least, is the explanation given for the monuments of a certain King Hor, found near the pyramid of Amenemhet III. However, a recent find at Tanis tends to place this king's reign under the Thirteenth Dynasty (P. Montet and H. Kees).

The case is clearer with Amenemhet IV; the monuments and the king lists show that he directly succeeded Amenemhet

III, his father, and reigned only nine years, three months and twenty-seven days (*Turin Papyrus*); even this brief stretch of time must include some period of coregency with his father. His reign was nevertheless a prosperous one, to judge by the number and quality of his monuments; Egyptian influence continued to penetrate Asia, for objects with his name have been found in a princely tomb at Byblos.

Sebekneferu or Neferusebek (1789–1786 B.C.)

The Twelfth Dynasty's last sovereign was a woman. Sebekneferu (the name should perhaps be read Neferusebek) was no doubt daughter to Amenemhet III and sister, or half sister, to Amenemhet IV. Her reign, according to the *Turin Papyrus*, lasted but three years, ten months and twenty-four days. Nevertheless a fairly large number of monuments bearing her name have been found. A woman on the throne—this suggests that the long line of Sen-Wosrets and Amenemhets had reached its end, that there were no more male heirs. This is why the dynasty comes to an end with Sebekneferu, and with it the Egyptian Middle Kingdom.

Egyptian Civilization in the Middle Kingdom

The Middle Kingdom has left us no monument comparable to the Great Pyramids of the Old Kingdom. In great part this is to be explained by the fact that the pharaohs of the Middle Kingdom used, in their constructions, materials less resistant to time than the enormous limestone blocks of the Tura quarries. But Greek travelers of the fifth century B.C. bear witness that these monuments, still standing in their day, were the equals at least of the architectural creations of the Old Kingdom.

Egyptian civilization, in fact, reached during the Middle Kingdom one of its most brilliant peaks. The restored monarchy helped spread Egyptian culture far beyond the borders of the land. From now on Syria-Palestine and Upper Nubia both, though not under the direct rule of the pharaoh, were more and more impregnated by Egyptian art and, no doubt, literature. As far as the Aegean shores of Europe, via Syrian ports in all probability, objects of Egyptian workmanship found a home. Such objects found in Crete, and Minoan pottery found in Egypt, while they do not support the perhaps exaggerated idea of the closeness of Egyptian-Minoan relations that has been formed, nevertheless testify to the reality of their existence. Europe, then, begins now to show dimly on the Egyptian horizon. It is, of course, quite wrong to speak of an Egyptian empire under the Twelfth Dynasty. Egypt's direct rule never extended beyond the southern border of Palestine, in this age, nor south of the Second Cataract in Nubia. And yet the Egypt of Sen-Wosret III cast its cultural shadow on every country in its neighborhood. And this, to a great degree, Egypt owed to the perfection of its art.

The temples of the Middle Kingdom were built, for the most part, with small limestone blocks. These have long since disappeared into the lime kilns of modern Egypt. Where, by some miracle, they have been preserved, as at Medinet-el-Maadi or at Karnak, in the foundations of a New Kingdom temple, we are able to appreciate how great has been the loss elsewhere. The surviving wall reliefs are the equals in every way of those of the Old Kingdom. Finds of jewelry at Lahun and Dashur demonstrate that Middle Kingdom craftsmen are as dexterous as those of the New Kingdom, and often have better taste. But it is in sculpture above all that the art of the Twelfth Dynasty attains its summit. The pharaohs of the Old Kingdom had been pictured as serene, impassive beings, veritable graven images; the sculptors of the Middle Kingdom portray their kings as men. And not just men, but men whose faces have been lined and molded by the vicissitudes of life and power—tragic, often tormented faces. The realism of the portrait sculptures of Sen-Wosret III and of Amenemhet III is eternal testimony to the humanity, the universality of Egyptian art.

For Egyptian literature, this was *the* golden age. Middle

381

Kingdom texts serve as literary models for the works of all later ages of Egyptian history; they are the classics of Egyptian literature. It has recently been shown (G. Posener) that many of them were inspired by the pharaohs for political ends, but this in no way detracts from their power and their charm. The *Story of Sinuhe*, for example, remains after four thousand years "one of the masterpieces of world literature"; it has been proven that the *Tale of the Shipwrecked Sailor* and the stories of the *Westcar Papyrus* lie behind certain of the tales of the *Thousand and One Nights*. For generation after generation, then, readers and listeners had fallen under their spell.

But there is more than fiction to the credit of Egyptian literature in the Middle Kingdom. To this age we owe scientific works such as the great medical papyri (*Hearst, Ebers*, and *Berlin Papyri*); they are preserved on New Kingdom papyri, but textual criticism has been able to show that these are copies of originals composed in the Middle Kingdom. The same holds true for the mathematical papyri (*Rhind* and *Moscow Papyri*). And, from a papyrus found at the Ramesseum, which gives lists of geographical, technical, and anatomical terms, of the names of crafts and professions and of fauna and flora, we find that the Egyptians, in the Middle Kingdom, had already attained a level of culture high enough to feel the need of—an encyclopedia.

The pharaohs, then, of the latter Eleventh and of the Twelfth Dynasty had restored to Egypt its lost unity, and given it an incomparable prosperity; this, in turn, stimulated a remarkable flowering of Egyptian culture in every domain. Nothing seemed so solidly based, so clearly destined for further progress, as Egyptian civilization in the early eighteenth century B.C. And nothing proved more vulnerable.

11

The Second Intermediate Period and the Hyksos Invasion of Egypt

There is no period in Egyptian history so impenetrable to modern eyes as that which falls between the end of the Twelfth Dynasty (ca. 1785 B.C.) and the beginning of the Eighteenth (ca. 1570 B.C.). We are very lucky indeed that we have these two dates, representing the death of Sebekneferu and the accession of Ahmose I, the first from Sothiac chronology (see pp. 281 ff.), the second from other sound evidence; without these, in attempting to estimate the lapse of time between the end of the Middle Kingdom and the beginning of the New Kingdom, we should be entirely at sea. This lapse is conventionally called the Second Intermediate Period, by analogy with that between the Old and Middle Kingdoms.

Had we been left with only Manetho's chronology to guide us, we should assign to the Second Intermediate Period a duration of 1,590 years; this would have seemed justified by the very great number of its kings, over 200. The figure of 217 pharaohs, who are definitely known to have reigned during the Second Intermediate Period, is confirmed by the ancient Egyptian lists—particularly the *Turin Papyrus*, our surest guide in these matters, which has preserved the names of at least 123 kings; to which must be added those pharaohs whom it does not mention, known to us from other king lists (e.g. the *Karnak Table*) and from contemporary monuments.

But, as we do know the two terminal dates of 1786 B.C. and

1567 B.C., the Second Intermediate Period cannot have lasted longer than 220 years. How are we to fit into this length of time the reigns of nearly 220 kings? By assuming for each a reign of barely over a year? We do know, from the ancient sources, that some of them actually reigned only a few months, Renseneb of the Thirteenth Dynasty, for example, or Antef VII of the Seventeenth. But we also know that some of them reigned for many years on end; for example, Merneferre held the throne for over twenty-three years, and Apophis I for more than forty. Besides, consider what the average duration of a royal reign was, in periods in which we can be reasonably sure of the order of succession and of the chronology of the reigns: for the Old Kingdom, seventeen years; for the Middle Kingdom, twenty-five years (the figure is high, because of the exceptionally long reigns of Sen-Wosret III and Amenemhet III); for the New Kingdom, sixteen years, at least under the Eighteenth and Nineteenth Dynasties. The extremely short reigns of the Second Intermediate Period require, then, some sort of political explanation. A maximally disturbed political situation, where one *coup d'état* succeeded another? Parallel dynasties, simultaneously ruling the crowd of tiny kingdoms into which Egypt must then have been divided? Some profound change in the nature of the institution of monarchy (W. C. Hayes)? A very great number of hypotheses has been put forward, utilizing one or more of the possibilities just outlined, to try to put some order into this confusion of kings and dynasties. Not one, if the truth be known, is convincing; we must await the discovery of new sources before we can, *perhaps*, attempt to write the history of Egypt in the Second Intermediate Period.

For the present, our sources for such a history are both too few and too fallible. Manetho is indispensable but untrustworthy; we cannot accept the chronology his excerptors have transmitted to us; his figures must be corrected. Worse, these unacceptable figures (they add up to 217 kings reigning a total of 1,590 years) are all he offers us; he has preserved no names. (A fragment cited by Josephus, as we shall see, is an exception,

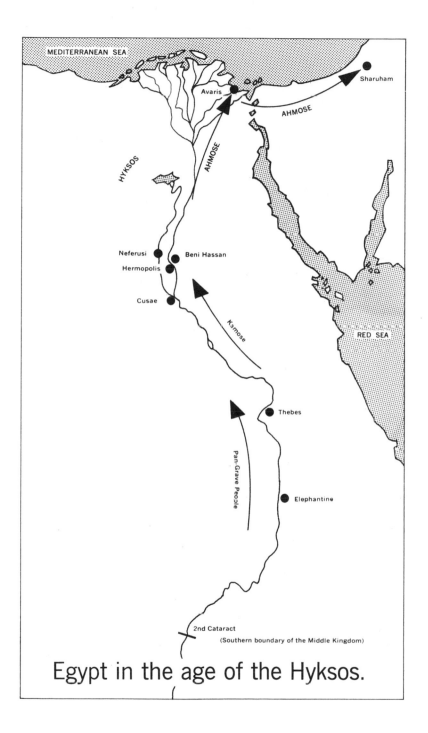

MEDITERRANEAN SEA

Sharuham

Avaris

AHMOSE

AHMOSE

HYKSOS

Neferusi

Beni Hassan

Hermopolis

Cusae

Kamose

RED SEA

Thebes

Pan-Grave People

Elephantine

2nd Cataract

(Southern boundary of the Middle Kingdom)

Egypt in the age of the Hyksos.

but not a helpful one.) The *Turin Papyrus* does give us some names, but unaccountably omits others. The *Karnak Table* does the same. The *Abydos* and *Sakkara Tables* ignore the period entirely. Contemporary monuments, on which we usually rely to check such facts and fill such gaps, are very scarce and generally of very little help. This is why Egyptologists have sought to draw as much information as possible from a source historians normally disdain: scarabs. The lowest order of Egyptian monuments, they often give the names of kings of whom we would not otherwise have heard; they are seals, amulets, or commemorative medals in stone or enamel, carved in the form of the scarab or dung beetle, the symbol of creation, regeneration, eternal life and the divine sun. Royal names are inscribed on them for their protective qualities, or as part of the commemoration of some event. They are very abundant for the Second Intermediate Period, but they are unfortunately often very difficult to date. The information they furnish therefore cannot, indeed may not, be used without the greatest caution.

Drawing on all the sources we have so far mentioned, we get a very rough outline of the history of the Second Intermediate Period, divisible into three phases (J. Vandier):

(A) Egypt before the Hyksos; Thirteenth and Fourteenth Dynasties (1786–1603 B.C.)
(B) The Hyksos: Fifteenth and Sixteenth Dynasties (1674–1567 B.C.)
(C) The Kingdom of Thebes and the expulsion of the Hyksos: Seventeenth Dynasty (±1650–1567 B.C.)

It must be understood that events will not always fit neatly into this outline, and that, as the dates given indicate, there is a good deal of overlapping in time between the three phases. The Hyksos, particularly, are infiltrating Egypt from the Thirteenth Dynasty on; their expulsion takes an equally long period of time. Nevertheless, crude as it is, this outline at least allows us to grasp the general direction of events in the Second Intermediate Period.

Egypt Before the Hyksos—Thirteenth and Fourteenth Dynasties

We have, as is so often the case, no certain indication of a violent break between the Twelfth and Thirteenth Dynasties. It is even possible (at least it is one of the many hypotheses that have been put forward, all quite unverifiable) that the first pharaoh of the Thirteenth Dynasty, Sekhemre–Khutawi–Amenemhet–Sebekhotep (=Sebekhotep I), was related by blood or marriage to the last rulers of the Twelfth.

The Thirteenth Dynasty, begun by Sebekhotep I, was to rule for a little over 150 years (1786–1633 B.C.). This number is obtained by correcting Manetho's figure of 453 to 153, assuming a Greek copyist's error by which Y (=400) was read for an original P (=100). During this time the throne was occupied by fifty or sixty kings, if we accept the list of the *Turin Papyrus*; but even that source has left out a certain number of names, as the *Table of Karnak* shows, so that a total of sixty sovereigns seems a minimum for this dynasty. This means an average reign of two and a half years, often a good deal less— some months, a few weeks. For the *Turin Papyrus* and the monuments agree in giving certain Thirteenth Dynasty kings three, four, seven, eight, ten and even twenty-three years on the throne, which cuts down sharply the average length of the remaining reigns. This ephemeral, May-fly nature of Egyptian royalty in this period has led many to picture the Thirteenth Dynasty as an age of anarchy, of chaos, of collapse.

Recent discoveries tend to present a somewhat different picture. In fact it has been suggested (W. C. Hayes) that the brevity of these reigns, the obvious lack of dynastic continuity, is merely an indication that these are not kings in the true sense of the word: They are puppets, set on the throne, perhaps by election, for a limited period of time, with the strings, and the real powers of the monarchy, firmly in the hands of the viziers. This is an extremely attractive hypothesis, but entirely impossible to prove. Of one thing, however, we can be quite sure: The instability of the central power slowly vitiated, and eventually destroyed, the economic prosperity of Egypt. But for about a century at least, the national unity was not endangered; nearly all of Egypt continued to be ruled by a single pharaoh, weak though he might be.

The kings of the Thirteenth Dynasty appear to have been of Theban origin; a desire to legitimate their claim to the crown may be seen by their names: Amenemhet, Intef, Sen-Wosret, Mentuhotep figure in the titulatures of several of these pharaohs; the most frequent name is that of Sebekhotep.

Under Sebekhotep I, Egypt continued to dominate Nubia up to Semneh, where this king's name was found carved on rocks beside that of Amenemhet III. His successor, Sekhemkare-Amenemhet-Senbuf, reigned over the whole of Egypt, for we have found his monuments in Lower as well as Upper Egypt. Still, it is possible that Egyptian power in the south had now begun to decline: The king's name is no longer to be found at Semneh, but at Askut, eighteen miles north of the border established by Sen-Wosret III. Egyptian influence is still making itself felt abroad under Sehetepibre II (second successor of Amenemhet-Senbuf), as the prince of Byblos recognizes the suzerainty of this king. His successors (Hetepibre, Sebekhotep II, Renseneb, Awibre-Hor, Kai-Amenemhet, Ugaf, Seneferibre-Sen-Wosret IV) are little more than names; the monuments merely confirm that they existed. The pyramid of Userkare-Khendjer, Sen-Wosret IV's successor, has been discovered at Sakkara, indicating once more that the dynasty's kings still rule Lower as well as Upper Egypt. Khendjer is in turn succeeded by a general, Semenkhare; he, too, still governs the Delta, for two colossi bearing his name have been found at Tanis.

The Thirteenth Dynasty continues, as does our almost total lack of knowledge of events, with the reigns of Sebekemsaf I, Sebekhotep III and Neferhotep. All of these kings are attested by contemporary monuments as well as by our later written sources. And from the monuments we learn that quite often these sovereigns are not of royal blood. Sebekhotep III, for example, was the son of two obscure Egyptians, Mentuhotep and Yauheyebu.

In spite of this rather monotonous turnover of almost seasonal kings, it does seem (or so certain papyri cause us to suspect) that viziers were able to hold on to their office during several reigns. A certain Ankhu, for instance, appears to have retained his charge from the reign of Userkare-Khendjer to that of Sebekhotep III. It is but a step from this to the conclusion that the vizier, not the king, holds the real powers. To take this step would explain for us how the Thirteenth Dynasty was able to last so long, while constantly, incessantly changing its kings.

There are, indeed, definite signs of a continuity of administration through all the round of momentary royalties. We have archives from this period, revealing the activities of the treasury and of the office of works. And from these archives we can draw a very little indirect information on what is going on in Egypt. A papyrus in the Brooklyn Museum contains a long list of agricultural laborers: It shows that, under Sebekhotep III, a great many Asiatics are in the service of officials in Upper Egypt (W. C. Hayes). It is impossible not to see the presence of these Asiatics on the Upper Nile as a sign of the Hyksos infiltration of Egypt, whether they are there as prisoners of-war, taken in skirmishes between the Egyptian army and nomads already seeking to enter the Delta, or whether they are individuals spontaneously seeking service in Egypt. In either case, their presence in the valley of the Nile cannot but have aided the eventual Hyksos seizure of power.

By carefully fitting together the evidence of monuments and of written sources, we have been able to date the reign of Khasekhemre-Neferhotep at 1740–1730 B.C. At this time, Egypt still has close relations with Syria, which implies continued control over the Delta. In the south, Elephantine and Aswan, where a statue and inscriptions of Neferhotep I have been found, remained obedient to the central power. It appears that the capital of Egypt was still Ittawi, as it was during the Twelfth Dynasty, and it appears that it was still mistress of the entire country, with a minor exception that we shall shortly examine.

Under the successors of Neferhotep I (Sihathor and Sebekhotep IV) the power of the Thirteenth Dynasty and of Egypt herself began to wither away. In a very short time, in fact, after the accession of Sebekhotep IV, the city of Avaris (the later Tanis) is occupied by the Hyksos, and the Delta is invaded by Asiatics. Little by little the succeeding Thirteenth Dynasty kings (Sebekhotep V, Mersekhemre-Neferhotep II, and Sekhemre-Seankhtawy-Neferhotep III) see their authority over the Lower valley reduced to nothing. Neferhotep III was even forced, so a stele at Karnak tells us, to defend Thebes itself against attack, an attack no doubt coming from the north. With Wahibre-Yayebi and Merneferre-Iy, the decline of the dynasty is accelerated. Very few monuments of this particular period have come down to us, although Yayebi ruled nearly eleven years, and Merneferre-Iy for over twenty-three years. The latter came to the throne about 1700. He may already have been a vassal of the Hyksos, for a monument with his name was discovered near Avaris, which had been in the Hyksos' hands for twenty years past.

The successors of Merneferre-Iy are the merest names to us, names copied from the *Turin Papryus*. It has been proposed, with considerable likelihood, to identify the pharaoh Djedneferre-Didumes with a king Toutimaios, whose reign, according to Manetho, saw the invasion of Egypt by the Hyksos. As these had been in occupation of the Delta since about 1720, it is probable that the "invasion" to which Manetho refers was the seizure of Memphis (W. C. Hayes). Didumes cannot have reigned earlier than 1674 B.C., i.e. almost half a century after the taking of Avaris by these outland invaders.

The fall of Memphis marked the fall of the Thirteenth Dynasty as well. The *Turin Papyrus* lists six more royal names, but clearly these are petty kinglets, vassals of the Hyksos, governing extremely limited territories in Upper Egypt, sometimes reduced to a single city (W. C. Hayes).

By about 1650 B.C., the decline of the Thirteenth Dynasty

is so manifest, so absolute, even in its native Theban region, that there a new dynasty rises up to try to save what is left of Egypt from the foreigner. This is to become the Seventeenth Dynasty, long acknowledging the Hyksos rulers as suzerains, eventually overthrowing their rule. However, Manetho and the *Turin Papyrus* both continue to regard the Thirteenth Dynasty as the legitimate royal line up to 1633, although, in all probability, from 1650 to 1633 the kings whom these sources carefully record are no more than local princes, allies or even vassals of the chieftains of Thebes.

Throughout the Thirteenth Dynasty, and for some years after its fall, the marshy territories of the western Delta, off the Hyksos invasion route to Egypt, remained more or less independent. This area was governed by the princes or kings of Xoïs (Kha-suut in Egyptian, the modern Sakha), who are Manetho's Fourteenth Dynasty. Manetho mentions seventy-six kings ruling for a total of 184 years. In our terms, they ruled independently of both the Delta and Upper Egypt from 1786 to 1603; aside from that, we know nothing of their history. The *Turin Papyrus*, listing the names of their kings, at least confirms the dynasty's existence.

The Hyksos—Fifteenth and Sixteenth Dynasties

Josephus, Jewish historian of the first century of our era, in his *Contra Apionem* quotes this passage from Manetho, describing the Hyksos invasion:

Unexpectedly, men of an unknown race from the east were emboldened to invade the country [Egypt] and, without a battle, easily seized it by force. . . . Their whole nation was called "hyksos," that is, "Shepherd Kings"; for "hyk" in the sacred language signifies "king," and "sos" is "shepherd" or "shepherds" in the common speech; "Hyksos" comes from joining these together.

This etymology has long since been shown to be only partially correct. *Hyk* comes, indeed, from *Heka*, "chief," "prince," etc., but *sos* cannot be a transcription of *shasu*, "nomad"; it is rather an abbreviation of *khasut*, "foreigners"; the expression *Heka-khasut* is known in Egypt as early as the Twelfth Dynasty, when it was used to designate the chiefs of nomad tribes who wandered the deserts of Syria-Palestine; under the Old Kingdom, it had been used for the sheikhs of the Nubian deserts. Both the *Turin Papyrus* and contemporary scarabs apply the term to known "Hyksos" kings.

The Hyksos invasion was certainly not as sudden as Manetho implies. Nowadays it is agreed that we ought to speak rather of a progressive infiltration than of an invasion in the strict sense. In addition, the invaders were not a single people; this was a heterogeneous concert of various inhabitants of Western Asia (Semites for the most part, but not entirely) who had been thrust out of their home pastures by Indo-European invasions of Anatolia and Upper Mesopotamia, either directly or indirectly. The Egyptians themselves call them various things: sometimes Amu, sometimes Setetiu, or Mentiu of Setet, or "men of Retenu"; i.e. all the old names used under the Old and Middle Kingdom for the Asiatic peoples who were Egypt's neighbors; which means they did not, like Manetho, consider them a hitherto unknown people, a new invading race.

It has occasionally been suggested that the Hyksos infiltration of Egypt may have begun in the Twelfth Dynasty. It is, however, now agreed (T. Säve-Söderbergh) that, although it is true there are many Asiatics in Egypt between the end of the Twelfth and the middle of the Thirteenth Dynasty, the infiltration of the Hyksos themselves, i.e. of the particular Asiatics who were to dominate Egypt, begins in the main after the reigns of Neferhotep I, Sihathor and Sebekhotep IV, i.e. from about 1720 to 1700. The Hyksos infiltration would, then, cover the reigns of Sebekhotep V, Neferhotep III and Wahibre-Yayebi. The first great step in this advance was the taking of Avaris.

We have been able to fix the date of this event by a monument known as the "stele of the year 400," for it commemorates the four hundredth anniversary of the reconstruction of the temple of the god Seth at Avaris. Now we know that the cult of Seth at Avaris was fostered by the Hyksos, who saw in this very old Egyptian god (he is attested under the First Dynasty) a local version of one of their own Semitic divinities, Ba'al or Resheph. There can be no doubt whatever that the reconstruction and enlargement of his temple were the work of his invading votaries. The fourth centennial of that work was celebrated about 1320 B.C., in the reign of the Eighteenth Dynasty pharaoh Horemheb, as the stele erected by Ramses II at Avaris states. This means that the temple was originally rebuilt in about 1720; in other words, by this date the Hyksos had laid hands on the far eastern parts of the Delta, quite close to the frontier, which is the region of Avaris.

It took them forty-six years more to extend their territory to Memphis. During this time they seized the nomes of the Delta, except for those of the west, where, as we have seen, the Fourteenth Dynasty retained its hold. Once they had got hold of Memphis, the Hyksos began, and continued thereafter, to consider themselves legitimate rulers of all Egypt, and are so counted as the Fifteenth Dynasty. Manetho (still via Josephus' *Contra Apionem*) has preserved a description of this event and its consequences:

Finally, they made one of themselves king; his name was Salitis. He resided at Memphis, taking tribute from both Upper and Lower Egypt, and leaving garrisons in the most advantageous places. Above all he sought to make the eastern region safe, foreseeing that one day, when the Assyrians [*sic*] had grown stronger, they would covet his kingdom and attack it. In the Sethroïte nome he found a city very favorably situated to the east of the Bubastite [branch of the] river, called Avaris after an ancient religious tradition. He rebuilt it, making the walls very strong, and installed a garrison of 240,000 heavy infantry to guard it. Every summer he would go there, to distribute rations and pay, and to put the troops through assiduous maneuvers to frighten off foreigners. After reigning nineteen years he passed away. After which a second [king] called Bnon ruled for forty-four years.

From this we can draw one immediate conclusion: Avaris was the fortified base of the Hyksos power. Under the Sixteenth

Dynasty, when the struggle with the south was well under way, Avaris was to be the Hyksos capital. A representation of the Hyksos kings has been seen in curious monuments, picturing rulers with lions' manes; but we now know that these sphinxes date back to the Twelfth Dynasty. The Hyksos kings left a few constructions in Egypt, but no portraits.

Manetho's Salitis would probably be the King Sharek or Shalek that a genealogical list of Memphis mentions in passing. This ruler lived a generation before the famed Apophis I, and two generations before Ahmose, the founder of the Eighteenth Dynasty (W. C. Hayes). It is also possible that he is the same as the pharaoh Mayebre-Sheshi, whose name appears on any number of scarabs and seal impressions.

The successors of Salitis, up to Apophis I, must have controlled, if not governed, the whole of Egypt from Gebelein, a little to the south of Thebes, to the eastern borders of the Delta. Their power or suzerainty may have reached to the First Cataract. South of that point began the kingdom of Kush, entirely independent when the war for the liberation of Egypt began. How long had it been so? It is difficult to say. It seems clear that, during the greater part of the Thirteenth Dynasty, Nubia at least down to the Second Cataract was still in the Egyptian orbit. At Semneh, at Uronarti, we have found seal impressions with the names of Thirteenth Dynasty rulers, which would seem to prove that the fortress system at the Second Cataract was still in Egyptian hands. The excavations now under way in Sudanese Nubia may tell us more.

For one thing, these Thirteenth Dynasty objects in the fortresses of the Second Cataract do *not* prove that the pharaohs still controlled them directly. The forts may have been occupied by Egyptianized natives, friends but not necessarily vassals of Egypt. The exploration of Mirgissa (in all probability the "Iken" mentioned by Sen-Wosret III, on his stele at Semneh, as an Egyptian trading-post) seems to show that those living in the town under the Thirteenth Dynasty, although heavily influenced by Egypt, were not in the main Egyptians. The further on one goes in time, the greater becomes the influence of the purely Sudanese culture of Kerma. Kerma itself, on the Third Cataract, seems to have had frequent relations with the Hyksos kings; scarabs and seal impressions with the names of Sheshi and other Hyksos rulers appear there.

With the reign of Salitis (whether he is Sheshi or no), the Fifteenth Dynasty begins. For his successors, the *Turin Papyrus* is fragmentary; we cannot read the length of their reigns, only the number of kings (six) and the total of their reigns (108 years). Salitis is succeeded by Meruserre-Yak-Ba'al, or *Yakub-Her* in Egyptian transcriptions. It is difficult to imagine how Yakub-Her might become the Bnon or Beon of Manetho; nevertheless he seems to have been the second Hyksos pharaoh. The Egyptian administration, to judge by the inscriptions, is now opened to foreigners: There is a treasurer named Hur, a typically Semitic name that the Egyptians write "Har." There are traces of his activities from Gaza to Kerma. Still there are Egyptians who remain in service under the invaders; another treasurer has the perfectly good Egyptian name of Peremwah.

King Khyan, Manetho's Iannas or Staan, succeeded Yakub-Her. He must have had a long reign—Manetho mentions fifty years, but the figure on the *Turin Papyrus* is illegible. Many monuments with the name of Khyan have been unearthed—in Egypt, from Gebelein south of Thebes to Bubastis in the Delta, and also abroad; the lid of an alabaster bowl discovered at Knossos carries his complete cartouche, "the good god, Seuserenre, the Son of Re, Khyan," and a small granite lion with his name turned up at Baghdad. From these it was once concluded that he must have ruled a vast empire, covering all of the Middle East. This is no longer thought to be the case. It is, in fact, unlikely that the power of the Hyksos kings in Asia extended much beyond the southern borders of Palestine. Commercial relations were another matter; obviously, these were very lively in the direction of Mesopotamia and the Mediterranean. In the direction of Nubia, the case is otherwise: No scarab, no seal impression with Khyan's name is to be found at Kerma. An independent native kingdom, it is thought, must have been established in Lower Nubia, ruling from Elephantine to Semneh. With rulers like a certain Nedjeh, friends of the southern Egyptian princes who were now seeking to regain their independence, employers of Egyptian scribes and officials, such a kingdom or kingdoms would have blocked relations between the Hyksos territories and the Kingdom of Kerma (T. Säve-Söderbergh and W. C. Hayes).

Auserre-Apophis I succeeded Khyan, and ruled, according to the *Turin Papyrus*, for more than forty years. "Apophis" is the transcription of an Egyptian name, "Ipepi," of which we have examples in Egypt from the Twelfth Dynasty onward. The Hyksos rulers, in other words, are becoming more and more Egyptianized. In the tomb of the Eighteenth Dynasty pharaoh Amenhotep I, a jar was discovered bearing the name of the Princess Herit, daughter of Apophis I; had she been married to one of the Theban princes? If so, then some drops of Hyksos blood ran in the veins of the great pharaohs of the New Kingdom (W. C. Hayes).

In any case relations between the Hyksos and the rulers of Thebes seem to have been fairly good under Apophis I; it was not until the very end of the reign that the south began to rise up against its Asiatic suzerains. A literary text (unfortunately fragmentary) has preserved an account of the outbreak of hostilities, in the reign of the Theban (Seventeenth Dynasty) king Sekenenre. "Sekenenre was then ruler of the city of the south" (=Thebes), while "the Prince Apopi was in Avaris" and received the tribute of all Egypt. Apophis took counsel with the counselors of the kingdom, and demanded that Sekenenre take measures (the obscurity of the text prevents us from knowing what), because the hippopotamuses at a pool in Thebes were keeping him (Apophis) awake. As the distance between Thebes and Avaris is some 500 miles, this passage has been interpreted as an insulting and unfulfillable demand, intended to justify recourse to war; but T. Säve-Söderbergh has shown that, in reality, Apophis, faithful worshiper of Seth, was anxious to protect the hippopotamuses of Thebes, for this animal was one of the material forms of his god, and the Egyptians traditionally, and ritually, went out at certain times of the year to hunt and sacrifice it. On receiving this message, then, Sekenenre called *his* counselors; at just this point the text breaks off, but the sequel can be guessed: Sekenenre rejects the Hyksos ultimatum, and the war of liberation is unleashed.

At Deir-el-Bahri, across the river from Thebes near the royal necropolis at the Valley of the Kings, the priests of the Twenty-first Dynasty hid the mummies of former kings in a single tomb to save them from graverobbers. In this "cache" was found the mummy of Sekenenre himself. It bears quite a number of ghastly wounds, which has led to the supposition that the king was killed in a battle with the Hyksos. A supposition, but no more; the wounds can be explained just as well by other means. Might they not be traces of an assassin's, rather than an enemy's, arms, indicating a successful palace revolution (H. E. Winlock)?

We cannot know how Sekenenre died. What is abundantly clear is that his reign marked the beginnings of the expulsion from Egypt of the Hyksos conquerors. The details of this struggle will be considered below, from the point of view of Thebes; as it continued, Apophis lost control of large parts of Egyptian territory; he was succeeded by other Hyksos kings, under whom the southern frontier of the Asiatics' realm was drawn at Atfieh, near the southern entry to the Fayum. The Thebans nevertheless were able to raid far into Hyksos territory, reaching Avaris itself. Ahmose, the second successor of Sekenenre, was able to drive the foreigners from Egypt entirely. The successors of Apophis I, then, Akenenre-Apophis II and Asekhre-Khamudy, were the last Hyksos pharaohs—their reigns must have been brief.

Along with the six Hyksos kings of the Fifteenth Dynasty, sometimes called the "greater Hyksos," other foreign rulers reigned simultaneously in Egypt, the "lesser Hyksos" of the Sixteenth Dynasty. Their power, it would seem, was limited to quite unimpressive territories; their names are for the most part unknown; only those of the kings Aken, Anat-her (formation with the name of the Semitic goddess Anat, whom the Hyksos made Seth's consort) and Semken will be mentioned; also that of the last ruler of this "dynasty," Nebkhepeshre-Apophis III, to whom a very beautiful bronze dagger, found at Sakkara, once belonged. The Sixteenth Dynasty kings appear to have been contemporaries of those of the Fifteenth Dynasty, but they are more local princes than true kings, and one wonders why on earth Manetho honored them with a dynasty of their own. Recently it has been proposed to simply strike them off the roll of the genuine and historically attested dynasties of Egypt (A. H. Gardiner).

Egyptian authors, from the scribes of the Eighteenth Dynasty to Manetho, all describe the Hyksos period as an age of abominations committed, by the invaders, against the Egyptian people and their customs. The facts do not seem to justify this. It is quite obvious that the Hyksos respected Egyptian civilization. It is clear that their appearance in Egypt was not the abrupt incursion of a barbarian army. We have long since given up thinking of it as the military victory of well-organized troops armed with superior weapons, the horse and chariot, the bronze sickle-sword, against which the Egyptians with their copper daggers could do nothing. We are no longer convinced by the supposed Hyksos "fortresses" in the Delta and in Syria-Palestine. Those most often mentioned, at Tell-el-Yahudiyeh and at Heliopolis, are clearly not fortifications but may be foundations, the foundations of temples (Ricke, as cited by T. Säve-Söderbergh). As for the war chariot, the new types of dagger and sword, the use of bronze and the composite bow, it is true that all of these were introduced into Egypt by the Hyksos—toward the end of their stay. The Hyksos had brought in these novelties to try to hold their own against their increasingly rebellious subjects, but they had not used them to conquer the country in the first place. That conquest appears to have been gradual; one can easily imagine small bands of armed Bedouins, hardened by the severe life of the desert, slipping farther and farther into a country whose national defense had been disorganized, imposing their authority in one locality after another on terrorized and defenseless peasants. The Hyksos domination was an episode, in other words, in the eternal struggle between the nomadic and the sedentary ways of life, with the temporary weakness of the one guaranteeing the temporary victory of the other.

This, to be sure, is guesswork, but the archaeological evidence seems to confirm it. Many tombs from the Hyksos period have been excavated in Egypt, and they do not give the impression of a massive intrusion of foreigners; there is no sudden change in funerary customs, the physical remains of the occupants are only very rarely of foreign, generally Semitic, type (T. Säve-Söderbergh). The pottery type called Tell-el-Yahudiyeh, long associated with the Hyksos invasion, actually goes back to the Middle Kingdom; it is imported pottery, and has nothing to do with the Hyksos, as it now appears (Säve-Söderbergh). The same is true for other pottery types thought to stem from the Hyksos.

Who were the Hyksos? No novel people from afar, as we have said; Manetho's impression will have come from the sources he used, hostile to the Hyksos and anxious to give them a bad pedigree. Hurrian and Indo-European elements have been seen among them, but the greater part of the Hyksos personal names that have come down to us are western Semitic; non-Semitic elements among the invaders can have been neither numerous nor dominant.

We can therefore say what the Hyksos domination was not. It was not a mass invasion by a numerous nomad people, bearing superior arms. What was it then? We revert to our imaginary picture of infiltrating Bedouin bands, able to seize power in one locality after another because of the political weakness of Egypt after the end of the Twelfth Dynasty. Manetho offers a hint that this was so: "Finally, they made one of themselves king." This would imply that previously there were several Hyksos chiefs, ruling parts of Egypt that they had seized on their own. Ultimately they united their strength under the leadership of one, and Egypt had a foreign pharaoh.

The Hyksos did not remain foreign for long. Their kings

399

use hieroglyphic script—so far, not a single cuneiform inscription has been found in Egypt that can be dated to the Hyksos period. They worship Egyptian gods; they have a special fondness for Seth, whom they identify with the western Semitic Ba'al or Resheph, but they are also perfectly willing to worship Re, although the later *Tale of the Quarrel of Sekenenre and Apopi* tries to insinuate the opposite. Khyan declares himself "Son of Re" on his cartouche; Auserre-Apophis goes even further, and calls himself "Bodily Son of Re" and "Living Image of Re on Earth." Furthermore, several Hyksos kings adopt names compounded with Re: "Great Is the Power of Re," for instance, or "Re Is the Lord of the Sword."

The Hyksos could not administer the land themselves; there were not enough of them to begin with, and among them there were surely not enough qualified scribes. Native Egyptians had to serve, and, as we see from Egyptian accounts of the war of liberation, served them faithfully. In general, the condition of the Egyptians under Hyksos rule was not nearly so abject as later Egyptian literature would like to make it out: A Theban prince, as we have seen, may well have married a Hyksos princess; the Hyksos rulers, pictured by the Egyptian sources as purely destructive barbarians, were responsible for the construction of temples and buildings. The statues, stelae and other works of art of the age, while falling short of the masterpieces of Middle Kingdom art, are nevertheless far from negligible; the Second Intermediate Period does not bring on the sharp decline in the arts that marred the First. Most important of all, perhaps, for forming a judgment on the effect of the Hyksos domination on Egyptian civilization, is the literary evidence: To the scribes of the Hyksos period we owe some of our best copies of Egyptian literary and scientific works, such as the *Rhind Mathematical Papyrus* (a copy dated in the year thirty-three of Apophis), the famous *Westcar Papyrus* with its folktales of Old Kingdom pharaohs, or the *Hymn to the Crown* (the *Golenischeff Papyrus*). It seems, then, that the Hyksos kings encouraged, rather than harmed, the intellectual life of Egypt.

The Hyksos borrowed much from Egypt. In return they made two essential contributions, as W. C. Hayes has forcefully reminded us. In the first place they entirely and permanently relieved the Egyptians of their superiority complex: No more would Egypt think of itself as a world apart from and far above its neighbors. In the second place they forced Egypt into close contact with Asiatics, themselves to begin with, but the change was lasting; from that time forward countless ties of blood, of culture, even of philosophy were formed between the Nile valley and western Asia, which the pharaohs of the New Kingdom sought not to break but to extend. Practical contributions the Hyksos made as well: The horse was known in Mesopotamia, perhaps also in Egypt, before the Hyksos period, but it was the Hyksos who introduced the horse and chariot into Egypt and spread its use. Far from being an unmitigated disaster, then, in a certain sense the Hyksos invasion even enriched Egypt, for it gave her the knowledge and the material means to acquire, under the pharaohs of the New Kingdom, an empire greater than Egypt had ever held before, or was ever to hold again.

The Kingdom of Thebes and the Expulsion of the Hyksos—Seventeenth Dynasty ($\pm$1650–1567 B.C.)

The Seventeenth Dynasty was destined to expel the Hyksos from the Egyptian land; but, until the reigns of its last three kings, it had no real independence, no authority over most of Egypt. As celebrated an Egyptologist as A. H. Gardiner has proposed to drop it from the historical list, for all its more than sixteen pharaohs. This would be unjust; vassals these rulers were, for the most part, and it may be loyal vassals, of the Hyksos kings; nevertheless these Theban princes, by reorganizing around their persons the nomes of Upper Egypt, acted as a catalyst to the national energies and prepared the way for the liberation of their country.

The first Theban princes appear about 1650 B.C, during the

reign, that is, of one of the first Hyksos pharaohs, and while the Thirteenth Dynasty was still theoretically sovereign, at least according to Manetho and the *Turin Papyrus*. The political situation, then, was confusion itself, when the rulers of Thebes first came to power.

The *Turin Papyrus*, in its intact state, listed fifteen Theban kings of the Seventeenth Dynasty. Nine of these are also named on the *Karnak Table* and on other New Kingdom lists. We know ten names from contemporary monuments; the existence of seven of these princes' tombs has been established in the Theban necropolis—along with that of an eighth ruler who is unknown to the *Turin Papyrus* (W. C. Hayes)—either by excavation of the actual tomb, or by the discovery of grave furnishings, or by mention in the depositions of funerary priests who inspected the royal tombs under the Twentieth Dynasty. By putting all this information together we have been able to establish the succession of reigns. One of the chronographers through whom we know Manetho lists the first five pharaohs of the Seventeenth Dynasty as a separate Sixteenth Dynasty, and this has sometimes been followed by modern historians (H. E. Winlock); we shall not join them.

The *Turin Papyrus* divides the dynasty's kings into two groups. There are eleven rulers in the first. The names of the first five would probably be: Nubkheperre-Antef V, Sekhemre-Wahkhau-Rahotep, Sekhemre-Wadjkhau-Sebekemsaf I, Sekhemre-Sementawy-Djehuti, Mentuhotep VI (according to H. E. Winlock and J. von Beckerath). After Djehuti, the *Turin Papyrus* lists six more kings in this first group, but only three of these are known to us from other sources. The kings in this group, taken together, seem to have ruled for forty-five years, the last reign closing about 1605 B.C., i.e. at the beginning of the reign of the Hyksos king Auserre-Apophis I (W. C. Hayes).

What part of Egypt did these princes govern? Probably no more than the first eight nomes of Upper Egypt, from Elephantine to Abydos. The other nomes of Upper Egypt would have been ruled by the successors of the Thirteenth Dynasty. Lower Nubia would have remained on good terms with southern

Egypt, but as an independent kingdom, the kingdom of Kush, governed by a Sudanese family one of whose members is known: Nedjeh. Buhen was possibly the capital of this state; its culture was much influenced by that of Kerma. Kerma, the territory to the south of the Second Cataract, was a larger country than it had been, but we still do not know whether it was ruled as a unified kingdom or as a collection of principalities. Northern Egypt was under direct Hyksos rule, but the entire country paid the Hyksos tribute, i.e. all of its rulers were vassals of the Asiatic pharaohs.

Thus the possessions of the princes of Thebes were limited. But within these limits they set to work to meet the difficulties of their situation. Both the north and the far south of the valley were in foreign hands, and, if this did not actually cut off supplies of wood from the Lebanon, limestone from the Cairo area and ebony, ivory and gold from the south, the flow of commerce must have at least been tightly controlled. For this reason the Thebans used as much as possible the materials available on home ground; the result was a provincial art, still in the tradition of the Twelfth Dynasty but somewhat crude—filled, however, with the energy appropriate to those who would reconquer Egypt.

The tombs of the Theban princes were still built in pyramidal form, as we learn from the inspection report of the Twentieth Dynasty, when these pyramids still stood. They appear to have been built of sun-dried brick, over a funerary chamber cut into the rock. The royal sarcophagi were made of wood, often sycamore wood, and are of a special type: *rishi* (literally "feathered") sarcophagi, referring to a prominent element of their painted decoration. Intellectual life seems to have been quite active, at least as active as that under the patronage of the Hyksos in the north. The famous *Prisse Papyrus*, today in the Bibliothèque Nationale at Paris, was originally found in the sarcophagus of Antef VI, in all probability; it contains the *Instruction of Ptah-hotep*, apparently quite popular under the Seventeenth Dynasty, for other copies have been found in contemporary tombs.

As good Egyptians, the pharaohs of the Seventeenth Dynasty were highly religious: Rahotep undertook the repair of the temple of Min at Coptos, one of the oldest sanctuaries in Egypt, and of the Osiris temple at Abydos.

There has been interminable discussion of the order of the reigns of the Theban princes, but it is now thought (H. E. Winlock and J. v. Beckerath) that the first was Nubkheperre-Antef V. (Antef I and III had ruled during the Eleventh Dynasty.) From the reign of this ruler we have some extremely interesting texts that cast a sudden light on the obscure history of this age.

It was long believed that the "enemies" mentioned in a decree of Coptos, dated in the third year of Antef V, must have been the Hyksos, and that therefore the war of liberation was begun by this king. We now know that these enemies were merely magical statuettes, stolen from the temple of Coptos by one Teti. The text (after J. Vandier) is nevertheless important for the picture that it gives us of the political condition of Upper Egypt at the time:

Every king of Upper Egypt, every chieftain who may show pity for him [the thief, Teti] will not be able to receive the white crown [of Upper Egypt], nor will he put on the red crown [of Lower Egypt]; he will not be able to sit upon the Throne of Horus of the Living, and the two goddesses [Wadjet and Nekhbet] will not be gracious to him as they are to those they love. Every commander, every official who may intercede in his favor with the king, his goods and his fields will be given to my father Min, Master of Coptos, as his property.

This text is addressed to the mayor-nomarch of Coptos, who is also head of the army, to the scribe of the temple, to the garrison of the town and all the clergy of the temple. It seems to show that under Antef V there were still local potentates, even local "kings" in Upper Egypt. These dynasts, elected or self-elevated, were certainly not as independent as has often been thought: The decree shows that the king of Thebes can intervene in their affairs. Superficially, the situation recalls that of the First Intermediate Period, when the nomarchs were

404

for all practical purposes independent, and made alliances among themselves to favor one or another pretender to the national throne. Under Antef V power was indeed localized, but the nomarchs were no longer at liberty to choose their allegiance, they were dominated by the princes of Thebes, and were to follow them when war against the Hyksos broke out (J. Vandier).

Antef V is also known by monuments he erected in Abydos and at El Kab, as well as by those at Coptos. His tomb was discovered at Dra-Abu'l'Nagga, in the northern part of the Theban necropolis. An inspection report of the Twentieth Dynasty informs us that it was still intact under Ramses IX. It was subsequently looted, but, while the funerary cave was being cleaned by modern excavators, there were found, near the royal mummy, two bows and six arrows, mute witnesses of the king's warlike past, which is also attested by the figures of Nubian and Asiatic prisoners engraved at Karnak under his name. Recent finds at Mirgissa show that he was in contact with the peoples of Upper Nubia (Kerma), whether he fought them or employed them as mercenaries. It was probably in his reign that the text known under the name of the *Song of the Harper* received its definitive form, although it goes back (doubtless) to the First Intermediate Period, and was to become very famous later on. An ancient source describes it as "the song that is in the tomb of King Antef, before the singer with the harp" (cited by W. C. Hayes); Antef V (unless an Antef of the Eleventh Dynasty is meant) is therefore connected with this work, one of the most celebrated in all Egyptian literature:

The generations pass away and others come to be since the time of
    the ancestors.
The gods who lived in former times [now] rest in their pyramids . . .
And those who built houses, their place is no more.
Behold what has become of them.
I have heard the words of Imhotep and of Hordjedef,
Of whom men speak so well:
Where are they [now]?

Their houses are in ruins, their tombs are no more, as if they had
   never been.
No one returns from there,
To tell us what has become of them,
To tell us what they need,
To quiet our hearts,
Until the day when we depart
For the place where they have gone . . .
Do what you desire as long as you may live . . .
Refrain: Make holiday, and do not tire,
Surely no man takes his goods away with him,
Surely none who go there ever return.

The successor of Antef V was Rahotep, the restorer of
temples at Coptos and Abydos (p. 404). Rahotep's successor,
Sekhemre-Upmaat-Antef VI, is sometimes referred to as Antef
the Elder. Antef VII (Sekhemre-Heruhermaat-Antef) is now
thought to have been Antef the Elder's successor; Antef VI
reigned only three years, his brother and successor Antef VII
only a few months, which would explain why the *Turin
Papyrus* does not mention him.

Sebekemsaf II had a reign of seventeen years, the longest
of the dynasty; the report of the inspection of his tomb, looted
under Ramses IX, calls him a "great king." The suggestion
has been made that it was he who pushed the Hyksos north
of Cusae (J. Yoyotte); this is ruled out by the opening lines of
the *Rhind Papyrus*, which tell us that the suzerainty of the
Hyksos pharaohs was still recognized in Thebes in the thirty-
third year of Auserre-Apophis (W. C. Hayes), i.e. under the
eleventh Theban successor of Sebekemsaf II.

Djehuti is, apparently, the successor of Sebekemsaf. His
name has been found at Deir, north of El Ballas. He is mentioned on the *Karnak Table*, although he reigned only one
year. He was followed by Mentuhotep VI (Mentuhoteps I-V
were Eleventh Dynasty kings; actually there were only three
of them, but numbers IV and V have been left in place by
modern historians to avoid confusion, of which there is surely
enough already).

Mentuhotep VI, too, ruled only a year, to be replaced by Sewadjenre-Nebirieraut I, who reigned six years. He is known for an important stele found in the Hall of Columns of the temple of Karnak. This is a legal document drawn up in the first year of the king's reign by one Kebsy, for the benefit of a relative. Kebsy hands over the office of nomarch of El Kab to discharge a debt worth sixty "deben" of gold (about twelve pounds by weight). We learn from this text something of the administrative organization of the Theban state: The vizier continues to play an important role. More important, we learn that the reign of Nebirieraut was about three generations later in time than that of Merhetepre-Ini of the Thirteenth Dynasty, who must have held the throne about 1680; Nebirieraut then would have ruled Thebes about 1620 B.C., some fifty years before the end of the dynasty.

Four rulers of whom we know nothing more than the names (from the *Turin Papyrus*) bring this first group of Seventeenth Dynasty princes to a close. The second group consists of five rulers whose names are lost from the *Turin Papyrus*; there can be no doubt, however, that the last three were the "liberators" of Egypt: Sekenenre-Taa I "the Elder" or "the Great," Sekenenre-Taa II "the Brave," and Wadj-Kheperre-Kamose. This order is assured by the monuments. The only problem is to determine their immediate predecessors. Until recently Nubkheperre (or Nebkheperre) -Antef V was placed here, wrongly as it now seems, to be succeeded by a Senakhtenre mentioned by the *Karnak Table*.

King Senakhtenre is attested only by the king lists; he appears on no monument, but his existence and his place in the succession of kings is taken as proven.

The *Abbot Papyrus*, our source for the inspection of royal tombs under Ramses IX, preserves a report of the tombs of *two* kings bearing the name of Sekenenre-Taa: "This makes a second King Taa," the report says after the name of one of them. In certain documents, Sekenenre-Taa II has added to his name the epithet "the Brave"; other simply call him Sekenenre, as does the *Sallier Papyrus I*, i.e. the *Tale of the Quarrel of*

Apopi and Sekenenre. The preamble to this text gives us a resumé of the political situation in Egypt: "It came to pass that the land of Egypt was in great affliction, and there was no lord as king of [that] time. And it came to pass that the King Sekenenre was then ruler of the City of the South (=Thebes). But affliction reigned in the city of the Asiatics, the Prince Apopi [=Apophis] was in Avaris. The whole land made offering to him with its tribute . . ." (after G. Lefebvre). The "affliction" (poverty?) of the Delta is simply a function of the author's hatred of the Hyksos; otherwise the situation described is historical: Sekenenre in the south is a vassal of the Hyksos king, who at least nominally rules all Egypt from Avaris, collecting tribute everywhere. This vassalage is confirmed by the last (surviving) part of the tale, where Sekenenre tells Apophis' messenger, whom he has given "all good things, meat, cakes" etc., to "return to King Apopi: 'Whatever you tell him [=me], I shall do it,' thus shall you say to him."

War between the Theban princes and their overlords broke out, then, in the reign of Sekenenre-Taa II. This ruler married his sister, Aahotep. Both were the children of Sekenenre-Taa I and of his wife Teti-Sheri, who seems to have lived on into the Eighteenth Dynasty, for her great-grandson Ahmose built a funerary chapel for her after her death, and endowed it with lands taken from the Hyksos in Lower Egypt. Aahotep, like her mother, survived her husband, and died under the reign of Ahmose. In her tomb have been found dress weapons of excellent workmanship. Taa II, "the Brave," died at about thirty, as the autopsy of his mummy shows; this, too, was found in the "cache" at Deir-el-Bahri, pierced by strokes of the sword. Kamose, his son, succeeded to the throne and carried on the struggle against the Hyksos.

The details and the drama of this struggle are known to us thanks to two Egyptian texts, actually one text divided in half, the first half of which has been known for quite some time, the second but recently discovered, and not yet fully published.

We have two versions of the first half. One is contemporary with the events, a hieroglyphic inscription on a stele dated in

Kamose's third year and found in the third pylon at the temple of Karnak; the other is written in hieratic, on a wooden tablet (*Carnarvon Tablet no. 1*) discovered in 1908 near Deir-el-Bahri, originally from a Seventeenth Dynasty tomb. Hieratic is a cursive adaptation of the hieroglyphic script, developed from the earliest dynasties onward for more rapid writing, with many changes in style as time went on. By the form of the letters we can give the *Carnarvon Tablet* a date quite close to the events it describes, certainly no more than fifty years after them (A. H. Gardiner). We therefore have, what is extraordinarily rare in Egyptology, two contemporary literary accounts of a series of historical events. The text is of the greatest historical importance in itself, and well worth citing; it begins with the date "Year Three of Kamose," lists all the titles of that king, and then proceeds as follows (after T. Säve-Söderbergh and A. H. Gardiner):

The king, mighty in Thebes, may be endowed with life forever, was an excellent king [so] Re [made] him the real king and gave him power in very truth. Now His Majesty spoke in his palace to his council of grandees who were in his following: "I should like to know, what good is my strength, when a prince is in Avaris, and another is in Kush, and I find myself associated with an Asiatic and a Nubian, each one in possession of his slice of this Egypt? And I cannot pass by him [to go] as far as Memphis, which belongs to Egypt, for he holds Hermopolis. No one is at ease, [each man] exhausting himself in servitude to the Asiatics. I am going to grapple with him, I am going to slit open his belly [for] my desire is to deliver Egypt and smite the Asiatics." [But] the grandees of his council replied: "Behold, all are loyal to the Asiatics as far as Cusae," [then] they lifted up their voices and spoke again in chorus: "We are tranquil in our part of Egypt. Elephantine is strong, and the middle part [of Egypt] is with us as far as Cusae. Men till for us the finest of their lands, our cattle [can] pasture in the marshes of the Delta. Barley is sent for our swine. Our cattle are not taken away and there is no attack against . . . He holds the land of the Asiatics and we hold Egypt. Yet [whoever] comes to us [to attack us], we shall rise up against him." But they displeased the heart of His Majesty.

The rest of the text is fragmentary. However we know that in it the king relates the beginnings of the campaign intended to expel his rival from Egypt. In the course of this struggle, the king took and razed Neferusi.

It has been shown (A. de Buck) that such a council meeting, with the counselors opposing the wishes of the king, was a literary device much admired by the ancient Egyptian scribes; it enabled them to display to better advantage, against the timorousness and blindness of lesser men, the courage and the foresight of a king. Nevertheless the following fact emerges: Kamose, like Sekenenre his father, still governs but a part of Egypt; much of the country is still under Hyksos rule, not only the Delta but also nearly all of Middle Egypt, from Memphis to Cusae (slightly north of the modern Manfalut). To the south, Lower Nubia is still ruled by the independent king of Kush. As for the attitude of the counselors, fictional or not it surely represents that of a great many Egyptians of the time—we have seen that the Hyksos domination was probably not as hateful to the Egyptians as the Eighteenth Dynasty texts would have us believe, and it has been noted that Kamose does *not* say that the people of Lower Egypt are being maltreated by the Hyksos (T. Säve-Söderbergh).

At the beginning of the war of liberation a part at least of the Egyptian subjects of the Hyksos remained loyal to their masters, siding with them against the Thebans. The first enemy whom Kamose attacks, for instance, is Teti the son of Pepi, obviously an Egyptian, who is in command of the town of Neferusi, which he has turned into "a nest of Asiatics." The local dynasties disappear one by one as the Thebans advance; it is likely that they put up some resistance to the southern armies, although an official text like the stele of Kamose will naturally pass over that sort of thing as much as possible, stressing the joy of the liberated populations instead (T. Säve-Söderbergh). Still, there are, as we shall see, a few discreet allusions to Egyptian resistance, warning us that this liberation partakes of the character of civil war.

The text of Kamose's Karnak stele and of the *Carnarvon Tablet* stops after the taking of Neferusi, north of Hermopolis.

Before it does so we learn that Medjayu, i.e. Nubians, are fighting on the Theban side. For any further information on the wars of liberation under Kamose, historians had to fall back on conjecture, until, in 1954, the continuation of the *Carnarvon Tablet* was found among the stone blocks serving as a foundation for a statue of Ramses II, near the second pylon of the temple of Karnak. This text is carved on a large curved stele; the narrative of Egypt's liberation, too long to fit on a single stele, had been carved on two; the first was that whose fragments were found in 1932 and 1935, the second, in much better condition, was that discovered in 1954, with thirty-eight lines of hieroglyphic text. The text has not yet been published in full.

The new text begins with a series of insults directed by Kamose against Apophis, reminiscent of those thrown out by Homeric heroes on the verge of combat. The Theban fleet has reached the region of Avaris. Kamose declares: "I shall drink wine from your vineyards that my prisoners, the Asiatics, will press for me." This is the result of a raid on Avaris, which nevertheless continues to resist, as Kamose now directs his eloquence at the women who "watch the battle from high up in the palace of Apophis;" he declares to them that "he will destroy the dwelling of Apophis and he will cut down his trees, he will lead his women into captivity and he will seize his chariots." Kamose then lists the booty taken on the raid, and concludes as follows: "I destroyed their cities and set fire to their dwelling places, so that they will remain hills of red earth forever, because of the damage that they did to Egypt, when they put themselves at the service of the Asiatics, forsaking Egypt their mistress" (after T. Säve-Söderbergh and A. H. Gardiner).

This fully confirms the presence of Egyptians on the Hyksos side in this war; the passage that follows is even more important for the political history of Egypt toward the end of the Hyksos period. Kamose is apparently the speaker:

I captured a messenger of his on the upper road of the Oasis, traveling southward toward Kush for the sake of [i.e. to deliver] a written dispatch. I found on it the following in writing from the ruler of Avaris: "I, Auserre, the Son of Re, Apophis, greet my son the ruler of Kush . . . Do you not see what Egypt has done against me? Her ruler, Kamose the Mighty, attacks me on my territory [although] I did not attack him, after the manner of all that he has done against you. He chooses these two lands to devastate them, my land and yours, [and] he has destroyed them. Come, set out at once toward the north. Do not be frightened! See, he is [occupied] here with me and there is no one who can oppose you here in Egypt, and [besides] I shall not let him go until you have arrived. Then we shall divide the cities of Egypt [between us] and our [two] lands will exult."

Kamose now resumes the narrative:

He had become frightened of me when I advanced toward the north, even before we fought together, even before I reached him. When he saw my fire, he sent as far as Kush to find someone who could save him. But I seized it [the message] on the road and I intercepted it. I sent it back to him, placing him [the messenger] on the eastern mountain near Atfieh.

Before returning to its base, Kamose's army makes a raid on the Oasis of Bahria. It seems that under Kamose, as in the Old and Middle Kingdom, the oases remained the traditional refuge for Egyptian rebels—this would explain the present raid. Another reason might be the Theban prince's desire to prevent a new exchange of letters between Avaris and Kush, or to block the access routes from the Sudan to Egypt proper. Indeed the oasis route will continue to be, even in the Middle Ages, one of the paths followed by Nubian raiders of Egypt.

It can easily be seen that the second Karnak stele is even more informative than the first. It shows us the danger that the existence of a well-organized state to the south of Egypt could constitute for Egyptian security. This lesson would not be lost on the Thebans; the rulers of the New Kingdom would know no rest until all of Upper Nubia was conquered and annexed. The text also alludes, however, to a conflict between Kamose and the ruler of Kush at some time before his campaign against the Hyksos. It is difficult to imagine what is meant by this. The first Karnak stele, in the speech of the counselors, pictures the situation south of Elephantine as peaceful. Further, Nubian mercenaries are a vital proportion of the forces Kamose leads against the Hyksos; is the king of Kush allowing his subjects to take service with a ruler who is his enemy? When Apophis speaks of "all that he has done against you," are we to think that he is merely referring back to the Nubian campaigns of the Twelfth Dynasty? The excavations now under way in Sudanese Nubia may answer these questions. For the time being the existence of a war between Kamose and the king of Kush rests on the weakest of proofs.

As for the Hyksos campaign of Kamose, the second Karnak stele allows us to follow it to its completion. The king reached the walls of Avaris; he was able to raid deep into Hyksos territory. "Raid" is the operative word, for Thebes was not yet strong enough to hold the north, and the army fell back on its base. Still, the frontier between Theban and Hyksos possessions had been pushed north to Atfieh, at the entrance to the Fayum near Memphis, for that is where Kamose leaves the Hyksos messenger to the king of Kush, by way of returning him to his master. From this point were to depart, doubtless, the campaigns of Kamose's successor, Ahmose. These are described for us in the autobiography of Ahmose of El Kab, the son of Abana, soldier of the Theban king; for many years the struggle between Hyksos and Thebans would continue on Egyptian soil. To follow it would take us into the history of the New Kingdom, and beyond the limits of this volume.

The second Karnak stele throws a flood of light on the end of the Second Intermediate Period. Until early in the reign of the Hyksos king Apophis I, Egypt was almost entirely in the hands of the invader. Sekenenre-Taa II "the Brave" was Apophis' vassal all through his reign, for his son, at the beginning of the next reign, was still in that condition. Kamose, then, did not truly become king of Egypt until his third year, with the reconquest of the country up to Atfieh; at that time his independence was recognized by Apophis himself.

413

With the death of Kamose, the Second Intermediate Period comes to an end. The Egyptian territory is not yet entirely cleared of the invader, but native Egyptian pharaohs have now recovered enough authority to justify the titles that Kamose took before his death: He revived the full titulature of the great pharaohs of the Twelfth Dynasty. He also appears to have composed his own eulogy (and here again he had some justification), which we read on one of his weapons: "The good god, master of the rites, Wadj-Kheper-Re, I am a valorous prince, the beloved of Re, the son of Ah [the moon-god], the child of Thoth and the son of Re, Kamose, conqueror forever." His Horus-name, written on the handle of an ebony fan, refers to the reconquest: "The Horus, Nourisher-of-the-Two-Lands." We do not know how this great king died nor how long he reigned. His tomb was still intact under Ramses IX, when the inspection of the royal tombs was made, but it was threatened shortly afterward; the funerary priests removed his sarcophagus for fear of graverobbers, reburying it on the Theban plain near the sepulchres of his mother, Aahotep, and of the two Antefs. There it was discovered in 1857. The mummy, unfortunately, was in such poor condition that it crumbled into dust before it could be examined by an anthropologist; we therefore do not know how old he was when he died, nor how he lost his life. The likelihood is that, like his father Sekenenre-Taa II, he had a fairly short reign. At least this seems to be indicated by his burial, on the orders of his son or brother Ahmose, in a very simple sarcophagus; there was no time to hold a solemn funeral, to prepare a sumptuous coffin; Egypt was still in the throes of war against the invaders who had interrupted her history.

Conclusion

When Egypt emerged, her unity once more restored, from the long and little-understood crisis we call the Second Intermediate Period, her situation was no longer and never again would be that which had obtained under the Old and Middle Kingdoms.

To the south, new peoples had settled, or old inhabitants had organized themselves; in any case they now constituted a danger to Egypt. To the east, the old and easy-going balance of powers had been shattered—new empires were rising, the whole Middle East was in turmoil. The Delta had proved much too close to all this turbulence; Egypt could no longer be indifferent to events in Asia. The Hyksos invasion had proved that a wall of fortresses along the frontiers, such as the kings of the Twelfth Dynasty had erected, was not enough to ward off the greed of nomad peoples on the move. Egypt in the Old and Middle Kingdoms had been autarkic, a society turned inward on itself; now in the New Kingdom she was to become aggressive—perhaps imperialist is the proper word—a society reaching out to all the lands around her for new provinces, new fashions, and new gods.

But, for the conquest of the northeast, the resources of the valley of the Nile were insufficient, both in raw materials and in men. The Hyksos, to defend their dying kingdom, had brought in a whole list of new resources: chariots and horses, weapons with a crueller cutting edge. The Theban rulers could never have overcome them but for the aid of mercenaries from outside Egypt, from the only part of the world to which their access was not blocked—Africa.

During the Second Intermediate Period there appears in Egypt, between Assiut and Aswan, in the heart, that is, of the region controlled by the princes of Thebes, a new people who seem to be of mixed Hamitic-Negroid type. More than fifteen sites in Upper Egypt have yielded up the graves typical of this people: shallow circular or oval graves, in the shape of a frying pan. For lack of a better name, they have been called "the Pan-Grave People."

From their tomb furnishings, we may conclude that these immigrants were closely linked, culturally, with Kerma and with the "C" group, agricultural and pastoral settlers in Nubia during the First Intermediate Period and Middle Kingdom (see pp. 375 ff.). The body, sometimes dressed in leather clothing, is laid in the tomb in the contracted position, with the head to the north, facing west. The pottery is for the most part deep bowls, red or black, more usually red with black edges and sometimes with incised decoration. Around the grave are buried animal skulls, goats' or sheeps' heads, decorated with spots of black, red or blue coloring. Deposited in the grave with the body are weapons—axes, daggers, arrows, etc.—and sometimes Egyptian jewelry in gold or silver. As a general rule, it is believed, these are mercenary soldiers, perhaps the Medjayu of whom Kamose's stele speaks: "Medjay troops watched from the roofs of the [ships'] cabins, to spy out the Asiatics and destroy their works." These mercenaries appear in Egypt at the end of the Thirteenth Dynasty. It was long believed that the Pan-Grave People were nomads of the eastern desert, related to but different from the sedentary populations of the southern Nile Valley. Their pottery and their burial rites were thought to resemble those of the "C" group, but here again differed in some respects. But the most recent excavations in Sudanese Nubia seem to clarify the matter. The incised pottery of the Pan-Grave People seems to be much closer than had previously been thought to that of the late tombs of the "C" group, and, around the Nubian tombs of this period, there have also been found painted animal skulls like those in the pan graves of Egypt. It is therefore not impossible that the Pan-Grave People, who appeared in Egypt at the end of the Thirteenth Dynasty, were descendants of the Nubian "C" group people contemporary with the Twelfth. If this is verified, then the mercenaries of the Theban princes were not only Medjayu, desert nomads, but also Nehesiu from the Upper Valley. This brings us back to the problem of the relations between Thebes and Kush. The king of Kush would have had little authority over the Medjay nomads in the neighboring desert, but the same would not apply to the settled populations of the valley. If these are Kushite mercenaries buried in Egypt, their presence would imply good relations between their homeland and the principality of Thebes.

The point, however, is this: To overcome the Hyksos, who were drawing upon Asia for new technical support, the Egyptians drew in turn on their African hinterland, and to a great degree—so much so that "the war of liberation gives the impression of a battle between Asia and Africa" (T. Säve-Söderbergh). This was to have consequences of immense importance; the whole later history of Ancient Egypt was colored by it.

When they came to power in 2000 B.C., the Theban rulers of the Twelfth Dynasty had placed their capital close to the Delta, in order to be able to rule all of Egypt. The pharaohs of the Eighteenth Dynasty, having reconquered all of the Nile valley, kept their capital at Thebes. Their reason for this is obvious: Egypt, in order to play the role of a world power, needed the resources of the Upper Nile. There and only there could she find the wood, the copper, the gold and above all the inexhaustible reserves of men that were henceforth indispensable to her greatness. But to conquer, to colonize and to control this African Eldorado she must set up her national headquarters as close as possible to her southern border at the First Cataract; the Delta was too far away. It was not by chance that the choice of Thebes as Egypt's capital corresponded with the conquest of the Sudan down to the Fourth Cataract. From these new provinces, Egypt was to draw her main economic and military strength from now on. And, from now on, Egypt was to find herself on the horns of a dilemma. To maintain her Oriental empire, to defend the Delta, the gateway into Egypt from teeming Asia, Egypt ought to mass her forces and place her capital in Lower Egypt, and was indeed to do so as time unfolded; but this was to leave the African provinces untended, to run the risk of losing them entirely, when they were the main sources of her national strength, the sinews of her empire.

For three centuries the pharaohs of the New Kingdom would be able to hold together an empire stretching from the Lebanon to the Sudan. Then the edifice would collapse, and the land once more be riven. Parallel dynasties would reign

417

in Lower Egypt, in Upper Egypt, and the Sudan—a repetition, in other words, of the history of the Second Intermediate Period, but a prolonged one. For there is this difference: After the Seventeenth Dynasty, there is a new golden age to come; after the Twenty-fifth and the Twenty-sixth, nothing but the slow and terrible death agony of a great civilization.

Notes

Chapters 1–5

1. The Chalcolithic age refers to a stage of development in which metal tools were used alongside the (more prevalent) stone implements.

2. High officials after whom the years were named in Assyria, but not in Babylonia. Originally determined by lot, the eponymous officials were later named in a regular order of succession. Kings also held the eponymate.

3. Higher dates, higher, that is, than those of the "middle chronology," would put Hammurabi of Babylon back as far as 1930–1888 B.C.; this would force an upward revision of our estimated dates for prehistory and the Protoliterate period, which does not seem justified.

4. The carbon-14 method calculates the age of remnants of wood, charcoal, and other organic matter by the amount of the radioactive isotope carbon-14 preserved in them. The carbon-14 method has resulted in a considerable lowering of many of the dates formerly assigned to finds of the prehistoric and Protoliterate periods.

5. R. S. Solecki, "Three Adult Neanderthal Skeletons from Shanidar Cave, Northern Iraq," *Sumer*, vol. XVII, pp. 71–96 (Baghdad, 1961).

6. E. Anati, *Palestine Before the Hebrews*, p. 245.

7. K. Kenyon, *Digging up Jericho*, plates 20–22.

8. C. F. A. Schaeffer, *Ugaritica*, IV, pp. 157 ff. (Paris, 1962).

9. J. Mellaart, "Excavations at Çatal-hüyük," *Anatolian Studies*, vol. XI, pp. 57–65; pls. XIV–XVIII (London, 1962).

10. A. J. Tobler, *Excavations at Tepe Gawra*, vol. II, pp. 41 ff. (Philadelphia, 1950); M. E. L. Mallowan and J. C. Rose, "Excavations at Tell Arpachiyah," *Iraq*, vol. II, pp. 22 ff. (London, 1935); S. Lloyd and F. Safar, "Tell Hassuna," *Journal of Near Eastern Studies*, vol. IV, p. 272, fig. 28 (Chicago, 1945); C. L. Woolley, "Prehistoric Pottery of Carchemish," *Iraq*, vol. I, pp. 147 ff., fig. 1 (London, 1934).

11. Pliny, *Naturalis Historia* (Editio Teubneriana) VI, 26, 122; see also XVIII, 162.

12. Fortified residence of Arab tribal leaders.

13. D. Stronach, "Excavations at Ras al 'Amiya," *Iraq*, vol. XXIII, pp. 95 ff. (London, 1961).

14. P. Delougaz, *Pottery from the Diyala Region (University of Chicago Oriental Institute Publications*, vol. LXIII), p. 23 (Chicago, 1952).

15. S. N. Kramer, "Sumerische Literarische Texte aus Nippur," *Texte und Materialien der Hilprecht-Sammlung*, Neue Folge, vol. III, pp. 10 f. (Berlin, 1961).

16. H. Helbaek, "Ecological Effects of Irrigation in Ancient Mesopotamia," *Iraq*, vol. XXII, pp. 186–96 (London, 1960).

16a. The usual spelling in older works, "ziggurat," has now been found to be a misreading of the original Akkadian word.

17. In Akkadian, raw bitumen is called *ittu*, i.e. "the (material) from Hit."

18. S. Lloyd and F. Safar, "Eridu," *Sumer*, vol. IV, p. 118, pl. V (Baghdad, 1948).

19. H. Lenzen, *XIV. Vorläufiger Bericht über die . . . Ausgrabungen in Uruk-Warka*, p. 26, pl. XLIIIa (Berlin, 1958).

20. S. Lloyd and F. Safar, *op. cit.* (n. 18), p. 118, pl. IV.

21. C. M. Otten, "Note on the Cemetery of Eridu," *Sumer*, vol. IV, pp. 125–27 (Baghdad, 1948).

22. C. S. Coon, "The Eridu Crania. A Preliminary Report," *Sumer*, vol. V, pp. 103–06 (Baghdad, 1949).

23. L. Le Breton, "The Early Periods at Susa: Mesopotamian Relations," *Iraq*, vol. XIX, pp. 81 ff. (London, 1957).

24. A. Moortgat, "Entstehung der sumerischen Hochkultur," *Der Alte Orient*, vol. XLIII, pp. 37 ff. (Leipzig, 1945); A. L. Perkins, *The Comparative Archaeology of Early Mesopotamia (Studies in Ancient Oriental Civilization*, no. 25), pp. 46 ff. (Chicago, 1949).

25. S. Lloyd, "Tell Uqair," *Journal of Near Eastern Studies*, vol. II, pp. 135 ff. (Chicago, 1943).

26. E. Heinrich, *Kleinfunde aus den archaischen Tempelschichten in Uruk*, pp. 15–28, pls. II–XIV (Leipzig, 1936).

27. H. Lenzen, *op. cit.* (n. 19), p. 37, pl. XLIIa; *idem, XVI. Vorläufiger Bericht über die . . . Ausgrabungen in Uruk-Warka*, pp. 37 ff., pls. XVII to XVIII (Berlin, 1960).

28. H. Lenzen, "Ein Marmorkopf der Dschemdet Nasr-Zeit aus Uruk," *Zeitschrift für Assyriologie und Vorderasiatische Archäologie*, Neue Folge, Vol. XI, pp. 85–87 (Berlin, 1939).

29. E. Heinrich, *op. cit.* (n. 26), pp. 17 ff., pls. IVb–XIII.

30. *ibid.*, pp. 15–17, pls. II–IVa, XXXVIII.

31. A. Falkenstein, "La cité-temple sumérienne," *Journal of World History*, I (1954), pp. 748–814.

32. H. Frankfort, *Cylinder Seals*, pl. IIId (London, 1939).

33. E. A. Speiser, *Excavations at Tepe Gawra*, vol. I, pp. 145 ff. (Philadelphia, 1935).

34. M. E. L. Mallowan, "Excavations at Tell Brak and Chagar Bazar," *Iraq*, vol. IX, pp. 31 ff. (London, 1947).

35. T. Jacobsen, *The Sumerian King List (Assyriological Studies*, No. 11), p. 76 (Chicago, 1939).

36. This threefold division, and the term "Early Dynastic," originate with Henri Frankfort.

37. This date is a working hypothesis. As before, we may also fix the dates of Hammurabi, according to the "low chronology," at 1728–1687.

38. For a discussion of the chronology of the Dynasty of Agade, see below, pp. 97 ff.

39. For a discussion of this terminology, see below, pp. 180 ff.

40. Most historians give the form *Mesilim*, as a conventional reading of this name.

41. The reading of this name is not certain.

42. Sumerian has no grammatical means to express the difference between masculine and feminine gender: *en* may therefore imply either.

43. T. Jacobsen, *Zeitschrift für Assyriologie*, Neue Folge, vol. 18 (1957), pp. 120 ff.

44. See Anna Schneider, "Die Anfänge der Kulturwirtschaft," in J. Plenge, *Staatswissenschaftliche Beiträge*, Heft IV (Essen, 1920); A. Falkenstein, *op. cit.* (n. 31), pp. 784–814.

45. For the most recent discussion see I. M. Diakonov, *Sumer: Society and State in Ancient Mesopotamia* (in Russian, with English resumé), Moscow, 1959, pp. 291 ff.

46. T. Jacobsen, *op. cit.* (n. 43), p. 100, note 11.

47. Compare the Old Testament report on Rehaboam, I Kings 12, 6–17.

48. *Eden* is from the Sumerian for "steppe." The "High *Eden*" (*an-edena*) was an elevated area between the cities of Uruk, Larsa, Badtibira, Umma, and Zabalam.

49. See W. F. Leemans, *Foreign Trade in Old Babylonian Times* (Leyden, 1960), pp. 159–166; *idem, Journal of the Economic and Social History of the Orient*, 3 (1960), pp. 23–30.

49a. This opinion may have to be revised when more work has been done on the Shuruppak texts, and particularly when the recently discovered Early Dynastic III tablets from Tell Abu Salabikh (of approximately the same date as the Shuruppak texts) come to be published.

50. Agade is the conventional spelling of the name of Sargon's capital. The northern part of Babylonia, to which the city gave its name, was called the "Land of Akkad."

51. The reading of the two last syllables of this name is not certain; the convention is to print such syllables in capitals.

52. This king is probably Erridupizir or Erriduwazir.

53. See T. Jacobsen, *The Sumerian King List*, pp. 110 ff. cols. VI, 28, to VIII, 3.

54. The historical data on the Second Dynasty of Lagash (see also above, pp. 94–95) are the result of Prof. A. Falkenstein's researches: this scholar very generously placed the manuscript of the introduction to his critical edition of the documents of this period at the disposal of the present author, permitting their use here.

55. I retain this translation, although "Shining Mountains" has been suggested, which, however, seems less sure to me.

56. For the change of meaning of the title *ensi* during the Agade period, see above, p. 111.

57. The Akkadian scribes introduced new names for the months, which the kings of Agade apparently enforced in the entire area under their control, at least in Mesopotamia.

58. A. Falkenstein, "Zur Chronologie der sumerischen Literatur,"

Compte rendu de la Seconde Rencontre Assyriologique Internationale (Leyden, 1952), p. 19.

59. The inscription published in the *Archiv für Orientforschung*, 10, p. 281, to which there has recently been added a duplicate (*Iranica Antiqua* 2, no. 29, p. 163), should be read in this way; KAL is the Sumerogram for *dannum*; it should not be affixed to the name, which is pronounced "Elul" (alternate form of the Elulu in the *King List*).

60. This is perhaps the Elamite reading of the name, which in Akkadian was written *Puzur-inshushinak*.

61. Lullu, Lullubu/Lullubi, later also Lullume (and even Nullu) are variants of the same native name for this people.

62. T. Jacobsen, *Journal of the American Oriental Society*, 59 (1939), p. 495, note 26.

63. In the empire of Agade, the custom had developed of naming years after a notable event of the current or the previous year, in order to date documents. The "date formulae" of individual rulers or of whole dynasties were gathered in lists. Annual date formulae were used in Babylonia, in the Diyala region, and on the Middle Eurphrates until about the end of the First Dynasty of Babylon. Later, dates were given by regnal years, after the pattern: "Year one, King X." On eponymous dating in Assyria, see above, p. 10, and note 2.

64. The reading of the name *Shid-tab* is not quite certain.

65. See H. Lenzen, *Die Entwicklung der Zikurrat von ihren Anfängen bis zur Zeit der III. Dynastie von Ur* (*Ausgrabungen der Deutschen Forschungsgemeinschaft in Uruk-Warka,* 4), (Leipzig, 1941).

66. The divine determinative is the cuneiform character for "god," written before the name of the god. If the determinative occurs before the name of a ruler, it indicates his divinization.

67. On the question of Dumuzi, see A. Falkenstein, *Compte rendu de la IIIe Rencontre assyriologique internationale* (Leyden, 1954), pp. 41–65 and T. Jacobsen, "Toward the Image of Tammuz," *History of Religions* I (1961), pp. 189–213.

68. See R. D. Barnett, *Journal of Hellenic Studies*, 83 (1963), pp. 20 ff.

69. See W. W. Hallo, "A Sumerian Amphictyony," *Journal of Cuneiform Studies*, 14 (1960), pp. 88–114.

70. So far almost 18,000 clay tablets of the Ur III period have

been published. The number of unpublished tablets in the store-rooms of the museums is many times that figure.

71. See T. B. Jones and J. W. Snyder, *Sumerian Economic Texts from the Third Dynasty of Ur* (Minneapolis, 1961), pp. 249–79.

72. An approximate translation of the Akkadian word.

73. The earliest examples of the transference of the name of the city of "Assur" to the surrounding region, Akkadian "Land of Assur," do not appear before the fourteenth century.

74. See G. Martiny, *Die Kultrichtung in Babylonien*, 1934.

75. For the *mushkenum*, see below, note 80.

76. Annelies Kammenhuber, *Zeitschrift für vergleichende Sprachforschung (Kuhns Zeitschrift)*, 77 (1961), p. 162.

77. For the details of the immigration of the Hittites and the beginnings of their history, see the next volume in this series.

78. T. Jacobsen and R. M. Adams, "Salt and Silt in Ancient Mesopotamian Agriculture," *Science*, 128, No. 3334 (1958), pp. 1251–58.

79. For details on the Empire of the Mitanni, see the next volume in this series.

80. Thus W. Von Soden, *Zeitschrift für Assyriologie*, Neue Folge 22 (1964), p. 133 ff. For another view, F. R. Kraus, *Ein Edikt des Königs Ammi-saduqa von Babylonien* (Leyden, 1958), pp. 144–55 (the *mushkenum* represents the mass of the free population, with the exception of an upper class called *awilum*, in the Old Babylonian period).

81. On this see F. R. Kraus, "Le Rôle des temples depuis la IIIᵉ dynastie d'Ur jusqu'à la Iʳᵉ dynastie de Babylone," *Journal of World History*, I (1954), pp. 518–45.

82. While we use here, and earlier, the word "priest(ess)," we must emphasize that although Sumerian and Akkadian employ a large number of terms for cult personnel, there is no general term for "priest."

83. W. F. Leemans, *The Old Babylonian Merchant* (Leyden, 1950), pp. 11–21, 96, 118 f.

83a. See H. Petschow, "Zur Systematik und Gesetzestechnik im Codex Hammurabi," *Zeitschrift für Assyriologie*, N. F. 23 (1965), pp. 146–72.

84. The translation gives the content of the Akkadian expression only approximately. See F. R. Kraus, *Genava*, Nouv. série, 8 (1960), pp. 285 f.

85. F. R. Kraus, *ibid.*, p. 292, mentions another, but less certain, case.

86. This of course refers to the apparent impermanence of a work like the *Code of Hammurabi*, which was *meant* to be permanent, and not to royal legislation, which was intended to be binding only temporarily.

87. A Kassite loan word in the Akkadian language.

88. See, in general, W. von Soden, *Zweisprachigkeit in der geistigen Kultur Babyloniens* (*Osterreichische Akademie der Wissenschaften, Phil.-Hist. Klasse, Sitzungsberichte* 235/1, 1960).

89. English translations of the *Gilgamesh Epic*: A. Heidel, *The Gilgamesh Epic and Old Testament Parallels*, second edition (Chicago, 1949); E. A. Speiser's translation in J. B. Pritchard, ed., *Ancient Near Eastern Texts Relating to the Old Testament*, 2d ed. (Princeton, 1955), pp. 72–99. On the Gilgamesh cycle in general, see P. Garelli, ed., *Gilgamesh et sa légende* (Paris, 1960). A comprehensive history of Sumerian and Akkadian literature has yet to be written. On the mythology of the Sumerians and the Akkadians, see most recently D.O. Edzard, "Mesopotamien," in H. W. Haussig, ed., *Wörterbuch der Mythologie*, vol. I/1, pp. 19–139; S. N. Kramer, *Sumerian Mythology*, 2d ed. (New York, 1961).

Bibliography

Chapters 1–5

ANCIENT WESTERN ASIA

Detailed studies are listed in the separate bibliographies for each chapter. For general orientation, the English-speaking reader may consult the following.

A. *Sources in English translation*:

Pritchard, J. B., ed., *Ancient Near Eastern Texts Relating to the Old Testament*, 2d ed. (Princeton, 1955). Historical, legal, religious and social documents from the entire Near East.

Thomas, D. W., ed., *Documents from Old Testament Times* (Edinburgh and London, 1958; New York, 1961).

B. *General works*:

Childe, V. G., *New Light on the Most Ancient East*, 4th ed. (London and New York, 1957).

Kramer, S. N., *The Sumerians: Their History, Culture, and Character* (Chicago, 1963).

Oppenheim, A. L., *Ancient Mesopotamia* (Chicago, 1964).

Saggs, H. W. F., *The Greatness That Was Babylon* (London and New York, 1962).

C. *Illustrations*:

Frankfort, H., *The Art and Architecture of the Ancient Orient* (Pelican History of Art Series, Harmondsworth, 1954).

427

Pritchard, J. B., ed., *The Ancient Near East in Pictures* (Princeton, 1955).

Chapter I

THE PREHISTORY AND PROTOHISTORY OF WESTERN ASIA

A. *Sources*:

Braidwood, R. J., and Howe, B., *Prehistoric Investigations in Iraqi Kurdistan* (Studies in Ancient Oriental Civilization, 31, Chicago, 1960).

Delougaz, P., and Lloyd, S., *Pre-Sargonid Temples in the Diyala Region* (University of Chicago Oriental Institute Publications, 53, Chicago, 1942).

Delougaz, P., *Pottery from the Diyala Region* (University of Chicago Oriental Institute Publications, 63, Chicago, 1952).

Falkenstein, A., *Archaische Texte aus Uruk* (Leipzig, 1936).

Frankfort, H., *Stratified Cylinder Seals from the Diyala Region* (University of Chicago Oriental Institute Publications, 72, Chicago, 1955).

Garrod, D. A. E., and Bate, D. M. A., *The Stone Age of Mount Carmel* (London, 1937).

Garstang, J., *Prehistoric Mersin—Yümük Tepe in Southern Turkey* (Oxford, 1953).

Genouillac, H. de, *Fouilles de Telloh*, vol. I (Paris, 1934).

Ghirshman, R., *Fouilles de Sialk près de Kashan*, vols. I–II (Paris, 1938–39).

Jacobsen, T., *The Sumerian King List* (Assyriological Studies, 11, Chicago, 1939).

Jordan, J., Nöldeke, A., Heinrich, E., and Lenzen, H., *Vorläufiger Bericht über die . . . in Uruk-Warka unternommenen Ausgrabungen*, Bde. I–XIX (Berlin, 1930–63).

Mackay, E. J. H., *Report on Excavations at Jemdet Nasr, Iraq* (Field Museum of Natural History, Anthropology Memoirs, 3, Chicago, 1931).

Mallowan, M. E. L., "Excavations at Tell Brak and Chagar Bazar," *Iraq*, 9 (1947).

Moortgat, A., *Vorderasiatische Rollsiegel* (Berlin, 1940).

Parrot, A., *Tello* (Paris, 1948).

Speiser, E. A., *Excavations at Tepe Gawra*, vol. I (Philadelphia, 1935).

Tobler, A. J., *Excavations at Tepe Gawra*, vol. II (Philadelphia, 1950).

Woolley, C. L., *Ur Excavations*, vol. IV: *The Early Periods* (London, 1955).

B. *General works*:

Albright, W. F., *The Archaeology of Palestine* (Harmondsworth, 1949).

Anati, E., *Palestine Before the Hebrews* (New York, 1963).

Bittel, K., *Grundzüge der Vor- und Frühgeschichte Kleinasiens*, 2. Aufl. (Tübingen, 1950).

Braidwood, R. J., *Prehistoric Man*, 5th ed. (Chicago, 1961).

Braidwood, R. J., and Willey, G. R., *Courses Toward Urban Life* (Chicago, 1962).

Childe, V. G., *Man Makes Himself* (London, 1941; 1955).

————, *What Happened in History* (Harmondsworth, 1952; 1954).

Christian, V., *Altertumskunde des Zweistromlandes*, Bd. I (Leipzig, 1940).

Ehrich, R. W. *et al.*, *Relative Chronologies in Old World Archaeology* (Chicago, 1954).

Frankfort, H., *Cylinder Seals* (London, 1939).

Ghirshman, R., *Iran* (Harmondsworth, 1954).

Jirku, A., *Die Ausgrabungen in Palästina und Syrien* (Halle, 1956).

Kenyon, K., *Digging up Jericho* (New York, 1957).

————, *Archeology in the Holy Land* (London, 1960).

Lloyd, S., *Early Anatolia: The Archaeology of Asia Minor Before the Greeks* (Harmondsworth, 1956).

McCown, D. E., *Comparative Stratigraphy of Early Iran* (Studies in Ancient Oriental Civilization, 23, Chicago, 1942; 2d ed., 1959).

Moortgat, A., *Frühe Bildkunst in Sumer* (Mitteilungen der Vorderasiatisch-Ägyptischen Gesellschaft, 40/3, Leipzig, 1935).

————, *Entstehung der sumerischen Hochkultur* (Alter Orient, 43, Leipzig, 1945).

Parrot, A., *Archéologie mésopotamienne*, vols. I–II (Paris, 1946; 1953).

————, *Sumer: The Dawn of Art* (The Arts of Mankind Series, New York and London, 1960).

Perkins, A. L., *The Comparative Archaeology of Early Mesopotamia* (Studies in Ancient Oriental Civilization, 25, Chicago, 1949).

Scharff, A., and Moortgat, A. *Ägypten und Vorderaisien im Altertum* (Munich, 1950).

Schmidtke, F., *Der Aufbau der babylonischen Chronologie* (Münster, 1952).

Soden, W. v., *Sumer, Babylon und Hethiter bis zur Mitte des zweiten Jahrtausends v. Chr.* (Propyläen-Weltgeschichte, Bd. I, Berlin, 1962).

Strommenger, E., and Hirmer, M., *Fünf Jahrtausende Mesopotamien* (Munich, 1962).

Van den Berghe, L., *L'Archéologie de l'Iran ancien* (Documenta et Monumenta Orientis Antiqui, 6, Leiden, 1959).

Westphal-Hellbusch, S., and Westphal, H., *Die Ma'dan, Kultur und Geschichte der Marschenbewohner im Süd-Iraq* (Berlin, 1962).

Wirth, E., *Agrargeographie des Iraq* (Berlin, 1963).

C. *Articles*:

Adams, R. M., "Agriculture and Urban Life in Early Southwestern Iran," *Science*, 136 (1962), pp. 109–22.

Braidwood, R. J., "Near Eastern Prehistory," *Science*, 127 (1958), pp. 1419–30.

Braidwood, R. J., and Braidwood, L. S., "The Earliest Village Communities of Southwestern Asia," *Journal of World History*, I (1953), pp. 278–310.

Braidwood, R. J., and Reed, C. A., "The Achievement and Early Consequences of Food-Production: A Consideration of the Archaeological and Natural-Historical Evidences," *Cold Spring Harbor Symposia on Quantitative Biology*, 22 (1957), pp. 19–31.

Helbaek, H., "Ecological Effects of Irrigation in Ancient Mesopotamia," *Iraq*, 22 (1960), pp. 186–96.

Le Breton, L., "The Early Periods at Susa: Mesopotamian Relations," *Iraq*, 19 (1957), pp. 79–124.

Mallowan, M. E. L., and Rose, J. C., "Excavations at Tell Arpachiyah, 1933," *Iraq*, 2 (1935), pp. 1–178.

Mellaart, J., "Excavations at Hacilar," *Anatolian Studies*, 8, pp. 127 ff.; 9, pp. 51 ff.; 10, pp. 83 ff.; 11, pp. 39 ff. (1958–60).

————, "Excavations at Çatalhüyük," *Anatolian Studies*, 11 (1962).

Nagel, W., "Zum neuen Bild des vordynastischen Keramikums in Vorderasien," *Berliner Jahrbuch für Vor- und Frühgeschichte*, I, pp. 1–125; II, pp. 111–53; III, pp. 155–215 (1961–63).

Chapter 2

THE EARLY DYNASTIC PERIOD

Cameron, G. G., *History of Early Iran* (Chicago, 1936).

Diakonov, I. M., "Some Remarks on the 'Reforms' of Urukagina," *Revue d'Assyriologie*, 52 (1958), pp. 1 ff.

————, *Obshchestvennyi i gosudarstvennyi stroi drevnego dvurech'ya: Sumer* (Sumer: Society and State in Ancient Mesopotamia [in Russian, with English résumé], Moscow, 1959).

Edzard, D. O., "Enmebaragesi von Kiš," *Zeitschrift für Assyriologie*, N.F. 19 (1959), pp. 9–26.

————, "Sumerer und Semiten in der frühen Geschichte Mesopotamiens," *Genava*, n.s. 8 (1960), pp. 242–58.

Falkenstein, A., "La cité-temple sumérienne," *Journal of World History*, I (1954), pp. 784–814.

Frankfort, H. and H. A., Wilson, J. A., Jacobsen, T., and Irwin, W. A., *The Intellectual Adventure of Ancient Man* (Chicago, 1946). Also published as *Before Philosophy* (Harmondsworth, 1949).

Gadd, C. J., *Ideas of Divine Rule in the Ancient East* (London, 1948).

————, "The Cities of Babylonia," *Cambridge Ancient History*, rev. ed., vol. I, ch. XIII (Cambridge, 1962—published separately).

Hinz, W., "Persia c. 2400–1800," *Cambridge Ancient History*, rev. ed., vol. I, ch. XXIII (Cambridge, 1963—published separately).

Jacobsen, T., "Early Political Development in Mesopotamia," *Zeitschrift für Assyriologie*, N.F. 18 (1957), pp. 91–140.

Le Breton, L., "The Early Periods at Susa: Mesopotamian Relations," *Iraq*, 29 (1957), pp. 79 ff.

Lenzen, H. J., "Mesopotamische Tempelanlagen von der Frühzeit bis zum zweiten Jahrtausend," *Zeitschrift für Assyriologie*, N.F. 17 (1955), pp. 1–36.

Chapter 3

THE FIRST SEMITIC EMPIRE

The principal sources are published in:

Thureau-Dangin, F., *Die sumerischen und akkadischen Königsinschriften* (Leipzig, 1907).

Barton, G. A., *The Royal Inscriptions of Sumer and Accad* (New Haven, 1929).

Hirsch, H., "Die Inschriften der Könige von Agade," *Archiv für Orientforschung*, 20 (1963), pp. 1–82.

For an outstanding discussion of the "literary tradition" of Sargonid history, see:

Güterbock, H. G. "Die historische Tradition und ihre literarische Gestaltung bei Babyloniern und Hethitern," *Zeitschrift für Assyriologie*, N.F. 8, pp. 1–91; 10, pp. 45–149 (1934, 1938).

An adequate illustrated guide to the art and archaeology of the period is:

Strommenger, E., and Hirmer, H., *Fünf Jahrtausende Mesopotamien* (Munich, 1962).

The most recently published historical study of this period, other than that to be found in:

Schmökel, H. *Geschichte des alten Vorderasien* (Leiden, 1957) is that of:

Gadd, C. J. "The Dynasty of Agade and the Gutian Invasion," *Cambridge Ancient History*, rev. ed., vol. I, ch. XIX (Cambridge, 1963—published separately),

in which a detailed bibliography is provided.

See also, in the same series:

Hinz, W., "Persia, c. 2400–1800 B.C.," *ibid.*, ch. XXIII (Cambridge, 1963—published separately).

Chapter 4

THE THIRD DYNASTY OF UR—ITS EMPIRE
AND ITS SUCCESSOR STATES

Edzard, D. O., *Die "zweite Zwischenzeit" Babyloniens* (Wiesbaden, 1957).

Falkenstein, A., "Zur Chronologie der sumerischen Literatur," in *Comptes rendus de la Seconde Rencontre assyriologique internationale* (Paris, 1951), pp. 12–28.

Falkenstein, A., and Soden, W. v., *Sumerische und akkadische Hymnen und Gebete* (Zürich and Stuttgart, 1953).

Gelb, I. J., *Hurrians and Subarians* (Chicago, 1944).

Jacobsen, T., "The Assumed Conflict between Sumerians and Semites," *Journal of the American Oriental Society*, 59 (1939), pp. 485–95.

Jacobsen, T., "The Waters of Ur," *Iraq*, 22 (1960), pp. 174–85.

Kramer, S. N., *The Lamentation over the Destruction of Ur* (Assyriological Studies, 12, Chicago, 1940).

————, tr., *Code of Lipit-eshtar*, in Pritchard, J. B., ed., *Ancient Near Eastern Texts Relating to the Old Testament*, 2d ed. (Princeton, 1955), pp. 159–161.

————, ed. and tr., *Code of Ur-Nammu*, with an appendix by A. Falkenstein, *Orientalia*, n.s. 23 (1954), pp. 40–51.

Kraus, F. R., "Le Rôle des temples depuis la troisième Dynastie d'Ur jusqu' à la première dynastie de Babylone," *Journal of World History*, 1 (1954), pp. 518–45.

Sollberger, E., "Sur la Chronologie des rois d'Ur et quelques probblèmes connexes," *Archiv für Orientforschung*, 17 (1954–56), pp. 10–48.

Speiser, E. A., "The Hurrian Participation in the Civilisations of Mesopotamia, Syria and Palestine," *Journal of World History*, 1 (1954), pp. 311–27.

Chapter 5

THE OLD BABYLONIAN PERIOD

Bottéro, J., "Désordre économique et annullation des dettes en Mesopotamie à l'époque paléo-babylonienne," *Journal of Economic and Social History of the Orient*, 4 (1961), pp. 113–64.

Driver, G., and Miles, J., *The Babylonian Laws*, Vols. I–II (Oxford, 1952; 1955).

Eilers, W., *Die Gesetzesstele Hammurabis* (Alter Orient, 30/3–4, Leipzig, 1932).

Falkenstein, A., "Zu den Inschriftenfunden der Grabung in Uruk-Warka 1960–1961," *Baghdader Mitteilungen*, 2 (1963), pp. 1–82.

Garelli, P., *Les assyriens en Cappadoce* (Paris, 1963).

Gelb, I. J., "Two Assyrian King Lists," *Journal of Near Eastern Studies*, 13 (1954), pp. 209–30.

————, "The Early History of the West Semitic Peoples," *Journal of Cuneiform Studies*, 15 (1961), pp. 27–47.

Goetze, A., *The Laws of Eshnunna* (Annual of the American Schools of Oriental Research, 31, 1956).

Harris, R., "The Organisation and Administration of the Cloister in Ancient Babylonia," *Journal of Economic and Social History of the Orient*, 6 (1963), pp. 121–57.

Hinz, W., "Persia c. 1800–1550," *Cambridge Ancient History*, rev. ed., vol. II, ch. VII (Cambridge, 1963—separately published).

Kraus, F. R., "Isin und Nippur nach altbabylonischen Rechtsurkunden," *Journal of Cuneiform Studies*, 3 (1951).

————, *Ein Edikt des Königs Ammi-saduqa von Babylon* (Leiden, 1958).

————, "Ein zentrales Problem des altmesopotamischen Rechtes: Was ist der Codex Hammurabi?" *Genava*, n.s. 8 (1960), pp. 283–96.

Kupper, J.-R., *Les Nomades en Mésopotamie au temps des rois de Mari* (Paris, 1957).

————, "Northern Mesopotamia and Syria," *Cambridge Ancient History*, rev. ed., vol. II, ch. II (Cambridge, 1963—published separately).

Landsberger, B., "Assyrische Königsliste und 'Dunkles Zeitalter,'" *Journal of Cuneiform Studies*, 8 (1954), pp. 31–73, 106–33.

————, "Remarks on the Archives of the Soldier Ubarum," *Journal of Cuneiform Studies*, 9, pp. 121–31; 10, p. 39 (1955–56).

Leemans, W. F., *The Old-Babylonian Merchant* (Leiden, 1950).

————, *Foreign Trade in Old-Babylonian Times* (Leiden, 1960).

San Nicolò, M., *Beiträge zur Rechtsgeschichte im Bereich der keilschriftlichen Rechtsquellen* (Oslo, 1931).

Walther, A., *Das altbabylonische Gerichtswesen* (Leipziger Semitistische Studien 6/4–6, 1917).

Chapters 6–11

ANCIENT EGYPT

For ancient sources, and for detailed modern bibliography, see the individual chapter bibliographies in:

Drioton, E., and Vandier, J., *L'Egypte* (Clio, Introduction aux Etudes Historiques, Les Peuples de l'Orient Méditerranéen, II, 4th ed., Paris, 1962).

See also the most recent general works:

Gardiner, A. H., *Egypt of the Pharaohs* (Oxford, 1961).

Hayes, W. C., *The Scepter of Egypt*, Part I: From the earliest times to the end of the Middle Kingdom (New York, 1953).

Smith, W. S., and Hayes, W. C., in *Cambridge Ancient History*, rev. ed. (Cambridge, 1961): vol. I, ch. XIV, "The Old Kingdom in Egypt" (W. S. Smith); *ibid.*, ch. XX, "The Middle Kingdom in Egypt" (W. C. Hayes); *ibid.*, vol. II, ch. II, "Egypt, from the death of Ammenemes III to Seqenenre II" (W. C. Hayes). Each chapter has been published separately.

The following are fundamental to an understanding of the civilization, art and religion of ancient Egypt:

Erman, A., and Ranke, H., *Ägypten und ägyptisches Leben im Altertum* (Tübingen, 1923).

Kees, H., *Totenglaube und Jenseitsvorstellungen der alten Ägypter: Grundlagen und Entwicklung bis zum Ende des mittleren Reiches* (Leipzig, 1926).

Smith, W. S., *A History of Egyptian Sculpture and Painting in the Old Kingdom*, 2d ed. (Oxford, 1949).

Vandier, J., *Manuel d'Archéologie Egyptienne*, 3 vols. in 6 (Paris, 1952–1958).

For very brief but up-to-date information on most aspects of Egyptian civilization, see:

Posener, G., ed., *Dictionary of Egyptian Civilization* (London and New York, n.d.).

Acknowledgments

DRAWINGS

FIGURE 1. *Pottery of the Tell Halaf culture*: a) after H. Schmidt, *Tell Halaf*, I (W. de Gruyter, Berlin); b) after M. E. L. Mallowan, *Iraq*, II, fig. 53, 1 (British School of Archaeology in Iraq, London)

FIGURE 2. *Clay bowl of the Samarra culture*: after E. Herzfeld, *Ausgrabungen in Samarra*, Vol. V, fig. 23, n. 23

FIGURE 3. *Clay bowl of the Eridu culture*: after C. H. Ziegler, *Die Keramik von der Qal'a des Ḥaǧǧi Mohammed*, pl. 14 (Gebr. Mann Verlag, Berlin)

FIGURE 4. *Pottery of the Ubaid culture*: a) after M. E. L. Mallowan, *Iraq* II, fig. 28, 2 (British School of Archaeology in Iraq, London); b) after *Journal of Near Eastern Studies*, Vol. II, pl. 19, 6 (University of Chicago Press, Chicago); c) after H. de Genouillac, *Fouilles de Telloh*, Vol. I, pl. 2ᴬ TG. 5440 (Paul Geuthner, Paris); d) after A. J. Tobler, *Excavations at Tepe Gawra*, Vol. II, pls. 126, 152 (University Museum of Pennsylvania, Philadelphia); e) after *ibid.*, 135, 265; f) after *ibid.*, 134, 252

FIGURE 5. *Pottery of the Uruk culture*: a) after A. Nöldeke, *4. Vorläufiger Bericht . . . Uruk*, pl. 18 Dg (W. de Gruyter, Berlin); b) after *ibid.*, pl. 18 Di; c) after *ibid.*, pl. 18 Dv; d) after *ibid.*, pl. 18 Cp; e) after *Sumer*, IV, pls. 3, 14 (Directorate General of Antiquities, Iraq, Baghdad); f) after A. Nöldeke, *op. cit.*, pl. 19 Bg.

FIGURE 6. *Temple at Eridu, Level VII*: after E. Douglas Van Buren, *Orientalia, Nova Series*, Vol. XVII, pl. 3 (Pontificio Istituto Biblico, Roma)

ACKNOWLEDGMENTS

FIGURE 7. *Temple at Uruk, Levels V–IVb*: after H. Lenzen, *Zeitschrift für Assyriologie*, N.F., Vol. XV, pl. 1 (W. de Gruyter, Berlin)

FIGURE 8. *Temple at Uruk, Level IVa*: after H. Lenzen, *op. cit.*, pl. 2

FIGURE 9. *The Anu Ziqqurrat at Uruk (restoration)*: after A. Nöldeke, *op. cit.*, p. 46, fig. 5 (W. de Gruyter, Berlin)

FIGURE 10. *Protoliterate cylinder-seal impressions*: a) after H. Lenzen, *op. cit.*, pl. 3, 1; b) after A. Nöldeke, *5. Vorläufiger Bericht . . . Uruk*, pl. 26b (W. de Gruyter, Berlin); c) after *ibid.*, pl. 27a; d) after H. Frankfort, *Stratified Cylinder Seals from the Diyala Region*, pl. 11, 94 (University of Chicago Press, Chicago)

PHOTOGRAPHS

1. Courtesy of Kathleen M. Kenyon, Jericho Excavation Fund, London
2. Courtesy of Kathleen M. Kenyon, Jericho Excavation Fund, London
3. Hirmer Verlag, Munich
4. Hirmer Verlag, Munich
5. From *Baghdader Mitteilungen*, II (Gebr. Mann Verlag, Berlin)
6. From *Baghdader Mitteilungen*, II (Gebr. Mann Verlag, Berlin)
7. Staatliche Museum, Berlin
8. Staatliche Museum, Berlin
9. The University Museum, University of Pennsylvania, Philadelphia
10. The British Museum, London
11. Louvre: photo Maurice Chuzeville, Vanves (Seine), France
12. The British Museum, London
13. Photo TELL, Paris
14. The Oriental Institute, The University of Chicago
15. Louvre: Service de Documentation Photographique des Musées Nationaux
16. The University Museum, University of Pennsylvania, Philadelphia
17. The University Museum, University of Pennsylvania, Philadelphia

438

18. The University Museum, University of Pennsylvania, Philadelphia

19. Louvre: Service de Documentation Photographique des Musées Nationaux

20. Louvre: photo Maurice Chuzeville, Vanves (Seine), France

21. Louvre: Foto Giraudon, Paris

22. The University Museum, University of Pennsylvania, Philadelphia

23. Directorate General of Antiquities, Iraq Museum, Baghdad

24. Photo TELL, Paris

25. Louvre: Foto Marburg

26. Louvre: Foto Marburg

27. The Metropolitan Museum of Art, New York

28. The Metropolitan Museum of Art, New York

29. Cairo Museum: Foto Marburg

30. Cairo Museum: Foto Marburg

31. Louvre: Foto Marburg

32. Courtesy J.-Ph. Lauer

33. Cairo Museum: Foto Marburg

34. United Arab Republic Tourist Office, New York

35. Cairo Museum: Foto Marburg

36. Louvre: Service de Documentation Photographique des Musées Nationaux

37. William Rockhill Nelson Gallery of Art, Atkins Museum of Fine Arts, Kansas City, Missouri

38. The Oriental Institute, the University of Chicago

39. The Metropolitan Museum of Art, New York

40. The Metropolitan Museum of Art, New York

41. The Metropolitan Museum of Art, New York

42. The Metropolitan Museum of Art, New York

43. Cairo Museum: Foto Marburg

44. The Calouste Gulbenkian Foundation, Oeiras, Portugal

45. Cairo Museum: Foto Marburg

46. Neues Museum, Berlin: Foto Marburg

47. The Metropolitan Museum of Art, New York

Index

441

NOTE ON EDITORS AND CONTRIBUTORS

JEAN BOTTÉRO is Professor of the History of the Ancient Near East at the École Pratique des Hautes-Études (Sorbonne) in Paris. From 1947 to 1958 he was in charge of research at the Centre National de la Recherche Scientifique of Paris. Together with other French and Belgian scholars, Professor Bottéro is currently at work on the deciphering of the royal archives of Mari.

ELENA CASSIN, a native of Italy, is at present in charge of research at the Centre National de la Recherche Scientifique of Paris. Her specialty is the economic and legal aspects of the history of ancient Babylonia, with particular reference to Nuzi. Madame Cassin is a contributor to the *Revue d'Assyriologie* and the *Annales*.

JEAN VERCOUTTER is a professor in the Faculty of Philosophy at the University of Lille, and a full member of the Deutschen Archäologischen Instituts of Berlin. Formerly a member of the Institute Français d'Archéologie Orientale in Cairo, he was the Director of the French excavations at Mirgissa (Sudan). His principal book, *L'Égypte Ancienne*, was published in 1947.

DIETZ OTTO EDZARD has taught Oriental studies at the University of Munich since 1963, and is the author of *Die 'zweite Zwischenzeit' Babyloniens* (1957). In 1961 and 1962 he was a guest lecturer at Harvard University.

ADAM FALKENSTEIN is Professor of Semitic Languages at the University of Heidelberg. Among his publications are *Die Archaischen Texte aus Uruk* (1936), *Neusumerische Rechtsurkunden* (1956–1957), and *Das Sumerische* (1959).